FRIENDSHIP *Reconsidered*

FRIENDSHIP
Reconsidered

WHAT IT MEANS
AND HOW IT
MATTERS TO POLITICS

P.E. Digeser

COLUMBIA UNIVERSITY PRESS
NEW YORK

Columbia University Press
Publishers Since 1893
New York   Chichester, West Sussex
cup.columbia.edu
Copyright © 2016 Columbia University Press

Library of Congress Cataloging-in-Publication Data

Names: Digeser, P.E., author.
Title: Friendship reconsidered : what it means and how it matters
to politics / P.E. Digeser.
Description: New York : Columbia University Press, 2016. | Includes
bibliographical references and index.
Identifiers: LCCN 2016002185 | ISBN 9780231174343 (cloth : alk. paper) |
9780231542111 (e-book)
Subjects: LCSH: Political science—Philosophy. | International relations—
Philosophy. | Friendship—Political aspects. | Interpersonal relations—
Political aspects.
Classification: LCC JA71 .D52135 2016 | DDC 320.01—dc23
LC record available at http://lccn.loc.gov/2016002185

Columbia University Press books are printed on permanent
and durable acid-free paper.
Printed in the United States of America

c 10 9 8 7 6 5 4 3 2 1
Cover design: Jordan Wannemacher

To the Memory of
Richard E. Flathman

CONTENTS

ACKNOWLEDGMENTS

I would especially like to thank Sue, Billy, and Nicholas, whose love, hospitality and friendship were invaluable during the writing of this book, and many thanks to Beth for her love, support, and willingness to read through the manuscript. Many friends directly and indirectly helped to make this book possible: Max, Kate, James, Peg, Dave, Amy, Catherine, Lorenz, Heather, Ed, Dick, David, Nick, Michael, Ross, Monica, Ivan, Tom, John, Nancy, Jackie, David, John, Rick, Tom, Bonnie, Jay, Dave, Ken, Andy, Roger, Bill, and Dennis. Special thanks to my parents for being who they are and thanks to Will Bensley for his work on the manuscript. I would also like to thank my colleagues for understanding the difference between toleration and acceptance and for so decisively choosing the latter in 2008. Finally, I have dedicated this book to Richard E. Flathman, who advised and supported me at Hopkins and throughout my career. His devotion and contribution to understanding the extraordinary thinkers and ideas that compose the tradition of philosophy and political thought, not to mention his generosity, patience, and love of freedom and individuality, have proved invaluable and inimitable.

Portions of chapters 1 and 2 are drawn from "Friendship as a Family of Practices," published in *Amity: The Journal of Friendship Studies* 1:34–52 (2013) and used with their kind permission.

INTRODUCTION

After having been exiled from political theory for centuries, friendship is making a comeback. Whether it is in exploring the pluralism necessary for politics, the character of feminism, the heteronormativity of the Greek model of political life, the revitalization of democratic citizenship, the failure of capitalism to recognize reproductive labor, the elemental attachments between persons or the predominance of neoliberalism, friendship has served as either a model or a touchstone for rethinking politics. Cognizant of its importance to ordinary life in providing bonds of emotional, psychological, and occasionally financial support, American legal thinkers have advocated that legislatures and courts recognize and, if possible, cultivate friendship. Responding to the perceived inadequacies of realist accounts for international cooperation, other thinkers have come to see the emergence of pockets of mutual trust and confidence as a form of international friendship. In most of these accounts, friendship is seen a desirable model for political relationships from the personal to the institutional to the international.[1]

Some of the reasons for the resurgence of friendship are close at hand. Ordinarily, friends are expected to settle their disagreements nonviolently and without rancor, to be attentive to one another's interests, to be open to frank speech, to forbear strategic thinking, and to act in a spirit of generosity. These are all practices that appear conducive to a peaceful, yet lively democratic politics oriented toward the good of oneself and one's friends. More generally, and perhaps more significantly, friendship is the sort of relationship that can draw and bind individuals together regardless of their kinship, tribe, ethnicity, race, class, or gender. There is nothing within the concept of friendship itself that necessarily precludes people of different religions, political ideologies, or moral philosophies from being friends. In a certain light, it becomes difficult to think of a nobler way for connecting politically, unrelated, diverse, and occasionally pigheaded people.

Despite this resurgent interest in friendship, powerful reasons remain for continued skepticism. First, assuming that friendship requires the mutual recognition of an appropriate set of motivations, the sheer size of the modern state precludes those bounds from extending very far. Without the mutual recognition of motives, one may have benevolence, civility, compassion, or care, but one will not have friendship. Even in a world in which there are only 3.74 degrees of separation between all Facebook users, the members of modern states are associations of strangers and not relationships of friendship.[2] The close-knit, emotion-laden character of friendship simply seems inappropriate in a political context.

Second, the bonds of friendship are powerful and real and for that very reason they may pull one in a biased or partial direction. Along with friendship come risks of cronyism, corruption, preferential treatment, exclusion, factionalism, conspiracy, and epistemic distortion.[3] Friendships challenge and may erode the necessary civil dispositions of impartiality, proportionality, and willingness to follow rules and procedures. Furthermore, the sentiment of owing more to our friends may leave us with little perspective as to how to treat strangers. To the extent that rules and procedures have become ways to ensure fairness, it is not surprising to see why friendship has been ignored or relegated to the private realm by a variety of perspectives.[4] Finally, the emotional components of friendship inhibit the flexibility needed to respond to continually changing circumstances (Baker 1999:164). Protecting or preserving one's friends may make it difficult to form political alliances or cut deals to advance a worthwhile political agenda. Friendship may handicap politics.

In diverse, complicated societies in which a premium is placed on a sense of fairness, the institutional need for impartial rules and procedures, and the importance of maneuverability places both kin and kith at arm's length. All of this must be conceded. Nevertheless, it is not enough to vote friendship entirely off the island of politics and political theory. A certain level of skepticism about the role of friendship in politics does not preclude seeing friendship as a relationship that tells us something about how human beings can and perhaps should relate to one another politically. The goal of this work is to carve out a position between whole-hearted endorsement and complete rejection of friendship as a political concern.

In fashioning that middle ground, this book illuminates the complex relationship between friendship and politics at a variety of levels: conceptual, individual, institutional, and international. First, this book abandons the pursuit of the necessary and sufficient conditions for friendship. It begins with the assumption that understanding the relationship between friendship and politics requires being alive to friendship's kaleidoscopic manifestations.[5] It takes up and explores a suggestion that friendship is a family resemblance concept. At the very least, this view implies that our generalizations about the relationship between friendship and politics have to accommodate the extraordinary diversity of understandings that exist over time and space. Specific conceptions of friendship are not the whole of the matter. Consequently, many defenders of a more robust role for friendship in politics are likely to be defending a particular ideal of friendship (and not friendship as such). Similarly, but from a very different perspective, skeptics may see friendship as inapplicable to politics because of the narrowness of their construction. If, however, we assume that the diversity of our conceptions of friendship is something to be celebrated, then we must also be aware of the ways in which politics and political/legal institutions may close down or inhibit that diversity. Thinking about the relationship between politics and friendship should not be limited to thinking about how friendship can be a handmaiden to political life.

Second, starting with the claim that friendship is a family resemblance concept does not mean that any relationship qualifies as a friendship. Fashioning this middle ground also entails setting out the ways in which that kaleidoscopic diversity finds expression in a family of practices of friendship. When seen through the lens of "practice," different friendships are composed of different motivations and different activities. Consequently, it is possible to have distinct kinds of friends with whom we act very differently. Those practices are identifiable as practices of friendship (as opposed some other sort of relationship) because we tend to agree upon a repertoire of ordinarily appropriate motivations and expected actions that must be recognized for friendship to exist. That repertoire and those actions, however, differ from culture to culture and across time. Consequently, all friendships need not be understood as creating rights and duties. All friendships need not be understood as solely motivated by altruistic reasons. All friendships need not be understood as existing between individual persons. Western, twenty-first-century practices of friendships, however, are conditioned by the mutual recognition of appropriate motivations and the subscription to certain adverbial requirements. These formal conditions distinguish friendship from related ideas of being a friend of or befriending, although they do not distinguish friendship from other close relationships. The latter distinction is found in the repertoire of motivations and actions that happen to be affiliated with "our" use of friendship.

The middle ground provided by this book is fashioned in a third way through the positive connections between certain practices of friendship and individuality. For many critics and defenders of friendship in politics, there is something about friendship and individuality that is like oil and water. For some defenders of friendship, recovering a notion of friendship is a way to overcome a modernity that is all too alienating and atomizing. Individuality is the problem. Friendship is the solution. For some critics of bringing friendship into politics, individuality is what is to be publicly encouraged and friendship is to be privately celebrated. At best, friendship should be, to use a word that Melissa Lane employs to discuss the Epicurean view of friendship, *infra-political* or "within or below the level of the political" (Lane 2014:230). In response to both positions, I argue that within our practices of friendship may be found not only support for a robust notion of individuality, but also a robust notion of individuality that can give rise to an ideal of friendship. Not all practices of friendship are at odds with individuality. Not all ideals of individuality preclude friendship. Political and legal institutions that are favorably disposed to individuality need not disable our capacity to be friends and vice versa.

Fourth, this book agrees with the skeptical view that friendship as a general model of citizenship is implausible. Nevertheless, the skeptics are wrong to dismiss entirely any role for friendship in understanding citizenship. Certain practices of friendship tell us something about an ideal of citizenship that can be realized only by smaller groups of individuals within a polity precisely because friendship requires the mutual recognition of motives. In the most challenging form of this ideal, civic friendship is neither simply friendship nor simply citizenship. As such, it pulls both terms out of their orbits in a distinctive manner. Civic friendship is a difficult ideal, but one that may facilitate the willingness of political opponents to continue to cooperate.

The view of civic friendship just considered implies a larger political/institutional context that is more or less stable. Our expectations and our ideals of friendship, however, may change if that institutional context is destabilized. The complexity of the relationship between friendship and politics is illuminated in a fifth way if we think about friendship in a delegitimized political environment. Once again, within the family of practices of friendship, one can find an ideal in which friendship cuts across deep political differences and works against the impulse that "you are either with us or against us." During times in which political practice and legal structure are able to protect diversity and minorities, such a role for friendship may be unnecessary. But there are dark times when friendship helps prevent a collapse and assimilation of people and positions. In effect, friendship can play a somewhat different political role by aiming to keep alive the opposition.

Turning back to institutions, the complicated place of friendship emerges in a sixth way when considering whether such relationships should garner political and legal recognition. In discussions of friendship and politics there is a temptation to instrumentalize friendship and see it as a handmaiden to politics. If, however, friendship is itself an end, then we must also ask what good (and bad) can politics (along with political and legal institutions) do for and to it. What legal and political institutions can do to and for friendship is not without its risks to our practices of friendship. The possibility of a law of friendship needs to be sensitive to both the intrinsic importance of interpersonal friendship and the multiple shapes it takes.

Finally, the complex, episodic political virtue of friendship also makes an appearance at the level of international politics. Here, I argue that states of a certain sort can be friends. To the extent that a state is minimally just, then its people and its officials have reason to protect and promote its own interests and basic policies. Those sorts of reasons apply to other regimes that meet those conditions. International friendships, then, are motivated by reasons to protect and promote just institutions and policies of other states. Given the nature of the institutions and stability of the regimes, these interstate friends may be more or less close. Within and between these alignments, interstate friendships will also generate a different sort of politics of friendship.

THE STRUCTURE OF THE ARGUMENT

The book is divided into three parts. The first part considers conceptual matters and defends an ideal of friendship that is compatible with individuality. The second part connects friendship directly or indirectly to political institutions and explores the idea of civic friendship, friendship during dark times, and the relationship between friendship and the law. The third and final section of the book considers friendship in an international context. It defends an account of friendship that applies to the relationship between states and considers the ways in which that vision of friendship will itself engender political agreement and disagreement. A more specific breakdown of the chapters follows.

Chapter 1 sets out what it means for friendship to be understood as a set of social practices that bear a family resemblance to one another. The core of the argument involves understanding Michael Oakeshott's notion of practice and responds to objections that could be made to applying that idea to friendship. Chapter 2 considers how practices of friendship structure our expectations both of the motives that must be mutually recognized by friends and of the actions that friends can expect of one another. Different practices of friendship are conditioned by different motives as well as by different adverbial rules governing the actions of the friends. If our practices of friendship are structured by mutually recognized motivations and the subscription to certain norms of conduct, chapter 3 considers the potential role of utility and obligation in friendship's motivational repertoire. While no one believes that friends should be useless to one another, relationships of pure utility are generally not thought to be friendships (at least in the contemporary West). Moreover, the role of obligation in friendship is deeply contested. In contrast, I argue that utility and obligation can be no more than "deficient reasons" for acting within a friendship and cannot bear the full motivational weight of friendship (although they can count as potent reasons for action vis-à-vis third parties).

Chapter 4 defends an ideal of friendship that both serves and is served by a robust conception of individuality. The motivational and adverbial features of our practices of friendship open up the possibility for a form of friendship that is consistent with Richard Flathman's notion of self-enacted individuality. In this ideal, friends work upon themselves to best assist the self-enacted individuality of each other. Because it emphasizes self-enactment, this ideal makes demands on the quality of our motivations for initiating and maintaining a friendship and supporting the individuality of our friends. To put it another way, it is a bridging/bonding relationship insofar as it requires both the bonding of mutually recognized sentiments and a bridging of the differences generated by individuality.

Part 2 of the book discusses various connections among friendship, politics, and institutions. Chapter 5 focuses on the idea of civic friendship and argues that in light of the considerations associated with the practices of friendship discussed in chapters 1 and 2, regimes of any significant size are unlikely to meet the condition that friends must mutually recognize the appropriate motivations of one another. Nevertheless, even if friendship cannot be incorporated into a general model of citizenship, it can be included in a civic ideal that some citizens may choose to enact with one another. Chapter 6 critically considers Hannah Arendt's view of friendship as a way to preserve pluralism in a delegitimized political environment. To address certain problems with her view, the chapter turns to Cornelius Nepos's "The Life of Atticus." The "Atticus" here is Titus Pomponius Atticus, a wealthy banker who was able to maintain friendships with all of the major players during the Roman civil wars. While historians and classicists have not been particularly friendly to Atticus, Nepos's biography can be read as advancing a political ideal of friendship that seeks to preserve those who have lost power by refusing to accept the choice between being "with us" or "against us." In fact, by violating that prescription, this ideal may open the door to political engagement and pluralism.

Chapter 7 concludes part 2 with a discussion of the ways in which political and legal institutions encourage and discourage interpersonal forms of friendship. Political institutions, public policies, and laws can formally establish barriers or reinforce social distinctions that make contact and hence friendship between individuals more difficult. Most of chapter 7, however, explores the question of whether the state should directly promote friendship. The discussion of friendship offered in the first part of this book, however, raises difficult issues regarding whether the law can recognize the diversity of friendships and keep up with their fluidity. Although the law can and should be friendlier to friendship, it will be an imperfect instrument for its enablement.

The third and final section of the book turns to the idea of friendship in the international sphere. The move from interpersonal friendship to interstate friendship is warranted by the diverse ways in which we use the notion of friendship. Since the time of Thucydides, terms such as *friend* and *friendship* have been part of the language of interstate politics.[6] Diplomats frequently draw on these words to characterize international agreements.[7] Politicians regularly toast, worry about, and aspire to maintain these kinds of relationships in their public rhetoric. Commentators often assess, challenge, and dissect international friendships.[8] Despite the importance of *friend* and *friendship* in the practical political vocabulary of state actors and observers, these concepts are only now receiving attention from scholars of international relations.[9] As Felix Berenskoetter notes, the understanding of friendship in international relations is "still in its infancy" (2014:51).

Chapter 8 explores the meaning of friendship when it is applied to state actors. In many ways, these terms are simply reducible to *alliances* and *partnerships* in which the security and self-interests of the parties are paramount. In all of these uses, the notions of friends and friendship do not carry any independent weight and are no more interesting than what appear to be their synonyms. The possibility that states can be motivated by reasons other than those of security and self-interest provides an opening to a more interesting idea of friendship between states. Chapter 9 defends such an understanding by arguing that the reasons that justify self-interest on the part of a state, also justify some interest in the interests of other states. To the extent that a state is minimally just, then its people and its officials have reason to protect and promote the basic interests of the regime. These international friendships of character, then, are distinguishable from mere alliances and partnerships to the extent that they are motivated by reasons to protect and promote more or less just institutions and policies of other states. With this understanding of international friendship in mind, it becomes possible to differentiate between levels or types of friendship depending on how stable and assured those regimes are of the quality and character of their institutions.

The final chapter considers what it would mean for states to take seriously the idea of international friendship. In so doing, it responds to a variety of objections that have been and can be made to the notion of minimally just states mutually recognizing a motivation to promote one another's just institutions and policies. In particular, it focuses on the possibility that international friendship would shut down politics by creating a sharply divided moral world of friends and enemies. Drawing on the work of Jacques Derrida, chapter 10 argues that international friendship would itself generate an international politics both because the character of state institutions can change and because the perception of the quality of a regime's institutions matters. Within a practice of international friendship, there will be a politics generated by being partnered with objectionable regimes (the "politics of penetration"). There is also a politics associated with the decision on the part of minimally just states to admit a previously unjust regime into an entente cordiale (a "politics of exclusion/inclusion"). There is a politics associated with managing the friendship that takes the form of distributing its costs and benefits as well as in deciding how far one will go in supporting one's friends (a "politics of entrapment and abandonment"). Finally, in the case of the strongest international friendships (those in which states see one another in a special relationship), there may also be a politics involved in seeking to preserve one's identity as an independent entity (a "politics of amalgamation"). To the extent that states can be motivated by reasons to protect and promote more or less just domestic institutions in other states and those motivations can be mutually recognized, then international friendships (and the attendant possibility for politics) are also possible.

The tangled relationship between friendship and politics discussed in this book is a function of certain facts about contemporary states and certain assumptions and claims about friendship. The "facts" about contemporary states (e.g., that they are simply too big to allow the mutual recognition of motivation, that the law can occlude and enable our capacity to recognize such motivations) are rather mundane. They are, of course, contingent and if (when?) they change, then it may be necessary to reassess the place of friendship. The attributes that will be associated with friendship in this work (e.g., its diverse meanings, its compatibility with individuality, its connection to social practices, and its adverbial character) are also contingent, but more contestable. The practices of friendship change over time and stretch (and contract) what may be recognized as bearing a family resemblance. Different groups and cultures have different repertoires of motivations and actions. Even the requirement that the appropriate motives of friendship must be mutually recognized is bound by time and place.

Within these contingencies, philosophical and popular accounts of friendship have offered various ideals of friendship. In this reconsideration of friendship, this work also sets out a series of ideals. The notion of bridging/ bonding friendship and its relationship to individuality is an ideal. The conception of civic friendship as a more restricted model of citizenship is an ideal. Nepos's account of Atticus is an ideal of friendship during violent times. Finally, the relationship between more or less just states is an ideal of sorts. At an individual level, the view of the friend as another self suggests that the tendency of friendship to generate ideals is driven by the desire to see in one's friend what one hopes to see in oneself. Without a doubt, the friend as a mirror is an important trope in our understandings of friendship.

Mirrored in the ideals of interpersonal friendship set out here, however, is not an exact reflection of oneself, but a disposition to protect and support what may be quite different from oneself. These are ideals less in the sense of advocating a vision that should be endorsed by everyone and more in the sense of expressing and building upon attributes of the practices of friendship that lead in a direction opposite to that of merely mirroring what one already happens to be. In the ideals of bridging/bonding friendship, civic friendship and the friendship of Atticus, the bounds of friendship hold across differences created by the pursuit of individuality, political goals, and, in the extreme, violent actions. Even in the case of international friendships, the relationship is not meant to be understood as a simple ideological alliance in which states are aligned with other states because they have the same institutions, culture, or historical experience. What is a more or less just regime can take a number of forms and hence international friendships should be open to those differences of circumstance and experience.

Friendships are a great good in life, but there is no essential understanding of friendship. Friendships are important to politics, but they cannot be a general model for citizenship. Friendships offer the hope of bridging a divide opened by violence and conflict but provide no guarantee for securing pluralism. Friendships can be manipulated and stymied by laws and policies, but they cannot be entirely shutdown or easily cultivated by political and legal institutions. Friendships can be held by states, but only if states are motivated by reasons of a certain sort. Friendships may ease the disruptions of an anarchic international environment and yet still generate their own forms of political disagreement and conflict. Friendships are wonderful, complicated relationships. It should be no surprise that their connection to politics, institutions, and states is neither straightforward nor easily understood. If, at best, this work has increased our understanding of friendship it will have also increased a sense of what we do not fully understand.

FRIENDSHIP *Reconsidered*

PART *one*

one
FRIENDSHIP AS A FAMILY
OF PRACTICES

Few things are likelier to kill a friendship quicker than a careful and strictly adhered-to theory of what qualities are needed in a friend.

—JOSEPH EPSTEIN, *FRIENDSHIP: AN EXPOSE*

Friends matter in politics. They are our allies, supporters, donors, partners, connections, or followers who are willing to help us as we are willing to help them. With any luck, they are plentiful and found in high places, across the aisle, or with deep pockets. More generally, they are useful and reliable: they can be counted on. Perhaps we may know them best when we know our enemies or when difficulties arise. If things go south and they fail to live up to our expectations, we may find ourselves let down or even betrayed by them. They may be good, bad, close, absent, loyal, true, long-time, best, or fair-weather. Through networks of and connections through friends, skids can be greased, doors can be opened, opportunities can be realized, and deals can be cut.

At least in English, not all of our friends compose friendships even though friendships do not exist without friends. For example, it is one thing to be friends of the earth, elephant seals, or submit an amicus curiae brief. It is something quite different to have a friendship with a planet, a pinniped, or a presiding judge. The friend we identify when distinguishing friend from foe may merely be on our side, wearing the same uniform or obligated to the same authority and not necessarily part of a friendship. A friend at work may simply be a colleague or a partner as opposed to a stranger or a competitor. These distinctions, however, may not be restricted to early twenty-first-century speakers of English. In a wonderful letter to his friend Titus Pomponius Atticus, the first-century B.C.E. Roman philosopher Marcus Tullius Cicero eloquently alluded to this distinction when he wrote:

> My house is crammed [in the] morning, I go down to the Forum surrounded by droves of friends, but in all the multitude I cannot find one with whom I can pass an unguarded joke or fetch a private sigh. That is why I am waiting and longing for you, why I now fairly summon you home. There are many things to worry and vex me, but once I have you here to listen I feel I can pour them all away in a single walk and talk.
>
> (CICERO 1999A:1.18)

Whatever motivations are associated with friendship, they seem to be more than what is recognized between mere friends. While friendships can be and usually are useful relationships, friends who are solely useful to one another do not appear to rise to the level of having a friendship—at least to us in the early twenty-first-century West and perhaps to Cicero as well.[1] This distinction between mere friends and friendships is a rough one and is subject to historical and cultural variation. This book is about friendships and not about the larger category of friends. Unless otherwise noted, when the word *friend* is used from here on out, it is meant to refer to the thicker relationship associated with a friendship.

Should friendships matter to politics? Unlike friends and politics, the relationship between friendship and politics is not addressed so easily. As noted in the introduction, there has been a resurgent interest in the idea of friendship, but there are also good reasons for being skeptical of its playing a substantial role in government or politics. The question, however, is an important one to ask not merely because of these differences of perspective, but because friendship is itself important.[2] Some have argued that friendship has become increasingly significant in societies in which traditional, kinship-based support systems have become less important. According to Laura A. Rosenbury, sociological evidence suggests that "more people are . . . living outside of domestic couplings, which necessarily changes their notions of intimate connection. Instead of relying on family within the home, people are relying on friends outside of the home" (2007:209). For Ray Pahl, our friends are part of a personal community that composes a "social convoy" that accompanies one through the hazards of life (2000:72). Friends are performing tasks that were once done by the family (8). This appears to be especially true of women who rely upon friends for emotional and material support particularly in times of emergency (Rosenbury 2007:210). People are turning to the networks of friends to help one another in ways that used to be done by couples or the traditional family. If these rough generalizations are correct, then we should be attentive not merely to the question of whether friendship should be important to politics, but whether politics should matter to friendships.

A focus on friendship is not intended to disparage the obvious importance of the larger category of *friend*. Rather it is to attend to a specific sort of relationship that is governed by its own motivations and forms of interaction that go beyond (but do not exclude) utility and self-interest. In light of this focus, many will dismiss any possible connection between friendship and the hard-nosed, calculating character of politics or between friendship and the impartial rules and procedures that seek to moderate the competition between political actors.[3] Perhaps even more implausible is the idea that friendship could have anything to do with the relationship between countries. In order to map out some of the connections between friendship and politics, I must first provide some account of friendship. These first four chapters perform that function and set up the discussion for the other two parts of this book.

This chapter begins by acknowledging the long-recognized diversity to our understandings of friendship and by endorsing the notion that friendship is a family resemblance concept. To understand some of the familial features that draw together these differing understandings of friendship, the second half of the chapter employs Michael Oakeshott's notion of a practice. In conditioning both our actions and our motivations, practices provide rules and expectations for how friends should interact with one another and the sorts of sentiments and reasons that can drive those actions. Different practices of friendship possess different rules of engagement and/or different sorts of motivations. This chapter concludes by responding to a number of objections to seeing friendship as a social practice and sets up for chapter 2 the discussion of the motivations and actions that compose current practices of friendship.

FRIENDSHIP AND ITS DIVERSITY

The basic elements of the theory of friendship offered here are rather simple: friendship is composed of a set of social practices in which certain norms and expectations govern not only the actions, but also the motivations of the friends. These practices bear no more than a family resemblance to one another. No essential action or motivation differentiates friendship from other social practices or unites the different practices of friendship. Supplementing these basic elements are certain features of practices. Like all practices, cultivating and having friends requires learning and subscribing to norms, conventions, and expectations that are then interpreted and employed with varying degrees of skill and success. Like many practices, the conventions associated with friendship are less about what to do at any particular time and more about how to go about doing whatever it is that friends wish to do for or with one another. In addition to these more general features of practices, friendships entail more specific conditions. For example, in their current Western manifestation, interpersonal friendships require the mutual recognition of appropriate motivations. If I believe that your actions toward me are motivated by the ordinarily appropriate sentiments of friendship and you believe the same about me and we act in a manner that is consonant with the adverbial conditions associated with a practice of friendship, then we have a friendship. As in the case of the actions that we expect from our friends, there exist multiple kinds of motivations that affect the tenor of the relationship. The practices of friendship are diverse, historically contingent, and adverbial in character. This understanding of friendship will be broad enough to encompass the wide variety friendships. Friendship is a flexible relationship whose boundaries are ultimately established only by the human imagination.

Evidence of the flexible and variegated character of friendship is not difficult to find at both an individual and social level as well as in some of the standard philosophical accounts of friendship. For example, at an individual level, not all of our friendships are the same and none is immune to change. The friends with whom we go to the movies, out to dinner, or celebrate the New Year may not be the friends at work or the bridge group or in the mosque. The friends that we have made simply because they lived next door may not be the friends with whom we confide our secrets and seek consolation. Our friendships at work may be extraordinarily important and, in many respects, fulfilling, but those may not be the friends with whom we feel most relaxed and ourselves. These differences that we experience are not hard and fast. Sometimes our closest friends fade out of our lives and other times a mere acquaintance, known for years, is transformed into a close and loyal friend. At any given time, different friends and sometimes the same friends play different roles. The diversity of the relationship is astoundingly rich and important to us.

At a societal level, what friendship means to children is very different from what it means to adolescents and adults (Pahl 2000:101). In addition, the ways of being friends may differ depending on the familiar distinctions of gender, class, and culture.[4] In part, these differences are a matter of the sorts of actions that friends do with or for another. The sorts of accommodations expected in guest friendships in ancient Greece are not the same expectations of a twenty-first-century reading group in Freeport, Maine. These kinds of friendships may also differ depending on the sorts of motivations that drive the relationship. In the Greek case, they are founded on certain tribal or familial obligations; in the latter case, they may be based on the mutual recognition of affection or a desire to have an enjoyable evening discussing ideas.[5]

The diversity of ways of being friends also tells us something about their importance to us. Given the range of things we want, the wealth of activities we desire to do, and the different sorts of people with whom we wish to associate, we also want relationships that are flexible enough to participate in the satisfaction and achievement of those wants, desires, and wishes. This is not to say that everything is better when done with a friend or that we never enjoy solitude, but that the sentiments and norms of friendship can accommodate the richness of human conduct and desire. Friendships can connect people in unexpected ways. Acquaintances and strangers can become friends. In their most resilient forms, the bonds of friendship can be as strong as or stronger than the bonds of family. This diversity is reflected in the sense that we value our friendships both intrinsically and instrumentally. We enjoy simply being with friends, but we also value our friends because they can aid, protect, encourage, and challenge us in many ways.

The diversity and flexibility of friendship is a puzzle that has fascinated philosophers from Plato to Jacques Derrida. For many ancient and modern thinkers, this diversity is a spur to discern the true form or the best type of friendship. In contrast, Derrida writes, "neither this tradition nor the concept of friendship within it is homogenous" (1988:634). He goes on to argue that the philosophical difficulties of setting down the necessary and sufficient conditions of friendship tell us something about the yearning for the presence of another (and ourselves) that can never be fulfilled. For the most part, the earliest attempts in the West to understand what friendship is (or should be) or how it is related to our condition in the world were relatively respectful of the diversity of friendships. For example, Plato's dialogue "Lysis" presents an account of philia that concludes without any clear answer. It is filled with false starts and the wreckage of alternative formulations. From one perspective, it is a warning for anyone who is foolhardy enough to try to pin down the meaning of friend. Reciprocity, mutuality, utility, goodness, beauty, similarity, difference, and belonging all fail to accommodate what seems to be such an obvious and commonly experienced relationship.[6] The dialogue forces upon us the question of whether we can be friends without fully understanding friendship. One way to read the dialogue's answer to this question turns on Socrates's suggestion that we can only be trusted with and have control over things that we fully understand (Plato 1991:209c).[7] If this is so, then Socratic ignorance regarding friendship warns us from trying to control or fully nail down a relationship that remains just beyond the reach of our understanding.

Few thinkers are more alive to the nuances and diversity of friendships than Aristotle. While it is true that the Greek notion of philia is much broader than the English concept of friendship, his categories of friendships of pleasure, utility, and virtue are familiar philosophical distinctions that have framed discussions of friendship for centuries. In addition, he was quite aware of how those distinctions were supplemented and complicated by further distinctions involving equality, justice, politics, community, family, the law, self-love, concord, benevolence, external goods, and fortune. While most scholars attend to what Aristotle thought to be the best or the highest form of friendship, it should be remembered that he was an acute observer of human ingenuity and diversity. For example, Aristotle noted that young people have differing expectations than the old with regard to the nature of their friendships. Commercial associates, in turn, develop their own forms of interactions. Friends who are equal seem to have a different kind of experience than friends who are unequal. Even though he said that friendships of utility and pleasure are friendship only by analogy to the best form of friendship, he was well aware that common usage is very broad. Whatever Aristotle thought about friendships that fall short of the ideal, he still saw them as friendships of a sort (Annas 1977:546–47; Lynch 2005:183; Smith 2011a:57).

FRIENDSHIP AS A FAMILY RESEMBLANCE CONCEPT

Twentieth-century interest in language and meaning provided a variety of ways to understand the flexibility and fluidity of our words and concepts. In the case of friendship, one particularly useful suggestion is to see friendship as a family resemblance concept. As separately suggested by Sandra Lynch, Diane Jeske, and Graham Smith, the idea is that when we seek to find some common element that joins together all of the ways in which we use the word friendship, we find similarities that "crop up and disappear" (Lynch 2005:21, 189–91; Jeske 2008:95–104; Smith 2011a:20). In effect, the similarities in these usages bear no more than what Ludwig Wittgenstein sees as a family resemblance to one another (1973:section 66). Just as we recognize certain familial traits (aquiline nose, high forehead, a set of facial expressions) among a group of family members, we may associate certain characteristics (affection, loyalty, care, joint activity) as part of the meaning of friendship. Nevertheless, not all of those familial traits may be shared by all the family members nor may any one of them be deemed an essential trait. Not all members of the family may have the "family nose" and some may merely have a high forehead, which others do not share at all. Similarly, not all friendships entail the sharing of secrets and some may involve common activities that other friendships do not entail at all. What joins together some uses of the word friendship will be unnecessary for other uses.

Seeing friendship as a family resemblance concept has a number of implications. First and foremost, it implies that "there is no determinate complete answer to the question, 'What is friendship?'" (Jeske 2008:96; Lynch 2005:22).[8] All understandings of friendship need not share some common attribute that differentiates it from all other relationships. Second, just as one conception of *game* (which Wittgenstein uses as one example of a family resemblance concept) is not in competition with another conception, so differing conceptions of friendship can coexist. We need not choose between conceptions of friendship in order to establish that this conception is *more of a* conception of friendship than some other. The fact that a friendship was motivated by respect, does not make it less than a friendship based on affection. Abandoning the search for the essence of friendship, however, does not mean that any sort of relationship is a friendship. It does not prevent us from distinguishing friends from lovers, partners, colleagues, comrades, customers, and acquaintances (let alone strangers, enemies, rivals, and foes). Third, the edges of the family are going to be blurry. The differences between a friendship and a partnership may sometimes be difficult to discern. Similarly, and certainly more fraught, the line between romantic entanglement and a caring friendship is also one for which clear distinctions can be elusive. These difficulties in identifying the conceptual boundaries of friendship are not necessarily to be seen as failures or inadequacies of the concept. Rather, the lines that we draw with regard to these matters may be no more than provisional and indicative of traditions, purposes, and norms that exist at a particular time and place. Finally, seeing friendship as a family resemblance concept does not preclude us from viewing certain forms of friendship as preferable to other forms of friendship. As in the case of the word *game*, we may prefer certain games over others. Those preferences, however, do not make the less preferred games something other than games and the less preferred friendships something other than friendships. In other words, employing the notion of a family resemblance does not preclude us from arguing that certain friendships are better or more desirable than others. It should make us wary, however, of saying that an ideal understanding of friendship is the only understanding of friendship.

Why should we accept or even entertain the possibility that friendship is a family resemblance concept? In Wittgenstein's view there is no better answer to this question than to go "look and see." Given the widespread experience of making, having, and sometimes losing friends, readers may want to consider whether all of their friendships, from childhood on up, share some set of features.[9] At a more theoretical level, the plausibility of seeing friendship as a family resemblance concept can be strengthened by considering a well-formulated account to the contrary: an account that argues that certain core or essential characteristics to friendship exist. As noted earlier, Elizabeth Telfer provides one such account and examining her position in chapter 2 will help illustrate the problems associated with attempting to set out the necessary and sufficient conditions of friendship. While these arguments hardly amount to a proof, they do suggest a certain level of skepticism toward finding the necessary and sufficient conditions of friendship.

Suggesting that friendship is a family resemblance concept may help diminish our expectations of finding a definitive account of friendship, but that is not the same as saying that no account can be given whatsoever. After all, friendship is a something and not an anything or a nothing. To have a friendship is to have a kind of relationship that is distinguishable from other sorts of relationships (although it frequently overlaps with a variety of other relationships and roles). In order to map out those distinctions, the following sections turn to Michael Oakeshott's conception of practice and apply it to friendship. Employing the notion of practice delivers a clearer sense of the nature of the variation of understandings of friendship as well as the ways in which friendship differs from merely friendly relationships and relationships of good will.

OAKESHOTT AND PRACTICES

Characterizing friendship as a social practice (or a set of social practices) is not new although little philosophical attention has been devoted to what that might actually entail.[10] Here, the idea of a practice refers to a set of shared rules or norms to which participants must subscribe if they are to partake of the activity in question. In his account of practice, Oakeshott writes,

> A practice may be identified as a set of considerations, manners, uses, ob-
> servances, customs, standards, canon's maxims, principles, rules, and offices
> specifying useful procedures or denoting obligations or duties which
> relate to human actions and utterances. It is a prudential or a moral adver-
> bial qualification of choices and performances, more or less complicated,
> in which conduct is understood in terms of a procedure.
>
> (OAKESHOTT 1975:55)

Moreover, he writes, practices "may range from mere protocol to what may be called a 'way of life.' . . . They may acquire the firmness of an 'institution,' or they may remain relatively plastic" (56). Practices that come to constitute institutions can take a formal character and be embodied in requirements that license sanctions or punishment if they are violated. In these cases, many of the rules and procedures that define the practice are formalized, ratified, and sometimes enforced by an identifiable authority. These practices may establish discrete roles or distinctive personae that one assumes at a particular time (e.g., a teacher, a lawyer, a doctor).

In contrast, the practice of friendship is much more plastic (to use Oake-shott's term). It is not institutionalized in the sense that there do not exist formalized ways of becoming or being a friend, at least in the contemporary West (Allan 1989:4; Jeske 2008:129). Like the practices of parenting or entertaining guests, friendship admits a variety of approaches that are largely free of a recognized authority. Nevertheless, it is necessary to sub-scribe to the conventions of friendship in order to be friends. To not abide by these conventions—either through choice, misunderstanding, or lack of competence—can mean not merely failing to participate in the practice, but suffering from informal sanctions that, in the case of friendship, can have unfortunate and sometimes heart-breaking consequences.

Oakeshott's claim that a practice entails rules that qualify or condition human actions and that those qualifications are adverbial in character will also be important to note. Practices do not specify performances. On Oakeshott's use of the term, a *practice* is defined less by what is pursued and more by how something is pursued. As a set of adverbial conditions, a practice does not tell us specifically what to do, but rather how to do it. Hence, central elements of practices may entail acting, "punctually, considerately, civilly, scientifically, legally, candidly, judicially, poetically, morally, etc." (Oakeshott 1975:56). For example, etiquette as a practice instructs us how to eat, not what to eat, not what to say, but how to say it. Subscribing to a practice of etiquette does not preclude any particular kind of meal, merely how it will be eaten. Similarly, it does not prevent or demand that we say anything in particular, but rather how we say what we want to say. How we are to understand the adverbial character of the practice of friendship will be discussed. As we shall see, it may be possible to distinguish different practices of friendship based on differences in the adverbial conditions that are expected in a relationship.

THE ACTIONS OF FRIENDS

Oakeshott's discussion draws our attention to two features of practices that will prove useful in this account of friendship. First, the rules that constitute the practices of friendship condition the *actions* of agents and second, they condition their *motives*. A focus on action presupposes a certain voluntary character to friendship in the sense that we must choose how to be with our friends. The norms and expectations of friendship are not self-executing in the sense that friends must interpret and apply them to specific people and circumstances. Friends must make choices. To do otherwise is to act thoughtlessly and to act thoughtlessly with our friends is to violate a common norm of friendship. In this regard, Oakeshott notes that a practice entails a language of self-disclosure. We tell the world something about ourselves not merely by having certain desires and interests, but by the way in which we pursue those desires and interests. As we shall see, friendships can be understood as requiring particular languages of self-disclosure that set them off from other sorts of relationships. In other words, we can distinguish practices of friendship from other practices (psychiatry, parenting, policing, and so forth), not so much by what is done with or for friends, but how they go about doing the things they do.[11]

The voluntary character of friendship is embedded in the notion that friendship conditions how we are friends. Some go further and argue that the voluntary character of friendship also extends to the question of whether to initiate a friendship. In support of this position, they argue that friendship is frequently distinguished from nonvoluntary relationships of blood. The expression "choosing a friend" or "making a friend" appears to point to a rather robust voluntary element in the creation of a particular friendship.

On the other hand, the voluntary view is sometimes contested by those who argue that we also "discover friends" or find ourselves in a friendship. Anthropological and historical evidence suggests that not all peoples understand friendship as a simple matter of choice (Cohen 1961; Friedman 1993:227–28; Bell and Coleman 1999:3). Even in the West, the practice of friendship may be a bit more nuanced than is frequently portrayed. While we may choose our friends, most friends come from the same socioeconomic background (Allan 1989:23). Furthermore, the practices of friendship may not only tell us how to be friends, but with whom we should and should not be friends (as we shall see in chapter 7, the state can coercively establish or reinforce those distinctions by limiting forms of association). Finally, to the extent that the motivations and sentiments of friendship are themselves not chosen, then the decision whether to be friends would also appear not to be wholly voluntary.

In this dispute over whether the choice of friends is really a choice, one could argue that whatever involuntary elements are part of a practice of friendship, they can never fully push out the voluntary elements associated with initiating and sustaining a friendship. Certain sentiments of friendship may spontaneously well up inside us. Certain social sanctions may exist for failing to be friends with someone from a certain tribe or class. Social status may define the opportunity set for friendship. Nevertheless, even when we "find ourselves" in a friendship because of an involuntary affection or social position, we must still choose to act upon that affection as well as sustain and maintain the relationship.[12] We may choose not to recognize the appropriate motivations in others or resist acting on our own motives and never initiate the relationship, or we may refuse to live up to the appropriate adverbial conditions for how we should be friends and destroy the relationship. Clearly, our choices are influenced by context, although it is unlikely in the extreme that they are fully determined by context. After all, no one is attracted to everyone with the same socioeconomic status. In contrast, one remains a sibling, even if one loses all (or refuses to have any) contact with a brother or sister. Not so with friendship. At least in the contemporary West, friends can always ask whether they are or should remain friends.

THE MOTIVATIONS OF FRIENDSHIP

The second rule-governed dimension of practices involves conditioning the motivations of participants. Oakeshott calls a focus on motivations, self-enactment (as opposed to self-disclosure). From his perspective, the motive of an action "is the action itself considered in terms of the sentiment or sentiments in which it is chosen and performed. An agent may, for example, choose to perform an action in a sentiment of greed, fear, compassion, resentment, benevolence, jealousy, love, hatred, kindheartedness, pity, envy etc." (1975:71–72). Because self-enactment refers to the choices of sentiments and because friendships need not rest on choices of this sort, I will simply refer to the *motivational requirements* that constitute friendship. Moreover, these motivational features can include not only sentiments but also duties, commitments, and self-interest. Oakeshott's more specific understanding of self-enactment, however, will come up again in chapter 4's discussion of a particular ideal of friendship and its relationship to individuality. In chapter 2, I will consider whether our practices of friendship are united by certain essential motivations (I will argue that they are not). In general, however, friendship will be understood as a set of practices in which there are certain rules that govern how friends interact as well as why they are motivated to be and remain friends.

OBJECTIONS TO VIEWING FRIENDSHIP
AS A PRACTICE

Before getting further entangled in the motivational weeds associated with friendship, it is important to note that the very idea of applying the notion of practice to friendship is not one that will be welcome in all quarters. There are at least four sorts of actual and potential objections that I will raise and then address in the remainder of this chapter. The first is that our relationships to our friends are so idiosyncratic that the expectations and norms that compose a friendship can hardly be portrayed as having the rule-governed quality of a practice. A second objection is that if there are rules and expectations associated with a friendship, they are constructed by the friends themselves. If this is the case, then friendship cannot be understood as a set of *social* practices. A third objection is that friendships require that we act for the sake of the friend and not because of a set of rules or out of a role that constitutes a practice. From this perspective, viewing a friendship as participating in a practice distorts its motivational requirement. A fourth objection is that to see friendship as a social practice is to ignore the degree to which it is an essential feature of all human life that must be connected to foundational notions of virtue and the good. Friendship tells us something about how to live the good life as such and hence is not merely a social practice. In what follows, I argue that each of these objections can be adequately addressed; preserving the possibility that friendship could be understood as a family of practices.

The spirit of the first objection makes an appearance in Montaigne's essay that honored his friend Étienne de La Boétie. Here, Montaigne asserts that the highest form of friendship is a joining of souls (1991:192). "Our friendship," he notes, "has no other model than itself, and can be compared only with itself" (193). It is a friendship "so entire, and so perfect that certainly you will hardly read of the like, and among men of today you see no trace of it in practice. So many coincidences are needed to build up such a friendship that it is a lot if fortune can do it once in three centuries" (188). It is a conception of friendship that not only turns upon the individuality of the participants, but also sees the relationship itself as distinctive and close to being inimitable. It is a vision of friendship whose virtues are to be found in the very fact that it departs from "common usage" (197).

It is certainly true that something that happens only once every three hundred years can hardly be described as a social practice. However, it is also clear that Montaigne does not understand this model of friendship as encompassing what he sees as common friendships. Consequently, the idiosyncratic character of Montaigne's ideal conception may not be as much of an objection to seeing friendship as a practice as an exception to a more general account. An alternative possibility is that it may be useful to consider a distinction between an ideal and a set of conventions and considerations that establish an ideal. The fact that there exists an ideal friendship (however rare) does not preclude that ideal from being part of a larger social practice. From this perspective, Montaigne does carve out a vision of friendship that differentiates it from other social practices that he associated with the natural, the social, the hospitable, and the erotic (188). In so doing, he is arguing that whatever friendship happens to be, it is not to be confused with these characteristics. More positively, he sees friendship as a relationship in which there is no ulterior end or purpose, but only a mutually recognized love that dissolves all competing obligations. In other words, his ideal friendship contains mutually recognized motivations (their mutual love) and adverbial forms of self-disclosure (lovingly, trustingly, willingly, and conjointly) that do point to a nascent practice.[13]

A version of the second objection could be drawn out of the claim that friendships are minimally structured interpersonal relationships. For example, Laurence Thomas writes that for friendship, "aside from the rules of morality, the nature of that interaction is not defined by this or that set of social rules" (1987:219). Pahl also notes that "there is an emerging modern ideal of friendship. This is not based on rules, regulations or any part of the institutionalized order. Individuals, out of their own volition, work out how they should behave with their friends" (2000:61; see also Vernon 2010:210). As a final example, the anthropologist, Robert Paine argues that what is deemed permissible or desirable in a friendship may be rule-governed, but "those rules appear not to be imposed from the outside, and, furthermore, they may be largely hidden from the view to all outside the relationship" (1999:41). Whether these sorts of claims could serve as objections to the notion of friendship as a practice depend, in part, on how antinomian or private the relationship of friendship turns out to be. On the one hand, Pahl notes that the emerging modern ideal of friendship is not based on rules. On the other hand, he also outlines certain standards and norms that accompany that ideal; namely that the exchanges between friends are not scrupulously monitored, the attachments are free from legal or administrative regulation, the feelings are not ones of obligation, and the origins and maintenance of the relationship is through conscious choice (2000:62). Without a doubt, these understandings are meant to admit a high degree of variability and individuality within the relationship. Nevertheless, characterizations of the sort offered by Pahl do point to things that look like conventions, if not rules that identify a practice.

Still, there is something to the claim that the expectations and considerations that govern our relationships with our friends are privately negotiated and established (as suggested by Paine). For example, in the case of one's closest friends, one friend cannot replace another. This attribute of friendship appears to point to the individuality of the friends as well as the possible uniqueness of each relationship. In response, one could argue that friends must understand themselves as being in a particular sort of relationship that is not just any kind of relationship. They share some kind of understanding that theirs is a friendship and not, say a mere relationship of employer to employee, or brother to sister, or lord to vassal. There is some set of social customs or mores that allow such differentiation.

In addition, the idiosyncratic character of a particular friendship is not precluded by the idea of a practice. The rules, norms, and conventions of friendship must be learned and hence presume a certain level of agency to acquire and apply those rules. Moreover, because they are learned, they can be learned well or poorly and practiced clumsily or adroitly. For some, making friends will come almost naturally. For others, it will happen in fits and starts. Because of choice or chance many will have no more than a taste of friendship. A few adepts will be so skillful as to be able to manipulate the conventions of friendship in order to establish the pretense of friendship. Out of these performances have come such assessments as true friends and false friends, close friends and fair-weather friends. Some of our friends are simply better at being friends. Just as not everyone who learns to play the clarinet can play like Artie Shaw, the learned character of the practice of friendship means that it will inevitably be practiced with a great deal of variability.

The variable character of our friendships is built into the idea of a practice in another, perhaps even more important way. As noted earlier, the rules of friendship, like all social rules, are not self-executing. They must be understood and applied to particular persons in particular circumstances. The rules of friendship take one by the elbow and not by the throat, so we must choose how we go about being friends with one another. As has already been suggested, while we do not choose the norms of friendship, we must choose how we go about being friends. In this way, the character of friendship must admit the idiosyncratic and the variable. The practice of friendship does not mean that all friends will respond to one another in the same way.

A third objection to applying the idea of practice to friendship can be found in Lawrence Blum's claim that the reasons for friendship are very much focused on the friends themselves and not on external criteria such as social rules. He argues that "the conception of friendship as a practice, on the model of a game or institution involving rules, defined roles, positions, and responsibilities, etc. . . . applies very poorly to large areas of our personal moral lives and experience" (Blum 1980:60).[14] Blum fills out this objection in a later essay in considering friendship as more like a vocation than like a role. He writes, "Thus if I appeal to the norms of friendship as a way of ensuring that I am able to regard myself as good friend, I am not really acting for my friend's sake. It can even be argued that appealing to the norms of friendship out of a genuine desire to *be* a good friend is too distant from a concern for the specific friend himself" (1990:186). Within a practice, it could be argued that one is provided with a given set of reasons for doing something with, or for one's friend, whereas in a true friendship, the only motivation that should count is acting for the sake of the friend. From this perspective, if Alan defends the name and reputation of his friend Denny not for Denny's sake but because the rules of friendship tell him to do so, then he is not really being a good friend.

Blum's argument points to a rather complicated feature of friendship involving the role of certain motivations in friendship. It also points to the question of the connection between the norms of friendship and friendship itself. On the one hand, the general thrust of Blum's position is quite correct: there is something about certain motivations that appear to be incompatible with friendship. As chapter 3 will argue, self-interest or utility cannot be sufficient motives for friendship. On the other hand, Blum's assertions that "acting for the sake of one's friend" is a necessary condition for all understandings of friendship and that this condition must preclude all other motivations are less compelling. Chapter 3 will also consider the possibility of friendships being based on motivations other than that acting for the sake of one's friend and that self-interest and utility can play a role without necessarily corrupting or disabling friendship.

At this point I want to consider more thoroughly Blum's claim that something has gone awry in a friendship if Alan is defending Denny because the rules tell him to do so. Obviously, how one responds to this claim depends on one's view of rules and rule-following. To simplify, if one subscribes to a mechanical view of rules in which they serve as a kind of algorithm, then Blum's observation makes sense. From this perspective, the rules of friendship may take the form of admonitions or imperatives such as "defend your friend from any and all attacks," "evenly split the bill whenever you go out for a meal together," or "keep no secrets from one another." These sorts of imperatives suggest that Alan should look to the rule and not to his friend. They substitute rule-mongering for judgment. If this is part of Blum's objection, then an adverbial conception of rules may help address it. Under an adverbial conception of rules, the rules of a practice of friendship condition, but do not determine, how the friends respond to and on behalf of one another. If Alan wants to defend Denny, then the adverbial rules of friendship (e.g., act loyally, considerately, openly) will guide Denny in a way that must be sensitive to a context that includes Alan, Denny, their circumstances, and the sort of friendship they possess. In short, an adverbial conception of rules requires judgment. It is open to the possibility that sometimes the defense of a friend may be unwanted, costly, embarrassing, or unjustified. Sometimes the full payment of a bill is the expression of generosity, unequal ability to pay, or of who ordered what. Sometimes a secret is kept in light of its insignificance, in light of its significance, or simply to protect the friend. If the actions of friends are guided by adverbial rules, then the rules cannot be the only things that matter, but neither can the friends simply look to each other (as perhaps Blum intimates). Alan must look to his friend, to himself, and to their circumstances in order to conclude which rules apply and then how to apply them.

A fourth objection to seeing friendship as a practice could come from those who see it as a universal or natural facet of human life. From this perspective, in order to live a fully human life, we need friends. To say that it is a social practice is not to say enough about its significance for a good life. Moreover, it ignores the degree to which friendship must be directed by a notion of nobility, excellence, or the good in order to be understood as true friendship. As James V. Schall argues, "When the friend does not exist in truth, that is, when both friends do not have a common good in which each exists, they become laws unto each other, precisely what they cannot be in friendship as Aristotle understood it" (1996:134). Seeing friendship as a social practice does not commit one to the claim that there is a best way of being friends that either expresses or cultivates an excellent human life. It does not bring one to the foundational questions of life.[15]

As Schall suggests, an example of this sort of position could be drawn out of Aristotle. Aristotle argues that while there are a number of ways to understand friendship, the most complete understanding is that of a friendship between individuals who are virtuous. Given the sort of beings that we happened to be, Aristotle argues that this is the highest form of friendship. On this account, friendship is not merely an expression of human excellence; it is also instrumental to cultivating human excellence. It is, he argues, necessary for living the best form of life: "no one would choose to have all [other] goods and yet be alone, since a human being is political, tending by nature to live together with one another" (Aristotle 1985:1169b15). More importantly, "having friends seems to be the greatest external good" (1169b10). On this account, friendship is necessary to achieve other, higher goods. In the case of moral virtue, "the excellent person will need people for him to benefit" (1169b10). The happy, relatively self-contained life of the magnanimous person is not complete unless he can assist others in the right way at the right time in the right amount. The virtue of assisting others in the right way can only happen if the excellent person knows and understands those whom he is assisting. Friends allow us to benefit other people in the right way, which can only happen if you understand who they are and the circumstances that they face. A version of this argument is found in Lorraine Smith Pangle's interpretation of Aristotle. She writes, "Friendship is important for Aristotle for much the same reason that virtue and philosophy are: Each in a different way is a perfection of man's potential as a rational being."[16] On this account, whatever goodness is associated with friendship is to be found in "the naturally social and political character of man" (2003:196) and not in the shared agreements or conventions that compose a social practice.

It is true that seeing friendship through the lens of a social practice will make one attuned to its historical and cultural variability. Still, one could concede that there is an ontology implied by any analysis that appeals to social practice. Whatever we happen to be, we happen to be beings that are capable of devising and living by rules and norms. This sort of ontological claim, however, does not say very much about the content of those rules and norms. Nor does it yield the judgment that all practices should be celebrated and valued, and even for those practices that are understood as valuable, they need not necessarily be understood as valuable for everyone. So although the notion of practice does not evade ontological or foundational presuppositions, those foundations settle very little.[17]

Perhaps the deeper problem with the open character of friendship as a practice is the one that Schall notes, namely that if friends do not share some common good—be it virtue or God—then they become a law unto themselves. And, most importantly, given the subject of this book, this means political trouble. As Cicero wrote, political conspiracies "can never be set afoot by one man without the aid of friends" (1991:95). One way to prevent friends from being drawn into nefarious or criminal activities is to define and bind friendship to virtue: "without virtue friendship cannot exist at all" (87). If this is taken to mean that true friends goad us toward the good and so-called friends lead us astray, then true friends would never ask us to do wrongful things. Only so-called friends lead us into conspiracies. Seeing friendship as a practice does not tie friendship tightly enough to some more foundational conception of the proper aim of human life.

On the other hand, the problem with defining friendship in terms of doing the right thing is that it blinds us to the virtues of adverbial self-disclosure that compose friendship itself, regardless of the particular ends that friends may seek. Moreover, it blinds us to the power of the loyalties and forms of courage that can accompany the relationship. We misunderstand an important part of human interaction if we fail to see that friendships—true, authentic friendships—can lead to conspiracies, wrongdoing, and harm. These may not be friendships that we want to encourage, but that does not require denying that they are friendships. In some sense, Cicero recognized this problem. For although he defined friendship in terms of virtue, he was well-aware that friendships posed a danger to

Rome. If friends could become a law unto themselves, then Cicero posed a law of friendship that required friends not to ask one another to do wrongful things (1991:95–96). In effect, he may be read as acknowledging that even if a relationship breaks the law of friendship, wrongdoers can still experience friendship.

Seeing friendship as a family of practices captures the diversity of friendships at both an individual and social level. Up to this point, however, the discussion of friendship as a family of practices has been little more than skeletal.[18] The importance of the motives and actions of friends to those practices does not distinguish friendship from very many other rule-governed social arrangements. Despite its formality, this chapter has addressed a number of objections to this conceptualization of friendship, but it has yet to tackle the objection that friendship can, in fact, be defined by a set of necessary and sufficient conditions. In other words, is it possible that there exist certain motives and actions that are essential to friendship? The next chapter begins to respond to this possibility by turning to Elizabeth Telfer's particularly concise and well-formulated account of friendship. Taking her view as illustrative of a philosophical attempt to nail down the conditions for friendship will illuminate difficulties with the claim that friendship can be identified by a particular motivation or set of actions.

two

MOTIVATIONS, ACTIONS, AND THE VALUE OF FRIENDSHIP

In arguing for a practice-based view of friendship, chapter 1 claimed that motivations and actions play an important role and that we unavoidably make choices over how to maintain our friendships and possibly whether to initiate them. It also claimed that we should not expect to be able to provide the necessary and sufficient conditions for friendship if it is to be understood as a family resemblance concept. This chapter digs deeper into that idea by discerning its implications for understanding the role of motivations and actions in our practices of friendship. It begins by noting that the philosophical call to provide a set of necessary and sufficient conditions for friendship has not gone unanswered.[1] Exploring the difficulties of one such account—offered by Elizabeth Telfer—will help to formulate the character of friendship's diversity. In many respects, the following discussion is indebted to Telfer's account even as it backs away from her stronger, essentialist-sounding claims. Responding to her position does not demonstrate the impossibility of setting out the necessary and sufficient conditions for friendship, but it does point to the difficulties of trying to set out those conditions.

After briefly summarizing Telfer's position, this chapter turns to her account of the motivations of friendship and argues that a plausible case can be made for widening the scope of appropriate motives beyond her discussion of affection and fondness to include desire, respect, appreciative love, and care. Instead of friendships being driven by an essential motive that defines the relationship, there exists of repertoire of motives (and actions) that can condition a friendship. Indeed, what is understood to be part of the repertoire of appropriate motives is a function of time and place. The "Essential Motivations of Friendship" section draws on Telfer's account in another way and claims that friends must recognize the appropriate motives in one another in order to be friends. As we shall see in chapter 3, mutual recognition of motives allows us to distinguish friendships from mere friendly actions as well as to identify false friends from actual ones. The "Mutual Recognition of Ordinarily Appropriate Motivations" section takes up the action conditions of friendship and the "Importance of Acting Friendly" section fills out Oakeshott's notion of self-disclosure as a way to understand those action conditions. Our practices of friendship are governed less by demands for the performance of specific actions and more by adverbial rules: the question is how friends should act toward one another as opposed to setting out specific actions. Because the term *self-disclosure* has been employed in earlier understandings of friendship, this section ("Adverbial Conditions of Friendship and Self-Disclosure") explores the differences in these understandings. The "Explanation, Justification, and the Practice of Friendship" section asks what we have gained in understanding friendship as a family of practices. Have we "explained" friendship? Have we provided a way to "justify" friendship? These questions bring us to the limits of a practice-based account of friendship as well as to issues surrounding the value of friendship. The remaining sections of the chapter defend the view that friendship itself can provide reasons for action by responding to Simon Keller's argument to the contrary. Friendships are intrinsically valuable, even if their value does not outweigh all others.

THE ESSENTIAL MOTIVATIONS OF FRIENDSHIP?

In her account of friendship, Telfer argues that friends must share activities. More specifically, she argues that friends need to provide reciprocal services (you shovel my driveway and I take in your mail when you are on vacation), have mutual contact (we talk, go to the movies, or simply spend time together), and have joint pursuits (we belong to the same book group, synagogue, community organization). She believes that these shared activities, while necessary conditions, are not sufficient. For, in addition to doing certain things, we must also perform them out of certain desires. In Telfer's view, these desires are the *"passions* of friendship." In other words, "friends must have affection for, or be fond of, each other." Telfer goes on to define affection "as a desire for another's welfare and happiness *as a particular individual.* This desire is thus to be distinguished both from sense of duty and from benevolence" (1991:251).[2] She argues that in a friendship, this affection is not connected to character (unlike what Aristotle saw as necessary in the most complete form of friendship). The characteristics of an individual may stimulate affection, but affection, at bottom, is irrational. Consequently, friendships are able to survive changes in character. It is difficult, she argues, to put our finger on why we like someone. It is not simply a matter of adding up a set of characteristics. Rather, it is something about the whole package that draws us to them (253). In addition to having affection for the person, Telfer argues that friendship is defined by a desire to be with our friends, to be in their company and not just "a desire for company as such" (252). Finally, Telfer argues that friends must not only have the passions of friendship, they must also choose to act on those passions (256). But the choice must be mutual. A friendship requires a kind of meeting of the minds. Hence, one cannot "choose to be a friend of just anyone." As she notes, what is also necessary is that "the existence of the passions of friendship in both parties, and the practice on both sides of acting on them, once established be *acknowledged* by the parties" (257). Or, in terms that have been used here, friendship requires the *mutual recognition* of the motives/sentiments of friendship.[3]

In a broad way, Telfer's focus on shared activities and the passions of friendship fit nicely into the formal structure of practices that includes both motivations and actions. The question now becomes whether *these* passions and *these* kinds of activities are necessary for friendship. If they are, do they offer a plausible account of the necessary and sufficient conditions of friendship? Undoubtedly, in some friendships, the elements discussed by Telfer are indeed essential. In such cases, if these conditions are absent, then the particular friendship would dissolve. Whether they are necessary for all friendships is not so clear. For example, Telfer claims that friends must have affection for one another. At one level, this claim seems to be undeniable. What would a friendship mean if there was no affection? Nevertheless, Telfer admits that "to some extent, of course, I am stipulating, rather than reporting, that the presence of the inclinations is a necessary part of friendship" (1991:256). In terms of how other thinkers have conceived of friendship, Telfer's stipulation would be largely accurate. For example, Preston King notes the importance of affection, but then writes, "At the end, what affection is, and whether it is genuine, and appropriate, may be best left to whoever owns it" (2007:131). Other thinkers place less weight on the importance of affection. For example, it is not at all clear that affection was a necessary condition for all of Aristotle's conceptions of friendship (Grunebaum 2003:38).[4] In his account of friendship between old people, he noted that they may not even "find each other pleasant" (Aristotle 1985:1156a25–30). Nor is it clear that affection is essential to Kant's conception (1991:216), or perhaps even C. S. Lewis's conception of friendship (1960:70–72).

If affection does not appear to be necessary to these other conceptions of friendship, then what else motivates individuals to become friends? An alternative motivation that is frequently mentioned is that of desire. But is not desire the same thing as affection? While the two ideas are frequently used interchangeably, it is possible to distinguish a form of desire that is not the same as affection in a way that is useful for understanding different kinds of friendship. Very generally, affection tends to be directed to the particularity of the object of affection. Kim-Chong Chong notes that,

> In the case of material objects, the object is valued in such a way as to express its uniqueness and irreplaceability. In the case of persons, one does not have an affection for another simply because he possesses certain qualities—someone may possess the most appalling qualities, and yet one may still have an affection for him. Similar qualities in another might, on the other hand, arouse dislike. Granted that the reason for this could be described, by pointing to more detailed differences, but this does not obviate the fact that not all that goes by the name of "affection" can be so described.
>
> (1984:354)

In contrast, desire can be focused, not on the particularity of the object of desire, but on the qualities of the object that fit it into a given class. On this view of desire, what matters are those qualities, and if another object or person possesses those attributes, then they can replace the original object or person.

Assuming such a distinction between affection and desire, it is easy to see how affection for another can serve as a motive for friendship. Indeed, for Telfer and, at least initially for Chong, there is a sense in which the particularity associated with affection is the sine qua non of friendship. After all, it is sometimes said that one friend cannot be replaced by another. For Chong, "unless there is or comes to be a care and concern for the other person in himself, there can be no close personal relationship to speak of" (1984:355). It would seem, then, that affection is necessary for the kind of close personal relationship that defines friendship.[5]

Despite these claims, however, Chong does not go so far as to claim that relationships that are desire-based cannot be friendships. For she also notes, "There are friendships which are not friendships in the full sense of the word, as we have described it. One may have a friend whose company one enjoys, but for whom one cares little or not at all, and some friends are friends whose companionship it would be advantageous and pleasurable for one to have. An egoist is not precluded from friendships of these sorts" (1984:355). What Chong is saying of the ethical egoist can be said of those for whom friendship is based on desire. What is being presumed in this discussion is that while these friendships may not encompass the "full sense of the word," they could still be understood as friendships. But why do they not qualify as full friendships? For Chong, the claim may be intuitive or merely stipulative, namely that care, affection, and commitment are essential features of friendship and that there is something lesser about "mere" companionship. She may very well be correct that there is something inferior about friendships motivated by desire as opposed to affection, but that does not preclude them from being friendships of a sort.[6]

To clarify further, it might be helpful to put this in an Aristotelian tripartite framework of friendship. Among friendships of pleasure, utility, and virtue, friendships of pleasure could be understood as friendships that are motivated by *desire* in Chong's sense of the term. These are friendships in which the parties see one another not as individuals in their particularity, but as persons of a certain sort—for example, they are good skiers, they enjoy partying, they are entertaining to be around, or they can tell a good story. Friendships of this sort are less a function of attending to the unique characteristics of the individual and more focused on the qualities that they happen to possess. In these kinds of friendships, the relationship is subject to the vicissitudes of those qualities. When they change, then the motivations for maintaining the friendship may disappear. Going fishing with George can be the basis for a friendship for Bill, but if Bill no longer enjoys fishing then the friendship may fade. There is something, as Aristotle noted, short-lived or unstable about friendships of pleasure. For our concerns here, whatever one may think of these friendships, they are still friendships, despite the fact that they are not motivated by affection. Desire, when distinguished from affection, can also serve as an appropriate reason for a friendship.

Even if one is unconvinced by a distinction between affection and desire, there are other motivations for friendship. A third possible motive for friendship is respect. In what Marilyn Friedman calls *particularized respect*, "someone is admired specifically for her worthwhile qualities, her excellences. . . . It may involve affection or fond feelings, but it need not" (1993:194). In this sort of friendship, the friends are drawn to one another because they are excellent musicians or excellent tennis players or just because they are smart. Perhaps through one's association with the other individual, one is challenged and made a better tennis player. This association may be enjoyable, but it may also be difficult and demanding. It does not require the kind of vulnerability in which one's secrets are brought to light, but rather a vulnerability in which one's weaknesses are potentially revealed. Perhaps a version of this motivation is implied by an older conception of being drawn to the nobility or virtuosity of another.[7] In this regard, it could be expressed in the kind of friendship between Aristotle's great-souled individuals.[8] Obviously, respect can be understood in a variety of ways. In this case, it is not the sort of generalized respect owed to all humankind, but a respect for excellence.

A fourth possible motivation for friendship that could be seen as a shade different from respect is presented in C. S. Lewis's work. In his essay on friendship, Lewis places great weight on friends acting in a particular way and sharing activities. Nevertheless, he is also quite clear that friendship is a form of love. In fact, it is a love that requires a fairly high degree of self-cultivation and restraint. It is not a love that is subject to jealousy (1960:67), and it is "is utterly free from Affection's need to be needed" (69); it tends to eschew gratitude (70). Rather, the love that motivates friendship is admiration or what he calls "appreciative love" (71). He writes, "In a perfect Friendship, this Appreciative love is, I think, often so great and so firmly based that each member of the circle feels, in his secret heart, humbled before all the rest" (71–72). While Lewis is adamant that friendship must be about something, in the sense that the friends share some truth or purpose, the motivation of appreciative love is distinct from affection, eros, and gratitude. To the degree that it is driven by a sense of humility (perhaps the Christian virtue of humility) it is also distinguishable from the notion of respect just discussed. It may very well be a conception of friendship that is unique to early to mid-twentieth-century Oxford dons, but it is still a conception of friendship.

A fifth motivation for friendship that may be distinguishable from these other motivations is what Blum calls "deep caring and identification with the good of the other." In many cases, we care for someone because of other feelings that we possess. We care for a friend because we love her or have affection for her. But it may be possible to conceive of care as a free-standing feeling which can be mutually felt and recognized by friends. In Blum's formulation, "caring means that if trouble arises between . . . [the friends], they will try to work it through." On this account, it is because the friends care so deeply for one another that they experience comfort and joy. Moreover, this sense of caring for the other is moderated by one's sense of separateness from and knowledge of the friend (Blum 1980:70).[9] Caring for someone as a motive is distinguishable from simply liking or having affection for them.

There may be other motivations for friendship that have existed, do exist, or will exist that are different from affection, fondness, desire, respect, care, and appreciative love. Kant, for example, thought that need was presupposed in every friendship (1991:213; see also Nixon 2015:128). The need here is not material, but a need for confidence in the other.[10] The larger point of this discussion is not simply to multiply the possible motivations, but to suggest that affection is not the only motivation for friendship. In fact, there may be no essential passion or passions of friendship. It may be more help-ful to argue that in any given culture there is a repertoire of motivations that are understood as necessary elements for interpersonal friendship. Within that repertoire, any single motivation, if it is mutually recognized, can meet the motivational requirements of the relationship. But these motivations can be present in various combinations and to various degrees. One may respect, have genuine affection for, and care for a friend. Alterna-tively, one may have a friendship in which one simply desires to be with him because he is fun. Moreover, the motives for a friendship can change over time. What began as a friendship based on desire could become one based primarily on affection or appreciative love (or some combination of motivations). As we shall see in part 3's discussion of friendship among states, even though the mutual recognition of sentiments is not necessary (or even possible), other sorts of reasons will still need to motivate the relationship.

THE MUTUAL RECOGNITION OF ORDINARILY APPROPRIATE MOTIVATIONS

The argument so far suggests that friendship is situated in a social context that sets out the repertoire of appropriate motivations. If individuals do not possess the appropriate motivations or fail to recognize them, then the friendship cannot get off the ground or, in the case of an existing friendship, it will have to be rethought or abandoned altogether. Telfer's view, however, points to an important feature of our current practices of friendship: friends must recognize appropriate motives in one another in order to be friends. Part of our practices of friendship involves conveying and recognizing something from that repertoire of motivations in others. If that capacity to read the sentiments and feelings of others is absent or disabled, as in the case of certain psychopathologies, then the possibilities for friendship diminish and perhaps disappear. Consequently, friendship requires that we are not entirely opaque to one another.[11]

How is this motivational requirement met? At some point, two individu-als arrive at the belief that their interactions are motivated by the right sort

of sentiments or reasons. This belief may be bolstered after a mutual decla-
ration of friendship ("You are such a good friend!"), but it is more than
likely to be reached by the parties inferring the motives of each other from
a series of actions and interactions ("Thanks for going out of your way and
picking me up at the airport . . . again"). The friendship, of course, is genuine if the inferences are correct. It is a misunderstanding or a charade (more
on this in chapter 3) if the inferences are incorrect.[12]

Once the friends believe that their interactions are motivated in the
right sort of way, must every interaction be properly motivated to sustain
the friendship? Such a high level of self-reflection may make sense in an
ideal of friendship (such as the one that will be discussed in chapter 4), but
most ongoing friendships are more likely to be sustained by continuing to
infer the motives of one's friend from her actions. Consider an ongoing
friendship between Cuddy and Greg. Even if Cuddy, with little thought,
invites Greg to her party or happens to be inviting him when she is angry
about something he did, her actions will continue to confirm (or disconfirm) their mutual belief that they are friends. If Cuddy does not act in a
way that is consonant with their friendship, or simply declares that she does
not want to be friends with Greg, then Greg (if he is not completely thick-
headed) will conclude that the friendship has come to an end.

The importance of the mutual recognition requirement combined with
the role of belief-sustaining actions has a number of implications. The first
is that the epistemic requirements for establishing a friendship are not insignificant. Even if the mutual recognition requirement can be eased or
evaded by the role of belief-sustaining actions, it points to the difficulties of
seeing friendship as a general model for citizenship (discussed in chapter 5)
and the problems of distinguishing friendships, friendly actions, and false
friendships (discussed in chapter 3). Second, recognizing the appropriate
motives for friendship helps to distinguish friendships from other sorts of
relationships (lovers, partners, associates, comrades) as well as to identify
different practices of friendship. Third, the importance of belief-sustaining
actions helps to differentiate the reasons for a friendship (which are trace-
able back to the mutual recognition of appropriate motivations) from reasons for acting within a friendship (which are understood to be consistent
with those motives because they accord with a mutually acceptable practice

of friendship). Cuddy does not always have to feel affection for Greg when she interacts with him. If she wants to remain a friend, however, she will need to act as a friend would act (enough of the time). Finally, the importance of belief-sustaining actions does not diminish the importance of the appropriate sentiments for the relationship itself. However friendly Cuddy may be to Greg, the relationship fails as a friendship if Cuddy does not recognize the appropriate motives in herself or Greg comes to disbelieve that Cuddy actually possesses those motives.

THE IMPORTANCE OF ACTING FRIENDLY

The role of belief-sustaining actions brings us to the importance of action in friendship. The mere recognition of a set of appropriate sentiments is not sufficient. For example, an announcement by Sue and Kathy that they respected one another would not be sufficient for friendship. As Telfer notes, friendship is not merely about the mutual recognition of appropriate motives, it is also about doing the sorts of things that friends do. In her account of friendship, the doings involve reciprocal services, mutual contact, and joint pursuits. While important to some understandings of friendship, these activities are not necessary for all friendships. Friendship does require mutual contact, but that is a condition for the existence of many types of relationships and is not a particularly helpful thread. Must friends engage in joint activities? In Kant's understanding of friendship in the "absolute sense," individuals open themselves up to one another (1991:214). This kind of relationship is perfectly intelligible as a form of friendship, but it is not one that requires joint activity. Must friends engage in reciprocal services? Once again, it is not evident that either Kant or Montaigne thought this was necessary. In addition, when friends are unequal, it may be very difficult for one friend to reciprocate, which may encourage the friends to avoid being useful to one another; i.e., placing the unequal friend in the embarrassing situation of having to reciprocate when she lacks the means to do so.

Nevertheless, it is impossible to think of friendship without friends interacting. Could one distinguish friendship from other relationships based on certain categories of activities? For example, what do we do with friends that we do not do with strangers, acquaintances, relatives, teachers, or psychoanalysts? Moreover, can we distinguish different types of friendship based on different types of activities? In the former case, perhaps friendships create an expectation that one will share one's secrets with one's friends, but not with a mere acquaintance.[13] In the latter case, perhaps some friends are for doing fun things, some are for doing useful things, and others challenge us to be the best sort of person that we can be. Does it make sense to focus on the sorts of things that are done with friends?

To some degree, focusing on specific activities to identify friendships is a plausible way to differentiate them from other sorts of relationships and to distinguish among different practices of friendship.[14] While plausible, this approach is not particularly parsimonious. The problem, of course, is that we can do many different things with the same friends without necessarily changing the character or quality of a friendship. Miles may be friends with Jack because they were college roommates years ago and because they occasionally go golfing together now. Miles's decision to take Jack wine tasting to teach him about the virtues of pinot noir need not transform their friendship. Alternatively, the activities that may define a friendship can also be done with nonfriends. I may share the deepest secrets of my life with my friend, but I may do the same with an analyst, a priest, or a prosecutor. We may seek to be friends with those who are useful to us, but not everyone who is useful is a friend. The virtue and zeal of St. Joan may be admirable, but being her friend might be unbearable. Basing friendships on activities points to something important, but differentiating practices in this way will either result in an unwieldy number of categories or be untrue to the flexible character of our friendships.

THE ADVERBIAL CONDITIONS OF FRIENDSHIP AND SELF-DISCLOSURE

As we saw in Oakeshott's discussion of practice, it is possible to differentiate practices not on the basis of what is specifically done, but on the basis of how actors should interact. The adverbial conventions of friendship establish a kind of protocol to which the friends subscribe when they are acting as friends and distinguish their friendship from how they go about interacting with those who are not friends.[15] For example, how Tony interacts with his therapist may be quite different from how he interacts with his friend Paulie. With his therapist, his interactions are governed by norms of professionalism. He may approach her deferentially (she is trained), expeditiously (she is being paid), and inattentively to her welfare (he has no other interaction with her). In contrast, when he tells Paulie about a secret in his life, he speaks comfortably and easily and is attentive to how the secret may affect his friend.

A set of adverbial conditions may not only distinguish friendship from other relationships, but also distinguish different types of friendships. On this account, a specific practice of friendship does not establish whether one goes to a movie or reveals one's secrets to another but how one does those things. For some friendships, interacting intimately, honestly, and authentically is prized while in other friendships interacting usefully, consistently, and reliably is seen as the norm. I may go to a movie with an old friend from college or with a friend from work, but how I (and she) will interact in that experience may be (assuming they are different sorts of friendships) quite different. In both cases, while we may share a cab, buy tickets, and talk about the plot, how we go to a movie can be performed differently. With the friend from work we may act reservedly, speak carefully, and eat popcorn moderately. In the case of an old chum, our actions and words may flow more freely, wholeheartedly, and unconditionally. Alternatively, how we tell a friend about a personal trauma may differ depending on whether the friend is someone from a reading group or someone we have known for years.

It is also possible that different practices of friendship are dependent on gender, class, sexual orientation, or ethnicity.[16] Perhaps the expectation of how fervently friends will converse is a function of gender. Friedman notes that while friends generally talk to one another, this is not always the case. The friends, she writes, "might be men, and might have been raised to avoid emotional expressiveness and intimate self-disclosure even in close personal relationships. Such patterns of noncommunicativeness in close relationship seem not to be part of the cultural conception or idealization of friendship but to derive instead from other contingently related social conditions, such as the practices of masculinity" (1993:226). In contrast, I am suggesting it may be possible to describe the norms of masculinity as having been incorporated into the cultural practices of friendship. The question of the number of different practices of friendship and whether those differences are correlated with such things as gender is an empirical question.[17]

The adverbial conditions associated with friendship are not, of course, always enabling. Sometimes they disable and preclude forms of friendship. Class distinctions, for example, may limit the interactions between individuals. Gendered distinctions may be governed by practices that are incompatible with the expectations for friendship or they may limit the ways in which individuals can be friends. Alternatively, how one interacts within a friendship may be conditioned by sectarian divisions. Crossing borders may entail grave risks for friends. Derrida, for example, notes that the dominant ethico-politico-philosophical discourse on friendship excludes friendships between women and between men and women. "This double exclusion," he writes, "of the feminine in the philosophical paradigm of friendship would thus confer on it the essential and essentially sublime figure of virile homosexuality" (1988:642).[18] If this is the theoretical world, the practice may be different. For example, Friedman writes that "friendship among women has been the cement not only of the various historical waves of the feminist movement but also of numerous communities of women throughout history who defied the local conventions for their gender and lived lives of creative disorder" (1993:248–49).

The idea, then, is that there are conventions for how we proceed with our friends that are different from how we proceed with acquaintances, strangers, teachers, police officers, and doctors and allow us to distinguish different practices of friendship. Our friends come to know us in terms of how we are friends; that is, how we go about living up to the adverbial conditions that define friendship (or a particular sort of friendship). It is, then, not inappropriate to use Oakeshott's description of this sort of activity as a form of self-disclosure.[19] Self-disclosure does not necessitate the opening of one's heart to another, the confession of one's inner-most secrets, the revelation of one's authentic self, or the finding of an individual who replicates oneself (although friendship could entail any of those actions). Rather, self-disclosure is much more prosaic. It is to be found in the choices made while acknowledging and subscribing to a set of adverbial rules that hang together in a manner that composes a social practice. Self-disclosure is achieved through the actions that we perform when living up to the conventions of friendship. It is judged in terms of quality of those performances and is frequently marked by such terms as whether one has been a good, bad, or merely fair-weather friend.

The idea of self-disclosure has been associated with friendship by a number of different thinkers. For example, Laurence Thomas argues that self-disclosure is the "predominant way in which companion friends can and do contribute to one another's flourishing, where the emphasis here is upon improvement of character and personality" (1987:227). By self-disclosure, Thomas means the reciprocal confiding of private information about our lives.[20] In contrast to Oakeshott's usage, Thomas's understanding of self-disclosure is a disclosure of secrets. By engaging in self-disclosure, we make ourselves vulnerable to one another and create the bonds of mutual trust that convey a sense of the special regard that deep friends have for one another (223).[21] It also signals to those to whom we have confided intimate information that we are willing to accept advice and counsel from them because they know us in a particular way. In contrast, Thomas argues that individuals who are public about everything in their lives—who are not discrete in their self-disclosures—have signaled to the world that they will accept advice from pretty much everyone and that they have neither special regard for nor trust in anyone in particular. Consequently, Thomas believes that they are incapable of deep friendships (224).

It is important to note that Thomas's account of friendship (and his conception of self-disclosure) is tied to an ideal of friendship and not friendship as such. Consequently, the differences in the meaning of self-disclosure can easily be understood as connected to differences in use. Perhaps what is more relevant for adopting Oakeshott's use of self-disclosure is a particular criticism that has been raised of Thomas by Cocking and Kennett. They argue that the problem with Thomas's account of self-disclosure as a condition for friendship is that it presupposes a very static and discrete conception of the self. As such, it precludes, what they take to be, the most significant facet of a deep friendship, namely that the self is itself a product of the friendship.[22] They argue that our most important friendships rest on what they call a "drawing account of the self" (1998:505), in which we are receptive to our friends' interests in a way that can change our own character and we are susceptible to our friends' interpretations of ourselves which can alter our self-conceptions.

Assuming that Cocking and Kennett are correct about the limits of Thomas's conception of self-disclosure and assuming that their alternative deep conception of friendship is in fact a valued and valuable conception of friendship, does Oakeshott's conception of self-disclosure foreclose the kind of ideal of friendship that they are suggesting? If it does, then Oakeshott's notion of self-disclosure may be unnecessarily preempting particularly important understandings of friendship.

Let us begin by assuming that Cocking and Kennett are carving out a plausible ideal practice of friendship. In that practice, there are certain expectations for both what the friends want and how they are going to get it. First and foremost, what they must want is the kind of friendship that Cocking and Kennett outline. In other words, they want a "deep" friendship in which their self-understandings will be susceptible to the interests of their friends (and not just anyone) and they take seriously the interpretations of themselves that their friends offer. If deep friendship is both a goal and a practice in an Oakeshottian sense, then its pursuit will be governed by a set of motivations and adverbial conditions. Consequently, it is not surprising to see that deep friendship requires acting responsively, openly, attentively, willingly, endlessly, flexibly, and acceptingly in addition to being motivated by affection and the desire for shared experiences (Cocking and Kennett 1998:524). From an Oakeshottian perspective, what distinguishes deep friendship from other forms of friendship are both the possible motivations that the friends mutually recognize (e.g., other practices of friendship could be motivated by appreciative love, respect, or desire) and the list of adverbial conditions that govern the relationship.

Still, Cocking and Kennett may argue that the adverbial conditions set out above do not define deep friendship as they understand it. Deep friendship is not a function of how things are done. It is not a matter of protocols and procedures. Rather, it is a function of doing something quite specific with another human: it is the establishment of a relationship in which there is the "emergence and acceptance of a degree of direction and interpretation of each by the other" (1998: 508). Perhaps this is true, but, as they also note, the problem with this condition is that it can be met by other sorts of relationships that are not friendships. For example, they point out that two psychoanalysts may also engage in interpretation and direction of each other. At this point, Cocking and Kennett argue that the difference between deep friendship and the relationship between the two analysts is that in the latter case their relationship will terminate once they achieve psychological health. In contrast, deep friendship is an endless engagement. When they begin to use this language, then it becomes clearer that the easiest way to distinguish deep friendship from other practices is to turn to either the motivations or the adverbial conditions that govern the relationship. In the case at hand, it is because the activity is *endlessly* engaged in. In addition, one could note that the analysts are motivated by psychological health and not affection. In any case, Oakeshott's formal notion of practice is flexible enough to accommodate a malleable, nonstatic conception of the self.

EXPLANATION, JUSTIFICATION, AND THE PRACTICE OF FRIENDSHIP

The last sections of this chapter step back to ask what this view of friendship achieves. If the idea of friendship as a family of practices is conditioned by the mutual recognition of ordinarily appropriate motives and adverbial conditions is at all plausible, what does it provide us? Is it an explanation of friendship? Is it a justification of friendship? Is it a description of friendship? Focusing on the conditions of the practice is not the same as providing a causal explanation for why the practice exists in general, or why it has the form that it does in any particular culture or period. Understanding the conditions of friendship should help inform how friends are friends, but it cannot establish that Denny and Alan's friendship, for example, was caused by the presence of these conditions or that these conditions caused Denny and Alan to maintain their friendship. Moreover, that certain kinds of motivations must be present or that certain forms of actions must be performed in order to have a friendship is not the same as providing the sort of justification that says that friendship is a good thing or that a particular friendship is desirable.

Nevertheless, even though elucidating the conditions of friendship is not a project of causal explanation or justification, explanation and justification are not far off (and therefore this exposition of friendship is not merely a description). Because friendship requires the presence and recognition of certain motivations, referring to those motivations (say, for example, a friendship based on mutual affection and respect) can provide something of an explanation for *why* Denny and Alan became and are friends: they have affection and respect for one another. Moreover, setting out the adverbial forms of self-disclosure also explains something about *how* they are friends: e.g., they interact honestly, openly, intimately, caringly, considerately, and affectionately.[23] Pointing to the motivations of a friendship may give us appropriate, perhaps even necessary reasons for a friendship, but those reasons may not be sufficient. Although they have affection and respect for one another, perhaps Denny is fighting on the other side of an armed conflict. Perhaps Alan has lied repeatedly to Denny. Perhaps Denny committed some horrible crime. Elucidating the character of our practices moves us only so far in sorting out those sorts of questions of justifying a particular friendship. The project of setting forth conditions of the practice of friendship will point to possible explanations of particular friendships, the plausibility of which can only be assessed empirically.

A practice-based account of friendship may also address features of the justification of friendship. If friendships draw on a certain repertoire of appropriate motivations (e.g., affection, fondness, desire, respect, appreciative love, care, need) and it is a prima facie good thing for human beings to act upon their desires and feelings, then it is a good thing for friendships to exist. These relationships allow us to cultivate and foster human desires and feelings. This is not to say that all desires and feelings are good or that all desires and feelings should be acted upon, but in the absence of countervailing reasons, I will presume that humans should not be frustrated or forestalled in doing what they want to do. It is one of the great joys of friendship that even if such relationships are not voluntary through and through, they do express a voluntary engagement with others that should not be disparaged or devalued. Friendship, then, is a prima facie good thing.

Because our practices of friendship also entail subscribing to certain adverbial conditions, the justification for entering into and maintaining a friendship may be connected to the value we attribute to acting in particular ways with other human beings. To be a friend to another may mean that we have to pursue our interests and desires in ways that we would not otherwise have to do or do in the same way. To strangers, acquaintances, colleagues, students, and fellow citizens, we have certain duties—for example, acting considerately, respectfully, courteously, peacefully, or perhaps professionally, helpfully, and so on. These are all worthy ways of acting and speaking with others and many of these ways of being are also shared with our friends or with certain sorts of friendships. That friendship adds to or intensifies these adverbial conditions by adding playfully, affectionately, caringly, critically, intimately, altruistically, etc., and that these are also valuable ways of interaction suggests that the practice of friendship opens up opportunities for other admirable forms of being in the world. Our friendships place demands on us that, while not always endorsable, do raise the bar. The fact that these conditions are not always met and that sometimes we fail to live up to the expectations of our friends can be seen as a tribute to the demands of the practices of friendship. In other words, these practices require that our actions live up to higher expectations of what we ordinarily understand to be worthy modes of action. This line of argument is further explored in chapter 4 where friendship is linked to the idea of individuality.

THE RELATIONSHIPS VIEW

In many ways, the position under consideration is consistent with the view that relationships of friendship themselves are seen as valuable. Seeing friendship as a family of practices reinforces the notion that human beings are creatures who value things in the world and value relationships between one another. Among those relationships is that of friendship. Of course, this does not mean that all friendships are valued equally or that friendship overrides all other values. Some friendships are closer and more significant. Other friendships may be judged to be harmful to the friends themselves or to other parties. Nevertheless, practices of friendship are important enough to us, that they seemed to be capable of generating what Samuel Scheffler calls "relationship-dependent" reasons for action (2010:104). It is precisely because we are in a friendship that we have reasons to act in particular ways.[24] Depending on the friendship, these reasons carry more or less weight vis-à-vis competing reasons for action. This *relationships view* is consonant with our commonsense view of morality; namely, whatever morality may entail, it should be able to incorporate reasons for acting out of friendship. Friendships are relationships that have intrinsic value which, in turn, can generate reasons (of variable magnitude) to act in a manner that favors our friends over others. Even if morality is deeply connected to impartiality, it should allow for reasons of partiality associated with friendship. This position raises the broader and more difficult problem of how the sort of impartiality prized in morality can accommodate reasons of friendship. This book begs off that meta-ethical question.[25] Chapter 7 takes on the problem of impartiality, but only as it relates to impartial legal and political institutions that pressure our practices of friendship.

Our practices of friendship, however, are complicated by the fact that they are rarely just intrinsically valuable. From friendships also come the pleasures of doing things together, the advancement of the interests and goods of ourselves and others, the comforts of shared experiences, the expectations of assistance and protection, the blessed release of secrets held, and many other goods that could be characterized as external or extrinsic. As I have suggested, certain practices of friendship may be deeply connected to such goods. For example, both historically and culturally, various practices of friendship have been and are valued primarily because they yield pleasure for or are useful to the friends. In addressing the question of the value of these various practices of friendship, I am left with a rather ragged set of assertions. In some practices of friendships, reasons for action are derived primarily from the relationship itself (i.e., the intrinsic value of the friendship). In other practices, reasons for action are tied to the instrumental character of the relationship. In many practices of friendship, however, the value of the relationship is both intrinsic and extrinsic.

One way to clean up this conclusion is to deny the possibility that friendships are extrinsically valuable. This possibility strikes me as deeply implausible. Such a view would mean that the external goods of friendship (e.g., that friendship may be useful for or bring pleasure to the friends) tell us nothing about the value of friendship. It is true, as I shall argue in chapter 3, that the role of those external goods in providing reasons for action is itself complicated by the fact that some of them have a friendship-undermining character. Nevertheless, it would be a mistake to claim that the external goods of friendship have no role whatsoever in the value we attribute to this relationship. The difficulty, tackled in chapter 3, will be to make sense of the nature of that role.

It is also possible to clean up the position by rejecting the possibility that friendships have any intrinsic value. Unlike the prior possibility, it is important to spend a bit more time sorting out this argument, particularly in light of a recent book by Simon Keller (2013) that powerfully argues just this case. Although what Keller has to say against the intrinsic value of friendship is framed in terms of a general argument about all partial relationships, I will focus on his arguments as they apply to friendship.

The heart of Keller's criticism is that we value friendship because of its importance for our needs, interests, and flourishing and not because of the relationship itself (2013:76). Keller writes, "If you ask why you have reason to do something special for your friend, then the answer, I say, is that your act would advance your friend's good, in some respect or other; it would further his best interests, manifest concern or respect for his autonomy, or help him to become a more excellent human being" (113). To grab onto the relationship itself (as writers such as Scheffler does) and its purported intrinsic value is to grab onto the wrong end of the stick. The individuals within the relationship are what matter, not the relationship as such. From Keller's perspective, to say that you have reason to do something special for an individual because she is your friend is both misleading and inadequate. It is misleading because the relationship itself does not itself carry any weight and inadequate because the real reasons have to be grounded on the value we attribute to the individuals concerned and whatever it is that they may merit. In the end, Keller argues that there is something "misanthropic" about the relationship view. More strongly, it "drags human relationships from their human context" (77).

Many of the arguments that Keller presents in support of his position lead to a *reductio* which strips away from a relationship all of the good consequences for the individuals involved in order to reveal the empty, inhumane nature of the friendship relation itself. In response, I do not argue that all practices of friendship are based on the intrinsic value of the relationship, but the intrinsic value of a friendship can certainly be a source of partial reasons for many practices of friendship. My defense of the relationships view will entail variations on the theme that Keller's reductio should be resisted. In other words, we cannot understand a relationship of friendship without understanding its motivational and action-related conditions as they apply to the specific individuals involved in the relationship. By stripping the notion of friendship to what Keller sees as its "bare structure," one is left with something of a "straw friendship." I would imagine Keller's responses to this move would, in part, be to claim that I have simply brought into the idea of friendship extrinsic matters of context and effects that are not necessarily part of the "bare relationship." In other words, my response has stacked the deck in favor of the possible intrinsic value of friendship. At this point, it is difficult to proceed without having a better sense of what the bare relationship of friendship actually entails. In the following section, I will explore Keller's arguments against the view that friendships have intrinsic value.

KELLER'S CASE AGAINST THE RELATIONSHIPS VIEW

The first argument against the relationships view is what Keller calls the "At Least It's a Relationship" argument. The basic idea is that if a friendship was utterly dysfunctional and entirely lacking of any external value, then, according to Keller, we "should not say, 'I can see that this friendship is not doing any good for anyone, but at least it is a friendship. At least it has that going for it. So there is something good about the relationship, even if there are bad things about it too.'" In other words, we should not say these things because in the absence of any external goods, there would really be nothing "to recommend the relationship" (2013:57).

Keller, of course, is correct. But, on the other hand, we should not say the opposite either. For example, we should not say, "I see this friendship between Greg and Wilson as abusive and harmful, but at least it's good for the individuals involved." We should not and would not say such a thing largely because it is not clear if their relationship would even qualify as a friendship. If interpersonal friendships presume that the friends hold certain beliefs about the motives of one another and that they mutually subscribe to a friendly manner of acting toward one another, then "friends" who believed and acted otherwise (for example, acting in an abusive manner) would be "friends in name only." Moreover, this response would accord with the idea that friendship must contain some element of intrinsic importance. Keller's judgment in the original case is correct, not because the friendship has no intrinsic value, but because either it is not a friendship (given that the ordinarily appropriate motives and action-conditions are not met) or because the intrinsic value of the relationship is utterly overwhelmed by the situation he describes. For example, suppose that Pretty Boy and Jesse are both real friends, but inept bank robbers. *We* would not recommend their friendship precisely because it has bad consequences for us and perhaps because it has bad consequences for them. *They* may eventually come to the conclusion that they need to end their friendship (they are constantly getting into trouble and thrown into jail), but that may be because those external effects have overridden the intrinsic value that they attribute to their friendship. From the perspective of the friends, it does not seem wildly implausible to think that they could still believe the relationship has some value to them (they are admired, liked, respected by their friend, and treated in a friendly manner) even though that value is overwhelmed by the unfortunate externalities suffered by others and themselves.

Keller's second argument against the intrinsic value of friendship is counterfactual. Imagine a people who lack the bundle of practices of friendship that have intrinsic value. In such a society, there would still exist friendships, but only of a certain sort. Perhaps people act benevolently toward one another because they enjoy it or because they believe that such benevolence will lead to their flourishing or to eternal salvation. In this imagined case, Keller argues that we should not regret the absence of the intrinsically valued friendships, nor judge such as society worse off than our own. Consequently, we would have no reason to rearrange such a society to create friendships that have intrinsic value. Keller writes, "Whether the society's arrangements are good or bad, and whether there is reason to change them, are matters of how the people within the society fare, not of how the bare structure of the relationships in which they participate" (2013:59).

But what is the bare structure of intrinsically valued friendships? I have suggested that in such relationships two individuals mutually recognize the appropriate motivations of friendship, subscribe to a set of adverbial conditions to guide their action and find something of intrinsic worth in the satisfaction of those conditions. In contrast to Keller, I believe that society is richer if that sort of relationship is possible. Does that belief commit me to the further claim that I should have reason to transform a society that lacked that sort of friendship? Perhaps. If achieving that possibility entails clicking my heels three times, that is one thing. If, as some sociologists argue, that possibility could only arise with the emergence of a free-wheeling capitalist system and that system results in the impoverishment of millions (perhaps it does or perhaps it does not), that is another thing. As a historical hypothesis, it is possible that in the West, seeing friendship as an intrinsically valuable relationship is something that emerged only in early modernity. Nevertheless, it is plausible to think that the world is a better place with the possibility of intrinsically valued practices of friendship, ceteris paribus.

A third argument concerns how we judge whether something has intrinsic value. Keller argues that we perform this task by separating what is claimed to have intrinsic importance from other values and "ask whether it holds value regardless of its consequences and context" (2013:61). Whether friendships can have intrinsic value and serve as the basis for special reasons depends on the possibility of being able to separate friendships from their context and other values. In Keller's view, this makes no sense. Whether a friendship is valuable cannot be separated from its context and effects. We simply do not set aside the external effects of the relationship in judging its worth.

In response, I think that Keller is correct with regard to our judgments about many friendships. We look to the presence or absence of external goods to determine whether our friends are behaving as they should. Consequences matter. If Bert becomes a stick in the mud and is simply no fun, then a friendship with Bert motivated by the pleasure of dancing in the park may evaporate. The situation is complicated by the fact that we also look to context and consequences to assess our beliefs about motivations of our friends. So, we may come to believe that what was a friendship was merely an exploitative relationship and hence no friendship at all. Alternatively, the idea of the intrinsic value of friendship makes more sense of the possibility that individuals may sometimes stick together through thick and thin. For some, the true test of a friendship may have been found in a context of pain and deprivation (such as during war or fighting wildfires) in which the friends continued to act as friends and are motivated by the appropriate sentiments of friendship. In such circumstances, the irrelevance of external goods to indicate the value of the friendship seems to point to its intrinsic importance.

In a fourth argument, Keller notes that sometimes we have reasons to end a special relationship: "Though I love my friend and he loves me, we may realize that we are incompatible, always interacting in ways that leave each of us bitter and depressed" (2013:61). As I understand this argument, Keller is claiming that this possible reason for ending the relationship cannot be produced by the friendship itself. You may have reasons to sacrifice a relationship for the sake of the individuals, but "you do not have reasons to sacrifice individuals so that the relationship, or its putative intrinsic value, can survive" (62).

Once again, Keller is correct in noting that there may be powerful reasons based on the functioning and consequences of the relationship for ending a friendship. It is also important to note that individuals may remain in relationships that have unfortunate consequences for bad reasons—inertia, maintaining a public image, weakness of will. On the other hand, could it not be the case that one of the reasons individuals remain in a relationship whose effects are troubling is because of the intrinsic value of the relationship? Overall, they may be mistaken in thinking that this is a friendship that should be preserved, but they may not be mistaken in thinking that the relationship is itself important. Does not the intrinsic value of friendship better account for why friends sometime stick together beyond the point that they should?

Keller's fifth argument is that while friends sometimes act for the sake of a friendship, we more often act for the sake of the individual with whom we are friends. More strongly, "A friend who is always thinking of improving your friendship, a colleague whose main concern is with the value of colle-giality, a parent who thinks mainly of how important it is to have a good relationship with his child—all of these characters are annoying to have around, and all of them seem to be missing what really matters in their re-lationships. In a relationship with such a person, you may feel that he cares less for you than for his relationship with you" (2013:63). Keller's singular insight here is worth the price of his book. He goes on to argue that the relationship itself usually does not motivate us to act (although Keller ad-mits that sometimes it does, but this is exceptional) and if it is motivating us, it will prove to be an irritant to our friends. In contrast, what usually motivates us or what usually should motivate us are the actual interests and needs of our friends. For example, if you hear that the town in which your friend lives has been flooded, you do not call her up saying that your friend-ship depends on it. Rather, you call because you want to be sure that your friend is okay. It is not the value of the *relationship* that motivates (or should motivate) us to act.

I understand Keller's argument to be the sort of objection that could be made to someone who loves being in love as opposed to someone who loves another person. His argument is that the relationships view is like the for-mer stance. Attributing intrinsic value to friendship is nothing more than loving to be in love. If this is true, then once again we can wonder if there is a relationship of friendship. If Wilson cares more about the "relationship" (where the word *relationship* does not include an implied reference to Greg) than he does about Greg, then it is unlikely that Greg would believe that Wilson is a particularly good friend. Absent is a shared belief that the friends are motivated by the appropriate sentiments of friendship. Absent a belief that those motives are present, there is no friendship. In this situa-tion, we should not say that the friendship with Greg is motivating Wilson because it is unlikely that he really has a friendship with Greg. Similarly, we should not say about the person who is in love with being in love that she is necessarily in love with her beloved.

Keller could argue that this is precisely why the relationships view does not work or why, if the relationships view works, it must separate the true reasons for action (the intrinsic value of friendship) from the motives for the action. In contrast, I am calling into question whether there is a relationship unless the description of the relationship specifies the individuals involved. To put this point another way: The reason why we must specify the individuals involved is because they exist in a special relationship to us. It is the intrinsic value of *this* friendship (and not any friendship in existence), meaning *this* relationship with *this* person (and not a stranger for instance), that explains why, when Cuddy hears that the town in which her friend Wilson lives has been flooded, Cuddy can explain that she wants to call to make sure that Wilson is okay. Wilson is not anyone, but her friend. To those who know Cuddy and Wilson, this friendship is already bound up with the person "Wilson." To those who do not know Wilson, she would say that he is her friend. It is the relationship with Wilson that motivates her action.

Perhaps Keller would be unconvinced. For Cuddy to say Wilson is her friend is not necessarily to say that Cuddy has an intrinsically valuable friendship with him. She could also be saying that she is especially concerned with Wilson's value "as an individual in her own right," which is Keller's preferred account, which he calls the *individuals view* (2013:74). On this view, Cuddy's motives for acting are "fully shaped" only because she knows that it is Wilson. To make this point clearer, one could imagine a situation (an example that Keller does not use, but I hope gets to the spirit of his argument) in which Cuddy learns that a town has been flooded and the list of the casualties have been posted in the local hospital. Cuddy has no reason to check the list because she does not know anyone from the town. An acquaintance of hers, however, tells her that, "I think a friend of yours was visiting that town on the day of the flood." When asked who it was, the acquaintance says, "I don't remember his name."

In this case, Keller would argue that on the relationships view, knowing that it is "a friend" will not be enough to fully shape Cuddy's motive. While Cuddy now has a reason to check the list, she will be "groping for more information" and feeling that she does not "know why exactly, this is such an important act to perform." Because she does not know who that friend specifically is, she would not fully know what her reason is for checking the list of casualties. However, if Cuddy's acquaintance suddenly turns around and shouts, "Oh, I remember, it's your friend Wilson," then Keller argues that her "motive will change in quality" (2013:96). Knowing that a relationship exists ("I think a friend of yours was visiting the town") will not focus and fully shape Cuddy's motive. At a phenomenological level, that focus happens largely because it is Wilson and not merely "a friend."

Because I have suggested that our relationships of friendship include reference to specific individuals, there is not much to distinguish my version of the relationships view from Keller's in the example of checking the list of casualties. On my formulation, once Cuddy finds out that it is Wilson, then her motive will be more focused and shaped, but it will be focused and shaped because she has a specific sort of friendship with Wilson. In large part, because of the variety of ways in which we can be friends, Cuddy's motives for looking at the list will be shaped by the sort of friendship she has. Not knowing the specific friend means that the quality of her motive is still open. Suppose Cuddy's acquaintance, who is bad with names, says, "Your best friend—I don't remember his name—was visiting the flooded town," then, it seems, that *would be* enough to fully form her motive. Perhaps one can read this possibility as either an argument in favor of the relationships view because it is "your best friend," or in support of Keller's individuals view because "your best friend" clearly identifies a specific individual, namely Wilson. In either case, the relationships view seems to be able to accommodate what Keller is trying to capture with his individuals view.

Keller offers one final argument against the relationships view: The relationships view cannot explain why my valuable friendships are of special significance to me, but Cuddy's friendship with Wilson is not equally valuable to me. If the relationship of friendship is the thing that counts and I have friendships and Cuddy has friendships, then why should I not care for Cuddy's friendships as much as my own (Keller 2013:118–19)? As Diana Jeske notes, we can ask not only why we form friendships in general and why we form this or that friendship, but also what reasons we have to care for a person with whom we have an intimate relationship that go beyond the ways in which we care about people with whom we are not intimate (2008:46). Why should we owe more to *our own* friends than to other friendships? The relationships view simply asserts that friendships provide agent-relative reasons in support of their special character. At best, it argues that we value our own friendships over the friendships of others because we subjectively value our own friendships. In short, it fails to provide an answer other than that our own friendships just are more important to us (Keller 2013:119).

The answer to Keller's query may be found in the structure of friendships and perhaps could be called the *practices view*. I have claimed that contemporary practices of interpersonal friendship share a structure in which the existence of the relationship depends on the following conditions:

1. The friends entertain the appropriate sentiments of friendship toward one another.
2. The friends believe that the others' actions are motivated by those sentiments of friendship.
3. The friends subscribe to a shared set of adverbial conditions that structure how they act toward one another—i.e., they interact in a friendly manner.

Keller asks why you should respond differently to the individuals "with whom you share special relationships, even though those individuals are no more inherently valuable than other individuals" (2013:124). Why should Cuddy's friendship to Wilson matter more for Cuddy than whatever friendships I may have? The practices view suggests the following answer: Cuddy cannot have a friendship with Wilson unless she accords some sense of appropriate priority to her own relationship with Wilson contingent upon Wilson responding in a similar way to Cuddy. That is what it means to participate in a practice of friendship. In part, it is a matter of understanding how the relationship is itself constituted by the manner in which individuals are expected to act. Cuddy should give special significance to Wilson's interests because that is part of the practice to which they subscribe. On the practices account, Cuddy would have a very difficult time if she were to attempt to have a friendship without subscribing to the conditions under which it is possible to have a friendship.

From a practices view of friendship, the question is not whether the relationship should generate special reasons for action. That is what the relationship is all about. To separate the possibility of special reasons from a practice of friendship is to misunderstand what it means to be in a friendship. To make this separation would be like saying, "I want to make a promise to be here tomorrow at 9:00, but can I get rid of all that baggage associated with creating an obligation?" From the practices view, the question about the partiality of reasons of friendship becomes a much broader question of why we should have a set of practices that create reasons of partiality. Asking this question, however, brings us to the limitations of a practices approach to friendship: namely, it will not yield an explanation or justification for the family of practices of friendship nor the shape of particular practices in a particular culture or time period. What a practices approach will stress is the idea that there are many different kinds of friendship. Not all friendships are intimate relationships. Not all friendships turn on the sentiment of affection. Not all friendships are based on the same level of concern (e.g., friendships motivated by desire versus those motivated by affection). The range of relationships that we call friendship, the kind of reasons or the weight of those reasons that support those relationships may differ quite a bit from relationship to relationship and over time within a relationship. Instead of focusing on whether there are reasons to give greater attention to friends over others or whether there exist special duties, I assume that such reasons and duties exist but that their weight varies. Assuming such reasons and duties, I argue in chapter 3 that how they function depends on to whom they are addressed.

A friendship, then, is a rather complicated relationship—historically contingent, dependent on a range of mutually recognized motivations, and realized in a variety of adverbial forms of self-disclosure, all of which can define distinctive and multiple practices of friendship. These practices are not united by any one sentiment or reason, by any given substantive actions, or by certain essential adverbial conditions. Rather, the practices of friendship condition friendships (as opposed to some other relationship) because they bear a family resemblance to one another. They share similarities that crop up and disappear. They do share the feature of being practices, but that feature does not distinguish them from other sorts of relationships. Seeing friendship as a family of social practices may help alleviate the temptation to close down or disparage different ways in which we can be and have been friends as well as open us to the meaningful use of friendship in other cultures and times. What distinguishes friendship from other practices is the repertoire of what are taken to be the appropriate motives and norms of self-disclosure that we recognize and enact as we more or less successfully make, lose, strengthen, or weaken our friendships. Further attention, however, needs to be devoted to the broader reasons for friendship and the place of self-interest and obligation as motivations for friendship. These issues are considered in chapter 3.

three

SELF-INTEREST, DUTY, AND FRIENDSHIP

A friendly action may mean one intended to be appropriately considerate of the interests of another or it may mean one done in a sentiment of friendship.

—MICHAEL OAKESHOTT, *ON HUMAN CONDUCT*

The relationship between friendship and such things as self-interest, duty, and utility is vexed. It is not entirely clear whether they can play a role in motivating friendship, and, if they play a role, what it entails. For example, some writers argue that friendship is not merely compatible with, but necessarily gives rise to certain obligations.[1] From this perspective, friendship must involve the acquisition of special responsibilities toward one's friends. In contrast, a powerful case has been made that the language of obligation sullies and perhaps undermines friendship (Wellman 2001). From this perspective, actions driven by duties are not the actions of friends. Similar disputes surround the place of self-interest, utility, and rights in our practices of friendship.

To help think about these relationships, this chapter begins by exploring the conceptual edges of friendship. Exploring these edges will illustrate how the conditions of friendship discussed in chapters 1 and 2 allow us to distinguish friendly actions from friendships and true friends from false friends. In many respects, these distinctions are enabled by a class of motivations that are understood as ordinarily appropriate for a friendship. Friendly actions that lack the mutual recognition of these motives are not enough for a friendship. Other motivations, however, are ordinarily understood as inappropriate. When individuals discern these latter motives to be in play, they are liable to describe their friends as false or no longer friends at all.

In addition to the distinction between appropriate and inappropriate motives, there are some reasons for entering into or sustaining a friendship that are deficient. It is into this class of motivations that utility, duty, and rights fall. These motives are neither sufficient for a friendship nor entirely inappropriate. They play a role in our current practices of friendship, but they are, by themselves, not enough to create or sustain a friendship. The bulk of the chapter focuses on the complex ways that duty serves as a deficient reason within our practices of friendship. Sorting through these matters reinforces the diverse character of friendship and sets the stage for the discussion and defense of a particular ideal of friendship in chapter 4.

FRIENDLY ACTIONS AND FRIENDSHIPS

One of the borders to our practices of friendship is created by the possibility that friendly action need not signify friendship. That this is the case is due to the role that mutually recognized appropriate motivations play in how current friendships in this culture work. As Telfer notes, a significant difference exists between *befriending* someone, that is, providing her with assistance and *having a friendship* with someone. Similarly, it is possible to be a *friend to* someone (say, out of pity or sympathy) without necessarily having the feelings of friendship (Telfer 1991:250). In most cases, acting as a friend would act is benign. For example, a stranger may stop her car to help me change my flat tire. That is certainly a friendly action and may be motivated out of a consideration of my interests. But it is not itself sufficient for a friendship. Even if this individual repeatedly helped me out and I helped her out, such interactions would still not be enough for a friendship unless the proper motivational requirements were met and mutually recognized. We may befriend another without there being a friendship (see also King 2007:132).

As simple as this cultural distinction may appear, it has three important consequences. The first is that we (here and now) are able to make the distinction between friendship and "befriending" or "being friendly to" because of the role played by the mutual recognition of motives in the former relationship. In other words, without that recognition, the distinction would collapse and being friendly would be enough for a friendship. Within the social/cultural context of this analysis, however, maintaining the distinction between acting friendly and having a friendship is important. Friendships are different precisely because the parties believe that certain sorts of motives and their mutual recognition play an important role in their relationship. Hence the motivational *requirement* is a requirement for how we have come to understand our practices of friendship.

The second implication is that in other cultures the "doing" part of friendship may be more important than the motivational aspects of the relationship. In these situations, the conceptual boundary between friendship and acting friendly is difficult if not impossible to discern. The anthropologists Sandra Bell and Simon Coleman argue that "the appropriateness of affect . . . in relations of friendship cannot be assumed to be universal" (1999:4). In support of this proposition, one can turn to various practices of friendship that deemphasize motive. For example, in the guest friendships of ancient Greece, the connections created by family and tribal connections appeared to be enough to establish a friendship. Those connections created obligations and those may have motivated parties to act in a particular way, but it was those connections that mattered more than the mutual recognition of particular sentiments. In other words, the obligations may have existed even if they were not recognized by one party or the other. Whether the parties lived up to those obligations, of course, was a different matter.[2] Similarly, Shmuel Noah Eisenstadt considers cultural forms in which friendship could be included in a class of ritualized personal relations (1956:90). He writes that "the main, and even explicit, reason for contracting this relationship seems to be . . . [a set of] potential instrumental benefits" (91). Kenelm O. L. Burridge notes that friendship among the Tangu in New Guinea "entails mutual aid, hospitality, informal gift giving" and can be inherited (1957:178, 179). Ruben Reina observed that for the Ladinos, a Mestizo community in Guatemala, a pattern of friendship called *cuello* "has practical utility in the realm of economic and political influence; this friendship is looked upon as a mechanism beneficial from the personal viewpoint" (1959:44). Relying on Reina's work, Wolf distinguishes between instrumental friendships and emotional or expressive friendships (1977:171–73). The anthropological ideas of instrumental, ceremonial, or institutionalized friendships tend to take the weight off of certain sentiments of friendship and their mutual recognition.[3]

A third consequence of a set of practices that distinguish friendship from merely friendly action is that the motivational requirements of friendship pose a significant obstacle to extending the idea of friendship beyond a circle in which those motivational elements can be mutually recognized. In particular, this limitation will be raised in chapter 4's discussion of the possibilities for civic friendship in large, anonymous societies. In effect, civic friendship cannot extend beyond a small number of individuals. Although citizen-strangers within a polity may or should act in a friendly manner toward one another, that kind of relationship is not the same as friendship.[4]

FALSE FRIENDS

Unfortunately, acting in a friendly manner toward another without a motive of friendship may also take a malevolent form. One may do the things that a friend does in order to achieve a nefarious end. In cases where motivations are incompatible with the appropriate motivations of friendship, such individuals can be revealed to be false friends. Obviously, false friends may be motivated by any number of purposes—money, power, prestige, security, and so on. The difference between a false friend and a friendly person is that a friendly person is motivated by sentiments or reasons (e.g., duty, pity, or a desire to be helpful) that are not incompatible with the appropriate motives of friendship, while a false friend seeks to misrepresent her motives. A false friend hopes that his friendly actions create the appearance of possessing the appropriate motivations leading the benighted individual to believe that she is in a friendship. In reality, however, the false friend is motivated either by malevolent reasons (e.g., they hope to harm the person or are indifferent to whether their actions will lead to harm) or reasons that are insufficient for friendship (more on this possibility follows).

Regimes of all sorts have created and relied on false friends who have acted as informants, spies, rats, and moles. Chapter 7 argues that the state's use of friendship in this way is problematic precisely because it makes it difficult for individuals to judge the motivations of others. More broadly, it raises the question of whether governments should be empowered to manipulate one of the most important sorts of relationships of human life.

SELF-INTEREST, UTILITY, AND FRIENDSHIP

Is there a kind of falsity in a friendship that is motivated by self-interest? As with the case of obligation mentioned at the beginning of this chapter, opinions differ. Some argue that the heart of friendship is found in Aristotle's statement that "in the case of a friend, they say that one ought to wish him good for his own sake" (Aristotle 1985:1155b29; see also Cicero 2009:109; Aquinas 1991:162, 168). Others argue that even for Aristotle, friendship is "shot through with the concern for one's own existence" (Pangle 2003:196). In the one case, "friendship is an altruistic phenomenon, and a locus of the altruistic emotions. This altruistic aspect is essential to friendship; a relationship based solely on mutual advantage (even if it involved mutual liking) would not in this sense be a friendship" (Blum 1980:43). In the other case, even the highest ideals of goodwill associated with friendship are driven by the effect that goodwill has on expanding and enriching one's self-interest.

This disagreement over the role of self-interest in friendship (and over how to interpret Aristotle) is reflected to some degree in common usage. In the early twenty-first-century West, individuals who are merely useful to one another are generally not deemed to have a friendship. They may be friendly toward one another and they may describe one another as friends, but it is unlikely that they or others would see a relationship based purely on exchange or an association solely driven by mutual advantage as a friendship. Because of the role of self-interest in such relationships, we are more likely to call it a commercial relationship, a cooperative venture, an association, a partnership, or simply a useful relationship.

In contrast, other sorts of friendships suggest that self-interest can play a central role. For example, individuals who enjoy one another's company, receive pleasure from being with one another, and act in a manner that friends act may very well be friends. Consequently, at least in certain practices of friendship, friendship and self-interest fit together quite easily. If the self-interest is not solely defined by material advantage (let us call these sorts of relationships motivated by material advantage "relationships of utility" as opposed to "friendships of pleasure"), then a relationship of friendship appears to exist. Whether we endorse Aristotle's argument that friendships of self-interested pleasure are not the highest of friendships, they are still friendships.[5] The difference between us and Aristotle on this matter is that we (here and now) are unlikely to accept his description of a relationship of pure utility as a friendship at all.

What further complicates the role of self-interest in friendship is that even those who see friendship as intrinsically valuable or see the altruistic sentiments as foremost do not expect our friends to be useless to us. All parties to the philosophical debate over friendship and self-interest concede that our friends can be useful and that this is a good thing. For example, notions of mutuality and reciprocity are commonly part of the expectations and norms associated with many of the practices of friendship. How, then, are we to make sense of the role of self-interest as a motivation for friendship?

In addition to different practices of friendship treating self-interest differently, it may also be helpful to distinguish between types of motivations for friendship. I have suggested that motives such as affection, fondness, desire, respect, appreciative love, and care compose a set of appropriate reasons for friendship. These motivations appear to be necessary to or an internal part of the practices of friendship (once again, this is a generalization bound by time and place). They are not, however, singularly or conjointly sufficient for a friendship insofar as they must be mutually recognized by the friends who must also subscribe to the appropriate forms of self-disclosure in their interactions. Moreover, they do not necessarily exclude other sorts of motivations from being part of the mix. Nevertheless, they are generally understood as *ordinarily appropriate motivations* for friendship.

Other motivations, such as utility, pity, eros, or charity, are not ordinarily appropriate motivations for friendship but can serve in the motivational mix if they are supplemented by an appropriate motivation. These motives can be compatible with our motivational repertoire and, in certain cases, can be an important component of a friendship. They cannot, however, stand alone in the sense that when recognized in one's friends, they are not enough to support the relationship or even specific actions within the relationship (qualified, as we shall see, in certain ways). In this sense, they are *deficient motivations or reasons* for friendship. Deficient motives are not part of the ordinarily appropriate repertoire of motivations even though in any given friendship they can play an important role. From this perspective, not only utility but also a sense of duty is a deficient motive for friendship. Without being accompanied by an appropriate motive, they cannot, on their own, support a friendship (although they may be able to support another sort of valued and valuable relationship).

To bring this discussion back to different practices of friendship, consider the observation that self-interest is within the ordinarily appropriate motivational set if it takes the form of nonmaterial desire or pleasure.[6] In other practices of friendship, however, self-interest may play a role, but its role is that of a deficient reason. To illustrate this claim, consider the kind of relationship that may arise between business associates. John and Henry may sometimes enjoy working with one another, but suppose theirs is truly a relationship of utility. If the business was not profitable, then they would have little to do with one another and they would care no more for one another than they would for mere acquaintances. If utility is considered a deficient reason, then the usefulness of their relationship cannot be the basis for a friendship. It can, of course, serve as the basis for an important and successful partnership or association.

By calling utility a deficient reason for friendship, I wish to capture the idea that it can still serve as some sort of reason for the friendship. The central idea, however, is that it cannot work alone. To alter the case of Henry and John, suppose that their relationship is not only profitable, but they also care for the other's well-being in important ways and they recognize that motive in one another. Even if they hit bad times or if the business went under, they would still try to ensure that the other was doing well. In this case, the ordinarily appropriate motivation of care is doing most of the work in the relationship. Henry and John are friends. The profitability of the relationship is important, but it could disappear without destroying their friendship.

The more complicated case is when the parties have mixed motives: the ordinarily appropriate motivations of friendship are present, but the deficient reasons are also a significant motivating factor. Suppose now that Henry and John not only mutually care about one another, but they are also motivated, to no small degree, by the fact that their relationship is profitable. Indeed, if the business failed, there is a good chance that their relationship would fail. Do they still have a friendship? If an ordinarily appropriate motivation is present, there is no certain criterion that could be used to rule out an affirmative answer. Human relationships are extraordinarily complicated, fluid things and to parse and dissect the role of particular sentiments is never easy. More strongly, if they believe that the other is generally acting out of the right sort of motives and they mutually subscribe to the appropriate adverbial conditions of friendship, then they have a friendship.[7] The fact that their friendship is a relationship in which the motivations are frequently mixed—with both appropriate and deficient reasons playing a role—is simply part and parcel of the relationship. If their relationship fails when the business fails, then we might say that theirs was not a very strong friendship. But they are still friends and their relationship can be understood by themselves and others as a friendship.

With this rough distinction between ordinarily appropriate and deficient motivations for friendship, additional complexities emerge. For one thing, how do we distinguish between the two types of motives? What elevates a sentiment or reason to the repertoire of ordinarily appropriate motivations? The philosophical/normative answer to this question is that there is no philosophical answer to this question. Whether a motive is ordinarily appropriate is a function of social practice. As the label is meant to suggest, what constitutes an ordinarily appropriate motive for friendship is a matter of what is ordinarily appropriate. Adopting this perspective implies that different peoples may identify different motivations as appropriate or deficient. For example, it is possible that in the ancient world and in other cultures, the motive of utility is a part of the repertoire of ordinarily appropriate reasons for friendship. In these other cultures, purely useful people who recognized one another as acting on self-interested material motivations could understand themselves as true friends. In contrast, it is not uncommon for contemporary theorists and philosophers to distinguish instrumental relationships and identify them as debased or failed friendships. I am suggesting, as a historical hypothesis, that this may be an artifact of a modern perspective. On this reading, the ancient Greek conception of a guest-friendship or Aristotle's conception of utility-based friendships could have been understood as an ordinary way to conceive of oneself as a friend—as opposed to a debased friend, or a false friend, or a less than sincere friend. In contrast, material self-interest is less likely now to be seen as the basis for friendship.[8]

An objection to a historicized account of the motivations for friendship could be raised if it were argued that we *should be* friends with another when particular conditions are met. That is, when we recognize certain characteristics of another human being (say their being virtuous), we should seek their friendship and (if they recognize the necessary characteristics in ourselves) they should seek our friendship. This view, however, would not push us very far from the view that these characteristics must be held or jointly understood as valuable, unless one could make good on the idea that such characteristics are good as such. At the individual level and in a pluralistic society this is not so easy to do. Piety, courage, charity, humility, not to mention commercial acumen and love are not easily harmonized. In the third part of this book, however, I will argue that at the level of the state, the character of a regime as being just does provide a general reason for friendship between political associations.

Before moving onto a discussion of the place of obligation in friendship, it may be useful to compare this account with certain aspects of Derrida's work on friendship (1997). Derrida suggests that pinning down the expectations for a friendship is always fraught, always subject to misunderstanding and confusion. In an important sense, this is part of what he calls the politics of friendship and it is more or less endemic to the relationship. In contrast, however, I am suggesting that this difficulty is rarely a matter of confusion and misunderstanding and that the kind of anxiety implied by Derrida's analysis applies to a fairly limited set of circumstances. More specifically, it applies to the case in which at least one of the partners no longer clearly recognizes the appropriate motives for friendship in the other, but they both still see their relationship as useful. In this situation, the relationship itself may need to be renegotiated and rethought. Is it is a friendship or merely a profitable association?[9] Outside of the case in which it is unclear whether one recognizes the appropriate motivations of friendship in another, it is not evident that ambiguities of friendship will be particularly troublesome. To a large extent, Derrida's analysis of the politics and anxiety of friendship depends on a notion that utility is incompatible with what are understood as more appropriate motives of friendship. But if we see deficient motivations as legitimate, but inadequate, then Derrida's account applies in a more restricted fashion.[10]

Now, as noted in chapter 2, the preceding analysis also suggests that there are multiple sorts of appropriate reasons for a friendship—affection, desire, appreciative love, respect, care, and so on. Given that diversity of motives, individuals can come together for different reasons. Andy may have genuine affection for Ken, while Ken is motivated by his respect for Andy's virtuosity in baseball. These differences in motivation may lead to differences in what they want to do (Andy just enjoys hanging out with Ken, but Ken constantly wants to play baseball), but there is no reason to think that they would necessarily have doubts they are each motivated by the sentiments of friendship.[11] In other words, these sorts of disputes between the ordinarily appropriate motivations of friendship are unlikely to generate the severity of misunderstanding that emerges when deficient or dishonest reasons are in play.

DUTIES AND FRIENDSHIP

As mentioned in the introduction to this chapter, many argue that moral duties are a natural part of our friendships, defining our friendships and distinguishing them from other sorts of relationships. Joseph Raz, for example, writes that the duties of aid and support are

> constitutive of the relationship. A relationship between people who enjoy amusing themselves in each other's company but do not owe each other any special duties is not friendship. To become friends with another is to enter a relation of a known and predefined kind, one consisting, alongside patterns of attitudes and expectations, of rights and duties. It is not a rigid framework. Within its established contours there is much scope

for individuals to define the nature of their friendship. But a framework there must be and it includes the normative components of friendship, its constitutive rights and duties.

(1989:19)

On Raz's account, the conventions and norms of friendship create not merely certain expectations that friends will behave in a certain way, but they also generate rights and duties. Duties of aid and support, for example, are constitutive of friendship and serve as reasons for acting. So, when Wilson is sick and Greg is busy, Greg may say to himself that he should go visit him. This "should" is not a mere expression of a norm associated with friendship. Rather, it is an expression of a duty to support his friend, which he is not (absent any competing claim that may override the duty) at liberty to ignore. Absent such a duty, Raz suggests, their relationship could not be considered a friendship.

For Raz, duty is not merely a reason; it is the most necessary reason for acting within a friendship. In contrast, Wellman (2001) argues that duty is no sort of a reason for acting within a friendship. If, when he visits his sick friend, Greg proudly says that he is doing so because he was obliged, Wilson may disappointedly reply, "I want you to be here as my friend, not because you *have* to be here."[12] Within our practices of friendship, duty appears to be one reason too many for action. If we wish to make sense of the expectations and desires associated with friendship, Wellman argues, we should not employ talk about rights and duties, but about virtue. If Greg disappoints Wilson by not visiting him, it is not because Greg has failed to live up to his duties to Wilson or that Wilson has a rights-claim against Greg, but that Greg appears to be self-centered if not selfish. The language of duty gets in the way of describing what matters in our friendships. Instead, Greg's desire to be a person of a particular sort (namely a good friend) should motivate his interactions with Wilson.[13]

I will argue that both Raz and Wellman have part of the story, but have mistaken the part for the whole. Raz is correct that duty can play a role in friendship, but he is incorrect that it is a necessary feature of all friendships and the primary motivating factor when it does come into play. Wellman is correct to be suspicious of duties and rights in friendship, but incorrect in thinking they have no place. To consider these claims, we can begin with the possibility that within the diverse practices of friendship, some friendships simply do not create or call upon duties. For example, in what Simon Keller calls "undemanding friendships," duty has no role to play. He writes, "Undemanding friendships can involve durable, genuine, mutual love and concern, without involving duties beyond those that hold between people generally" (2013:51). In contrast to Raz, Keller suggests that it may very well be the absence of such duties that lend themselves to the attractiveness of undemanding friendships. In support of this possibility Keller argues that just because we value something (even intrinsically), we need not associate the notion of duty with it (2013:50). To use an example from Wellman, we may value a great work of art or a natural wonder without generating a duty to appreciate it (2001:226). Similarly, we may attribute intrinsic worth to a friendship without also appealing to the language of duty.

If there are practices of friendship that do not rely on duty at all, are there practices of friendship in which duties or rights can be the primary motivating factor? Diane Jeske, for example, does not find an appeal to duty as troubling as Wellman does. She argues that acting from duty reflects the fact that we have many competing and conflicting commitments to ourselves and to others. For this reason, the deployment of the language of duty is consistent with the value that we place on the relationships we have with our friends. An appeal to duty is a reaffirmation of the value placed on the relationship and its relative position given competing commitments and relationships. Jeske goes on to argue that acting from duty is a way to acknowledge that our emotional ties (although deep and genuine) are not unconditional because we have competing commitments and ties. More-over, she notes, duty may motivate us when our "occurrent affection" for a friend is running low. Dredging up an obligation calls to mind the friendship and all that it may entail (1998:71). When we are rushed, or tired, or have other things to do, Lynch suggests that "we might expect friends to act 'as if' they feel affection" (2005:117). There is a pretence that must be adopted to get one to move when the ordinary sentiments of friendship are lacking. In both signaling moral urgency and revitalizing or mimicking affection, acting out of duty in friendship is troublesome only if our friends have the unreasonable expectation that the relationship is unconditional or that the sentiments of friendship must always motivate our actions toward our friends.

Jeske's argument regarding the role of duty as a way to rank commitments is an important insight, particularly when a duty-claim is deployed against a third party. What this means and why it is important will be considered in the next section. At the moment, it is important to note that the role of duty vis-à-vis one's friends, even on Jeske's account, still seems fraught. For example, suppose Greg mentions to Wilson that he is at Wilson's bedside because he has a duty to be there. In such a case, the words *duty* or *commitment* do not necessarily signal urgency or the importance of their friendship. Rather the call of duty could signal to a friend, "I am here because no other commitment outranked my commitment to you." Jeske argues that this sounds strange only if our friends have unreasonable expectations about our friendships. In contrast, I am suggesting that friends simply do not expect duties to be the primary motivations in their interactions. On this reading, it is not that friends expect their relationships to be unconditional, rather it is that they do not expect their relationships to be mediated by claims of justice.[14] Duty is a strained way to convey the importance of a friendship. Greg may do better simply by showing up or doing what needs to be done, or by saying "Being here is what is important" or that "we're good friends."

What are we to make of Jeske's idea that duty may motivate us when our "occurrent affection" for a friend is running low? The occurrent affection problem helps bring into focus the question of for whom duty is really an issue: Greg, who is acting on duty or Wilson who is the beneficiary of Greg's support? Or both? The disappointment created by Greg's acting out of duty is first and foremost Wilson's. Wilson's friendship with Greg depends on Wilson's belief that Greg is primarily acting on the appropriate motives of friendship and not solely out of duty. Greg's internal appeal to a sense of duty owed to Wilson may motivate Greg to act when his occurrent affection for Wilson is running low, but he will strive to act as friends act, i.e., consistent with the ordinary motivations of friendship. As noted in chapter 2, how we act toward our friends goes a good distance in confirming whether the friendship is based on the ordinarily appropriate motives. Much of the argument of chapter 2 is that it cannot go the full distance in establishing or maintaining our practices of friendship. If duty can help motivate Greg's action within a friendship, it must motivate him to act in a way that is consistent with the norms of friendship and with sustaining the belief that duty is not the primary motive of the friendship.

For Greg, acting out of duty is less of a problem. Nevertheless, given our current practices of friendship, it remains a deficient motivation. Consequently, if Greg comes to believe that the only reason why he is doing things for Wilson is out of duty, then that should (within contemporary practices) eventually lead him to reassess the relationship. Within an ongoing friendship, the immediate problem with duty has to do with its uptake and the potential for breeding the disappointment mentioned earlier. In the longer run, it can also become a troubling question for the friend who is always acting out of duty. In other words, why is Greg friends with Wilson?

Among other things, this analysis may give rise to two questions. First, why is the perception of acting out of duty such a problem for our contemporary practices of friendship? Second, does a perpetual possibility for a kind of falsity or hypocrisy in the friendship arise from the disconnect between Wilson's perception that Greg is acting out of the ordinarily appropriate motives of friendship and Greg's real motivation (duty)? Who are one's real friends in such a world? One way to address the first question is to argue that when Greg gives Wilson the news that he is solely driven by duty, Wilson is not only disappointed because he wants Greg to want to visit him, but also because he wants Greg to visit him in a certain way—freely.[15] This is part of the reason why friendship is so valuable to us. Within many Western practices of friendship, the notion of agency is placed at a premium— an ideal that may not hold everywhere and for all time. Nevertheless, within this context, the notion of obligation as *the* motivation for acting within the relationship seems to chip away at the voluntary nature of the relationship. Hence, it is important that Wilson continues to believe that Greg is motivated by the appropriate sentiments even if he is motivated by duty. This explanation helps, but as I shall discuss it is not entirely satisfactory. Sometimes it is important to make explicit a claim of duty.

Is the difference between Greg's being moved by duty and Wilson's perception that Greg is being moved by sentiments of friendship a problem? The answer is yes if this is not the exception. Moreover, even when it is the exception, being moved by duty is a deficient reason. It is still a reason for acting, but it is not ordinarily understood as an appropriate motivation. This position is different from the one offered by Wellman, for whom there is something inherently objectionable about duty serving a reason at all. After all, as even Wellman notes, it is not uncommon for people to speak of duties of friendship (2001:225) and (perhaps not as frequently) people also speak of rights of friendship (235n26; Meyer 1992:478–79). Instead of seeing such talk as wrong-headed (as Wellman suggests), the idea of seeing *duty* and *rights* as deficient reasons accords with how we use these terms. Under this possibility, duty cannot appear to stand alone as the primary reason for acting within a friendship without creating disappointment. But disappointment need not be same as a denial of the relationship. When faced with a dutiful friend such as Greg, Wilson may then seek some confirmation that Greg does possess the appropriate sentiments of friendship.

An alternative account of the peculiar role of duty within a friendship is offered by Sandra Lynch. She argues that "the fact that friendship is a preferential relationship does not invalidate the notion of duty in friendship; rather it makes friendship a relationship in which the notion of duty is particularly indeterminate." It is indeterminate, she suggests, because it demands "indirection of intention" (2005:118). Duty requires indirection because friendship cannot be, on her account, pursued with any ulterior motive, otherwise it will collapse (100): "Friendship must do away with purely instrumental reasoning in the sense that friendship cannot aim at a particular outcome" (149). In a friendship, one must act as if other aims (such as interest, personal advantage, pleasure) were "transcended." As I understand her argument, the same applies to duty. There is a self-effacing character to duty as a reason for acting within friendship. We may have duties of friendship, but we cannot be understood (by our friends?) as acting directly upon them.[16]

The idea of duty as self-effacing suggests that the real reasons for action are one thing, while the desirable motives for action are something else (Keller 2013:82). Lynch is trying to capture the idea that we may really be driven by duty, but the truth is corrosive of the relationship. In contrast, I suggest that the motivations for friendship need not be pure (i.e., duty free) as much as they need to be appropriate. This requirement does not mean that utility and duty are transcended but that they must be supplemented by more appropriate reasons. In an ongoing friendship, it is just as, if not more important that Greg's appropriate motives are being conveyed to Wilson. For if Wilson comes to believe that Greg is only acting from duty, even when he is not, then the relationship may go south. So, Greg must act in a way that is consistent with the ordinarily appropriate motives of friendship. Duty may be playing a role in any given instance, but it will be unfortunate for the relationship if it is perceived as the sole motivating force. If Greg comes to visit Wilson reluctantly, dragging his feet, and complaining about the expense of the visit, then Wilson may believe that Greg is simply fulfilling an obligation. Because of the importance of self-disclosure and the belief-sustaining role of actions, how Greg visits Wilson is just as important as the fact that he does visit him.

One difficulty with Lynch's suggestion that duty must be self-effacing is that in certain circumstances it does not hold. What is interesting about the language of duty in our practices of friendship is that while it is corrosive of the relationship when used between friends, it can signal something different when deployed outside the relationship. In addition, the corrosive character of duty does occasionally have a place in the relationship between friends. Sometimes friends do makes demands on one another and claim what is perceived as due in the attempt to restore a friendship. These possibilities suggest that the role of duty is even more complicated than what is implied by the view that it is self-effacing or that it is a deficient reason for action.

DUTIES OF FRIENDSHIP AND THIRD PARTIES

The language of duty in friendship functions differently in different contexts. For example, suppose that when Greg is approached by his boss, Cuddy, she tells him not to take any time off to see his sick friend Wilson. Greg, however, responds by saying that Wilson is his friend and he has a duty to support him. As Jeske's analysis suggests, in making this claim, Greg is trying to convey a sense that, given all of the demands on his time, seeing Wilson is the most urgent. Regardless of whether, at that moment, he is motivated by the ordinary sentiments of friendship, his friendship outweighs whatever competing responsibilities he may have and that others (particularly his boss) should recognize his duty to his friend. Greg is trying to convey a notion that he should not, without fairly compelling reasons, do otherwise than visit his friend. The claim of duty is meant to get Cuddy to back off. Moreover, if Wilson heard that Greg made such a claim to Cuddy, he may be a bit embarrassed, but he is unlikely to be disappointed. Vis-à-vis Cuddy, the duty card may count for something. Vis-à-vis his friend, the duty card is a disappointment.

Not only is duty less problematically deployed against third parties, it can also be deployed, to some extent, by third parties. Suppose in a somewhat different scenario Cuddy wonders why Greg has not visited his sick friend Wilson. As it turns out Greg is balking at the thought of going to his bedside (he does not like the smell of hospital rooms). In response, Cuddy first reminds Greg what his visit to Wilson would mean to his friend. When Greg continues to offer a litany of excuses, Cuddy admonishes him by saying that it is his responsibility to support his friend—that is what it means to be a good friend. In this case, Cuddy's third-party admonishment does not appear to be corrosive of the relationship of friendship between Greg and Wilson (although Greg may be irked by Cuddy's admonishment). Rather it is meant to shake Greg out of a sense of complacency about his friendship. Once again, the notion of duty is less troublesome when it is not used between the friends.

THE CLAIM OF DUTY AS A *PHARMACON*

This chapter concludes by briefly considering two additional ways the language of duty may enter into our practices of friendship: as a means to disrupt the complacency of a friend and as connected to an expectation that friends should be more willing to forgive one another. In the first case, the language of duty may be paradoxically deployed by friends against other friends in order to end the friendship or to secure it. Michael Stocker notes that "Duty seems relevant in our relations with our loved ones and friends, only when our love, friendship, and affection lapse" (1976:465n8). In certain circumstances, the use of duty within a friendship acts like a *pharmacon* in which it may either remedy or poison the relationship.[17] In a sense, the deployment of duty comes to resemble the way in which one talks to a third party. In so doing, the ordinarily appropriate sentiments are no longer (or appear no longer to be) doing any of the work in motivating a friend's actions. After a while, Wilson may notice that while he has supported, encouraged, and aided Greg on a number of occasions, Greg has rarely reciprocated. Wilson finds himself in a situation in which he needs Greg's support. At that moment, he may call him to task by saying, "You have to do this for me." Ordinarily, Wellman is correct in arguing the idea that a "demand" appears foreign to the functioning of a friendship. Within a friendship, Wilson may certainly implore his friend, guilt-trip him, say how great it would be to see him, but the notion of demand simply seems inappropriate. Nevertheless, this is not always the case. When Wilson does make a demand on Greg, he may very well be claiming that Greg is not at liberty to do otherwise and that Wilson has a right to Greg's assistance. By claiming what is understood to be due in the friendship, Wilson is trying to bring Greg to realize that this is how friends act toward one another, but he may also be asking whether there still exist the appropriate sentiments of friendship.[18] Such appeals and claims may shake Greg into action or they may signal the end of the relationship. It is precisely because obligations (and rights) sit uneasily within friendships that they can play this ambiguous role of a *pharmacon*.

FRIENDSHIP AND FORGIVENESS

Finally, many practices of friendship place a premium not merely on the voluntary character of the relationship but also on the sentiment of loyalty and the willingness to forgive one's friends. At an interpersonal level, forgiveness entails a willingness of the injured party to work on herself to remove whatever feelings of resentment may have resulted from the injury, as well as to act in a way that restores the parties to their previous relationship. In many friendships, the elasticity of the relationship—that is, its capacity to withstand the bumps and challenges of life—is due in part to a certain willingness of the friends to work out their differences and either simply let things drop or forgive one another for injuries they may have inflicted. Does a stronger sense of duty enter the relationship through this notion of elasticity? A case can be made that many practices of friendship include the expectation of some "give" in the relationship. Nevertheless, this "give" need not be connected to a duty to forgive. Instead of using the language of duty, one could ground this expectation in terms of the desirableness of the relationship, the loyalties that friends develop over time, and the character of the injury that may have occurred.

Within the practices of friendship in which this sense of give is prevalent, Greg's failure to live up to the norms of friendship may be accompanied by his sense that Wilson will "give him a break" or "cut him some slack" and forgive the injury or let the matter drop. Greg may realize that he has certain responsibilities to his friends, but also expects that his friends will forgive him for injuries of a certain sort. If, however, Greg is minimally attuned to the adverbial practices of friendship, he may also realize that there are limits to those expectations. The injuries and harms to Wilson that he has caused may be so severe or so recurrent that Wilson comes to call the relationship itself into question. In effect, Wilson may come to believe that Greg has taken advantage of his friendship and that enough is enough. One need not claim that all practices of friendship contain a duty to forgive in order to understand these complicated facets of the relationship.

The notion of friendship as not merely a voluntary relationship, but also one that is frequently characterized by a willingness to forgive or forget injuries and repair the relationship will come up again in chapter 7 when considering whether friendships create legally enforceable obligations. If the law can enforce the duties of friendship, then it will also override the norms of *give* that exist in a relationship. As noted earlier, those norms are not absolute: loyalty has its limits and injuries can be unforgiveable. Friendship is not a realm that should be understood as free of legal entanglements, but it cannot be argued that the role of the law in the enforcement of the duties of friendship is one that will necessarily protect or promote the relationship.

Friendship is a social practice, formally structured by a set of ordinarily appropriate motivations and certain adverbial rules for how friends should interact. As a practice, it is unavoidably suffused with contingency. Friends must decide whether to act on their motives and how to disclose themselves to one another. Friends must recognize the appropriate motivations in one another, but these do not preclude secondary motivations that may not, by themselves, be necessary or sufficient. The conventions and protocols that define the appropriate forms of self-disclosure are historically contingent and culturally variable. It is on the basis of those conventions, however, that we are able to distinguish friendly actions from false friends and discern the complicated relationship among self-interest, duty, and friendship. Do these conventions and protocols point to a particular ideal of friendship? The next chapter seeks to answer this question by arguing that in light of the contingent and variable character of friendship there is an ideal that is both an expression of and consonant with human individuality.

four

FRIENDSHIP AND
INDIVIDUALITY

Because it was he, because it was I.

—MONTAIGNE, *ESSAYS*

Chapters 1 and 2 considered the idea of friendship as a family of practices that are conditioned by the mutual recognition of ordinarily appropriate motivations and the participation in the adverbial rules of self-disclosure. Chapter 3 explored how a difference in types of motivations may help clarify the role of self-interest, utility, and duty in friendship. This chapter sets out a particular ideal of friendship and its relationship to individuality. The ideal involves friends attending to the character of their own motivations in a more conscious manner than is ordinarily expected. Much of this ideal draws on a vision of "self-enacted individuality" developed by Richard Flathman and will be referred to (with the less than felicitous expression) as a "bridging/bonding friendship."[1]

The first part of the chapter dives into an account of an ideal of friendship that is related to the engagement of self-enactment. The second part summarizes Flathman's ideal of self-enacted individuality and considers his brief discussion of how this ideal of self-enacted individuality is compatible with the ideal of friendship offered by Montaigne. I argue that while individuality is the highest ideal for Flathman, it is also possible to understand an ideal of friendship that both serves and is served by individuality. The last part of the chapter responds to the sorts of criticisms of bridging/bonding friendship and individuality that could be leveled from the perspective of an Alexis de Tocqueville or George Simmel.

Before proceeding, it should first be noted that in setting out an ideal of friendship, I am not arguing that this is the only way to understand friendship. Nor am I arguing that there are no other ideal conceptions of friendship. I do, however, argue that bridging/bonding friendship expresses some of the central characteristics found within our practices of friendship in a more complete manner. That is, it makes friendship more thoroughly chosen and voluntary. Whether one sees this as a good thing, of course, will depend on whether extending agency in the manner suggested is plausible and how important one believes agency to be.[2]

THE IDEA OF SELF-ENACTMENT AND AN IDEAL OF FRIENDSHIP

We do not lack ideals of friendship. Philosophers love to spin them out. The traditional reading of Aristotle is that a virtue-based friendship is superior to those based on pleasure or utility. For Montaigne, the ideal friendship is a blending and mingling of souls. For Kant, it is a friendship of sentiment in which friends unburden their hearts to one another (1991:214–15). For Ralph Waldo Emerson, it is a tenderness and sincerity that is fit for good days and for bad. For C. S. Lewis, it is found between "men at their highest level of individuality" (1960:60). For the most part, these ideals of friendship focus on forms of self-disclosure. In the ideal, friends act a certain way with one another or do certain things with one another—share secrets, care for one another, act loyally, etc. In these ideals, while friends are motivated by the appropriate sentiments of friendship, the hard work of achieving the ideal is to be found in acting in a particular manner vis-à-vis one's friends. For the most part, the motivations are what they happen to be—affection, desire, care, respect, need—but the full expression of the ideal is found in the interaction of the friends.

In contrast, the ideal I wish to carve out is broadened to include not merely the mutual recognition of the appropriate motivations (which is a condition for all sorts of friendship), but the mutual recognition of a willingness of one's friends to work on their motives. While most discussions of friendship tend to presume the given character of those motives, this ideal presumes that friends can engage in a form of *self-enactment* (a term that I will say more about later) in which they attend to, shape, and choose their motives. Without a doubt, we often find ourselves simply liking some people and disliking others. Perhaps by making a friend we seem to be acting on some initial form of attraction—affection, a desire to be in their company, respect for their virtuosity. In some instances, a friendship can seem to spring up almost instantly as friends recognize common interests and a mutual attraction. These experiences suggest that our motivations have a brute or given character to them. Nevertheless, even in these instances we may always ask whether we should have affection for another or whether we should desire his company or have respect for her. These questions are somewhat different from asking whether we should act on a given set of desires and motivations. In asking the former sorts of questions, we are not conjuring up an alternative sentiment out of whole cloth. Nor need we assume that we can simply dissipate a set of feelings on command. Such questions suggest the possibility that we can control, moderate, or transform the sentiments that we do possess. In addition, these questions suggest that we could explore alternative sentiments and feelings which we may have not attended or cultivated.

In the type of friendship I am conceiving, friends look to their own motivations for initiating or maintaining a friendship and seek to cultivate, alter, maintain, or expand the sentiments of friendship despite the ordinary challenges that may be presented to the existence of those feelings. For example, imagine an instance of an ongoing friendship between Alan and Denny. One day, Alan observes Denny engaging in rude behavior toward a colleague. Alan then decides to let Denny know that he does not approve of that kind of behavior and that Denny should apologize to his colleague. Suppose further that when Alan initially witnesses Denny's behavior he (Alan) is very angry. Also, suppose that when Denny first listens to Alan's correction of his (Denny's) behavior Denny is indignant. For both friends, the ideal assumes that it is possible for the friends to choose the sentiment in which they are going to act vis-à-vis the other. The fact that the initial event made Alan angry and that Alan's correction made Denny indignant does not mean that in their interactions, the one is destined to be motivated by anger and the other is programmed to be motivated by indignation. Alan and Denny still care for and respect one another. These are the central motivations of their friendship, but they may not always be readily accessible or the most pressing of motivations. For Alan not to be motivated by anger or Denny not to be motivated by indignation may take a great deal of control and self-discipline. They may have to say to themselves that they do not want to be the sort of individuals who react to their friends based on those kinds of motives. Moreover, they may strive for such a self-improvement, but find themselves slipping back into anger or indignation. Once again, the claim is not that anger or indignation somehow go away (they may, of course, fade, or they may not), but that Alan and Denny are able to work on themselves in such a manner that they act with different sentiments in mind.[3]

In addition to attending to the motivations associated with the friendship itself, this ideal of friendship values the engagement of self-enactment more generally. Such friends can recognize in one another the value of self-enactment in other facets of their lives. As we shall see herein, this engagement can be understood as a form of what Richard Flathman calls self-enacted individuality which can then become part of the motivations for the friendship itself. Such a friend is like oneself in the formal sense of valuing his or her individuality. On the other hand, the existence of this individuality means that these people are friends because, in part, they are unlike one another.[4] The connections between and the challenges created by individuality and friendship will be more fully set out in the sections that follow. At this point, it may be enough to note that individuality as understood by Flathman and adopted here is a function of both how we respond to the adverbial conditions that govern the practice of friendship and to the complex responses and feelings within ourselves. In Foucault's language, our individuality is to be found in a certain care for the self. Friendship can be based on a mutual sense of such care.

As with Aristotle's ideal of friendship, the bridging/bonding ideal is very much a character-based form of friendship. By character, however, I am focusing less on the "to act" part of the "disposition to act in a particular way" and more on the "disposition," although both motivation and action are packaged together in a complex way, as we shall see. That is, the bridging/ bonding ideal requires that Denny is willing to work on himself and that Alan is willing to do the same. In their own ways, each strives to be motivated as he believes he should be motivated. Each sees himself as not having a set of brute or given sentiments and motivations, but rather as a being that sees those sentiments as things that can be altered or countered with alternative sentiments. It is an engagement of a struggle for self-command or autonomy which is never completed or fully "won."

The basis for this ideal of friendship is drawn from Oakeshott's notion that individuals may not only choose to do this or that action they may also choose the sentiments or motivations in which they act (1975:76). In this regard, Oakeshott argues that human agency can be expressed in our external actions (self-disclosure) and internally: We can decide to act on certain motives and not others. How is this possible? To answer this question, it will be useful to consider Oakeshott's account of self-enactment. The presumption here is that sentiments have some cognitive component such that they can be emblems of self-command (75). Consequently, sentiments are not to be understood as "organic impulses or urges." Although Oakeshott notes that our motivations may be inextricably mixed and that "it may be difficult for the agent himself to be confident about the sentiment in which he is acting," he also claims that "choosing an action is always meaning to procure a satisfaction in a motive of some sort" (72). There is some motive (or motives) that is (are) always attached to an action, hence we engage in self-enactment when we permit ourselves to act on certain motives and not others.

In distinguishing self-disclosure from self-enactment, Oakeshott is interested in "the differences which distinguish conduct in respect of its being an agent seeking what he wants [i.e., self-disclosure] from conduct in respect of its being an agent thinking as he chooses to think and enacting or re-enacting himself as he wishes to be [i.e., self-enactment]" (1975:72). There are those who would argue that it is impossible for us to shape or choose our motivations. Alternatively, there are those who argue that we are consistently self-deluded by our motivations (there is a way to read Hobbes or Freud along these lines) or that we are fundamentally opaque to ourselves (which Augustine and Arendt seem to suggest on occasion). From these perspectives, a commitment on the part of an agent to act out of compassion, benevolence, love, pity, or charity could never be kept and to believe that one did choose to act generously instead of self-interestedly could be nothing more than a rationalization of one's conduct.

Oakeshott is not particularly concerned with responding to these skeptics. His claim is that if we understand ourselves as agents, where agency is an exhibition of intelligence, then our motivations are exhibitions of intelligence (as opposed to brute impulses or autonomic response like the blink of an eye or a twitch in one's arm) to the extent that they are a function of self-command. The assumption is not that they are always a matter of choice and deliberation. Sometimes we do not attend to them. Sometimes we may not even understand them. Perhaps most of the time we drift along, acting out of a given set of motives that we do not question or examine. Perhaps we perform our actions spitefully or perhaps we perform them with kindheartedness. In these cases, the specific choices that we make to pursue this or that satisfaction may be made without deliberating about our motives. Nevertheless, as agents, motivations *can be* exhibitions of intelligence—they *can be* reflectively understood and shaped.

If we attach the idea of self-enactment to an ideal of friendship, then there is an alternative response to those who reject the capacity to shape or choose our motives: this will not be their ideal. For whatever reason, it may very well be the case that for some people this ideal is implausible or impossible because self-enactment is implausible or impossible. On the other hand, there is no reason why an ideal of friendship must be an ideal for everyone. Nor does it mean that alternative ideals which preclude self-enactment are not ideals. What this view does rule out are ideals that unduly narrow the possible practices of friendship.

Because this ideal of friendship is so dependent on Oakeshott's conception of self-enactment, it may be useful to note that there is no necessary connection between motivation and self-disclosure. The lack of a necessary connection reinforces earlier, and more general, claims about the relationship between our motives and our actions. For example, within an ongoing friendship Greg need not actually have an occurrent, ordinarily appropriate motive in order to act in a friendly manner to Wilson. In this way, our action can sustain a belief that the friendship is based on those sentiments even if they happen to be absent on a given occasion. The lack of a necessary connection between motive and action also means that it is possible to take advantage of the practices of friendship and create the false impression of a friendship. Oakeshott puts the matter more starkly: our sentiments (e.g., "greed, fear, compassion, resentment, benevolence, jealousy, love, hatred, kindness, pity, envy") in which we act, spin independently of the action. Loren may pursue his career motivated by resentment and bitterness, distaining his colleagues and students. Despite these sentiments, it is still possible that his actions accord with the ordinary codes of conduct associated with being a colleague and teacher. Of course, it is also possible that his motivations may find an expression in his mutterings, curt responses to colleagues or harsh treatment of students. But these sentiments do not necessitate such actions. Oakeshott writes,

> No doubt it is the case that the sentiment in which an agent acts may be, somewhat indistinctly, betrayed in the manner of his acting, in his facial expression, his tone of voice, a gesture, or an attitude. . . . But the sentiment has no direct relation to the action as an intention to procure a satisfaction. A man may kill in a sentiment of compassion or of hatred; he may mean to keep a promise in a motive of greed, of gratitude, or of resentment; he may concern himself with another's wants out of fear, kindness, pity or contempt.
>
> (1975:72)

On Oakeshott's account, our characters as associated with self-enactment are first and foremost a function of motivations that we choose to adopt in pursuing what we want to pursue. Character enters the scene because the emphasis in self-enactment is placed on self-command and not external success. While one has a certain set of goals in mind when one acts (say to get promoted), the failure to achieve those goals is not itself a failure of character if one is able to maintain one's integrity through the process. Alternatively, one may successfully achieve one's end, but at the sacrifice of one's character (e.g., one's integrity).

In the example of Alan's correcting Denny, Alan may choose to be motivated out of friendship—he cares for Denny's reputation—instead of anger at a perceived injustice. How he actually speaks to Denny is not determined by that prior choice. To Denny's ears, Alan may sound quite angry. He may speak forcefully, his voice may be raised and he may use sharp words in expressing his disapproval. All of this may lead Denny to ask Alan if he is angry at him and Alan, in all honesty, may say no (assuming that he is not motivated by anger). Depending on the nature of the friendship, Denny could say that this is no way to treat a friend, i.e., Alan is violating the norms of self-disclosure associated with their practice of friendship.

Alternatively, Alan may be angry as a hornet, but speak to Denny in a controlled, reassuring manner—effectively masking his feelings and perhaps abiding by the adverbial expectations of the relationship. How Alan acts can certainly flow from his feelings, but that is not necessarily the case. To the extent that an ideal of friendship focuses solely on self-disclosure, it also focuses on a standard for conduct. It seeks to govern how Alan and Denny interact: in this case, Alan's speaking calmly to Denny. To the extent that an ideal of friendship also focuses on self-enactment, then it also requires that Alan sets a standard for himself regarding his own feelings and sentiments toward Denny and recognize the same impulse to self-enactment in Denny.

While there is no *necessary* connection between what one does and the specific sentiments that one possesses, Flathman has offered an account of self-enactment that points to the existence of important *contingent* connections. After all, one cannot engage in self-enactment without some form of self-disclosure. In addition, a case could be made that the disciplines of self-disclosure may help us engage in future forms of self-enactment. By responding to Denny in a certain manner (say calmly), Alan may also reinforce certain choices to be motivated by certain sentiments (say with concern for Denny). Our own external actions may be resources to be drawn upon in shaping the sentiments in which we act. It is possible that agency at one level (as expressed in our forms of disclosure) can help us achieve a level of agency at another level (as expressed in self-enactment). This possibility does not deny Oakeshott's claim that self-disclosure is distinguishable from self-enactment, but it does suggest that connections can be made.

In line with Oakeshott's notion of self-enactment, the standards associated with this ideal of friendship need not be understood as a creation of the friends themselves.[5] The repertoire of ordinarily appropriate motivations provides a sense of what the friends should be working toward. Nevertheless, no one can do that work of self-enactment other than the individual herself—although our friends may assist us in various indirect ways. One must seek to live up to those standards and must negotiate her own responses and feelings as they arise vis-à-vis her friends. In the struggles and choices she makes with herself, bridging/bonding friendship more fully encompasses the voluntary attributes found in our practices of friendship. Not only do we frequently choose our friends and must choose how to interact, we can (by taking up the ideal of bridging/bonding friendship) also choose the sentiment in which we engage in those interactions. To the degree that we value the voluntary character of friendship, we may also value the opportunity (perhaps the burden) to mold our own characters in our interactions with our friends. From this perspective, a friendship focused on self-enactment is a more complete form of friendship as it embodies a central feature that we may value in other forms of the relationship.

The ideal here is one in which friendship supports the individuality of the friends and the individuality of the friends is a prime motivation of the friendship. On the one hand, it is possible that our friends may encourage and reinforce our projects of self-enactment by celebrating our individuality. This relational component will be considered in the discussion of Flathman's conception of self-enacted individuality.[6] On the other hand, the exercise of self-enactment can be part of the motivations for the friendship. Alan's attempt to engage in a form of self-command can motivate Denny to engage further in the practices of friendship with Alan. *How* Alan is being a friend (both in terms of his motivations and his actions) says something about Alan's individuality and character. It says something about who he is. In this friendship, individuality of this sort is mutually recognized and mutually prized (see also Friedman 1993:192). The *bond* of their pursuit of individuality is not a mere reflection of the other (the friend as another self). Rather, their individuality is both an opportunity and a challenge to friendship which must be periodically *bridged* through forms of self-enactment. Consequently, it is an ideal that can be called a "bridging/bonding friendship;" one that celebrates and builds on the individuality of the friends as expressed in the engagement of self-enactment.

Like Aristotle's conception of friendship, bridging/bonding friendship is an ideal that is based on the mutual recognition of virtue. Moreover, like his ideal, it presumes that the friends already know quite a bit about each other. In Aristotle's case, realizing that one's friend is just, moderate, courageous, or wise (or all of the above) requires seeing one's friend in a variety of circumstances. In the case of bridging/bonding friendship, the friends need not merely recognize a set of sentiments of friendship, but they also need the time to recognize what has gone into the formation of those motivations. They need to understand that this friend, for whom they have affection, respect, care, or simply the desire to be with, is engaged in a more difficult task of self-enactment. It is a recognition that may be signaled not merely by her interactions with oneself, but also through her interactions with the rest of the world. She is seeking to carve out her own individuality.[7] This requirement does not mean that friends are fully transparent to one another, but it does demand that we know enough to recognize a sincere engagement of self-enactment when we encounter it.

In response to this ideal, it could be argued that the reflection and self-formation that is part of bridging/bonding friendship eliminates the spontaneous character of friendship. There is too much work involved in self-enactment for it to be any kind of an ideal. In a way, it recreates the kind of problem we encountered in the discussion of duties of friendship. To go back to the example discussed in chapter 3 with Greg's trying to decide whether to visit his friend Wilson (where Greg is reluctant to do so), is it any better from Wilson's perspective for him to hear of Greg's struggle with himself and ultimate choice to be motivated by feelings of friendship? Does not that struggle besmirch the action as much as Greg's saying that he is visiting Wilson out of a duty to do so?

In response, one may recall that the problem with acting from duty was not so much that it killed the spontaneous character of the action, but that it suggested that Greg had no option but to visit his friend and that he was motivated by a deficient reason for friendship. In the case of a bridging/bonding friendship, Wilson recognizes Greg's struggle with himself. Moreover, he recognizes Greg's attempt to be the best friend that he can be and in that recognition, in part, Wilson is motivated to sustain his friendship with Greg. Instead of sullying the friendship, Greg's struggle with himself may actually strengthen it.

Of course, Greg may not want to visit Wilson and cannot muster any sort of countervailing wish to act as a friend would ordinarily act. Greg may reach the conclusion that he does not respect Wilson, nor like him, nor care for him, nor have any desire to do things with him. Bridging/bonding friendship does not mean that Greg then seeks to manufacture a set of sentiments. Alternatively, Greg may no longer recognize any of the appropriate motivations of friendship in Wilson. Without that recognition, bridging/ bonding friendship is impossible. As Telfer writes, "If the friends change in such a way that they cease to like each other or have anything in common, the friendship is at an end—not in the sense that it would be wise or usual to break it off, but by definition" (1991:255).

That there exists some kind of relationship between individuality and friendship is a theme that is frequently part of modern conceptions of friendship.[8] As Badhwar notes, "The mutual concern and respect of friends who love each other as ends involves a mutual acknowledgement that each is a separate individual, with her own ends and powers of decision and a moral claim to each other's—and other people's—concern and consideration" (1993:14). The connection between Oakeshott's notion of self-enactment and individuality and that between individuality and friendship has been most fully set out in the work of Richard Flathman. While Flathman sees individuality as "the highest ideal of liberalism" (1992:158n46; 1998:xvii) and one that can be served by friendship, I will suggest that individuality is a high ideal of liberalism, but so is friendship. Moreover, from this pluralistic perspective, friendship is not to be understood as merely instrumental to one's individuality, but that individuality also serves and enhances friendship. The relationship between these ideals, however, can be extraordinarily challenging.

FLATHMAN ON INDIVIDUALITY

Flathman believes that the less said about the content of the ideal of individuality, the better. For one thing, this ideal is not a hammer to bludgeon individuals into different ways of life. Like the practices of friendship noted in earlier chapters, Flathman emphasizes the diverse, adverbial, and formal character of individuality. While the writers that Flathman most admires talk of "imagined forms of individuality" (Hampshire), self-made individuality (Montaigne), and free-spiritedness (Nietzsche), he tends to settle on an Oakeshottian conception of self-enacted individuality. Flathman argues that the actual engagement of self-enactment brings into being the plurality of "selves each of whom enacts herself in distinctive ways" while satisfying the distinctive moralities of self-enactment and self-disclosure (2005:129).[9]

Although he is reluctant to give this ideal much content, Flathman's discussion does suggest various ways in which this chosen activity of self-enactment cultivates individuality. First, it is important to note that his conception of individuality differs from other conceptions insofar as it forgoes any kind of claim to the existence of an authentic self that must emerge independently of social practice and convention. Whatever individuality may mean, it does not necessitate belief in an entity that is able to transcend its social circumstance and time (as he has argued in his other work, this is a self that is always "situated"). After all, a self-enacted individual still subscribes to some set of social norms and expectations that govern both self-enactment and self-disclosure. Second, Flathman's conception of individuality does not demand that one arrive at a totally unique vision or way of acting in the world. Individuality does not require a radical form of originality in which one brings into being a perspective or lifestyle that is totally new. Third, while individuality requires some notion of standing apart from others, it does not necessitate the belief in a self that can serve as a master center of control or inner citadel. Instead, self-enactment requires either that I resist already given feelings and desires or make a positive commitment to choose certain motivations over others when I find myself being pulled in some other direction. One way or the other, self-enacted individuality entails a self-overcoming. This presupposes a view of the self as a many-in-one or what Flathman also calls a self that is "for and against itself" (2003:7). Flathman writes,

> I have found distinctions such as between lower and higher order, better and worse desires, volitions, and the like to be useful in thinking about the components of thinking and acting and about the selves who think and

act. Making use of such distinctions, however, neither must nor should involve positing some continuing 'Master' or Sovereign self that draws the distinctions and employs them to ride herd over all other aspects and characteristics of the self of which it is supposedly the master.

(167)

With no master or sovereign, the strife within oneself is a messy, anarchic affair. Individuality is possible only because of this inner struggle.[10]

Fourth, individuality is also not a letting-go or self-indulgence. Flathman writes that "self-control, moderation, magnanimity, respect for 'forms' and adverbial considerations, and conditions of life conducive to these are elements in all strong voluntarist conceptions of individuality" (1992:211). It requires an element of discipline and as an ideal, individuality is an achievement and not an inevitability. Given its self-enacted character, it requires the most difficult sort of work on oneself because it entails a self-executed, self-overcoming that is never easy. Nor is it the case that once one has attended to one's character one can simply slap one's hands together and say, "Well, now that I've done that, what's next?" Whatever may be achieved in shaping one's character is always a work in progress.

Flathman's position appears to suggest that whenever one engages in self-enactment, one is expressing one's individuality. From this perspective, the point is to think about the kind of character one wants to have. If my default setting, so to speak, is that I am rather a self-involved, embittered, resentful colleague, then by self-overcoming those motivations and seeking to be more positive and buoyant, I am enacting an individuality by forging myself. I am not accepting the character that comes "naturally" and I am seeking to dampen those "automatic" responses by constructing a second nature (although they may dissipate or disappear over time, or they may not). Or, to take another example, I may be deathly afraid of speaking in public. Overcoming that fear does not mean that fear is purged when speaking in public, but rather that fear is disciplined by other desires, such as the desire to be in command of oneself or being internally calm and collected. The individuality that emerges from this perspective is not that no one else in the world acts optimistically or confidently. Nor is it that I am constructing a new virtue or virtú of cheerfulness or self-command. Rather,

I am engaged in an activity that in the end, no one else can do. No one else can choose these motivations or choose my character for me. One might add that for Flathman (and perhaps Oakeshott), no one else can judge whether I have lived up to those standards. By engaging in self-enactment, I am no longer adrift, but actually putting my own stamp on myself instead of simply going with whatever has been branded onto me by my urges, culture, upbringing, or immediate circumstances. But, of course, this is a bounded activity in which there are available certain social conceptions of what is a good, respectable, worthwhile character. Those boundaries can themselves be challenged, but there is a sense in which they could never be entirely overthrown. In addition, there is sense that in order for this to be part of my character, some time needs to pass. Singularity also requires a certain stretch of diachronic identity. If I cannot sustain this character for some amount of time, then it is no character. This self-branding, however, need not be permanent and one can always seek to shift one's character. These shifts would also be part of one's individuality.

FRIENDSHIP AND INDIVIDUALITY

Much, if not most, of what I take Flathman's conception of individuality to entail is compatible with the notion of bridging/bonding friendship discussed at the beginning of this chapter. As mentioned, the central difference is whether friendship must play a subservient role to individuality.[11] It is clear, however, that Flathman believes his ideal of self-enacted individuality is compatible with the kind of ideal of friendship offered by Montaigne. More specifically, Flathman argues that Montaigne's ideal of friendship while lofty is formal and unique: "He [Montaigne] identifies qualities of character and relationship that are essential to friendship but their content will vary from one friendship to another. Just as the value of friendship is incommensurable with all other relationships so every friendship is incommensurable with all others" (2006:352n21). There is a kind of singularity to every friendship—a unique plurality. On Flathman's view, Montaigne's discussion of his friendship as "one soul in two bodies" and as a "fusion of wills" does not determine anything about what those souls are necessarily like or what those wills are willing. Nor does it mean that the fusion of wills is total in the sense that true friends lack any independent will.

Flathman also argues that Montaigne's ideal is compatible with individuality insofar as his conception of friendship is connected to the struggle and self-overcoming that is part of self-made individuality.[12] As already noted, individuality requires struggling "with and against elements and forces that, given the unavoidably situated character of our selves, are almost certain to have installed themselves deeply within us." The possibility for engaging in a sustained form of this "combat can be enhanced by true friendship" (2006:125). How so? Flathman does not provide many details or examples. He does, however, note Montaigne's claim that "friendship gave him the resolve, the courage, to continue" (121). Along these lines one could imagine additional possibilities: being inspired by a friend who has gone through her own struggles for individuality; being encouraged by a friend to cultivate the potential for virtuosity in one's character; being reminded by a friend to think about what is important to oneself; being chided by a friend when we fail to live up to our better selves; being shored up by a friend when one is faced with rules, norms, or conventions that are destructive of one's individuality. The possibility of being inspired, encouraged, reminded, chided, challenged, and shored up all carry significant weight in a relationship whose practice can include trust, frank speech as well as mutually recognized motivations such as care and concern, a desire to be in one another's presence, and an other-regarding sensibility. Friendship can provide the kind of support, security, sounding board, and mirror that can foster individuality.

Despite or alongside these possibilities, Flathman then writes that this enhancement of individuality through friendship "depends above all on sustaining—no easy thing to do—the conviction that 'You are as much a god as you will own / That you are nothing but a man alone'. . . . This is the ideal that Don Calogero glimpsed in the life of Don Fabrizio" from Lampedusa's *The Leopard*. The quotation is itself taken from Montaigne, who writes that the Athenians honored the Roman general Pompey with this "inscription" when he entered their city. The upshot of the quote, Montaigne notes, is that it is a mistake to put too much stock in conditions or advice outside ourselves. What Don Calogero says about Don Fabrizio is that he found in Fabrizio "a disposition to seek a shape for life from within himself and not in what he could wrest from others" (Flathman 2006:98). Presumably the lesson to be gleaned from these references is that while one can turn toward one's friends to enhance one's individuality, one should remember that the ultimate judgment and arbiter of how to live one's life or "enjoy our being rightly" must rest with us. That this is, "no easy thing to do" seems to suggest the ever-present possibility of being tempted or seduced away from our individuality by friendship itself.[13] Such a seduction could result in the surrender of one's judgment, the reinforcement of the unwanted desires and elements of the self or simply the reestablishment of the status quo ("I like you the way you are! Don't change anything about yourself!"). The quote from Lampedusa suggests that the risk to individuality from a friendship is a failure to seek a shape for life not from within oneself but in the interaction with one's friends.[14]

Where does this discussion leave the relationship between individuality and friendship? In describing Montaigne's position, Flathman writes that "it is not an easy thing to let one's self go as it comes, to let the self be first and foremost for itself. This is because the idea of doing so as with the idea of true friendship is not merely an idea but a soaring ideal, a vision of what fully human, fully humane lives—in all their diversities— would be like. The first of these is the ideal that Montaigne urged upon himself. As I read him, the ideal of friendship is subordinate to, a means of achieving, the first of these ideals" (2006:125). I think Flathman says "as I read him" only because there are elements in Montaigne that could be read as seeing friendship as the highest ideal and not individuality (e.g., Montaigne writes that "the ultimate point of the perfection of society is this [that is, friendship]" [120]). This interpretative question, however, does not cloud Flathman's position in which there is little or nothing to suggest individuality is not the highest idea for him and for his conception of liberalism. I do not think that it is much of a stretch to say that in Flathman's vision of liberalism and individuality, friendship can be a soaring ideal, but it is instrumental or subordinate. Should I endorse this position?

SELF-ENACTED INDIVIDUALITY AND BRIDGING/
BONDING FRIENDSHIP

Flathman's ideal of self-enacted individuality further illuminates how friendship can cultivate and maintain individuality. That one's friends may not merely tolerate but celebrate one's idiosyncrasies has been recognized by other writers as well. Marilyn Friedman notes that "friendship is more likely than many other relationships to provide social support for people who are idiosyncratic, whose unconventional values and deviant life-styles make them victims of intolerance from family members and others who are unwillingly related to them" (1993:219, 248). Or, as Alexander Nehamas writes, "Friendship provides . . . a place where one can try, not necessarily consciously, new ways of being—of acting, feeling and thinking. The palpable comfort that is characteristic of spending time with a friend springs from the awareness that one is in a safe haven where it is possible to strike out in new directions without knowing what the final destination will be" (2010:289). That friendship can be an instrument for protecting and fostering individuality is enormously important. That Denny maintains and reaffirms his friendship with Alan because Alan so enjoys Denny's quirkiness (which is part of his character) and vice versa is not to be underestimated. Theoretically, it also points to the extent to which at a micro-level, individuality need not be reduced to a cartoon vision of atomism that is sometimes drawn by its critics.

Nevertheless, if the discussion of chapter 3 is persuasive, then the instrumental properties of friendship in advancing individuality can serve as no more than a deficient reason for the friendship. If Denny's sole motivation for being friends with Alan is because Alan fosters Denny's individuality, then something important has been lost. Even when it serves the high ideal of individuality, friendship must still be accompanied by the mutual recognition of appropriate motivations. From this perspective, friendship to be friendship has to have a degree of separateness from other ideals. It must stand, in important ways, on its own, even (or perhaps especially) in instances when it is useful.[15]

Thinking about the degree to which friendship can support an ideal of individuality, Flathman also correctly points to the possible temptations posed by friendship that can undermine individuality. The sources of these temptations are many, but some of them reside within the practice of friendship itself. For example, they may be found in such notions of the friend being another self, in Montaigne's fusion of wills, in Augustine's sense of one soul in two bodies, and in Nietzsche's warnings of "going over" to one's friend. These impulses may lead friends to seek and impose conformity on one another.[16] The friendship as a clique can have this sort of flavor. Other elements may be found in the care and affection for a friend that may be challenged by the changes of self-enacted individuality. In the extreme, letting a friend be is not an easy thing when one believes that she is running a risk of destroying herself.[17] In less extreme cases, when a friend chooses a path that is unexpected or unusual, it may not be surprising to try to call her back to the person that one once knew as opposed to who she is trying to become.[18]

There is, as Flathman sometimes notes, a Nietzschean pathos of distance that accompanies these ideals of friendship and individuality. This distance is also expressed in Emerson's essay on friendship. He writes, "Treat your friend as a spectacle. Of course he has merits that are not yours, and that you cannot honor if you must needs hold him close to your person. Stand aside; give those merits room; let them mount and expand" (1991:229).[19] The trick is to say neither too much nor too little. The ideal of bridging/bonding friendship, then, must be one that is attentive to the risks of falling on either side of this line.

Something of this connection between individuality and friendship lies just below the surface of Oakeshott's conception of friendship. He writes,

> To discard friends because they do not behave as we expected and refuse to be educated to our requirements is the conduct of a man who has altogether mistaken the character of friendship. Friends are not concerned with what might be made of one another, but only with the enjoyment of one another; and the condition of this enjoyment is a ready acceptance of what is and the absence of any desire to change or to improve. A friend is not somebody one trusts to behave in a certain manner, who supplies certain wants, who has certain useful abilities, who possesses certain merely agreeable qualities, or who holds certain acceptable opinions; he is somebody who engages the imagination, who excites contemplation, who

provokes interest, sympathy, delight and loyalty simply on account of the relationship entered into. One friend cannot replace another; there is all the difference in the world between the death of a friend and the retirement of one's tailor from business. The relationship of friend to friend is dramatic, not utilitarian; the tie is one of familiarity, not usefulness; the disposition engaged is conservative, not 'progressive.'

(1991:416–17)

As an ideal, Oakeshott's view is compelling. At the same time, however, as an account of friendship in all of its manifestations, it unduly narrows our practices of friendship. For some people, friendship may very well be understood as an opportunity to improve another human being, and for many practices of friendship, utility is not entirely inconsistent with friendship. Alternatively, it may also be the case that one skiing buddy comes to replace another who has lost interest in the sport. None of these friendships live up to or even seek to live up to the ideal of bridging/bonding friendship, but they are still friendships.

For the most part, this discussion has focused on the extent to which Flathman's conception of self-enacted individuality is served by friendship. Flathman's discussion brings this aspect of the relationship into focus while his idea of individuality as the highest value, de-emphasizes how individuality may be built into and serve a particular ideal of friendship. We can, however, also highlight the ways in which the perceived individuality of one's friend heightens and strengthens friendship. From this perspective, what I celebrate, what I find so interesting and so compelling about you is your distinctive character: your take on the world, your voice. What I love about you is your courage, your willingness not to take the easier path, your ability to resist social pressures and norms. You are an original. Individuality in this case, serves as a motivation for friendship. Individuality may enliven the sentiments and feelings of friendship directed toward a specific person. In contrast, we can drift, so to speak, into a friendship with another. This is neither unusual nor something to disparage. There is something about friendship that should make it easy to be benevolent, generous, affectionate, caring, and so on. This ease does not preclude reflecting on why one has or should have those sentiments. Nor does this reflection necessarily mean that we would adopt other sentiments.[20]

INDIVIDUALITY, FRIENDSHIP, AND CONVENTIONAL MORALITY

One question that the combination of friendship and individuality raises is whether this individuality-infused friendship should be molded to the demands of ordinary morality. There are at least two sorts of questions embedded in this issue. The first concerns whether we should follow or support our friends even when they violate what is conventionally understood as right and wrong. The second is whether friendship should be conditioned by our friends' moral character. With regard to the first question, Cicero's law of friendship encapsulates what could be considered the conventional response: "we must not ask wrongful things, nor do them, if we are asked to" (Cicero 1991:95). One of Cicero's central concerns in *De Amicitia* is that friendships can lead to conspiracies and conspiracies can lead to treason (a theme that will be considered in chapters 6 and 7). Consequently, conventional forms of right and wrong must put the brakes on friendship. Against Cicero's law, one can place E. M. Forster's much quoted comment that if given the choice between betraying his friends and his country, he hoped that he would have the strength to betray his country (1938:68). The deeper difficulty raised by the relationship between friendship and ordinary morality, however, is one that cannot be handled by Cicero's law or by Forster's testament. For it is one of the effects of many sorts of friendships that we may find ourselves rethinking what we understood as right and wrong or good and bad. While Nehamas's claim is overstated as a generalization for all friendships, he is correct in noting that friendships may lead us into territory that we never thought possible: "We never know exactly what friendship promises, whether its promise will be fulfilled, and whether, once fulfilled, it will be for better or worse" (2010:279). Yet this is one of the wonderful and troubling things about friendships—that they do have the potential to lead us to question ourselves and what we believe. In the case of bridging/bonding friendship when one is calling into question and seeking to shape one's sentiments, this is particularly true. It is, then, no accident that philosophical conversation and friendship have been linked since Plato. In friendship we may be led to think beyond the conventional and the legal. It is also this very character that generates certain risks and rewards. With regard to the first question, we may conclude that the ordinary rules of morality do not trump the ideal of bridging/bonding friendship, nor does the ideal necessarily trump ordinary morality.

But suppose that a friendship does not lead us to rethink our sense of right and wrong. Suppose we come to the conclusion that our friend really has done wrong—violated the ordinary rules of morality, the law, or the basic requirements of humane treatment of others. Should we be or remain friends with those who have done wrong? Should we support their actions? Offer them aid and comfort? The questions can be answered in different ways. For example, if the wrongful actions violate the conditions noted in earlier chapters (i.e., the wrongdoer no longer subscribes to the adverbial conditions of self-disclosure or reveals that her motivations are no longer those that were compatible with friendship), then obviously the friendship is over. Suppose, however, the wrongful action does not violate those conditions for friendship? In the case of the ideal of bridging/bonding friendship, there is nothing that requires disassociation with a friend because she has done wrong (a related issue occurs in chapter 6 with the discussion of Atticus's friendships with the various players during the Roman civil war). Of course, the social pressures for such disassociation may be extraordinary. Guilt by association is not an unusual form of judgment. On the other hand, nothing about the ideal of bridging/bonding friendship requires endorsement or approval of all actions done by a friend. As Lynch notes, disagreement, conflict, and disappointment are also part of friendship (2005:113).[21] These features of friendship raise again Telfer's question regarding precisely what it is about a friend that supports the friendship. The discussion from chapter 3 and highlighted further in the ideal of bridging/bonding friendship is that one can be attracted *to how* another engages in the world. That their character is such that they strive to be motivated by generosity and care and that they seek to act generously or caringly is an expression of their individuality and a reason why they are friends.[22]

These kinds of answers, however, bring us to the second question of whether moral character should make a difference for bridging/bonding friendship. This ideal is most certainly linked to character (as understood in terms of self-enactment) and hence the quality of character should make a difference. As was noted earlier, however, while bridging/bonding friendship is a character-based friendship, it is largely adverbial or formal. It is possible that a friend's pursuit of her individuality could have deeply objectionable substantive results. Should one break off a friendship with an autonomous racist? On the one hand, no one has a duty to be friends with anyone. Consequently, one need not remain friends with an individual with whom the ordinary motivations for friendship no longer exist. On the other hand, one does not have a duty to break off a friendship with such an individual. One may still have affection or care for her and that affection and care may be returned. The existence of such a friendship does not mean that one need not work against the manifestations of a friend's racism, even if the ideal of bridging/bonding friendship precludes a commitment to reforming or remaking her attitudes. Still, bridging/bonding friendship is an ideal and exists alongside one's other commitments and values. Even if one comes to believe that some other values override one's friendship with a racist, the ideal friendship is not overridden. Something of value would be lost in such a decision.

What emerges as a central value in bridging/bonding friendship is not merely my own individuality, but the individuality of someone else. When we think about the implications of these moves for liberalism, an argument can be made that they reassert a commitment to moral pluralism (there exist competing moral values that may not be fully commensurable) and they present an alternative to the view of liberalism as a lonely, atomistic doctrine. Our individualities can be enhanced and sustained through friendship and our friendships can be deepened and enriched through the pursuit of our individuality. The practices of generosity and acting for the sake of another, far from being estranged from liberalism's celebration and pursuit of individuality, can be accommodated, even if tensions and conflicts always remain.

SIMMEL AND TOCQUEVILLE ON
FRIENDSHIP AND MODERNITY

The association between individuality and friendship would not, however, be welcome by all. The sociologist George Simmel could argue that bridging/ bonding friendship simply reinforces an already pervasive form of fragmentation that defines much of modernity. By emphasizing the connection between individuality and an ideal friendship, I am moving friendship farther away from the possibility of "absolute psychological intimacy," an intimacy that was once part and parcel of friendship (Simmel 1950:325). Alternatively, from a Tocquevillian perspective, the ideal of bridging/bonding friendship could be seen as simply adding to a pernicious form of individualism that further saps public virtue and reinforces the alienating facets of an egalitarian society plagued by a tyrannical majority. Perhaps more troubling, it could be argued that seeing any form of friendship as an ideal will further protect and entrench the power of elites. The circle of attachment around one's friends is already well-drawn and protected by those with the resources to help those they want to help. In contrast, what is really needed in political theory is not an account of friendship and its ideal, but more attention to our universal obligations or attachments that are owed to strangers.

In response to the last objection, I have not attempted to make the claim that friendship is the only form of association that has some claim to our attention. The history of liberal thought is largely one of trying to discern the principles or institutional structures that could secure the allegiance of individuals with diverse conceptions of the good life who frequently find themselves in conflict with one another. The value attributed to friendship or individuality is not meant to deny the value of minimally just institutional structures. Nor is it to deny the existence of responsibilities to others who are not our friends. Undoubtedly friendship has certain unfortunate effects (as Cicero recognized), but that does not mean that friendship always has those effects nor does it mean that we should be unconcerned with the effects of political institutions on friendship. The argument is that even in a liberalism that lends enormous weight to individuality, friendship (or a particular ideal of it) will also be of intrinsic and instrumental importance. The question, taken up in chapter 7, is whether friendship is so important that it calls for greater institutional recognition. Should, as some have argued, law and policy be more cognizant of encouraging and protecting friendships?

The Tocquevillian critique raises the question of whether bridging/bonding friendship would undermine the kind of diffuse support necessary to sustain a worthy political life. Is friendship that turns upon individuality dangerous to a good politics? Should we be friends of liberty first and interpersonal friends second? In chapter 5 I seek to address this question by making the case for a very circumscribed conception of civic friendship. The bulk of that chapter, however, examines whether the notion of friendship can serve as a general model for citizenship. This view, most fully expressed in the work of Aristotle, but resurrected in the work of contemporary thinkers, is one that I will reject. Tocqueville may be correct in thinking that interpersonal friendship can pull us away from and potentially challenge and disrupt the public sphere. That is not necessarily a bad thing for politics or a good thing for friendship. The quality of our politics may be improved by such disruptions, but interpersonal friendships may be corrupted by our public life. The question is not merely the possible consequences of friendship on political and legal institutions, but the possible implications of those institutions for friendship.

In many writings on friendship, authors sometimes point to Simmel's comments regarding the role of friendship in modern life (Pahl 2000; Epstein 2006; Lynch 2005). Simmel argues that the relationships of both marriage and friendship are built on the idea of "the person in its totality" within which we are able to encounter fully another human being (1950:325). Modern culture and society, however, are characterized not only by a high degree of differentiation, but also by a pervasive sense that around every individual is a sphere that should not be penetrated, "unless the personality value of the individual is thereby destroyed" (321). Simmel believes that preserving our identities in modern life requires preserving and controlling secrets about ourselves. In contrast, he claims that "the ideal of friendship" as it "was received from antiquity and developed in a romantic spirit . . . aims at an absolute psychological intimacy, and is accompanied by the notion that even material property should be common to friends" (325). Simmel is willing to entertain the historical realization of this ideal (when it flourished is not exactly clear) but then claims that "such complete intimacy becomes probably more and more difficult as differentiation among men increases. Modern man, possibly, has too much to hide to sustain a friendship" (326). In Simmel's view, a fragmentation of friendships results. Some of our friends are drawn together by affection, others by religious affiliation, and still others by intellectual pursuits. There is no point at which the whole of who we are is encountered in any friendship.

For Simmel, an additional problem with modern friendship is that these different realms of friendship remain distinct. The friends with whom we take daily walks should not explore our feelings and spheres of interest associated with our friends from high school, and those old chums should not concern themselves with our newly made friends from the community band. The reason for this compartmentalization is that if our friends *did* *seek* to understand these other friendships, it would "make them feel painfully the limits of their mutual understanding" (Simmel 1950:326). In other words, they would realize how much of their friend's "total personality" they do not comprehend. Simmel concludes this discussion with the observation that, despite such limitations, modern, compartmentalized friendships do emanate from the center of one's identity and they can inspire the same depth of affection and willingness to sacrifice found in the ancient/romantic ideal.

As a description of prevailing practices of modern friendship, Simmel's account is extremely sketchy. For example, it is not clear exactly who defined this ancient/romantic ideal of friendship in which one self is totally revealed to another. It sounds like Montaigne, but even Montaigne never thought this was actualized very often. Apart from its origins and its highly gendered character, who subscribes to this particular ideal of friendship? Is it as pervasive as Simmel suggests? More importantly, what does it mean for one person to reveal totally her personality to another? Would such a disclosure make sense even in a society in which there is not some (any?) level of social differentiation?[23] These questions point to problems in using Simmel's position to establish any kind of normative leverage against modern friendship or connecting friendship with individuality.

One can, however, approach Simmel's position from another perspective. It is possible that the sort of fragmentation that Simmel notes may be no more than different practices of friendship. From this perspective, Simmel is indeed witnessing distinct realms of self-disclosure, but those realms are indicative of the richness of a cultural life and not its impoverishment. They reveal diverse ways in which different styles and forms of friendship have emerged. But Simmel could respond by arguing that the Oakeshottian account of practice and self-disclosure upon which my account of friendship as a family of practices is based, rests on a form of self-disclosure that merely reveals a particular *persona* and not the whole person.[24] The motivations and adverbial conditions that structure our expectations regarding a particular friendship will be different from the sorts of conditions that define other practices. Friendships are different from other sorts of relationships—teacher/pupil, employee/employer, parent/child, and so on. What is disclosed to our friends will inevitably be different from the self disclosed to a judge, a teacher, a coach, a colleague, or a fellow member of a mosque (assuming that one is not both friend and colleague, etc). In this regard, Simmel is correct. There is no relationship in which all of the possible forms of self-disclosure come together. Social differentiation has multiplied our personae.

Why would this be deemed objectionable? Behind Simmel's account may be a yearning for a social relationship in which one human being is entirely present to another. For Simmel, marriage has become the one relationship in which the totality of personality is revealed. One way to respond to this yearning is to argue that he is largely correct in his description of friendship as it is a relationship in which a yearning to be completely present to another can never be satisfied. Nevertheless, this is not a condition to be regretted (even if the ideal of bridging/bonding friendship falls short of "absolute psychological intimacy" or a commanding view of our friend's personality), not because Simmel's ideal of total disclosure is impossible (as say Derrida would suggest), but because even if were possible it would be undesirable. Nehamas suggests this sort of response when he draws on Nietzsche and argues that "the sense that our knowledge of our friends, and everyone we love is always provisional and incomplete is a constant incitement to come to know them better" (2010:289). Bridging/bonding friendship adds an additional dimension to this provisional understanding. Drawing on Flathman's notion of self-enacted individuality and the idea of a self that can be divided in ways that one may not fully understand, the ideal of individuality presumes that self-enactment is itself also an adventure whose course cannot be fully laid out or understood from the beginning. It opens up the possibility that our friends may see things in us that we do not initially recognize. As Jeske notes, "Our friends come to know certain facts about our characters before we are aware of them—friends help us to understand our own characters. It is not unusual to have an epiphany about ourselves and then, upon sharing it with a friend, have them respond that they had realized that fact about us long ago" (2008:57).

From this perspective, one is seeking to understand oneself and others. This seeking presupposes that neither oneself nor one's friends need be completely transparent. Nehamas takes this position a bit further by arguing that,

> If we are friends, I am of course attracted to what I already know about you, but I also expect that what I don't yet know will be attractive as well and, with that expectation I want to come know to you better and more intimately. Friendship, like every kind of love, is a commitment to the future, based on a promise of a better life together than either one of us can have alone. If ever that commitment wanes, if one day you find yourself feeling that you already know everything that matters about me, that there is nothing more you want to learn—on that day our friendship will be over.
>
> (2010:278)

As with the response to the extended quotation from Oakeshott, one can endorse the value Nehamas attributes to provisional and incomplete character of our self-understandings and understandings of others without having to accept a stronger claim that all practices of friendship must be driven by notions of commitment or perhaps even by the presumption that friendship would be over if we believed that there was nothing new to learn about our friends. In these sorts of comments, Nehamas may be carving out an ideal that need not be for everyone.

If we see our practices of friendship as unavoidably possessing certain voluntary features, then it is possible to construct an ideal of friendship in which those features are extended and elaborated. Consequently, it is possible to understand a practice of friendship that was conditioned not only by the adverbial norms that structure our actions but also by the demands of self-enactment that a friend must take upon herself. In this ideal of friendship, the friends are attracted to one another because of their engagement in self-enacted individuality. Bridging/bonding friendship is an ideal in which individuality can condition and motivate the bonds of friendship. On the other hand, and just as important, this sort of friendship may also enhance and encourage the individuality of one's friends.

PART *two*

five

CIVIC FRIENDSHIP

I hope that America's ideological opposites in Congress, on the airwaves, in cyberspace, and in the public square will learn that being faithful to a political party or a philosophical view does not preclude civility, or even friendships, with those on the other side.

—ORRIN HATCH, "THE TED KENNEDY I KNEW"

If interpersonal friendship is understood as a family of practices in which the participants subscribe to certain adverbial conditions to guide their actions and recognize certain motivations in one another, in what way or ways could it be connected to politics? The next three chapters explore this question from three different angles. This chapter concentrates on the most obvious of those connections, namely that friendship, or some practice of it, can serve as a general model for citizenship and political action. Chapter 6 looks at the role of friendship as a model for interaction in situations of political unrest and, chapter 7 considers whether political and legal institutions should be cognizant of and attempt to foster interpersonal friendship. The overall theme of these chapters is that the place of friendship in our political life at both a personal and institutional level is and should be complex. It should not only be sensitive to the multiple understandings of friendship, but also to the political environment and the capabilities of our institutions. In short, friendship has a (qualified) role to play in politics and our political and legal institutions have a (qualified) role to play in our friendships.

Can friendship serve as a general model for citizenship? More specifically, is the idea of civic friendship or political friendship (and I will use the terms interchangeably) applicable to the complex, enormous states that exist today? In the West, an ancient tradition sees friendship as a general model for citizenship. The most important source of that tradition is Aristotle's discussion of political friendship in the *Nicomachean Ethics* and the *Eudemian Ethics*. The Aristotelian tradition of thinking about political life through the lens of friendship can then be found in Cicero's *De Amicitia* and to some extent in Aquinas (Schwartz 2007). For a variety of reasons that need not be considered here, that lens was largely discarded in later Western political thought.[1] More recently, however, political thinkers have begun to recover these models of civic friendship and adjust them to modern realities. Although this chapter rejects seeing civic friendship as a way to knit a society together, civic friendship does represent an ideal of political interaction that, while difficult, should be taken seriously even by liberals who tend to be cool on the whole notion.[2]

Why the renewed interest in civic friendship? Are not the dangers of cultivating and celebrating friendships in politics (cronyism, partiality, favoritism, corruption) enough to warn us away from a serious theoretical exposition and defense of civic friendship?[3] Those who have sought to revitalize interest in it have done so for different reasons. For a number of thinkers, an interest in friendship is driven by a desire to move away from conceptions of politics that seem to separate and, on some accounts, atomize us. For example, Alasdair MacIntyre sees friendship as an avenue for acknowledging and sharing our vulnerabilities to and our dependence on one another (1999:150–51, 164–65). Through friendship, we learn to speak on behalf of those who cannot speak for themselves (150). For others, a concern with friendship is motivated by a desire to understand a bond between citizens that is both respectful of difference and able to withstand the disagreements that citizens may encounter when discussing or pursuing public business. For example, Sybil Schwarzenbach claims that we need to reconsider the notion of civic friendship and the motivation of philia in order to provide a sufficient level of unity to the modern state—a state increasingly divided by disparities of wealth and the rising tensions between religious and ethnic groups (Schwarzenbach 2009:1). In contrast, Danielle Allen argues that friendship solves the problem of division by converting "rivalrous self-interest" into "equitable self-interest" (Allen 2004:126). One of the goals of civic friendship on Allen's account is "antagonistic cooperation" in which citizens can tussle over their differences, while nonetheless sustaining their connection (118). Although his aspirations may not be as high, Jason Scorza (2004) sees friendship as providing lessons for how we should talk to one another while maintaining our disagreements and divisions.[4]

These contemporary accounts tend to see something about friendship that can provide a scalable model for civic interaction. For Allen and Schwarzenbach, civic friendship expresses an encompassing sense of good will among citizens. By either wishing one another well or acting "as if" we wished one another well, conflict can be moderated. Differences continue to exist, but because of civic friendship we are not inclined to take the ball and go home. The atmosphere of civic friendship may be necessary either because it is believed that the existing informal manners, norms, and expectations of civility no longer work or because the claims of justice and the rule of law are too blunt. What motivates the reappearance of civic friendship is a desire to forestall or mitigate a general level of enmity that renders cooperation impossible and to cultivate a political culture that permits differences to flourish while strengthening just arrangements.

One response to this turn to civic friendship is to argue that conflict and, yes, enmity, are simply part of politics, even in the best of circumstances. Susan Bickford's rejection of civic friendship as a grounding for democratic political deliberation is largely based on such a claim. We may be drawn to Aristotle's metaphor of fellow travelers on a ship and think that somehow being in the same boat will foster mutual well-wishing and concern, but, Bickford argues, even given a shared interest in staying afloat, "I am as likely to make an argument for pushing some people overboard (say, the people who will not give up the best cabin) as I am to develop for everyone 'a fairly extensive and powerful sense of mutual concern'" (1996:39). Whether one believes that the attitude of throwing others overboard is "as likely" as mutual concern, the point is well-taken. Still, defenders of civic friendship are not blind to the level of conflict and disagreement in society.

Their argument, in part, can be read as an attempt to provide reasons for why we should develop civic friendships in the face of such disagreement and not to deny its existence or pervasiveness.

A central claim in this chapter is that while Bickford's view of politics may be closer to reality, even if it were not, civic friendship as a general model for citizenship would fail. Although I will argue that civic friendship is important, it is not necessary to sustain political cooperation and just institutions. Its primary importance is not derived from its instrumental qualities (say, its usefulness in sustaining a general background of good will), but from the values of the bonds of friendship and its potential compatibility with individuality; a compatibility which suggests that difference and close social connection can find some overlap, and that these connections establish a limited, episodic ideal or form of virtù in our political life.

As a general matter, friendship is unnecessary for political cooperation for a couple of reasons. First, the need for a general background of good will to sustain just arrangements is contestable. The question of what binds a people brought together by choice and chance is deeply disputed within the history of political thought and political science more generally. For some thinkers what is important is not a background of good will, but a shared cultural experience or set of traditions that have survived the test of time. Other thinkers have argued in favor of the utility of fear and the significance of consent. Still others have turned to willfulness or the cultivation of a tough-mindedness associated with agonistic democracy. For example, John Rawls employs the duties of justice, public reason, and civility in order to bind citizens together. Michael Oakeshott points to the recognition of authority. Susan Bickford draws upon "the practice of decision-making in a conflictual context, along with a sense of justice of the practice" (1996:38). If it is not evident that a general background of mutual concern is necessary, then it is not evident that what can generate that background is necessary.

A second, and perhaps more compelling, reason why civic friendship is not and cannot be a necessary condition for social cooperation and justice is because the mutual recognition of the requisite motivations for friendship is impossible in large, complex societies. Even if one believed in the importance of a general background of good will, civic friendship cannot get us there. Although civic friendship could be a limited ideal of citizenship, it is not scalable. The next section offers an argument as to why this is the case.

SIZE MATTERS

The heart of the argument against civic friendship as a general model of citizenship is simple: size.[5] To the extent that civic friendship requires the mutual recognition of the appropriate motives of friendship, such recognition is virtually impossible in a polity with a large population.[6] Wellman's argument against employing friendship as a useful political relationship is an example of this critique (Wellman 2001:222). For Wellman, civic friendship requires a widespread form of intimacy which is impossible in contemporary states.

For defenders of civic friendship, a critique based on scale would come as no surprise. In response, they have argued that friendship in a political context is simply not the same as what is found in ordinary interpersonal relationships. For example, Aristotle did not conceive of the citizens of a polis as having the sort of knowledge of one another required by virtue-based friendships. Similarly, Sybil Schwarzenbach argues that in politics, "where one assumes no ties of intimacy, of individual knowledge, or of personal affection," friendship will be based, in part on reciprocal advantage and equality. Personal friendship is not the same as political friendship. In addition, she argues, it is not merely a love of advantage that drives civic friends. The motivational tie of civic friendship "is evidenced . . . by a general concern and attitude in the everyday lives of its citizens and works via the constitution; it is recognized in legal and social norms regarding the treatment of persons in that society as well as in the willingness of fellow citizens to uphold them" (Schwarzenbach 1996:109; 2009:54). From a somewhat different perspective, Danielle Allen (2004) argues that political friendship must be shorn of emotion and affect if it is to find a place in politics. Most defenders of civic friendship are thus aware that political friendship, whatever else it may mean, cannot rest on the sentiments associated with ordinary friendship.

THE MUTUAL RECOGNITION
OF MOTIVATIONS

The criticism based on size offered here, however, is somewhat broader than what would be addressed by shearing intimacy and emotion from political friendship. It order to further secure their positions, defenders of friendship as a general model of citizenship must also argue that political friendship need not require the mutual recognition of motives. As we shall see, removing the necessity of mutually recognizing motivations will have important consequences. It is necessary for supporters of civic friendship to make such a move, however, because individuals may not be able to judge the motives of one another in large societies. Indeed, if we take the lessons of social psychology seriously, it is difficult to judge our own motives.[7] Not only are motivations frequently ambiguous, but also the perception of the motives of others is frequently biased (Heider 1958; Malle 1999). In the case of biases, we tend to be subject to so-called attribution biases regarding the motives of others. For example, we frequently attribute negative motives to others who hold positions that differ from our own (Reeder et al. 2005). In addition, "when we explain what others do, we tend to invoke low-level dispositional explanations—the person is cowardly, or generous, or fair-minded—rather than explanations that refer to pressures of the particular situation of the agent" (McGeer and Pettit 2009:59–60). Conversely, when we explain our own behavior, we tend to emphasize the particular situation. Because of this bias, we may be more willing to attribute to our fellow citizens motives of good will or craven self-interest when, in fact, they are merely responding to the pressures of a particular situation. In sum, we have problems correctly identifying the motives of ourselves and others. These sorts of complexities and biases do not mean that human beings are opaque to one another or to themselves, but that overcoming these difficulties requires knowing more than what people are doing. Political associations of any significant size make it impossible for citizens to accurately judge the motivations of one another. Such judgments do not demand intimacy (although we hope that in our intimate relationships we understand something of the motives of our partners and friends). They may, however, require time and contact—conditions which cannot be met in large societies.

To protect themselves from these sorts of criticisms, defenders of civic friendship have several options. One option is to argue that if the mutual recognition of motivations is obstructing friendship from serving as a general model of citizenship, we might simply abandon the need for mutually recognizing motivations. There are two versions of this approach. The *thinnest theory* of civic friendship simply associates it with civility. Alternatively, the *thin theory* of civic friendship sees it as an ethos that citizens adopt in their interactions regardless of the motives of the other. The latter theory conjoins civility with friendliness. I will argue that despite the attractions of these views, they fall short of friendship. A second option is to surrender the aspiration for seeing civic friendship as a general model of citizenship. Civic friendship is still friendship, but it is not a relationship that all can have toward all. Instead, civic friendship should be viewed as a bounded ideal of citizenship. A third option is to try to find a way to deal with the motivational critique that avoids the first two options. This third possibility gets us into the weeds of the current debate over civic friendship and considers in more detail the positions of Schwarzenbach and Allen as well as the interpretations of Aristotle that have become part of the debate. In the end, I argue that the mutual recognition of motivations remains an insurmountable barrier and hence the second option may be the best we can do in thinking about civic friendship.

THINNEST AND THIN: CIVIC FRIENDSHIP AS CIVILITY AND AS FRIENDLINESS

If the general problem is that we cannot reliably assess the motives of our fellow citizens in polities composed of millions of individuals, why not see civic friendship as independent of that mutual recognition and more dependent on the actions that friends perform for and with one another? In such a scenario, civic friendship would amount to a kind of civility. The manners of citizens would matter more than their motives.[8] Hence, whether one is motivated by fear, virtue, the desire for security, agonistic competitiveness, or institutional incentives is independent of whether one is acting civilly. That is, citizens are doing the sorts of things citizens should do:

respecting the rights and liberties of other citizens, obeying the just laws of the land, living up to their obligations, and acting respectfully.

There is much to be said for this move, particularly if one assumes that what should primarily count in politics are actions and not motivations. While we may have more confidence in an official who performs her duties out of a sense of justice, it may be enough for her to do the just thing, even if her motivation is to get re-elected.[9] Similarly, in the case of citizen strangers, what matters more is how we are treated and not the specific sentiments that motivate the treatment. In the following, I will suggest that connecting the idea of citizenship to civility is not a bad place to start. Nevertheless, if civic friendship was nothing more than civility, then talk about friendship would be superfluous. We could adequately describe, encourage, or admonish citizens for acting civilly (or not) without saying that they should be establishing and maintaining friendships with their fellow citizens. Like the notion of love, once the idea of friendship enters the scene, it is difficult to talk about the relationship without some reference to motive.

A thicker, but still thin, conception of civic friendship could bring motivation back in, but frame it more as an ethos. Perhaps G. A. Cohen offers such a vision when he suggests that while we cannot be friends with millions of others, "it suffices that I treat everyone with whom I have any exchange or other form of contact as someone toward whom I have the reciprocating attitude that is characteristic of friendship" (2009:52). In other words, I have the reciprocating attitude even if that attitude is unknown or unrequited. The central advantage of this account of civic friendship is that it does not require the mutual recognition of motivations, but merely a commitment on the part of citizens to engage in a form of self-enactment that could be described as "good will" toward all plus a form of self-disclosure in which one is friendly or civil to another. This view of civic friendship is a form of civic friendliness motivated by an ethos of generosity.

As in the case of civility, there is much to admire in such an ethos of civic friendliness. Nevertheless, from Aristotle forward, there is a sense that the possession of good will by itself is not friendship. He claimed that friendship was not merely good will, but reciprocated good will (1985:1155b30–35).[10] Preston King echoes this view, noting that "friendliness, as important as it is to oil the machinery of social interaction and to forge political cohesiveness,

is not itself friendship" (2007:143). King further argues that seeing friendship as a mass phenomenon is both mistaken and dangerous. He argues that
there can be "no *mass* of friends, no *pile* of pals, no heap of *close* relations, no
total and indistinct unity of all citizens. There can be no family or city or
region in which everyone is equally a personal friend to everyone else. This
cannot be. Nor should we aspire to it" (142–43). The attempt to aspire to
friendship as a society-wide phenomenon is a recipe for despotism (143).

Even if the aspiration of mass civic friendship is not as risky as King
suggests, equating *civic friendliness* with *civic friendship* would erase the distinction between the two terms. In part 1, I argued that the distinction
between *friendliness* and *friendship* underscores the importance of motivation and perhaps even self-enactment to our practices of interpersonal
friendship. But should we maintain this distinction in our political interactions? Why not simply accept a theory of civic friendship that means little
more than an ethos of civic friendliness? Part of the answer is that motives
matter not merely for judging the presence of a friendship, but also for
grounding the value we attribute to the relationship. Motives matter in
the sense that the value of the bond of friendship and our willingness to see
it as a bond depends on discerning something more than friendliness in the
actions of our fellow citizens. Our sense of connection and loyalty to
other citizens (as opposed to loyalty to abstract ideas) comes from believing
that our compatriots are also acting for the appropriate motives and that
they believe we are doing the same. The bond bears the weight of civic
friendship and it is the mutual recognition of motivations that secures that
bond. Contemporary conceptions of political friendship tend to see friendship as providing the basis for both bonding individuals and bridging differences. Friendship suggests not merely that I believe that I am acting
generously, but that I believe that others are doing the same.

King's argument is more nuanced than the claim that friendliness should
not be confused with friendship. On his view, the two need to be distinguished because something about interpersonal friendship opens the possibility for a larger ethos of friendliness. He argues that the dyadic character
of friendship can teach us about how we should interact with others.[11] King
writes that "dyadic friendship has a universal substratum, as in the example
that it sets, the ethic that underlies it, the unilateral offshoots that spring

from it, and the generalized friendliness it can bestow upon society at large as a regnant morality." He goes on to say,

> The particular knot of dyadic friendship contains the germ of its own sublimation. This germ is the element of affection for another or others, of caring for these, of seeking their happiness and well-being, of being welcoming and kindly—even should one reach the point where these dispositions are not reciprocated, or cannot be reciprocated, or where reciprocity is simply not sought. We draw nearer to the idea of friendship as a mass phenomenon, within society as a whole, when we concentrate upon this abstracted germ of affection, this unilateral offshoot, this generalized species of friendliness, in which the reciprocity itself is grounded.
>
> (2007:134)

This idea of a "generalized friendliness" is more than civility insofar as it turns on concern or affection for others, but it is less than dyadic friendship insofar as it is unilateral. In short, generalized friendliness "ought to be viewed as the universal moral imperative deriving from these dyads" (144).

For King, the most that we can expect from civic relationships is generalized friendliness, but we can get that only because of our experience with friendship. For the concerns of this chapter, however, it is enough to say that even for King, a generalized notion of friendliness is not a conception of civic friendship. Emphasizing this distinction is not meant to reject the importance of an ethos of friendliness, which presents its own challenges as a form of self-enactment. Rather, it merely means that even if we do endorse it, it does not offer us a theory of civic friendship. Whether there is a coherent idea of civic friendship that acknowledges the importance of motivations remains the question. The next section defends a particular ideal of civic friendship as a more bounded relationship that recognizes the limitation of mutually recognizing motivations.

THE VIRTÙ OF CIVIC FRIENDSHIP

If the thin theories of civic friendship are not placing enough weight on the implications of the idea of *friendship*, perhaps civic friendship is an ideal that will be worthwhile for some: more a virtù than a virtue. As an ideal, its provenance is not found in the anonymous interactions of citizens in large states. Rather, it is realizable by some set of citizens that is small enough such that they can recognize one another's motives. From this perspective, civic friendships are like islands in a larger sea of citizen-strangers and -acquaintances. These civic friends are individuals whose actions entail more than obeying the law, but who understand and mutually recognize the appropriate feelings of friendship among one another. They are individuals who are involved in the public business, in either an official or unofficial capacity, but choose to see their relationship to one another in a manner that is inflected by the ordinary practices of friendship. They may be members of a Senate, union officials, or fellow soldiers. They may find themselves working in the bureaucracy, holding appointed positions, volunteering for a campaign, or in the same foxhole. They may be working in concert, on different sides of the aisle, or fighting in the same unit. However they are situated politically, their motivations and actions toward one another go beyond the requirements of mere civility and friendliness. It is an ideal of behaving and feeling that can be very difficult to enact and sustain, especially when the friends find themselves in opposition. Nevertheless, it is an expression of the more familiar values that we associate with ordinary practices of friendship and ordinary citizenship. Civic friendship entails the mutual recognition of the appropriate sentiments, but if it is a civic friendship, then it differs from other sorts of friendship. But how does it differ?

One possible, albeit, mundane difference is that civic friendships are ones in which the friends do civic-related stuff. Just as one can have friends from one's job, school, or club, one can have friends from the campaign office or in the assembly or the union. These are friendships that happen to occur at particular place or in a particular set of circumstances.[12] In these cases, the word *civic* adds nothing to the word *friendship* beyond signaling a context out of which they arose or occur. Is civic friendship only this mundane understanding?

The rejection of civic friendship as a general model for citizenship may provide a way to begin to answer this question. If it is implausible to think that we should define citizenship through the lens of friendship, then we have a good reason to advance notions of citizenship that do not require friendship. That is, we have a good reason to imagine conceptions of citizenship that would guide the interactions between individuals who would otherwise see one another as strangers or merely useful or who are not only indifferent to but possibly detest one another. Civic friendship differs from other forms of friendship insofar as it seeks to combine the cool civility of being a citizen with the warmth of friendship.

The view of citizenship that I am employing to inform the meaning of civic friendship uses civility as a starting point. The principle advantage of starting with civility is that it does not demand that citizens have certain feelings toward one another. Rather, in a move familiar to many liberals, acting as a citizen entails acknowledging others as free and equal despite feeling indifferent, adverse, or favorable toward them. The case for offering an understanding of citizenship that swings freely of the motivational demands associated with friendship rests on the assumption that it is either impossible to ensure that citizens function with the right motives or that to instill the right motives would be dangerous and/or costly.[13] To put it in the Oakeshottian language of part I, the generalizable notion of citizenship offered here requires forms of self-disclosure that recognize the freedom and equality of others, but not forms of self-enactment.

This is, admittedly, a very watery notion of citizenship, one that could be easily accommodated by rules for interactions between those who are not even fellow citizens. Consequently, the civic interactions of citizens must require more than mere civility. Citizens, of course, are citizens of some place with its own particular history, culture, advantages, and disadvantages. That place is controlled by institutions and those institutions are guided by purposes, ideals, and principles. To talk of being a citizen of the world as the ancient Stoics did is still to express adherence to some set of principles and the territory of the earth, even if institutional arrangements are lacking or merely emerging. Fellow citizens share a sense that they should be governed by some set of institutional arrangements or basic principles and ideals and that they have obligations to those arrangements or principles. These institutions and principles may be more or less well defined and certainly contested in various ways without calling into question one's rights or obligations as a citizen.

On this account, the norms of citizenship include civility, acknowledging the authority of a given set of political institutions, as well as accepting what John Rawls calls the "facts of pluralism" (2005). We differ over the formulation of basic political principles, over the weight of the values that those principles embody, over how best to embody those principles in basic institutions, as well as over how they should be enacted in laws and policy. These differences are precisely why civility is an important component of how citizens should interact. Understanding these differences is part of the responsibilities of citizenship. As citizens, people should treat one another as free and equal and attempt to secure institutions that protect and enable those values. We can discern institutional arrangements as being more or less just depending on whether those institutions take this view of citizens. Setting out these matters has defined much of Western political philosophy since the emergence of the state system. For the purpose of this argument, it is enough to say that citizenship requires the appropriate forms of self-disclosure (e.g., acknowledging and respecting the freedom and equality of other citizens) along with obligations and rights vis-à-vis a shared set of institutional arrangements and basic principles roughly conceived.

As a sketch of a general model of citizenship, this view is not meant to require or rest on civic friendship, but neither is it meant to preclude the possibility of individuals seeing civic friendship as a civic ideal. In light of this view of citizenship and the discussion of friendship from part 1, "civic friendship" is neither simply friendship nor simply citizenship. Within civic friendship there is something about the character of citizenship that affects friendship and there is something about friendship that is affecting civility. The larger and obvious lesson from this discussion is that civic friendship is very much dependent on other, broader commitments and understandings of how people can be friends and citizens.

CIVIC FRIENDSHIP IS NOT MERELY FRIENDSHIP

Given this admittedly rough discussion of citizenship, the somewhat mismatched features of *civic* and *friendship* intimate a tension that, in the end, may be part of the ideal of civic friendship itself. Citizenship tugs at friendship and friendship pulls at citizenship, creating a hybrid whose orbit is different than either of its components. What effect does citizenship have on friendship? The general view of citizenship offered thus far brings with it no specific motivational demands and consequently it makes little difference to the motivational aspects of friendship. Citizenship does affect, however, the actions ordinarily deemed appropriate within many visions of friendship. Three examples come to mind. One has to do with the way citizenship may alter the privileges of friendship. A second has to do with how the duties of citizenship may affect the attachments and loyalties associated with friendship. The third is connected to the adverbial conditions and expectations that govern how civic friends will interact.

As we saw in chapter 4, friends, because they are friends, may have the sensitivity and wherewithal to endorse and support what we have endorsed and hence endorse our better selves, sometimes even in opposition to our presented projects and interests. In so doing, they may call into question judgments and actions that appear to undermine or defeat our own attempts to live more autonomously or deliberately. In many respects, these are difficult and trying judgments for friends that walk a fine line of paternalistic interference. Consequently, they are hazardous engagements for a friend to undertake and place the friendship at risk. Nevertheless, these sorts of engagements, which should never be taken lightly, are part of the many (although not all) practices of friendship.

What may be trying and difficult in the context of a friendship is deeply disturbing if licensed in the relationship of citizens. Citizens should take one another as they are, not because they cannot understand the possibility that their fellow citizens lead complex internal lives, but because it is not the place of a citizen to dismiss the presented identity of an individual in favor what they (the actors) understand to be their better or higher selves (assuming third parties can make this judgment correctly). While citizens may appeal to the better angels of one another's nature, they may not dismiss or disregard other facets of our presented identities on the claim that we may not endorse them under more ideal conditions. Civility entails respect for what has been publicly presented. This is not an epistemological argument regarding what citizens can or cannot know about each other. The argument is rather that what can be appropriate for friends to do is not

CIVIC FRIENDSHIP · 119

appropriate for citizens and (perhaps most importantly) unlike the actions of friends, the actions of citizens may be accompanied by the coercion of the law. This, of course, is a very old argument about the dangers (and incoherence) of forcing individuals to be free. It is also an argument about respecting the complexity, internal struggles, and individuality of adults. Civic friendship, then, calls into question this license (if it exists) of friendship. Within the idea of civic friendship is incorporated a distance associated with civility.

A second way in which the civic components of civic friendship tug at friendship involves the force of one's political obligations on the attachments associated with friendship. It is not surprising that the affections that bind friends together can create expectations that the interests and projects of friends will be supported and promoted when possible. I have argued in chapter 3 that if there are obligations associated with friendship they are of a deficient nature, unable to support the relationship on their own. Nevertheless, the felt loyalties associated with friendship can be fierce depending on the nature of the friendship. From the perspective of citizenship, citizens have certain duties to obey the law and follow authoritative commands and policies under the right sorts of circumstances. As citizens, those obligations may be overridden or disappear depending on the character of the regime and or the character of particular authoritative acts. Our civic obligations are neither absolute nor require a surrender of judgment. Nevertheless, they are very real (at least in the right sorts of circumstances). Citizenship brings to and elevates within civic friendship obligations that would otherwise be deficient reasons within friendship alone. In this sense, civic friendship is a form of friendship in which obligations potentially play a greater role and in which friends' bonds to one another are entwined with their obligations to support the minimally just, specific institutional arrangements which govern them as citizens.

Civic friendship is a kind of friendship that has a different sort of tenor than the one implied by E. M. Forster when he writes:

> If I had to choose between betraying my country and betraying my friends,
> I hope I should have the guts to betray my country. Such a choice may
> scandalize the modern reader, and he may stretch out his patriotic hand to
> the telephone at once and ring up the police. It would not have shocked

Dante, though. Dante places Brutus and Cassius in the lowest circle of Hell because they had chosen to betray their friend Julius Caesar rather than their country Rome.

(1938:68)

In Forster's view, however difficult it may be to support one's friends, it is clear that the better choice (if a choice is required between one's friends and one's country) is to betray one's country. Civic friendship differs from this sort of friendship insofar as the civic friends are friends precisely because they look outward toward some shared, more or less definite sense of justice. As we shall see, in gazing outward, they are not merely having a patriotic moment or sense of civic virtue (and consequently civic friendship is not the same as patriotism and civic virtue) because the civic friends genuinely respect or like one another (whereas patriots love their country but not necessarily each other).

Forster's bumper sticker view of friendship is wrapped in the hope that he would betray his country and not his friends. In civic friendship, the friends' civic obligations to the ideals, principles, institutions, laws, or policies are built into the friendship. While it would be an exaggeration, for the reasons discussed next, to say that in civic friendship in sacrificing one's country one is sacrificing one's friends, there is a sense that a betrayal of one's country could simultaneously be a betrayal of one's friends. In betraying England, the British spy Kim Philby also betrayed his civic friends, even those who may not have been directly harmed by his actions (this case, however, is muddied by the fact that all of his English "friends" were taken in by his charade of being a friend and public servant, a case that is considered in more detail in chapter 6). To let one's country down is to let one's friends down.[14] The phrase, "sacrificing one's country is sacrificing one's friends," is an exaggeration in part because the obligations of civic friendship are complicated by what is meant by one's country. Is it necessarily *these* institutions or reflected in *these* policies and laws? Or is one's country a set of principles that may or may not be embodied in certain prevailing institutions and commands? One's civic friends need not necessarily agree on the justness of particular laws and policies. The effort to change those laws or, in more extreme cases, engage in civil disobedience may strain the civic friendship, but need not break it. The obligations associated with civic friendship do not necessitate that the friends are in full agreement and working shoulder-to-shoulder on a common cause in support of the same policies, laws, and institutions. The differences and pluralities of public life mean that when such a friend says, "Here, I must stand," that is a call that should be acknowledged, perhaps supported or perhaps resisted, but it need not be the end of a civic friendship.

More strongly, the obligations of civic friendship bring with them a respectful treatment of difference. As suggested earlier, civility is itself an acknowledgment of the fact of pluralism. Civility can be had across the aisle and across party lines. This is so largely because it is a matter of self-disclosure. This is not to say that it is easy, but rather that it is possible. Civility itself provides an orientation that a relationship can be had with those whom one disagrees, sometimes deeply (of course, if the disagreement is deep enough, one may no longer feel that civility is warranted). Civic friendship can be built on that opportunity to interact and come to know those on the other side. Within a civic friendship, the interaction can be cooperative, but it can also be competitive. In the latter case it entails acting in a manner that acknowledges and respects the differences that may exist.

Finally, civic friendship may shape the adverbial conditions and expectations governing how friends will interact. To see what this may entail, we can use Ross K. Baker's (1999) discussion of friendship in the U.S. Senate. Through interviews conducted in the 1970s and historical analysis, Baker argues that the most prevalent form of friendship in the Senate was what he calls "institutional kinship."[15] In this form of friendship, senators drew on certain adjectives used to describe one another. These included seeing their friends as possessing empathy, integrity, diligence, and restraint (66). However, it is not much of a leap to imagine viewing institutional kinship as a kind of civic friendship in which senators are expected to act toward one another empathetically, honorably, and temperately. Senators who subscribe to this practice of friendship were disposed to place themselves in the shoes of their friends, to keep their word, and not take policy differences as the basis for personal animosity. Diligence refers to how seriously senators discharge their responsibilities as opposed to how they interact with one another. In any case, these conditions could be said to establish a disciplined notion of civic friendship that is distinguishable from other practices of friendship outside the Senate, practices that may require friends to act generously, selflessly, inquisitively, joyfully, kindly, nicely, or openly as opposed to empathetically, honorably, and temperately. In the Senate's practice of civic friendship, senators do not expect that their senatorial friends will open their hearts to one another.

The adverbial characteristics that I have drawn out of Baker's discussion of senatorial friendships are not meant to exhaust the possible adverbial conditions associated with civic friendship. The general claim is that civic life can, in various ways, come to define how friendships are conducted. The manifestation of civic friendship in a male-dominated institution composed of one hundred individuals, who are elected every six years, may not be the same as the manifestation of civic friendship in other institutions or political arrangements. In her discussion of friendship between women in the U.K. Parliament, Sarah Childs notes that "the form and importance of the friendships, at least in these MPs' views, are distinct from friendships in other places of work" (2013:136). They are also distinct from their friendships with their male colleagues. Although she does not frame their interaction in these terms, it could be argued that the female MPs of Childs's study see themselves as interacting supportively, understandingly, nonthreateningly, and attentively (135–37). Such a list of adverbial conditions, once again, is not meant to be exhaustive but to indicate that different practices of civic friendship may exist. The conceptual point is that for a friendship to be *civic*, it must be conditioned by the political or legal environment in which it is happening and in the case of women MPs, this environment is one that is not entirely friendly to women holding power.

CIVIC FRIENDS ARE NOT MERELY COMPATRIOTS

In civic friendship, the nature of citizenship tugs at the concept of friendship. What does the friendship side of the equation contribute to the concept? How does it affect citizenship? First, it adds an affective dimension. Civic friendship, because it is friendship, requires the mutual recognition of the appropriate motivations. Civic friends are friends because they are fond of one another, or have respect for one another, or care for one another and so on. They do things with and for one another because they want to. It is true that obligation and utility are in the mix, but so must be something from the repertoire of acceptable motivations for friendship. The warmth of friendship strengthens their civic bonds.

In addition, friendship brings citizens out of themselves. The other-regarding character of friendship pulls citizens toward actions that may be incompatible with their own self-interest and favor the interest of their friends. It can put them at odds with themselves and to that extent makes sense of acts of self-sacrifice for one's friends. In civic friendships, the friendships themselves may alter one's interests. This may help increase the possibilities for cooperation or, when the friends disagree, to continue to work with one another. In performing these functions, civic friendship may contribute to the maintenance of political institutions. At the very least, these relationships can diminish rancor and personal animosity between friends insofar as their relationship calls for self-restraint. In speaking broadly about friendship in the Senate, Baker writes, "It is demonstrable that many of these relationships cross party lines, and whatever they may do for [the] individuals involved, they contribute in important ways to the cohesion of the U.S. Senate" (1999:9).[16]

As a possible example of civic friendship, we can consider the relationship between Edward Kennedy and Orrin Hatch in the U.S. Senate. In late-twentieth-century American politics, Senator Kennedy from Massachusetts was sometimes known as the liberal lion of the Senate (Simon and Luther 2009).[17] During his forty-six-year senatorial career, he worked on and passed legislation involving health care, education, labor laws, civil rights, and immigration. In contrast, Hatch, the conservative Republican senator from Utah, claimed that one of his motives for being elected to the Senate "was to fight Ted Kennedy" (Davidson 2009). And they did indeed fight. But they were also friends. After Kennedy's death, Hatch wrote, "We did not agree on much, and more often than not, I was trying to derail whatever big government scheme he had just concocted." He also noted that,

> Disagreements over policy, however, were never personal with Ted. I re-call a debate over increasing the minimum wage. Ted had launched into

one of his patented histrionic speeches, the kind where he flailed his arms and got red in the face, spewing all sorts of red meat liberal rhetoric. When he finished, he stepped over to the minority side of the Senate chamber, put his arm around my shoulder, and said with a laugh and a grin, "How was that, Orrin?"

(2009)

Despite their disagreement they were able to pass legislation on medical insurance for children, federal funding to fight AIDS, and a national volunteer service program. The Kennedy-Hatch connection thus moved beyond civility in the sense that they genuinely liked one another.

One could reasonably ask, however, what makes this a "civic friendship" as opposed to a friendship that is merely happening in the Senate.[18] At a personal level, Hatch counseled Kennedy to quit drinking when the nephew of the Massachusetts senator was accused of raping a woman after he had been drinking with his uncle (Davidson 2009).[19] Kennedy, in turn, helped Hatch's grandson when he needed surgery by contacting top surgeons at Massachusetts General Hospital (Canellos 2009:333–34). These interventions seem to express a friendship without the *civic* modifier. What may make this friendship a "civic friendship" is that it appears that they took one another politically as each understood himself. Kennedy remained a liberal to the end, and Hatch has remained a conservative. At the level of friendship per se, perhaps there was a "license" for Hatch to confront Kennedy about his drinking or that enabled Kennedy to show up at the funerals for Hatch's parents. But these permissions did not extent to Hatch's attempting to remake Kennedy into a conservative or to Kennedy's attempting to remake Hatch into a liberal. Civility provides a distance that should be respected.

On the face of it, civic friendship is not necessarily an *agonal relationship*, if by that term one means rivals who come to respect one another in the midst of struggle. For one thing, civic friendships may arise more readily from political agreement. Second, even if they are rivals, civil friends are also friends. When there is political disagreement and the agonal relationship results in a mutual sense of respect within a given civic framework, then that relationship can also become a civic friendship. Respect is part of the repertoire of ordinarily appropriate motivations for friendship. When it is mutually recognized in an opponent then it is difficult to see why the notion of civic friendship could not apply, assuming that there is also mutual subscription to the appropriate adverbial conditions governing their actions. As friends, they may struggle with the competing imperatives to acknowledge their differences and maintain their friendship, which is only to say that between opponents, civic friendship will be both rare and excellent.

OVERLAPPING NETWORKS OF CIVIC FRIENDS

Yet, civic friendship may not be so rare between partisans. This may suggest an avenue to generalize civic friendship. Perhaps overlapping networks of civic friends could knit together a civil society. Perhaps the sentiments of friendship within parties and across the aisle can compose a polity in a way that is more compelling than the mere aggregation of interest or ideological similarity. On this account, not everyone needs to recognize the motivations of everyone else. Rather, the conditions of civic friendship in a large political association can be met in a more piecemeal fashion. Although there is little to support such a position in Aristotle, civic friendship may have taken such a form in ancient Greek and Roman practice. For example, Hauke Brunkhorst writes of antiquity, "there are many networks, and through closely meshed networks, the various individual friendships make the bond of harmony among *all* citizens more and more resistant to being torn" (2005:13). On this account, civic friendship exists when there are enough overlapping networks of individuals who share and mutually recognize the appropriate sentiments. For example, Butch and Waldo mutually recognize the appropriate motivations of civic friendship and Waldo and Darlene mutually recognize the appropriate motivations of civic friendship and Darlene and Cubby do the same. They are drawn together even though Butch and Cubby are strangers. Civic friendship is present when there are enough overlapping connections among friends.

This is a useful way to understand how civic friendship could function in a large society. It should, however, be clear that the notion of overlapping networks of friendship does not qualify as a general model because it does not support a view that citizens should see other citizen-strangers and

-acquaintances as friends: friendship is not a transitive relationship. Darlene's friendship with Annette and Annette's friendship with Cubby does not mean that Darlene will be friends with Cubby (King 2007:134). Even though Darlene may come to realize that Annette and Cubby mutually recognize the appropriate motivations of friendship vis-à-vis one another, that does not mean that Darlene and Cubby will have a similar understanding of one another. Darlene may still mistrust Cubby, and Cubby may still believe that Darlene is wholly driven by self-interest no matter what Annette may say. It is, of course, true that out of respect for Annette, Darlene may be disposed to act a particular way to the friends of her friends, but that disposition does not go very far. In addition, it could be argued that these chains of friendships provide a certain connection to one another, particularly because a society in which such relationships are able to flourish is worthy of some level of respect. It may, however, overstate the case to claim, as Preston King does, that these chains of friendship tie communities and the world together (King 2007:144). The absence of transitivity to these relationships suggest otherwise. The idea of civic friendship as a network of mutually recognized friends creates islands of friendship, but it does not necessarily create larger civic bonds.

TWO CONTEMPORARY VIEWS ON CIVIC FRIENDSHIP

So far, I have argued that civic friendship can be understood as a limited ideal. The second half of this chapter considers two contemporary views of civic friendship that see it as a general model of citizenship. In light of the discussion up to this point, I will focus on the general issue of how these positions respond to the problems raised by size and motivation, arguing that the mutual recognition of motivations remains a problematic part of their theories. After providing a general overview and critique of each position, the argument turns to how these and other contemporary thinkers have deployed Aristotle's conception of political friendship as a way to bolster their own positions. In the end, I argue that Aristotle fails to provide the necessary backup to these arguments. Without that backup, the limited view of civic friendship offered above may be the most plausible account of civic friendship.

In her richly argued book, *On Civic Friendship: Including Women in the State* (2009), Sibyl Schwarzenbach turns to the ancient Greek notion of philia. Before explicitly discussing the idea of political friendship, she emphasizes the ways in which philia can be understood in a reproductive relationship of care for others.[20] This feature of philia is key to her understanding of civic friendship. A central goal of her work is to open up a space for the sort of activities that women have always done. She thus includes women in the state by shifting what she sees as the predominant economic metaphor from production to reproduction. Unlike production, reproduction entails an emotional response of caring for the other. The shift to a focus of reproductive labor and the practice of care is important because friendship is reproductive labor's "proper end," unlike a purely productive model of labor. For Schwarzenbach, "not only are virtuous mothers and children genuine friends" but she goes on to say that "such friendships (in the ideal case) reciprocally aim at the independence and equality of the other when conceived over a complete life" (1996:101).[21] We care for others with the aim of restoring their independence and (re-)establishing their equality.

Ordinarily, Schwarzenbach acknowledges, reproductive labor and care is expressed in an intense emotional bond that requires intimacy. In contrast, she argues that, for Aristotle, civic friendship did not require such a bond or intimate knowledge (2009:53). In politics, she claims, "where one assumes no ties of intimacy, of individual knowledge, or of personal affection," it will be based, in part on reciprocal advantage and equality. But it is not merely a love of advantage that drives civic friends. The motivational tie of civic friendship "is evidenced . . . by a general concern and attitude in the everyday lives of its citizens and works via the constitution; it is recognized in legal and social norms regarding the treatment of persons in that society as well as in the willingness of fellow citizens to uphold them" (1996:109; 2009:54). The presence or absence of care can be found in the degree to which we are concerned (or not) about what happens to our fellow citizens. Although care originates in the household and close personal relations, one need not have a personal relationship in order to care for someone else. In effect, citizen-friends can be strangers because we can care about strangers and they can care for us without either knowing the other personally.

Schwarzenbach updates Aristotle's approach. Motivated by care, citizen-friends interact with one another in a way that is different from what Aristotle suggested. We move from "a more stringent Aristotelian concern with the moral virtue of one's fellow citizens . . . to a more tolerant enlightened concern primarily now with their political character" (Schwarzenbach 1996:113). Lacking agreement over a comprehensive conception of what is good, civic friendship now focuses on whether our fellow citizens are tolerant, subscribe to universal principles of respect, and support the constitution and basic political and legal institutions. In contemporary political life, civic friendship can be expressed in a doctrine of rights in which "citizens acknowledge and express their general concern and goodwill toward the interests of each particular individual in the concrete. A doctrine of individual rights, far from revealing mere conflict or indifference between citizens, may be seen to embody a fundamental regard—if not love—for the special interests of every human being" (114).

As with Aristotle and Cicero, Schwarzenbach believes that without friendship, "genuine justice becomes impossible" and that civic friendship is a "necessary condition" for justice. For example, when we are required to do the just thing and "yield ground in the name of fairness," but we do not trust the motivations of others, then our propensity to favor ourselves will generate the perception of being treated unjustly. By themselves, just institutions are not enough. It appears that we need to believe that people have the right sorts of motivations when we are being asked to do the just thing. Without that belief, truly just decisions will be perceived as "nothing more than the imposition of the interests of the stronger." The resulting resentment and potential humiliation means that civic friendship is also a necessary condition for genuine peace and "any good society" (Schwarzenbach 2009:55). A political atmosphere of ill-will and distrust ultimately fragments society.

Injustice also undermines civic friendship. If citizens perceive that there are injustices and that individuals are being treated unequally, then they cannot be civic friends (Schwarzenbach 2009:54). We not only need civic friendship in order to have a sense that one is living in a just state, but we also need just political arrangements for friendship. As with Aristotle,

Schwarzenbach traces out a virtuous circle: Just institutions support civic friendship and civic friendship reinforces justice. Consequently, Schwarzenbach argues, civic friendship constitutes and strengthens a just society.

Similar sentiments appear in Danielle Allen's book, *Talking to Strangers* (2004). She, too, sees Aristotle as an important source for understanding our civic relationships but centers her view on his analysis of the human desire to have more than someone else or what the Greeks called *pleonexia*. For Allen's Aristotle, *pleonexia* is at the heart of many political disappointments and frustrations. Enmity and conflict are driven by a self-interest infused with rivalrous desires (124). Responding to the deleterious effects of *pleonexia* can take a variety of forms. Educating the citizenry in virtue, cultivating homogeneity, and establishing a just legal system are all possible responses, but the first and second are unrealistic for a large population and the third is insufficient. On her reading of Aristotle, the solution is to turn to friendship. Friendship "teaches us when and where to moderate our interests for our own sake. In short, friendship solves the problem of rivalrous self-interest by converting it into equitable self-interest, where each friend moderates her own interests for the sake of preserving the relationship" (126).

At least initially, Allen's account looks much like the thinnest theory of civic friendship discussed earlier. She writes that good citizenship amounts to "interacting with strangers in ways that look like friendship even if, since they lack the emotional charge, they don't feel like friendship" (127). In other words, civic friendship is "bereft of affect" (128). At one point, she notes that the danger of pursing ordinary friendship in politics is obsequiousness (129). Instead of turning to emotion, political friendships rests on a sense of equality of burden and benefit, equality of recognition, and equality of agency. She argues that

> the core practices that are necessary for a relationship to count as friendship are practices to equalize benefits and burdens and power sharing. Strangers can converse or even hang out with each other, but if they don't act equitably toward each other, or are unwilling to share power with one another, they don't count as friends.

(130)

Political friendships are not about virtue, but utility (see also Yack 1993:111–12). More specifically, they are about practices of reciprocity in which the friends learn to exchange and bargain in a manner that does not require the terms to be spelled out and enforced to the letter. Following Aristotle, she notes that "politics thus constantly opens exchanges that remain open for difficult lengths of time, or even forever, and nothing but ethical reciprocity can make such delay bearable" (Allen 2004:133). Friendship makes this bearable because it extends our selves to include and incorporate the interests of another. This ability to extend the self, which is part of the practice of friendship, forms the basis of what Allen calls "equitable self-interest." "Friendship," she writes, "is the extension of one's interests to include someone else's in ways that annihilate loss" (133).

There is a kind of sacrifice associated with not knowing when (or whether) the burdens that one has accepted politically will be reciprocated or alleviated. Seeing oneself in the other, however, ameliorates the burdens. The "equitable" part of "equitable self-interest" exists in the attention that citizens devote to the benefits and burdens that they are imposing on one another and the effect that that balance is having on political agency. Friendship is a "crucial component" to good citizenship (136). Only through friendship can rivalrous self-interest be converted into equitable self-interest. And, only through friendship do we have the right orientation toward others, the proper understanding of the problems of rivalrous self-interest, the correct form of attention and habits directed toward equity, and the development of the psychological state of good will that Allen also calls "consent" (137). Friendship preserves and transforms the notion of self-interest. It sustains and advances the idea of justice. It shores up the trust that sustains our political bonds. From Allen's perspective, the problem is not self-interest per se, but unrestrained and inequitable self-interest.

MOTIVATION IN THESE CONTEMPORARY ACCOUNTS

Do these understandings of civic friendship as a general model of citizenship rest on the mutual recognition of motives? Neither of these theories specifically addresses this issue, although both respond to the challenge raised by size. As briefly noted toward the beginning of this chapter, Schwarzenbach argues that civic friendship can overcome an objection based on size if we keep in mind the distinction between personal and political friendship. Nevertheless, different elements of her theory do appear to require the mutual recognition of motivations as a condition of civic friendship. Three of these elements include reciprocal liking, good will, and care. Perhaps the strongest argument that her view turns upon the mutual recognition of motive is connected to her claim that public institutions (contrary to Allen's position) should be engaged in the cultivation and education of our emotions.

Schwarzenbach claims that all forms of friendship rest on three conditions: "reciprocal awareness and liking, good will, and practical doing." She also suggests that in the case of civic friendship, these conditions manifest themselves somewhat differently than in personal friendships. Are they different enough, however, not to require the mutual recognition of motive? In the case of the first two conditions, the answer is no. Schwarzenbach argues that the political expression of reciprocal liking entails not affection (as it does for personal friendship), but rooting out "any and all" prejudices they may have about each other. In other words, she claims that citizens "like" one another when they abandon their stereotypes of one another (2009:61). Although the absence of prejudice may stretch the notion of "liking" a bit, it does suggest some attention to the motives of one's compatriots in the sense that citizens believe that their compatriots are not *motivated* by prejudice. Presumably, in order for this kind of liking to be "reciprocal," citizens would have to know something about the quality of their fellow citizens' motives.

In bringing friendship into politics, Schwarzenbach wants to create a background of "general concern and good will between citizens, which works through society's constitution, a doctrine of individual rights, and public standards of acceptable civic behavior" (2009:141). The existence of such a background appears to imply that civic friendship requires us to believe our fellow citizens are motivated by good will toward us and vice versa. A similar claim appears to be part of Allen's use of "good will."[22] This condition of mutual awareness becomes the difficult hurdle, one that thinkers such as Schwarzenbach and Allen have sought to overcome.

Schwarzenbach's position does not appear to abandon the idea that there must be the mutual awareness of good will. Indeed, she argues that her view can overcome what she calls "motivational utopianism" (2009:170). In other words, such a background of good will is possible if we are willing to construct the "social and political institutions that emphasize and encourage collectively reasonable feelings (friendship, security, trust, and so forth) and that minimize irrational and destructive ones (humiliation, fear, hatred)" (114, 237). Civic friendship requires a form of political education of emotions. Consequently, it seems to require some awareness that that education has been successful in shaping the internal lives and motives of our compatriots.

Finally, in expressing that notion of good will, citizen Mary knows that citizen Jean-Jacques cares for her if his reproductive labor is performed at least in part for her good (Schwarzenbach 2009:152). Although Schwarzenbach conscientiously notes that her use of care is not merely a disposition or feeling, but a practice, it still requires certain motivations and not others. Or, to put this point another way, even though it is not merely a feeling (but much more than that), it is still a feeling whose mutual recognition would seem to be required for civic friendship to flourish. On this account it is difficult to see how civic friendship can emerge unless there also exists a mutual awareness of the good will and care of one's fellow citizens.[23]

Still, one could argue that Schwarzenbach's account of civic friendship does not necessarily fail because it rests on some level of mutual awareness of motivations, even if their true character may be difficult to discern. In certain ways, Schwarzenbach's position turns on a particular reading of Aristotle offered by John Cooper. In order to respond to Schwarzenbach, it will be useful to consider whether Cooper's view of Aristotle offers a way out of the problem of mutually recognizing motivations.

In his interpretation of Aristotle, Cooper is well aware of and conscientiously seeks to solve the mutual recognition problem. He argues that civic friendship, for Aristotle, "involves mutual good will, trust, well-wishing, and the mutual interest that fellow-citizens have in one another's characters [that] is part of that good will and well-wishing" (1993:319; Smith 2011a: 66–67). For Cooper, the problem of discerning motivations can be overcome because it is possible to infer them from a variety of sources: citizens' knowledge of the constitution, their support of the political structures, and their expectations of one another's behavior vis-à-vis the law. He writes,

> One should bear in mind that in describing in very general terms the conditions that hold good for friendships of whatever type . . . Aristotle says only . . . that friends must both wish their friends well for the friends' own sake, *and know this fact about one another* [emphasis added]—not that they must be intimate with one another, or even know each other in person. Intimacy and personal knowledge are not the only ways of knowing (or anyhow reasonably coming to believe) that such mutual good will exists, and they are not even the normal way such mutual good will gets communicated in every contest where it exists. In the political context, knowledge of the nature of the constitution, of the general level of support for it among the different elements of the population, and of what's generally expected of people in that society is the normal way of knowing about these things, and it is sufficient, sometimes, to establish a reasonable presumption of good will on the part of one's fellow-citizens generally.
>
> (320n18)

For Cooper and for Schwarzenbach, through such inferences citizens could be said to mutually "like" one another, even though they do not know one another. Does the inference argument work?

Cooper makes a good case that our motivations in general and toward our friends in particular are usually inferred from our deeds and sometimes from our words. Cooper wants then to argue that because we can witness the deeds and words of our fellow citizens, we can discern their motives. However, not only does this presume that observed actions can reliably reveal specific motivations, but also that citizens are actually witnessing the actions and words of their compatriots in a regular fashion. Once one moves beyond a face-to-face society, one cannot be confident of the motivations of one's fellow citizens: we simply do not have the opportunity to observe repeatedly how very many of them act.

Perhaps it is because such direct observations will be infrequent that Cooper argues for inferring individuals' motivations from their general knowledge of the constitution, the degree with they support it, and (or?) from our expectations regarding how they will act (presumably lawfully and respectfully). Nevertheless, that move is unlikely to work. Even if we assume that we have some inkling of what our fellow citizens know of the constitution (how much of it must be understood?), it is not at all clear how knowledge of the regime and its basic principles reveals their motivations toward one another. Nor is it likely that support for a regime's basic principles reveals much about a person's motives beyond the fact that she supports them. It is just as plausible to suppose that our fellow citizens follow and abide by the constitution and its laws out of habit, fear, or patriotism as much as out of a desire to improve the lot and character of their fellow citizens. For example, we may expect that most of our fellow citizens will pay their taxes, but that action tells us little about their motivations for doing so. More specifically, it does not tell us that they are paying taxes out of a desire to wish us well. Alternatively, we may observe foreigners abiding by laws of a host country, but from that behavior we cannot conclude that the native citizens love them or that the visitors love the natives. We may hope for the best with regard to the motivations of other citizens, but that hardly amounts to recognizing that they are motivated one way or another. Neither Cooper nor Schwarzenbach provides us with the wherewithal for accurately recognizing the motivations of philia in our fellow citizens—assuming, once again, that the mutual recognition of motives is necessary and that many or most of our fellow citizens are strangers or mere acquaintances.

Instead of inferring our motivations, perhaps we can save the notion of civic friendship as a general model of citizenship by pushing harder on Cooper's suggestion that it is *reasonable to presume* that our fellow citizens have the right kind of motives. Civic friendship, on this account, does not require that we actually identify the motives of strangers. Rather, the establishment of a background of good will requires that enough citizens presume that they are acting out of motives of friendship. In a more or less just regime where we have the expectation that people will abide by the basic institutions, processes, and laws, it is not unreasonable to think that people are being motivated by the better angels of their nature. A version of this argument may be found in Allen's view of political friendship. She writes,

> A polity will never reach a point where all its citizens have intimate friendships with each other, nor would we want it to. The best one can

hope for, and all one should desire, is that political friendship can help citizens to resist the disintegration of trust and achieve a community where trust is a renewable resource. But to accomplish this, citizens must set their sights on what lies beyond their reach: goodwill throughout the citizenry. If they do, here and there citizens who were perfect strangers to each other will become friends simply by acting as if they were friends. More important, however, even in the vast majority of cases where citizens do not become intimates, they will at least have achieved a guiding orientation that will help make them more trustworthy to each other.

(2004:156)

By acting "as if" we recognized the sentiments of friendship in one another we can generate a sense of good will between those engaged in the interaction. Having an orientation or being disposed to act as if one was a friend vis-à-vis others will itself create good will.

As I understand the argument, a practice of civility combined with a presumption that one's fellow citizens are people of good will or are worthy of our trust is enough to bootstrap the community into civic friendship. With such an orientation, we will be less likely to accuse our opponents of bad faith, or burn our political bridges, or feel that we have been unfairly burdened when we are actually being asked to pay our due. To further strengthen the argument, Allen could claim that we should assume the best motivations about our fellow citizens until we learn otherwise.

Is a presumption of the motives of friendship on the part of our fellow citizens reasonable? If social psychologists are correct about our attribution biases, then it may be unreasonable to suppose that we will, in fact, be able to see our fellow citizens as necessarily having the right sorts of motivations. Moreover, in a culture that valorizes self-interest and its pursuit, seeing our fellow citizens as motivated by good will toward us will be a tough sell. The difficulty with Allen's position is that she sees rivalrous self-interest as not merely a cultural artifact, but as an endemic and enduring feature of political life. If so, then the reasonable presumption on the part of citizens is not that their fellow citizens are motivated by equitable self-interest, but that they are driven by *pleonexia*. At this point, it is not clear how to proceed. Is the solution to ignore what is reasonable and simply assume that others are motivated the right way because the rewards are so great? If so, then Allen is not offering a reason for political friendship as much as a leap of faith.

The objections regarding our biases and the significance of rivalrous self-interest smack of what Schwarzenbach calls the charge of motivational utopianism, which she believes is possible to overcome if we move to a re-productive metaphor of labor and devise institutions that attend to the edu-cation of our emotions. From her perspective, it may not *now* be reasonable to presume that our fellow citizens are acting out of friendship, but it can be reasonable in the future under the right sorts of conditions.

To the extent that Schwarzenbach's position rests on Aristotle, the pos-sibility for such a future's emerging would seem to be undercut by other elements in Aristotle's account of political friendship. More specifically, Aristotle's civic friendship is a friendship of utility. In the *Eudemian Ethics*, he wrote,

> Political friendship exists because of utility above all else. People seem to come together because they are not self-sufficient, though they would also have come together for the sake of living together. But only the friendship of a political regime and its deviant form go beyond being friendships and are also communities based on friendship. The others are based on superiority.
>
> (2013:1242A5–10)

Later, he notes that "political friendship is based on utility; just as cities are friends to each other, so too are citizens. 'Athenians no longer recognize Megarians' and it is the same with citizens, when they aren't useful to each other; their friendship is a cash-in-hand transaction" (1242b20–30).

If civic friendships are friendships of utility then the characteristics that Aristotle attributed to utility-based friendships also apply to civic friend-ships. There is both good news and bad once political friendship is seen in the light of a utility-based friendship. The bad news is that such relation-ships are a great deal more fractious than virtue-based relationships. The good news is that it may move the discussion of political friendship away from a concern with mutually identifying (what early twenty-first-century Westerners take as) the ordinary motives of friendship. First, the fractious character of utility-based friendship was noted by Aristotle. He wrote that these kinds of friendship are more liable to disputes of unfairness or injustice than other sorts of friendship. Aristotle wrote, "Accusations and reproaches arise only or most often in friendships for utility. . . . For these friends deal with each other in the expectation of gaining benefit. Hence they always require more, thinking they have got less than is fitting; and they reproach the other because they get less than they require and deserve" (1985:1162b5–20). If we accept Aristotle's claim, then it may not, in fact, be unreasonable to presuppose that our fellow citizens are being motivated by *pleonexia* (or the desire for more) instead of philia. Self-interest and personal advantage are not only more than likely to taint the motives of our fellow citizens, but mean that we will frequently accuse our fellow citizens of being motivated by self-interest. Built right into political friendship is a tendency for charges of unfairness. Instead of calming and moderating those charges, looking into the hearts of our fellow citizens may simply inflame them (because we are liable to think that others are motivated by a desire for more). Civic friendship does not appear to provide the sort of calming background condition Schwarzenbach suggests.

From within an Aristotelian worldview, there may be two ways to go.[24] One way is to concede such a tendency to charge utility-based friendships with unfairness, but that tendency can be counteracted and moderated in the case of political friends. Bernard Yack takes this route by arguing that the disputes associated with civic relations drive people to accept impartial rules and laws. Citizens, first and foremost, share standards of political justice (Yack 1985:105–6). Citizens may presume that their compatriots will act as virtuous friends, but they are bound to be disappointed. They may presume to trust their fellow citizens and hence presume an ethical form of friendship, but find themselves thrown back on a legal, interest-based form of friendship. Such presumptions create expectations that will inevitably be disappointed. Even under the conventional forms of friendship, Yack argues that for Aristotle, "we need political justice to resolve the problems that arise within political friendships. . . . The political form of justice, with its legal standards and public deliberation, grows out of the political form of friendship" (1993:112). As with all things Aristotelian, there is always the possibility for a virtuous circle: friendships of mutual concern can "develop out of citizens' sharing in the practices of political justice." By sharing similar experiences and ends citizens come to develop a sense of mutual concern for one another; out of this mutual concern "a sense of friendship should grow." The polity rests less on shared beliefs and principles and more on "sharing in the particular kinds of processes and interactions that particular communities establish as forms of political justice" (1993:125).

According to Jill Frank, the problem with Yack's response is that if civic friends need to turn to the institutions of justice to work out their perceived differences regarding what is due to them, then they have effectively stepped outside of friendship. She writes, "Turning to external measures to settle differences . . . even if by agreement between the parties, generally spells the end of their *friendship*. It signifies that the friends could not themselves come to terms, something that friends, even quarrelsome ones, must be able to do if they are to remain friends" (2005:151–52). Instead of claiming that those who have justice need civic friendship in addition, it appears that that those who have civic friendship need justice.[25] In effect, this reading of Yack implies that what now counts are not our fellow citizens' motives—which appear unstable and easily swept away by a desire for more—but the willingness of the parties to accept the decisions of regulators, mediators, and judges, that is to say, justice.

Nevertheless, Frank argues that it is possible to save the argument even if citizens stay within the bounds of utility-based political friendships. In responding to Yack, she argues that such friendships do have the internal resources for settling their disputes. Internal to utility-based and political friendships is a notion of virtue and the common good, even though they also are driven, in part, by self-interest. Contrary to Cooper and Schwarzenbach, Frank embraces exchange relationships as a way to understand what is happening in political relationships. Her willingness to embrace exchange relationships turns on the claim that no such exchange could ever be solely based on self-interest. Even in mundane relationships of commercial exchange, the participants already have some nascent understanding of justice in order to engage in the action itself. The exchange requires not only some prior understanding of what constitutes a fair or just exchange, but some degree of trust. The parties must trust one another enough to believe that the other is not misrepresenting the nature of the exchange item

(2005:153; a point, it is important to note, which Yack also makes [1993:114–15]). Because an exchange relationship presumes some minimal conception of virtue and justice, appealing to an idea of justice to settle a dispute does not go outside the relationship. Consequently, she argues that Yack is mistaken in thinking that civic friendships cannot resolve the inevitable conflicts that are part of the relationship.

More importantly, Frank argues that utility-based friends (say, buyers and sellers), "need not be, and usually are not particularly oriented toward one another: they need not particularly like one another nor need they be especially virtuous" (2005:153). If their friendship is to continue in the face of conflict, they must be oriented "to the thing" (as Aristotle put it), which, in this case, is their agreement for exchange that yields their mutual advantage. Their understanding of justice in this exchange is provided by the agreement and their virtue exists in their willingness to uphold their end of the bargain. The agreement is their common good.[26] From this perspective, the charge of self-interest is not much of a charge at all insofar as self-interest is probably driving the exchange—but it is not the only condition of the exchange. They must share some notion of what is good. Reproaches and difficulties arise not because one of the parties accuses the other of acting out of self-interest, but because one charges the other of violating their sense of the common good as presupposed in the exchange relationship.

Frank takes this logic and applies it to political friendship. Political friendship is also a friendship based on utility. But because it is based on utility does not mean that it is devoid of virtue or a sense of the common good. Exchange and political relationships are utility-based friendships or "use friends" and "act not for the sake of one another but with a view to the thing" (161). "The thing" in politics is the constitution or the way of life.[27] By acting in this manner, each citizen advantages herself and others. Political friendship does not require the virtue of a virtue-based friendship, but it does require good judgment and moderation in the pursuit of their particular goods. She writes, "The constitution, a result of cooperation among political friends based on self-interest and oriented also to their common good, is, as such, able to govern their relations not only under cooperative conditions but also in the face of conflict" (162). Political or civic friendship does not rest on identifying the motives of one's fellow citizens. Rather, it depends on citizens being disposed to act in a particular way and recognizing that they are advantaged by the current constitutional arrangements. The common good appears to be the result of aggregating the particular assessments of individual citizens—each sees the constitution as advancing his or her good. Later writers in the civic virtue tradition may add "in the long-run." From this perspective, Aristotle's civic friendship looks more like civic virtue: what is loved is not one's fellow citizen but liberty or the constitution or a way of life.[28]

A contrast with Schwarzenbach's position may be useful here. In her discussion of the U.S. Constitution, she writes,

> If we consider the attempt to embody a doctrine of universal equality between persons in legal institutions of right (again attempted in the Constitution), we have a clear instance of what I call "civic friendship." Here I do not personally know the vast majority of these other persons, nor am I ever going to; nonetheless, I wish them well. I seek a general system whereby any rights and privileges that I seek for myself are granted to them also (including even to my personal enemies).[29]

(2009:188)

On the reading of Schwarzenbach offered above, not only do I wish my fellow citizens well, but I believe that they have the same motivation toward me and that others believe the same about my motivations. In contrast, I read Frank as arguing that I may believe that my fellow citizens are wholly motivated by self-interest, but that does not preclude civic friendship. Civic friendship requires that citizens believe that they find the Constitution to their advantage and act moderately and with good judgment. The central point, however, is that *neither* position yields a robust notion of civic friendship that can serve as a general model of citizenship. In Schwarzenbach's case, I have argued that the mutual recognition of motivations required is simply too demanding in a state of any significant size. Why should I have any confidence that my compatriots wish me well (or have any particular feelings toward me, for that matter)? In Frank's case, while her account yields something that could be called civic friendship, it is more easily identified as civic virtue—a love that does not need to be acknowledged by the beloved thing in order to exist. In short, civic virtue need not depend on civic friendship. Perhaps the larger problem with positions that have turned to Aristotle's conception of civic friendship is the one identified by Julia Annas: "It is hard to avoid the conclusion that Aristotle has overstretched the concept" (1977:553).

A FORMAL TEST FOR CIVIC FRIENDSHIP

I will consider one last conception of civic friendship as a general model of citizenship. It occurs in Schwarzenbach's notion of a formal test of civic friendship. Under this test one asks:

> *Would you allow a particular type of action to be done to a genuine friend* (e.g., allow your friend to be lied to, exploited, or left untended)? If not, then perhaps it is your duty to see that your government (through its laws, practices, and institutions) does not allow any of your fellow citizens to be treated thus either.
>
> (2009:245)

Such a test appears to be much more than simple civility but less than what is required in assessing the motivations of others. On the face of it, it appears to be a plausible middle point between focusing merely on what people do and requiring the mutual recognition of why they are doing it.

As appealing as such a formal test may appear, its force rests on blurring our expectations regarding personal friendship with our expectations of political friendship. It also blurs the notion of civic friendship with what justice may require. The heart of the problem is that our civic duties should not rest on what we would allow to happen to our friends. For example, although one hopes that one would not allow a friend to be lied to, exploited, or left untended, that does not mean that government's role is to prevent and punish all lies, forms of exploitation, and neglect. It is one thing if the source of the lies being told to a friend is another individual that causes no significant harm, it is quite another if the harm is significant or the source of the harm is the government, a corporation, or a powerful group. The fact that a friend would not *allow* either harm does not mean that government should also not allow either harm. The expectations of friendship tend to be higher then the expectations associated with governmental protection.

Protecting others from maltreatment should not rest on how one would treat one's friends, but on a complex understanding (depending on the treatment) of how anyone should be treated as well as the nature of the harm.

In addition, aside from fairly extreme actions, friends do not ordinarily use or threaten to use violence to protect one another from lies and neglect. In contrast, behind state action is coercion. In sorting through these issues, the idea of genuine friendship appears to muddy our ideas of justice, harm, and the nature of the law. At some level, this may get to the heart of why friendship is so important to Schwarzenbach (and to others arguing for a more robust notion of friendship in politics). On her account, an ideal of friendship exists which can serve as a general standard or model of human interaction or sociality. In contrast, my position is that friendship is not the same as justice or equality or freedom and, assuming its family resemblance character, could never be fully assimilated to these other values.

While civic friendship may not be an appropriate general model of citizenship, friendship does offer an ideal of citizenship. In this ideal, our role as citizens pulls at our conception of friendship and vice versa. The result is a difficult relationship that bonds partisans and can bridge political differences without calling into question the differences themselves. This scaled-down vision of civic friendship cannot knit a society together, but it may provide openings for cooperation between political opponents. This possibility comes to the fore in considering the place of friendship in a delegitimized political environment. This is the topic of chapter 6.

six

FRIENDSHIP DURING DARK TIMES

I have always operated on two levels, a personal level and a political one.
When the two have come into conflict, I have had to put politics first.

—KIM PHILBY

Every man's character makes his fortune.

—NEPOS, *ATTICUS*

Should politics trump friendship? In a pluralistic, more or less stable political environment that has become increasingly polarized, friendships
between those holding alternative political viewpoints may not only be less
common, but also frowned upon. We may be puzzled by how one could be
friends with someone who holds diametrically opposed positions on the
central and most heated issues of the day. The "rightness" of one's political
positions may become a litmus test for friendship. In contrast, the ideals of
bridging/bonding friendship and civic friendship suggest that political differences should not preclude friendship. These ideals complicate the choice
that you are either "with us or against us" or that the idea of difference is an
anathema to friendship. From the perspective of those ideals, one's political
commitments should not serve as a litmus test for friendship.

The idea that politics should not trump friendship may seem even clearer
in extreme conditions of political instability and despotism. In 1939, my

father's mother, who had immigrated to the United States, returned to Germany to bring her father-in-law back with her to America. At one point, my Catholic grandmother encountered a Jewish friend in a department store. When they met, her friend told her not to talk to her or be seen with her because it was too dangerous. My grandmother never saw her again. In this instance, it may be relatively easy to judge that there is something wrong with a regime that is threatened by friendship: It is one more piece of evidence of its deep injustice. Once again, it appears that politics should not trump friendship.

We may, however, feel less confident about this conclusion when the friendship appears to be with someone on the wrong side. For example, imagine a former general of a corrupt, despotic regime remaining friends with members of that regime while fighting on behalf of the rebels. In war, a friend of my enemy looks much like an enemy. Is not giving aid and comfort to the enemy the sine qua non of treason? If the cause is the right cause, should not we dissolve our friendships with those on the wrong side? In extreme times of political instability and violence, should not the admonition of either being "for us or against us" mean that those who are "with you" become your friends and those who are "against you," your enemies?

It would be a mistake to see a politically charged, Manichean friend/enemy distinction as necessarily governing the understanding of interpersonal friendship. Even for a thinker such as Carl Schmitt, for whom deciding who is your friend and who is your enemy is the definitive act of politics, the ordinary motivations of friendship need not be recognized in his friend/enemy distinction.[1] One identifies one's "friends" by the existence of a common cause and not by the common sentiments of friendship. Those sentiments may, of course, be cultivated by fighting the good fight together, but they may also never come into being. In Schmitt's friend/enemy distinction, just as one's enemies may not be disliked, one's friends may not be liked.

If, however, we focus on the family of practices associated with friendship, then the history of political philosophy offers two tendencies for characterizing the relationship between friendship and politics during times of despotism and civil war. On the one hand, there is a long tradition which suggests that tyranny makes ordinary friendship virtually impossible to sustain. For example, Cicero suggests as much in his discussion of friend-ship. It has led thinkers such as Sandra Lynch to make a strong connection between political/legal institutions and friendship. In her discussion of friendship, Lynch writes that

> Cicero's commentary on friendship and his exclusion of friendship from the tyrannical order suggest that some form of egalitarian political organ-ization and some degree of political stability may be necessary if friend-ship is to endure, in either the public or private sphere. The fear and resentment that characterize tyranny will necessarily undermine the trust that is essential, at least to some degree, to all friendship. This in turn suggests—contrary to Aristotle's view—that friendship is not, and cannot be the foundation of the kind of stable and egalitarian political life that Aristotle considered the citizens of the polis to share. Rather, some mea-sure of stability and equity in the socio-political order of a community or state may be a necessary pre-condition of friendship.
>
> (2005:58)

Lynch expands this claim, arguing that "close personal friendships are most coherently seen as built on the foundations of a broader and more imper-sonal relationship, such as Aristotelian civic friendship or Kantian practical love might constitute" (108). In other words, an impersonal, perhaps more or less just, public sphere provides a necessary background for friendship. Friendship during dark times is impossible.

Judith Shklar, however, offers the opposite view. She argues that in des-potic or anarchic situations, friendships are especially acute: "Friends form their private polity which protects them against the state and gives them an alternative moral universe. Here freedom and spontaneity reign, while op-pression and hypocrisy are the universal rule in the larger society" (Shklar 1998, 14). In these small societies of friends, there is the possibility of com-fort, sharing, and trust. She argues that it is very much a situation of the friend being another self: of one soul in two bodies. Tyrants may come to see these friendships as a threat to themselves, but the friendships that survive are particularly intense. Moreover, she argues that the claims of friendship far outweigh the duties of politics and when one friend acts in opposition to the regime it is as if the other friend did it as well (1998:14). It is perhaps not surprising that despots are so willing to make claims of guilt by association—because at least in some of those associations the deeds may be deeply and firmly supported by a friendship.[2]

Obviously, friendships cannot be more acute under tyranny if tyranny renders them impossible. In support of Shklar's claims, it is reasonable to think that in a delegitimated political environment individuals are thrown back onto whatever resources they can muster in order to preserve themselves and (some degree of) independence. Those resources may include not only friendships, but also familial, tribal, ethnic, or religious connections. This sort of plausible empirical generalization suggests that friendships are made acute by the severity of the fractures in a despotic or anarchic situation.[3] As such, ordinary, interpersonal friendships can be pressed into the service of unifying the opposition or perhaps even stabilizing the position of those in power.

Accepting Shklar's position also seems to suggest that in a delegitimated political environment we should expect friendships between those on the same side to deepen and intensify. The logic of "you are either with us or against us" would render friendships with the enemy impossible. Politics would trump friendship. But should it? In order to explore this further alternative, this chapter focuses on the place of friendship in Hannah Arendt's essay "On Humanity in Dark Times: Thoughts about Lessing," and in the Roman biography of Titus Pomponius Atticus (112/109–35/32 B.C.E.). Arendt presents a nuanced view of friendship during dark times. Although her comments do not amount to a full-blown theory of friendship or a description or prediction of how friendship does or will function under despotism, they do offer an account of how friendship can and should enable the possibilities for politics.[4] In brief, the core of her notion is that friendship secures the plurality that is a condition for politics by establishing what she sometimes calls the world that lies in-between people.[5] Part of her argument rests on a notion that friendship is deeply linked to discourse. Another part of her argument rests on the claim that ideas such as fraternity and compassion either are inadequate or destroy the space needed for politics. A final part of her position depends on a view that claims of truth or principle should not trump friendship. The combination of these positions suggests a view of friendship that rejects the "with us or against us" mentality that so easily and frequently pervades desperate situations. Nevertheless, her account comes at the cost of ordinary elements of friendship that go beyond discourse and include the sort of intimacy that is a familiar part of many practices of friendship. Arendt opens the possibility of seeing friendship as a way to engender plurality, but she does so without distinguishing the context of a delegitimized environment from that of a more settled environment.

In contrast, Cornelius Nepos's biography of Titus Pomponius Atticus has been read as offering a self-consciously uncivic form of friendship. In response to this interpretation, I argue that the biography can be understood as offering an ideal of friendship during extreme times. This ideal resembles Arendt's account insofar as it is compatible with preserving pluralism, but it differs in significant ways. It is a conception of friendship that is compatible with intimacy, not blocked by the exercise of violence or unconditionally applicable beyond extreme circumstances. Despite its Roman origins, it is an ideal that suggests an anti-Machiavellian account of necessity, virtù, and *fortuna*. Political friendships during dark times do not guarantee anything, but they do provide an opening for cooperation and perhaps even reconciliation.

ARENDT ON FRIENDSHIP

The heart of Arendt's view of friendship depends on a particular way of reading the Greek conception of philia.[6] She claims that for the Greeks, "the essence of friendship consisted in discourse. They held that only the constant interchange of talk united citizens in a polis. In discourse, the political importance of friendship, and the humanness peculiar to it, were made manifest" (1968:24). Friendship, she argues, is at the heart of politics, but should not be confused with modern notions of friendship as a relationship of intimacy, in which friends open their hearts to one another. Unlike the Greeks, Arendt thinks that we tend to believe we reveal ourselves only in our face-to-face encounters. The intimacies associated with contemporary friendships are not so much connected to eros or romantic love, but to the desire to talk about ourselves—how we are doing, our successes and failures, our secrets and dreams. In contrast, the Greeks see discourse as the essence of friendship. The polis is sustained through talk about the common world. Her understanding of friendship can be read in the context of her larger views on the character and conditions of political action. Without getting into those views, it is sufficient for this discussion to emphasize the degree to which she believes that politics is only possible when individuals with multiple perspectives are able to appear before and talk to one another. A human and humane world is created within that "in-between" space where individuals are able to bring their own perspectives before others and potentially join with them in common action. Pluralism, then, is utterly essential to politics and because friendship fosters pluralism through its emphasis on discourse, it is also essential.[7]

Unlike the ancient Greek conception of friendship, Arendt also believes that the ideal of fraternity or feelings of compassion do not preserve and respect distinctive perspectives. On the one hand, it is difficult to base political unity on feelings of compassion. These feelings tend to weaken with changes in circumstance. On the other hand, fraternity and compassion bring us too close together. Unlike friendship, they have the unfortunate effect of closing down the sort of discourse that Arendt believes defines political life. At least in part, the thought appears to be that they do not allow the sort of room needed for individual perspectives to flourish. Both compassion and fraternity join us together in a way that vitiates difference.

The causes that can collapse the public space were constant concerns for Arendt. In her essay on Lessing, appeals to truth or a conception of scientific rectitude can have the same unfortunate effects.[8] They have these effects, in part, because we believe we have a duty of objectivity to the truth that should override relationships of friendship. If truth or rightness calls for us to break off a friendship, then we tend to believe that we should do so. One may wonder under what sorts of conditions this might occur. One possibility would be if we were pressured to break a connection with a friend because she held false beliefs—say she belonged to another religion or held objectionable political or moral beliefs. Arendt, however, focuses less on this sort of situation and more on the case in which appeals to the truth demand that we persecute people for who they are, some of whom happen to be our friends. In an extreme example, she writes,

Suppose that a race could indeed be shown, by indubitable scientific evidence, to be inferior; would that fact justify its extermination? But the answer to this question is still too easy, because we can invoke the "Thou shalt not kill" which in fact has become the fundamental commandment governing legal and moral thinking of the Occident ever since the victory of Christianity over antiquity. But in terms of a way of thinking governed by neither legal nor moral nor religious strictures . . . the question would have to be posed thus: *would any such doctrine, however convincingly proved, be worth the sacrifice of so much as a single friendship between two men?*

(1968:29)

She concludes the essay by suggesting that truth must be "humanized by discourse" (30). In this humanization there are "many voices" and each individual says "what he 'deems truth.'" This humanized telling of truth is not aimed at reaching a Millian convergence or consensus over what is true.[9] Rather, she writes, it both "links and separates men, establishing in fact those distances between men which together comprise the world" (30–31). In other words, the truth is also put in the service of creating a human and humane world. Truth that has not been humanized by discourse is dangerous

because it might have the result that all men would suddenly unite in a single opinion, so that out of many opinions one would emerge, as though not men in their infinite plurality but man in the singular, one species and its exemplars, were to inhabit the earth. Should that happen, the world, which can form only in the interspaces between men in all their variety, would vanish altogether.

(31)[10]

In effect, friendship preserves the sort of pluralism that can be closed down by notions of truth and by a sense of being right insofar as one's willingness to be a friend to others should not be conditioned by them.

Bracketing her views on truth, Arendt's account of friendship during dark times raises a number of issues. The first, and most obvious, concerns the strong link she makes among philia, discourse, and the unity of the polis. As noted in earlier chapters, philia was a very rich idea for the ancient

Greeks. It is, however, something of a stretch to say that the *essence* of the term was "discourse." For example, according to Julia Annas, for Homer, *"philia* was very largely a matter of inherited guest-friendships depending little if at all on the individual's personal preferences" (1977:552). Moreover, she notes that in its "non-mutual" senses it could apply to quail, wine, and philosophy (533). In other words, one could experience philia toward inanimate objects or ideas that lacked the capacity to talk back. In its mutual senses it refers to some notion of affection (Konstan 1997:73; Nussbaum 1986). While Aristotle does associate our humanity with the capacity to talk about how we should live, the philia of his citizens (as we saw in chapter 5) is connected to the utility of their relationships and not to discourse per se. In short, neither for the Greeks nor for us is friendship (or philia) defined by discourse. Moreover, if politics depends on discourse, it does not appear that discourse depends on friendship, if friendship requires the mutual recognition of certain sentiments and the subscription to appropriate adverbial conditions in action. There is no reason to believe that the mutual recognition of the sentiments of friendship is needed for us to talk with or to one another. As for the claim that friendship holds the polis together, the argument of chapter 4 against civic friendship as a general model of citizenship weakens that argument in the case of a polity of any significant size. The forces of truth and right may divide friends, but that division bears little on the possibilities for politics.

Alternatively, assume that the connections among friendship, discourse, and politics hold. Even under those circumstances, Arendt's discussion in her essay on Lessing is strangely silent about the effects of violence on the possibilities for friendship. On her account, politics and violence are antithetical. Discourse, the diversity of perspectives, the capacity to act in concert, and the "world" itself are eroded if not erased by violence. But what of our relationship to those who have turned to violence? Obviously, if one is the object of the violence of a so-called friend, then the friendship is over (it being difficult to conceive of a practice of friendship that sanctioned such violence). The question, however, is more difficult when one's friends are doing the killing. Moreover, the question arises in its most difficult form when one's friends are killing other friends. For example, does Arendt's notion of friendship exclude friendship with tyrants? Should one keep talking to participants of a civil conflict who have resorted to cruelty? On the one hand, it could be argued that given her sharp delineation between violence and politics, we should not talk to despots, particularly if friendship is understood in terms of discourse (as opposed to truth or force). From this perspective, Arendt's position permits friendships with ideologues, but not with thugs. On the other hand, she appears to approve Lessing's stance in which "any doctrine that in principle barred the possibility of friendship between two human beings would have been rejected by his untrammeled and unerring conscience" (1968:29). So, if the "no friends with thugs" stand is a principled one and she endorses Lessing's (principled?) position against principles overriding friendship, then perhaps Arendt would be open to the sort of practice of friendship that could sustain friendships with those who are killing one another.

The risks of such friendships are, of course, enormous. In matters where the parties are divided by ideology and are willing to use force to achieve their aims, to be friends with one side may very well mean being seen as an enemy of the other. In circumstances of civil war or despotism, all parties will be tempted by the judgment that a friend of an enemy is an enemy. A friend who remains a friend of an enemy is thus seen as expressing disloyalty of the worst kind. Such a friend may be perceived as hedging her bets or succumbing to a character defect—perhaps cowardice or weakness. From the state's perspective, one cannot honor Polynices without dishonoring Eteocles (or hunt with hounds and run with the foxes for that matter). Under such circumstances we assume that political opposition trumps personal friendship. As objectionable as Kim Philby's remarks at the beginning of this chapter may be, there is an enormous temptation to rank politics over friendship precisely when the chips are down.

While it is clear where Arendt stands on the view that friendship should be able to overcome ideological divisions, it is less obvious where she stands once those divisions are covered in blood. In either case, to the extent that she endorses the view of friendship as connected to discourse, the value of friendship appears to be primarily associated with its capacity to create a world that is by and for humans. In this way, friendship is less instrumentalized and more constitutive of political life. There is a value associated with friendship, but not forms of friendship linked to intimacy. Public friendship is clearly important, which raises an obvious question: If one's private friendships clashed with one's public friends, do one's intimate friends suffer the same fate as truth and scientific right? Suppose that one's intimate friends were shocked that one has remained willing to talk to a Nazi ideologue. Suppose that they were so shocked that they refused to remain friends as long as you did not denounce and cut off all connection with the ideologue. Would an Arendtian choose the public friendship? At the least, one could argue that there is not very much in Arendt's work that would tip the scale in favor of one's intimate friends (although the case of her friendship with Heidegger is interesting in this regard).

A final feature of Arendt's comments concerns the scope of their applicability. Nothing about her notion of friendship changes if the times change. On her view, it appears that the practice of discourse associated with friendship during dark times points us to the larger significance of friendship during less troubled and troubling times. The circumstances themselves do not appear to dictate the expectations that we may have about the nature of friendship.[11] In contrast, it is not impossible to think, as Shklar suggests, that friendships under despotism or anarchy have a different tenor or cast to them. This possibility, however, is not entertained in Arendt's essay.

At this point, I turn to an ideal of friendship that can be drawn out of Cornelius Nepos's biography of Atticus. In order to discern this ideal, it will first be necessary to consider how the biography has been traditionally received. I then consider how Nepos portrays Atticus as a man who repeatedly refused political engagement. The argument, however, is that these refusals are part of a larger project in which Atticus sought to protect his friends when they were in trouble, but not help them when they were more or less secure and still in the pursuit of political gain. Nepos's biography suggests a way of understanding friendship and plurality without the drawbacks associated with Arendt's position.

READING NEPOS

Cornelius Nepos (ca. 99–ca. 24 B.C.E.) wrote a set of biographies (*De Viris Illustribus*) of famous Romans and foreigners. His biography of Atticus can be and has been approached from a variety of perspectives. As a historical document, it tells us something about the life of a very wealthy, highly educated Roman citizen, a member of the equestrian order, a lover of philosophy and literature, who refused to take sides in the significant political clashes of his day and remained friends with many of the major players who were bitter enemies of one another. As a literary text, it tells us something about the emergence of biographical writing and the character of style of the times. As Fergus Millar notes, however, it is also a statement of Roman values. In his view, these values were "taken up, distorted, and deployed in the propaganda of the Augustan regime" (1988:40). In sum, Nepos's biography is an important survival from the past and hence is evidence of the literary styles, beliefs, events, and individuals of the time.

J. C. Rolfe (1929) suggests that biography of this sort was meant not only to entertain its readers but also to convey a moral to the general public. The reading of the biography presented here will presume that Nepos was attempting to formulate some kind of ideal. Unless we are to read "The Life of Atticus" ironically, and there is no evidence to suggest that this is the case, it is clear that Atticus is presented in a very favorable light. From this perspective, the "real" Atticus is less important than what that ideal could have possibly entailed. In passing, it is important to note that the historical Atticus has not been treated kindly by many modern scholars. For J. L. Moles, it is clear that Atticus was "a man whom many obviously regarded as a toad" (1992:315). In their introduction to Cicero's correspondence, Robert Tyrrell and Louis Purser write, "That he was the lifelong friend of Cicero is the best title which Atticus has to remembrance. As a man he was kindly, careful, and shrewd, but nothing more: there was never anything grand or noble in his character. He was the quintessence of prudent mediocrity" (quoted in Ramage 1967:318). More recently, Kathy Welch argues that Atticus was a behind-the-scenes manipulator; a self-interested, wealthy banker who always hedged his political bets: "Atticus should be seen as a discreet, diplomatic and constant political and financial brain who sought at all times to be influential with the powerful. He was not without affection or opinions, but these were always subservient to interest in prosperity and necessity in adversity" (1996:471).

As we shall see, Nepos's biography does provide evidence to support these historical and largely critical readings of Atticus. In part, this reputation is founded on the shock one has when realizing the nature of his friendships during the civil wars. For example, how could Atticus provide support to Gaius Marius the Younger and be friendly toward to the man who defeated him and his father in battle? How could he be, on the one hand, an intimate friend of Pompey and on the other hand a friend of Caesar, the man who defeated Pompey at the Battle of Pharsalus? How could he be the man to whom Caesar wrote "what he was doing, what, above all, he was reading, in what place he was, and how long he was going to stay in it" and also be "much beloved" by Marcus Brutus, the man who murdered Caesar? How could he be much beloved by Brutus, provide financial support to him when Brutus was forced out of Rome and yet provide legal and financial support to Marc Antony's wife Fulvia, when Antony had been declared *hostis* (or an enemy who could be killed by anyone without it being a murder)? How could he be considered a friend of Antony when he was on such good turns with Brutus and Cicero? How could he be friends of both Cicero and friends with Antony, the man who murdered Cicero? If this be friendship, it looks to be an oily, opportunistic kind.

Part of the reaction to Atticus, of course, is a result of being able to see the whole story. One could, of course, be a friend of Caesar and Brutus because Caesar and Brutus were friends—or, at least, Caesar thought so. Whether Pompey and Caesar were friends, they were political allies that formed the First Triumvirate, before they were at each other's throats. But should Atticus have been a friend of Caesar after Pompey's death? Should he have been a friend of Brutus after Caesar's assassination? Or a friend of Antony after he murdered Cicero?

The story told of Atticus combined with our conventional "either/or" sensibility toward political friends and enemies makes it difficult to see how Atticus's apparent glad-handing personality could possibly be an ideal. Hence, the plausibility of Millar's reading that Nepos's Atticus embodied the quietistic, politically disengaged virtues of a relatively powerless people living under a monarch—more specifically under the monarchy of Octavian (Gaius Julius Caesar Augustus, 63 B.C.E.–14 C.E.). In contrast, I suggest that the biography carves out an ideal of friendship during violent times in which the character "Atticus" refused the choice between being "with" or "against" various individuals and factions. In fact, by violating that prescription to choose one set of friends over another, the ideal may open the door to political engagement. In making this case, we must still begin with what one first encounters in the biography; namely the number of times when Atticus refused to become politically engaged.

ATTICUS'S REFUSALS

After beginning with a brief discussion of his family and education (he went to school with Lucius Torquatus, Gaius Marius the Younger, and Marcus Cicero), the biography jumps right into his first refusal to get involved in politics.[12] Around 85 B.C.E., when he was about twenty-seven years old, he fled from Rome to Athens after his brother-in-law, Publius Sulpicius, was assassinated. According to Nepos, the reason for his departure was that Rome "was in disorder because of the rebellion of Cinna, and that no opportunity was given him [Atticus] of living as his rank demanded without offending one or the other faction—for the feelings of the citizens were at variance, some favoring the party of Sulla, the others that of Cinna—he thought it was a favourable opportunity for gratifying his tastes, and went to Athens" (Nepos [1929] 2005:2–3). The "disturbances of Cinna" to which Nepos refers concerned the relationship between Lucius Cornelius Cinna (d. 84 B.C.E.), elected as a Roman consul in 87 B.C.E., and Lucius Cornelius Sulla, the prior consul. Cinna had sought to secure the rights of "new citizens" and forced Sulla out of Rome. Cinna himself was then exiled and stripped of his citizenship by the other consul, Octavius, Sulla's supporter. When Cinna raised an army and joined Gaius Marius against Octavius and Sulla (138–78 B.C.E.), the result was civil war. Marius died in 86 B.C.E. and Cinna died in 84 B.C.E.

These details are important because another civil war erupted when Gaius Marius the Younger (Atticus's schoolfellow) became consul in 82 B.C.E. In his biography, Nepos notes that Atticus "assisted young Marius, when declared an enemy, by such means as he could, and relieved him in his exile with money." This assistance may have happened when Gaius Marius the Younger went into exile with his father in 88/87 B.C.E. Being declared an enemy in Rome was no minor thing. It legally placed the individual outside the protection of the law. More importantly, by supporting Marius the Younger, Atticus was supporting not just an enemy of Rome, but Sulla's enemy.

A second refusal occurred when Sulla was on his way back from Asia in order to take Rome (perhaps 85–84 B.C.E.). While in Athens, Sulla stayed with Atticus. Nepos notes that Sulla was impressed by his politeness and knowledge. He then wanted Atticus to go with him to Rome. Atticus, however, replied, "Do not, I pray you, try to lead me against those with whom I refused to bear arms against you but preferred to leave Italy" (Nepos [1929] 2005:4). In other words, Atticus left Italy in order not to join the opposition to Sulla and now he did not want to join Sulla to be against those who opposed him. Perhaps it is a few years after this time that he provided financial support for Sulla's enemy, Marius the Younger, when Marius was in exile because of Sulla.

A third political refusal occurred while in Athens, when he refused Athenian offers of citizenship and honors. In this refusal, he wished it to be clear that he remained a citizen of Rome. Nepos notes that as long as Atticus stayed in Athens, he prohibited any statue of himself from being erected to recognize his service to the city. Reasons for these honors will be discussed in the section that follows.

A fourth set of political refusals came when he had returned to Rome after spending fifteen years in Athens. Nepos writes, "He accepted the prefectures offered him by numerous consuls and praetors on the condition that he should accompany no one to his province, being content with the honour and disdaining to increase his means. He would not even consent to go with Quintus Cicero [Marcus Cicero's brother] to Asia, although he might have had the post of his lieutenant-governor. For he did not think it becoming, after having declined a praetorship, to become the attendant of a praetor" (Nepos [1929] 2005:6).[13] Similarly, Nepos implies that Atticus never accepted offices from Pompey. Even though political positions were available, he never availed himself of them. Nepos writes that such offices could not be had without corruption or used for the good of the country without danger to oneself, so Atticus stood back.

A fifth refusal comes after Caesar is assassinated. A proposal was made for the equestrian class to set up a private fund to aid those who assassinated Caesar. Nepos writes that

> Gaius Flavius, a friend of Brutus, appealed to Atticus to consent to take the initiative in the enterprise. He [Atticus], however, thinking that he ought to render service to his friends, but not join parties, and having consistently held aloof from such measures, replied that if Brutus wished to make any use of his means, he might do so to the limit of his resources, but that he would neither confer with anyone on the subject nor meet with anyone. Thus the unanimity of that clique was broken by the disagreement of this one man.
>
> ([1929] 2005:8)

Atticus's refusal to "join parties" suggests a clear preference to refuse to play a great, but dangerous game.

A sixth refusal occurred when Antony had been declared an enemy of Rome and fled. In this case, Atticus refused to join those who sought to act against Antony or against his wife, Fulvia, and their child (despite being friends with Brutus and Cicero). Antony's enemies were endeavoring to strip Fulvia of her property and put his children to death. Nepos notes that no one thought that Antony had a chance of return. The suggestion here is that it was difficult to imagine how such actions could benefit Atticus. For his response, "criticism of him arose from some of the aristocrats, because in their opinion he was not sufficiently hostile to bad citizens [*malos cives*]" (Nepos [1929] 2005:9).

A final refusal worth mentioning is raised at the end of the biography. While it is not political, it does point to themes that compose this ideal of friendship, particularly those related to questions of fortune that will be considered in the discussion of the ideal that Atticus represents. Nepos writes that when Atticus was seventy-seven years old, he became ill. For three months, Atticus fought the illness with various remedies until he had done all that could be done to try to cure himself. Because he believed that further food and drink would simply prolong the pain and the inevitable end, he decided not to take in food. In opposition to his family and friends, he undertook this course of action. After of couple of days, however, the fever abated and the pain became less oppressive. Nepos then writes, "Nevertheless, he persisted in his resolution, and so died, on the fifth day after he had made his decision, which was the thirty-first of March in the consulship of Gnaeus Domitius and Gaius Sosius" (Nepos [1929] 2005:22).

Given the tenor of the times, Atticus's political refusals combined with his love of literature and philosophy is reminiscent of a line in Plato's *Republic*, when Socrates is discussing the situation of philosophers during violent times:

> Now the men who have become members of this small band have tasted how sweet and blessed a possession it [philosophy] is. At the same time, they have seen sufficiently the madness of the many, and that no one who minds the business of the cities does virtually anything sound, and that there is no ally with whom one could go to the aid of justice and be preserved. Rather—just like a human being who has fallen in with wild beasts and is neither willing to join them in doing injustice nor sufficient as one man to resist all the savage animals—one would perish before he has been of any use to the city or friends and be of no profit to himself or others. Taking all this into the calculation, he keeps quiet and minds his own business—as a man in a storm, when dust and rain are blown about by the wind, stands aside under a little wall. Seeing others filled full of lawlessness, he is content if somehow he himself can live his life here pure of injustice and unholy deeds, and take his from it graciously and cheerfully with fair hope.
>
> (1968:496C–E)

There is much to this passage that appears useful for understanding Atticus. He was reputed to be intelligent and loved Greek thought (hence the name "Atticus"). As in Socrates's discussion of the philosophers, Atticus saw that the pursuit of office could not be done "amid such unlimited bribery and corruption without violence to the laws, nor administered to the advantage of the state without risk in so debauched a condition of public morals" (Nepos [1929] 2005:6). All of this led Atticus to act prudentially. As Nepos writes, "But if that pilot is extolled with the highest praise who saves his ship from the storm in a rock-strewn sea, why should not that man's skill [*prudentia*] be regarded as without parallel, who from such numerous and terrible civil tempests comes safe into port?" (Nepos [1929] 2005:10).

Nevertheless, other aspects of Atticus's actions discussed in the biography do not fit the Socratic account. Unlike the Socratic philosopher, Atticus's refusals may have been informed by an Epicurean disposition to avoid politics in general. D. R. Shackleton Bailey writes, "Much has sometime been made of his [Atticus's] adherence to the philosophy of Epicurus. No doubt it appealed to his temperament, though he was certainly no fervent disciple like his contemporary Lucretius. The Epicureans attached great importance to friendship" (Bailey 1999:18). From this perspective, Atticus's refusals appear consistent with Epicurus's admonition that, "We must liberate ourselves from the prison of routine business and politics" (Long and Sedley 1987:126). As Bailey notes, Atticus "avoided overt political activity, apart from a demonstration of support for Cicero in the Catilinarian crisis; it seems he did not even like voting at elections" (1999:18).

While Atticus's Epicureanism will help illuminate certain aspects of his understanding of friendship, we need to proceed cautiously in using that connection to draw out an ideal from within the four corners of Nepos's text. The most important reason for this caution is that Nepos never mentions that Atticus was an Epicurean. The most that Nepos says on this matter is that Atticus "had so thoroughly mastered the precepts of the great philosophers, that he made use of them in the conduct of his life and not merely for display" (Nepos [1929] 2005:17). Moreover, aspects of the biography do not fit so neatly into an Epicurean life. Not only was Atticus deeply involved in the "prison of routine business" as a prominent banker, but also his suicide "was not following the mainstream of his school's teaching" (Griffin 1986:67).[14] If Nepos can be read as setting out an ideal of friendship and its relationship to politics, that ideal was not meant to rest solely on the precepts of Epicureanism, although it is reasonable to imagine that his audience was well versed in those precepts.

In addition to his Epicureanism, Atticus differs from Socrates's prudent, but hunkered-down philosophers in another way. Despite his refusals, Atticus did intervene in significant ways.[15] Atticus assisted Marius the Younger, Cicero, those who were assisting Pompey, Brutus, the family and friends of Antony, as well as those who were being harmed by the proscriptions Antony issued.[16] Millar believes that "Nepos presents this even-handed generosity as having a moral basis, that is the maintenance of private *officium* [duty] regardless of circumstances. But it also had another purpose, of course—that of personal survival through drastic swings of fortune." (1988:45). Millar then quotes Nepos's admiration for Atticus's prudence.

The idea that self-interest motivated these interventions is carried a step farther by Kathy Welch who argues that Atticus was a player: "Part of Atticus's talent, however, was to retain those friends he had made even when they appeared to have lost their usefulness. Early experience of civil war, and, I will allow, some measure of the humanity so overemphasised by Nepos, had taught him that one never knew when the circle would turn" (1996:454). Because the times were so uncertain, Atticus continued to support friends who were political losers. The rationale was that losers could always become winners. Consequently, there was no clear distinction between public and private. For the most part, Atticus's drive for personal gain explains his conduct. Whether this is true of the historical Atticus, it would not be the best reading of Nepos if he was indeed seeking to set out an ideal. In order to sort through that alternative account, it will be useful to first consider Atticus's political interventions.

ATTICUS'S POLITICAL INTERVENTIONS

The biography notes a number of occasions in which Atticus's actions could be construed as having enormous political significance. For example, after living in Athens for a while, Atticus provided significant financial assistance to the city. Nepos writes that "when the state needed to negotiate a loan and could not do so on fair terms, he always came to the rescue, and in such a way that he never exacted from them excessive interest, nor would he allow them to remain in debt beyond the stipulated time" (Nepos [1929] 2005:2). Later Nepos notes that the Athenians "found him an adviser and help in all the administration of their state." Second, he made a conscious decision to turn down an offer to become an Athenian citizen because it might jeopardize his standing as a Roman citizen (3). The political/legal status of being Roman was clearly important to him. Third, in Roman politics, he used to come to the elections of his friends, "and was at hand whenever any important action was taken"—suggesting political and/or financial support (4). Fourth, Nepos writes that even though he did not aim for political office, "in public life he so conducted himself as always to be, and to be regarded, as on the side of the best men [*optimarum partium*—the senatorial party], yet he did not trust himself to the waves of civic strife" (6). This does not suggest an individual who was indifferent to politics or refused to have any say whatsoever. In being on the side of the senatorial party, it is clear that he had known political positions. Fifth, he clearly acted against public judgments that established someone as an enemy of Rome. He assisted those who were proscribed by the triumvirs. Although he may have been motivated by a private sense of duty, that may not in and of itself have rendered the act nonpolitical. One does not need to go far below the surface to discern the political nature of many of his actions discussed in the biography.[17]

THE IDEAL THAT ATTICUS REPRESENTS

What is the moral of Nepos's story? Part of what Atticus represents can be found in the traditional, ordinary virtues: "He never lied, nor could he tolerate falsehood. Hence his affability was tempered with austerity and his dignity by good-nature, so that it was difficult to know whether his friends felt for him greater love or respect" (Nepos [1929] 2005:15). Beyond those virtues, Atticus was not merely a scrappy survivor who hedged his political bets. Instead, there was something unusual about his character and the conduct of his friendship that was also of value. Part of this ideal may be connected to how Atticus (or, at least the literary construction of Atticus) viewed political tumults and instability. Atticus, Nepos writes, refused to take sides in the turmoil of the day because he "did not trust himself to the waves of civil strife, since he thought that those who had delivered themselves up to them had no more control of themselves than those who were tossed on the billows of the sea" (6). The Epicurean perspective in this statement is clear enough.[18] As such, it opens the possibility that Atticus may have been motivated by an understanding that avoiding tumult was itself a form of pleasure. The Epicureans believed that pleasure entailed not merely the presence of good sensations but the absence of unpleasant sensations and existence of a sense of tranquility.[19] On the other hand, this possibility is not entertained by Nepos, whose ideal appears to be more directly related to the familiar notion that, at times, fortune is in control of politics. While individuals may carefully plan and muster their resources, their fate is, under especially dire circumstances, not under their control. In this respect, the quote from Plato's *Republic* mentioned earlier is apropos and, yet, not entirely descriptive of Atticus's response to his situation. His actions and refusals do appear to be in accord with a belief that there are occasions in politics in which a collective madness takes over, in which people—the "majority," according to Plato or very powerful individuals and factions for Atticus—lose control of themselves and the situation. The difference between Atticus's response and Plato's is that Atticus recognized that these individuals were still his friends and consequently he was willing to intervene. They were being tossed around by the violent waves of politics and did horrible things to one another, but they were not animals as Socrates suggests.[20] They may have acted like wild animals, but that did not nullify their capacity for friendship.

The reason their friendship was not nullified may be because in such difficult times it is *as if* their agency was swamped by fortune. Nepos conceived of an Atticus who interpreted the actions of his friends during the civil wars with a kind of generosity. On the one hand, Nepos did not have Atticus justify his friends' actions. For example, Atticus remained friends with Brutus, but not because he thought that Brutus was justified in murdering Caesar. In fact, Atticus refused to give money to the equestrian "friends of the assassins fund." If he condoned Brutus's action, perhaps Atticus would have been willing to support such a fund. In contrast, Atticus's actions broke up the possibility of the fund. In short, Atticus did not justify the crimes committed by his friends.

Alternatively, it would not be quite correct to say that, from Nepos's perspective, Atticus excused his friends. They did not kill one another by accident or by mistake. If they had a failure, it was a failure to understand how little they controlled their situation. They acted, but their actions released a set of events that overwhelmed their intentions. In Nepos's view, Atticus saw his friends as plunging into the waves of fortune. In that metaphor, he distanced Atticus from their circumstances and their actions. It is neither a justification nor an excuse but closer to an expression of sympathy for their losses and failures. For example, Brutus may have thought that he was taking charge and attempting to control events on the Ides of March, but from the perspective that I am attributing to Nepos's construction of Atticus, Atticus treated Brutus as if he were a plaything of fortune. Atticus refused to jump into the fray and join the wave that seemed to be in Brutus's favor, but he *was willing* to throw him a life preserver if it looked like Brutus was going to drown. Atticus was willing to do this because he still recognized Brutus as a friend.

NEPOS AND MACHIAVELLI

In order to draw out and highlight the sort of ideal of friendship implied by Nepos's biography, I will place Atticus in conversation with the much later thought of Niccolò Machiavelli and then return to Arendt. This is not as peculiar as it sounds insofar as Machiavelli was also drawing on a Roman conception of fortune. Machiavelli is useful, however, because his notion of fortune and the related terms of necessity and virtù stand in stark contrast to what Nepos may have had in mind. The account that I will give depends on placing not only a great deal of weight on the role of *fortuna*, but also on Atticus's concern for character, and on seeing his even-handed interventions as providing a possible opening for political reconciliation.

Nepos offers a very different sort of relationship to *fortuna* and political action than what is offered by Machiavelli. For Machiavelli, one way to attract and control fortune is through the exercise of virtù. If Machiavelli is known for anything, he is known for understanding that virtù is not virtue as the Christians came to understand it. In exercising virtù, one must not be constrained by the ordinary conventions, rules, or religious scruples that tie the rest of us down. In part, virtù requires a willingness to do whatever is necessary to secure the state. For example, from Machiavelli's perspective, it is likely that Brutus thought that it was necessary to kill Caesar, that Antony thought that it was necessary to kill Cicero, and that Antony's enemies thought that it was necessary to persecute Antony's wife and children. In addition, it is reasonable to think that the triumvirate thought it necessary to place certain individuals on an enemies list. For Machiavelli, the world of necessity is a world independent from the ordinary rules of morality. The realm of necessity triggers a form of political justification in which one believes that sometimes you need to break a few eggs to make an omelet. From within this hard-boiled political realism, necessity paradoxically becomes a form of liberation and a release from the binding ties of what is ordinarily expected.

Nepos's Atticus did not use the language of necessity to describe the situation faced by Cicero, Caesar, Pompey, Antony, Brutus, and so on. For Nepos's Atticus, the Machiavellian realm of necessity was not a realm of freedom for the strong; rather it was a realm in which both the strong and the weak had lost control. Instead of freedom, the experience of necessity is that of being subjected to forces that one cannot direct, contain, or master. Instead of the Machiavellian prince who has the guts or virtù to do whatever is necessary to remain an actor, the realm of necessity signals a form of subjectivity where success and failure are matters of luck. It is a realm where one is carried by currents and winds that do not follow one's commands. In an unstable political environment, Atticus saw his friends as riding a tiger which they could not dismount. Consequently, under such circumstances, Atticus was reticent to join the fray. Refusing (although, as we shall see, not totally refusing) to participate in the turbulent world of civil war was not a function of keeping his hands clean, but of trying to retain his capacity to act. In preserving that capacity and intervening in a limited way, Atticus could be read as altering the fortunes of some of the players.[21]

During times of political chaos, refusing to participate is one way to avoid entering a world controlled by fortune. More strikingly, however, it is not the only action that one can perform. One can also act against fortune by assisting those who have been laid low by the storms of politics. For example, from the perspective of those who received Atticus's aid, it may have looked like good luck. But from Nepos's perspective, Atticus was intervening in the course of events that the participants could no longer direct or manage. His action as a friend was not conditioned by any response: there was nothing to his service that suggested a repayment of a debt or even, according Nepos, the expectation of future gain. He was acting out of friendship and in so doing acting outside the arena of political turmoil. It was a "divine" action in which Atticus created (or sought to create) good fortune for others. And, unlike Machiavelli's prince, it was an action that was motivated not by glory, but by the virtue of friendship.

In this political environment during which Atticus helped his friends, one is struck by how lucky he seemed to be. Why did not one side or the other execute Atticus or appropriate his wealth in response for assisting the enemy? Here we should consider the saying that is repeated twice in the biography: "Each man's character makes his fortune" (Sui cuique mores fingunt fortunam hominibus). The idea that *mores*—in this case, character, disposition, or habits—can make one's fortune sounds quaint and aristocratic to our ears: an aphorism more appropriate for those who already have made their fortunes and hence can afford to mind their manners. It strains credulity to think that somehow good luck is linked in any way to one's disposition. Moreover, this view stands in stark contrast to a Machiavellian vision of virtù in which the prince must beat down fortune or act in an audacious manner in order to attract her. Nepos's emphasis on character is unlike Machiavelli's view that acting in politics requires the ability to step away from one's character. For Machiavelli, princes who lack that ability will be successful only if the times happen to match their characters. A successful prince, in contrast, needs to be able to appear differently in different situations. If the situation is an unsettled, delegitimized political environment, the ability to act beyond and against one's character is indispensable.

It is true, of course, that Machiavelli also points to the importance of prudence. Success can be due to the fact that one has built one's dikes and dams well before a political cataclysm. Similarly, as noted earlier, Nepos writes that Atticus's *prudentia* saved his ship in the rock-strewn seas of the political storms that surrounded him. But prudential action is only one modality of action for Machiavelli, while a concern with character seems to be everything for Nepos. In the unsettled, violent political world occupied by the larger than life characters of Caesar, Pompey, Brutus, and Cicero, all of whom are endlessly seeking to gain control of events, Nepos's Atticus offered a counter-virtù. Both Machiavelli's prince and Atticus are seeking to act in an unsettled political environment. Both believe that fortune can be controlled or fashioned to some degree. They differ, however, on the degree to which it can be controlled, on the means they are willing to employ, and on the ends that they are seeking to achieve.

Why did Nepos believe that character can make one's fortune? Millar is correct in noting that "this attitude of neutrality and non-partisanship cannot of itself explain why things turned out as they did." Millar then notes that undoubtedly many Romans "remained throughout passive, uncommitted, and neutral, preferring private *officia* and the glories of the past to the urgent issues of the present" (1988:53). To describe Atticus as passive and uncommitted, however, is mistaken on this account. In contrast, I am suggesting that to the extent that he was committed to his friends and the families of his friends, his commitments were not ordinary political commitments. More importantly, by aiding his friends when they were in deep political trouble, he was not passive. It cannot be denied that his prudent actions may have allowed him to steer a course that saved himself and his position, but (once again) what difference could his character make?

The answer to this question lies in Nepos's claim that "before fashioning his fortune, Atticus so fashioned his character as to make it impossible for him to be injured justly" (Nepos [1929] 2005:xi, 6). Note that his *mores* did not prevent him from being unjustly injured. Rather, it secured him from just forms of punishment. In other words, his character did not secure him from all attacks. Rather, his character was such that he avoided doing wrongful acts and did the right things vis-à-vis his friends. Consequently, Nepos's view appears to be that in the violence of an unsettled political environment the most that one can do is ensure that one is not justly harmed and that one acts as one should toward one's friends.

Perhaps Atticus's actions can be interpreted in a more favorable light. Perhaps by doing the right thing vis-à-vis his friends, he did the politically unexpected thing. Whatever else it meant to support his friends who found themselves at odds with one another or publicly aid individuals such as Antony's family when Antony was exiled, it is clear that Atticus's actions were not particularly prudent. Indeed, given the circumstances, and the stakes, his actions could be characterized as audacious. He might have secured himself from being justly harmed, but his actions made him vulnerable to unjust harm. If this reading is plausible, then perhaps it is the surprising, audacious character of publicly protecting one's friends when they are down and out that constituted the political intervention that paradoxically saved him. This description begins to look more like Machiavelli's prince. The audacious action, however, is not aimed at the consolidation or legitimation of power but at securing one's character and friendships against the extraordinary pressures of politics. This reading of Nepos, which to some degree runs against the current of the biography, suggests that Atticus's character made his luck because he was disposed to perform actions that few would expect anyone to do.

In order to sharpen the point and contrast it with an alternative interpretation, we can return to Millar's suggestion that what saved Atticus was his turn to private *officia*. For Millar, this turn away from the public realm has enormous political significance. He writes, "The philosophic quietism and neutrality, which Atticus observed and Nepos praised, only served to smooth the path to monarchy. Under that new monarchy political neutrality was to be the enforced fate of everybody; and an antiquarian interest in the Roman past could be put to use in the propaganda of the newly-established dynasty, and immortalized in stone in the monuments which it put up in the centre of Rome" (1988:53–54). In effect, Millar argues that the value structure that Nepos appears to be celebrating is one that would support the kind of monarchy that was embodied in the reign of Augustus. But supporting one's friends, regardless of their political stance when their political fortunes are ebbed, is not quite the same as quietism. Moreover, it is not a view that is conducive to a form of monarchy that seeks uniformity or the subjection of the political opposition. Rather, it is a position whose effect is to keep the opposition alive. For Nepos's Atticus, it was at the moment when his friends were on the outs politically that he provided political intervention and support.

To continue this, perhaps, fanciful line of thought, one could argue that it suggests a vision of politics in which the political opposition should never be entirely defeated. In contrast to Millar's reading, Nepos's view looks less monarchist and more subversive and pluralistic. In making this suggestion, the sort of ideal of friendship offered here now begins to resemble the conception of Arendtian friendship discussed earlier. The similarity of the two views on friendship extends not merely to the fact that both conceptions found expression during "dark times," but that each could see friendship as a way to establish and maintain multiple points of views within the political arena. Moreover, to the extent that ideological differences separated the factions of the civil war, it is clear that Atticus did not see political ideas or ideals as overriding friendship.

Unlike Arendt, however, Atticus's politically consequential friendships were, or appeared to be motivated by affection and affective relationships. In his letters, Cicero repeatedly expressed his affection for Atticus. The relationship between Caesar and Atticus, at least on Nepos's account, could qualify as intimate and hence does not seem to be political in the Arendtian sense. More generally, Nepos's biography focuses less on what Atticus might have said and witnessed politically (as Arendt emphasizes) and more on what he did for his friends: e.g., legal support to Fulvia, financial support to Cicero, the refusal to join a faction supporting those who killed Caesar. The contents of Atticus's actions do not have the same resonance as what Arendt understands as constitutive of politics. These friends were private as much as they were public.

In addition, while there were sharp ideological differences between the factions of the civil war, these were also men driven by power and position. Despite their willingness to kill one another, Atticus remained their friends. In Nepos's ideal, Atticus did so not out of self-interest, but out of character.[22] To be clear, that implied practice is not one which says that one should be friends with thugs and tyrants, but that thuggery or tyranny is not itself sufficient to preclude or break off a friendship.[23] Friendship of this sort is possible and laudable despite the level of violence, a possibility that may be closed down in Arendt's conception of politics and certainly runs counter to the practice of many forms of ordinary interpersonal friendship.[24]

Finally, it may very well be the case that Atticus's refusals and interventions in politics were a function of the times during which he lived. Nepos notes that Atticus would have participated if the system was not so corrupt. In desperate times, one aids one's friends whenever they are needed even if that violates the rules and laws of those who claim legitimacy. In less desperate times, however, this sort of reasoning is less compelling. Shklar argues that in a free society, where the duties of citizenship are relatively just, they outweigh the duties of friendship. In other words, one should not hide one's friends from the police in a more or less just regime. This ranking makes sense because in a free society the protection that Atticus sought to offer his friends is institutionalized (or, at least, one hopes that it is). In effect, it is a feature of a minimally just society that it should secure the position of a political opposition and guarantee that those who have violated the law are subject to a process that is due to them as citizens.[25] This institutionalization does not mean that friends need not worry about each other or abandon each other when they have lost politically or when they have committed a crime. Rather, it means that the impulse to rescue a friend from the seas of fortune in a free society is less likely to arise if the proper protections are relatively secure. In a stable, minimally just society, Atticus's actions are less necessary because of the nature of the institutions. The answer to the question of whether to stick by a friend who is wanted by the police depends not only on the larger duties of citizenship, but on the judgment that the appropriate mechanisms are in place to protect one's friend. In noting that this is a matter of judgment, I am arguing that such assistance could be justified if one believed that there were systemic and persistent violations of protections of the politically vulnerable or defeated. The claims are more ambiguous in a free society, which suggests that one may not take for granted that the opposition (in its various forms, criminalized or not) is protected in important ways.

This way of looking at the question implies that Nepos's ideal tells us something about friendship in rather extreme political situations that has a certain reflection upon the operation of just institutions. In contrast, Arendt's discussion of friendship in dark times is of one piece with a more general discussion of friendship within a functioning polis. In dark times, friendship is less about rescuing them and more about keeping discourse alive or not sacrificing them. This makes the loyalties of friendship in Atticus's case difficult to achieve and to generalize. After all, Atticus's wealth, talent, and situation are unique. Perhaps the challenge that Nepos's ideal poses for individuals is that it creates a demanding conception of friendship in which one does precisely what others do not expect. One embraces one's friends at the moment their political fortunes have ebbed. This is not a form of civic friendship, but of friendship imbued with a form of courage that stands in the way of the prevailing political currents. It is not meant to be hidden or surreptitious or conspiratorial. It entails the public association and acknowledgment of another person who has, in the case of Atticus's friends, been declared *hostis* or a public enemy and, in the case of my grandmother's friend, was placed in a modern version of that category.

But so what? To go back to case of my grandmother, what difference would it have made if she had embraced her friend, taken her dinner, gone out to a movie? Should she have given her money? Attempted to smuggle her out of Germany? Perhaps these possibilities are part of a higher ideal of friendship and form of self-enactment to which few may subscribe and even fewer embody. Alternatively, what was served by Atticus's friendships with individuals who were enemies? The Roman civil wars did not stop. At worst, his support allowed adversaries to survive and fight beyond what they would have done without such support, prolonging the turmoil. It seems that because Atticus was saved by his unexpected actions, saving his own skin must have been his intention. Alternatively, Nepos could be suggesting that whatever political differences existed between the great adversaries during these civil wars, friendship was still possible. Our enemies do not turn into wild animals, and consequently, it is still possible to pull back—to extricate oneself from the tumultuous seas of political fortune—even when one friend has murdered another. That Atticus's approach failed to shake the parties out of their passions and the madness of the civil war is not surprising.

There is one final element to the phrase that "character makes one's fortune" that deserves mention. As we saw in chapter 1, friendship is not solely a function of friendly actions, but it is also about the mutual recognition of the appropriate sentiments or feelings. In the ideal of friendship set out in chapter 4, friendship is understood as a form of self-enactment in which one chooses the appropriate motivations to act and acts upon them. In contrast, self-disclosure is "choosing satisfactions to pursue and pursuing them" (Oakeshott 1975:76). In the pursuit of a chosen end or purpose, one acts in the world and with (and sometime against) others. It is, Oakeshott argues "immersed in contingency, it is interminable, and it is liable to frustration, disappointment, and defeat" (1975, 73). When friendship is viewed through the lens of a moral practice entailing friendly actions, those actions are subject to the actions of other individuals who may defeat or alter it.

Atticus may send money to Cicero or to Marius or to Brutus but that assistance may never reach its destination—the messenger is robbed, a boat conveying the money is lost at sea, and so on. But to the extent that Atticus wishes to see himself as a good friend and seeks to act out of a sentiment of friendship, then his

> conduct is released from its character as a response to a contingent situation and is emancipated from liability to the frustration of adverse circumstances. For, what the agent chooses to think is related to his understanding and respect for himself, to the integrity of his character, and not at all to his understanding of a contingent situation to which he must respond by choosing an action.
>
> (OAKESHOTT 1975:73)

From the perspective of self-enacting features of friendship the idea that one's character makes one's fortune acquires a somewhat different twist. Because the engagement of self-enactment is relatively immune to contingency or fortune, one places oneself more or less outside of its reach. As an exploit in self-enactment, the existence of a friendship requires the recognition of the appropriate sentiments, but it does not require their generation. One cannot require another to be one's friend or to choose the appropriate sentiments upon which to act. In this way, this particular ideal of friendship operates beyond the reach of the political. As with other forms of self-enactment, this ideal of friendship is not subject to fortune's wheel.

I have argued that Nepos's biography of Atticus can be read as presenting an interpersonal form of friendship that sees itself as different from a politics defined by the political admonition that "either you are with us or against us." It is an ideal that remains connected to politics in certain respects and disconnected in others. By intervening in order to support one's friends in their political misfortune, it may keep alive an opposition and pluralism. In so doing, it runs counter to the winds of fortune and moves beyond a sort of quietism. In addition, by sustaining friendships between those who are enemies, it raises the possibility of political reconciliation. While that possibility may fail or never be taken up by the parties, the actions of Atticus suggest that political divisions need not be insurmountable rifts between individuals. If it is possible to be friends to those who see one another as enemies, it is always possible for those enemies to step back from political turmoil and refuse the realm of necessity and its corresponding abandonment of action. Finally, the friendship of Atticus suggests a somewhat different stance toward fortune and the contingent character of political action. If we see political turmoil as a realm dominated by the hazardous effects of violence, then friendship is one way to step beyond those hazards. Supporting one's friends when they have lost politically is both a form of self-enactment insulated from contingency and an unexpected act that may shock and alter the course of events.

This discussion of Atticus began with his political refusals. At the end of that list was a refusal related to his own death. In the biography, Atticus is described as deciding to end his life after having done what he could to effect a cure. After having abstained from food for two days, the fever abated and the disease "began to be less violent. Nevertheless, he persisted in a his resolution, and so died on the fifth day after he had made his decision" (Nepos [1929] 2005:327). The refusal to take up food exhibited a choice to die in a manner of his choosing. Once again, he stood on the brink of the realm of necessity, a realm defined by illness, in which one does whatever one can to save one's life. His refusal to do what was necessary, however, had the unexpected consequence of slowing his death. By sticking to his resolution, however, he befriended death with his life.

seven
INSTITUTIONS FOR AND
AGAINST FRIENDSHIP

CASSIUS: You love me not.

BRUTUS: I do not like your faults.

CASSIUS: A friendly eye could never see such faults.

BRUTUS: A flatterer's eye would not, though they do appear
As huge as high Olympus.

—WILLIAM SHAKESPEARE, *JULIUS CAESAR*

For the most part, theoretical accounts of friendship and politics focus on how friendship could serve or erode important political values and arrangements. In chapters 5 and 6, we saw how this approach can yield certain conclusions regarding civic friendship and the role it can play in an unstable political environment. The high value that we attribute to friendship, however, also reminds us that any discussion of the relationship between politics and friendship should also consider how our political arrangements and ideals can serve or erode friendship. Because of its importance, friendship should not be seen as a mere handmaiden to politics. This chapter takes up and explores the various ways in which legal and political arrangements can undermine or promote friendship.

To begin with the obvious, the more impartiality is valued and achieved in the functioning of public institutions, the less room for friendship exists in their operation. A basic sense of fairness seems to require that political and legal institutions governing free and equal citizens should avoid partiality and favoritism. Should, however, our political and legal institutions strive to root out all forms of partiality? If so, then there is a sense in which the procedures and rules of a more or less just system of government will seek to dampen or discourage friendships and the connections and advantages that they may bring in the area of governance. This matters a great deal in the application of rules and laws and in the appointment of individuals to offices and positions. Allowing considerations of friendship into both of these matters creates obvious risks: unfairness and corruption in appearance or reality. The first part of this chapter briefly explores these risks in light of the general principles that the law should be impartially applied and that offices and positions should be open to all. I argue that although these general principles are compelling in most cases, good reasons exist for creating space for permitting friendship to play some role in the appointment process.

In the rest of the chapter I turn to whether policies and laws should indirectly or directly encourage friendship. The middle sections of the chapter consider how laws and policies indirectly affect friendship because they reinforce inequalities or manipulate the interactions of individuals. These, in turn, can affect the possibility for friendships by reducing the ability of individuals to mutually recognize the motivations of others. Here, I suggest ways in which the state can indirectly promote friendship by reducing or removing barriers to many of the practices of friendship.

The last and longest sections of this chapter focus on whether the state should play a more direct role in promoting friendship. This possibility has arisen in the context of a legal debate over whether there should be a law of friendship that recognizes and enforces certain privileges and obligations among friends. Despite the advantages of such recognition, the difficulties of the legal recognition of friendship are significant enough such that we should be skeptical of such a project. Some of these difficulties rest on the claim that friendship is a family resemblance concept and that the law lacks the flexibility to identify its diverse and mutable character. In addition, the law's emphasis on rights and privileges—which can be understood as deficient reasons for friendship—raises the question of the potential costs of the law's playing a positive role in promoting friendship.

IMPARTIAL INSTITUTIONS AND FRIENDSHIP

The idea that the law should be impartially applied and that offices and positions should be open to all is a familiar one within liberal theory (Rawls 1971:53). In this ideal, personal relationships to those in power should make little difference to who is appointed to public office and how laws and policies are applied. For example, when positions are distributed on the basis of "connections" and not on fair procedures, their distribution and the distribution of whatever power, prestige, and pecuniary rewards that follows from them, appear arbitrary and hence unjust. The familiar complaint that "it's not what you know, but who you know" in being hired or appointed is a basic expression of this feeling of injustice. More generally, in the application of laws and policies, it is not uncommon to believe that officials should recuse themselves not only when their friends are involved, but also when their friends' interests are involved. All of this is familiar enough and suggests that the values of impartiality and formal equality should rule out friendship as a basis for appointment to office or play any role in the application of rules and laws.[1]

It is important to highlight that an emphasis on rules and procedures is meant, among other things, to diminish the power of kith and kin in the application of the law and in appointment to office. In the procedural republic, friendship simply should not mean as much as in other sorts of regimes: The intense bonds of friendship are cooled by rules and procedures. What is gained is a sense of fairness and impartiality, but what is lost is the potential importance of friendship when dealing with clerks, officers, judges, and officials. This sort of tradeoff makes sense because in a free society the protection that someone like Atticus sought to offer his friends is institutionalized by laws and administrators who are perceived as fair. In a more or less just regime, Atticus surrenders his friends to the law in the belief that they will receive the process that is rightfully due to them.

Moreover, a belief in the fairness of a system of rules and policies is furthered bolstered by the perception that friendship (or kinship) does not matter or "count" in the application of the law or in the appointment to office. In a sense, the law is "fair," in part, precisely because it deflates to some degree the importance of friendship and then attempts to keep personal relationships at arms' length. This distance is especially important in the application of laws, procedures, and policies. Even if it is true that no one may know more about the motivations or capacities of an individual than a friend and that this information may be relevant to the proper application of a law or policy, there still remains something troubling about having an official decide a matter that concerns her friends. Whatever advantages that could conceivably be derived from friendship do not appear to outweigh the necessity of protecting the appearance of impartiality.[2] In the fair application of the law, friendship carries the taint of corruption. It violates an ideal of equal treatment to which citizens are entitled.[3]

Similarly, the expectation that friends act supportively, usefully, and loyally runs headlong into the ideal that appointments to offices and position should be made fairly. Multiple reasons support the ideal that offices and position should be open to all and hence preclude friendship as a relevant reason for appointment. First, to the extent that offices and positions require some set of qualifications, there seems to be little reason to think that friendships track the relevant qualities needed for office. Consequently, the distribution of offices to friends is arbitrary. Second, to the extent that we are considering public offices and positions, their distribution based on friendship violates a notion that citizens as citizens should be treated equally. Third, allowing considerations of friendship into the decision of who should hold office appears corrupt in the sense that one's own interests are very much connected to advancing the interests of those who are closest to oneself. Just as the idea of using an office to feather one's nest is ethically troubling, so one's friendships can be seen as part of that same nest. Finally, if the arguments of Simon Keller (2004) and Sarah Stroud (2006) are correct, then some understandings of what it means to be a good friend imply a kind of epistemic bias. As Keller writes, "when good friends form beliefs about each other, they sometimes respond to considerations that have to do with the needs and interests of their friends, not with aiming at the truth, and that this is part of what makes them good friends" (2004:333). The danger of legitimizing the appointment of friends to office is that they not only are, but in some cases should be (from the perspective of the friendship) willing to place friendship ahead of what is true or what the evidence may indicate. If a good friendship can entail that we see the world in a way more favorable to or supportive of our friends, then that may create problems in any official situation that demands a clear-eyed view of things. In short, on the side of keeping "offices and positions open to all" lie equality, impartiality, qualification, fairness, and justice.

The arguments for keeping friends at arms' length in applying rules and procedures as well as in appointing people to office are strong. Nevertheless, despite the powerful reasons listed thus far and unlike the general case of applying the law, I suggest that an argument can be made for admitting friendship as an acceptable reason for appointments to some public offices. In other words, friendship should not be ruled out *tout court* from questions of appointment to every public position. The central argument for permitting friendship to enter the scene of appointment is that there are aspects of some friendships that could be related to holding particular positions. These include such attributes as trust, loyalty, and frank speech. In friendships that have these attributes, it is not difficult to see how they could be important in offices whose tasks involve providing advice and counsel. In other words, built into some practices of friendship may be qualities that are useful for the office. For example, in the United States, we frequently refer to those positions in which such virtues are emphasized to be political appointments. The idea is not that all political appointees are or will be friends of those who make the appointments, but that the discretionary nature of such appointments creates a space for friendship within institutional structures that ordinarily attempt to push it out or keep it at bay. One does not need to be a friend to be loyal or to be trustworthy or to speak freely. On the other hand, one may look to one's friends when one is seeking these qualities and in a set of circumstances in which these qualities are valued, friendships can be cultivated.

If certain sorts of friendships do track some of the qualifications of office, then the appointment of friends need not look so arbitrary. Still, it could be argued that whatever value is associated with friendship is outweighed by the fact that such appointments violate a sense of equality, imply a kind of corruption, and risk creating potentially harmful forms of bias. Can these objections be overcome? If friendship is a permissible reason for appointment to office, then by definition the appointment is not open to all. Even if we expand the interpretation of the phrase "open to all" to mean that careers are open to talents under conditions of fair equality of opportunity (Rawls 1971:271), that still does not admit friendship into the mix. In a state of any significant size, it is difficult to see how the talents associated with a political appointment could be recognized under conditions in which everyone could have a friendship with the officeholder. In a fundamental sense, permitting the appointment of one's friends means that a personal connection is violating respect for equal citizenship. In light of this conflict with equality of treatment, the appointment of friends should be, at best, the exception and not the rule. The exception can be justified only if the qualities associated with some forms of friendship are especially desirable for the office.

Nevertheless, even if it is the exception and the qualities of the friendship do track the qualifications of office, such appointments still look corrupt. One way to respond to that difficulty is to argue that friendship should not be the only qualification for office. If some minimal set of qualifications are needed for the office beyond those associated with the virtues of friendship, the appointee must demonstrate them. Friendship cannot be a sufficient reason for an appointment to an office or position. The difficulty is that even if the friend is qualified, the friendship itself can lead observers to call into question the qualifications of the individual. The taint of corruption may never be eliminated in the appointment of friends, particularly in a competitive politicized environment.

Finally, the problem of epistemic distortion is also an important challenge.[4] As mentioned earlier, Keller and Stroud raise the possibility that a good friend may be one for whom the truth is not the most important thing. Consequently, friendship can result in people saying what they believe others want to hear or what will bolster them or prop up their resolve. In an official capacity, friendship can slide into flattery and flattery may slide into a biased or dishonest appraisal of a situation or of one's friends. One can see this tendency in the exchange between Brutus and Cassius at the beginning of this chapter where Cassius claims that friendship implies a kind of blindness to his faults.[5] In response to this objection, it can be argued first that the adverbial conditions that may lead to an epistemic bias—for example, acting supportively and loyally—can themselves be satisfied in any number of ways that do not necessarily lead to such a bias. Perhaps the best sort of loyalty to a friend is expressed in a willingness to tell the truth, even when it may be difficult to hear. As Brutus's response to Cassius indicates, practices of friendship exist that place a premium on frank speech (Keller 2004:334). Being able to say honestly and openly what is on one's mind is a difficult but important task for those who have been hired to provide counsel.

Second, the existence of an epistemic bias does not mean "willfully believing the false, or the incontrovertible" (Stroud 2006:506). If a bias exists, it can take different forms. For example, Keller thinks of it in terms of the sort of relationship one has with a coach who provides "motivation and encouragement" and not simply the cold truth about all the obstacles that stand in one's way (2004:329). In such instances, the bias could, but need not be disturbing for those holding office. The friendship between an adviser and an official need not mean that the adviser will refuse to acknowledge the reality of their situation. It may mean, however, that the adviser is more willing to encourage her friend to overcome whatever impediments she faces. Obviously, this may be good or bad, depending on the situation. The same, however, may be said of an adviser who is not in a position to offer such encouragement.

Third, if Stroud and Keller are correct and this kind of epistemic bias is a norm in many practices of friendship, then it may very well be the case that some friends intuitively grasp this bias and filter out the most enthusiastic forms of support that friends provide. In other words, friendship may entail seeing our friends and their actions in a certain light, but knowing that our friends respond in this way may, on the one hand, be supportive, but on the other hand be discounted because such a norm exists. Finally, it can be argued that the problem of epistemic bias is not currently perceived as so severe that political systems take steps to remove people from office once they become friends. If the dangers of friendship were overwhelming, it seems that the practice of appointments would include this sort of safety mechanism. Epistemic distortions may be a risk of friendship, but not so great as to preclude friendship from being a reason for appointment to office.

The case for partiality that I am making here turns upon competing values that can be easily swamped in the pursuit of formally just arrangements. In opening the door to appointments that are partly based on friendship, we may not have impartiality, fairness, or even justice, but we may be able to secure other virtues that improve the conduct of the public's business. The case of friendship simply reaffirms that impartiality is not the only value. This argument does not resolve the tension between the demands of justice and friendship and, in fact, suggests that those tensions may remain a part of politics. In the appointment to offices and positions, the value of impartiality does dampen the flame of friendship but, I argue, need not seek to extinguish it.

THE CHILLING EFFECT OF LEGAL AND POLITICAL INSTITUTIONS

When we turn to the effects of the laws and policies created by political and legal institutions, we can see various ways in which they have historically and (in many cases) unjustly discouraged or undermined friendship. Three sorts of obstacles deserve mention here: establishing barriers to association; creating or reinforcing legal, social, or economic inequalities; and placing friendships in the service of state ends. In all of these cases, friendship is still possible, but not probable. This improbability is due, in part, to the role these obstacles can play in preventing friends from performing acts of self-disclosure associated with ordinary practices of friendship. However, the greater difficulty is that law and public policy can make it extremely difficult for individuals to reliably recognize in one another the appropriate motivations of friendship. All of these instances are ones in which laws and policies have a chilling effect on friendship. Paradoxically, they also point to ways in which laws and social policies can indirectly promote friendship. To the extent that the law removes barriers to association, encourages forms of equality, and refrains from engaging in manipulative behavior, it may create opportunities for friendship. However, just as law and policy may not render friendship impossible, it also cannot ensure that friendships will flourish.

Legal and political institutions and policies can affect the possibility for friendship by establishing new or reinforcing existing barriers to association. Obviously, if individuals are successfully prohibited from having contact with one another, they cannot be friends simply because they cannot do the sorts of things that friends ordinarily do. Laws that prohibit groups of individuals from marrying, socializing, or being educated together will diminish the opportunities for those groups to establish friendships. On the other hand, not just any sort of repeated social contact opens the door for friendship. The question becomes the quality and character of that contact and whether individuals can mutually recognize the appropriate motivations.[6]

Inequalities of all sorts may also diminish the prospects for friendship. On some accounts of friendship this is so because equality is understood as a necessary part of friendship. Aristotle, for example, presented it succinctly in the phrase, "amity is parity" (1985:1157b36). Horace wrote, "What good friends say inside: equal with equal, equally met" (Sharp and Welty 1991:48). For Kant, "The relation of friendship is a relation of equality. A friend who bears my losses becomes my benefactor and puts me in his debt. I feel shy in his presence and cannot look him boldly in the face. The true relationship is cancelled and friendship ceases" (1991:213–14). Mary Shanley argues that John Stuart Mill's "belief that equality was more suitable to friendship than inequality was as unalterable as his conviction that democracy was a better system of government than despotism; the human spirit could not develop its fullest potential when living in absolute subordination to another human being or to government" (1993:281–82).[7]

There are various ways to understand equality, but the form of inequality that appears most destructive of the opportunities of friendship is that found in relationships of domination and subordination. Laws or social policies that establish or reinforce political, economic, or social relationships in which one individual can exercise power over another also generate significant obstacles to friendship. There are a variety of reasons why this may be the case. For example, Marilynn Friedman argues that the existence of domination and subordination are conditions that "override the consent of one or both parties and, thereby, undermine the voluntariness of the relationship" (1993:211). Power forces people into relationships that are best understood as not being matters of choice. While Friedman is correct in noting that voluntariness is a problem, it may not be the whole story. As we shall see, in the case of flatterers, domination undermines consent in a very indirect manner. The distortion caused by the difference in position can also result in dissimulation. Differences in power complicate our ability to judge the motives of others. Without being reliably able to assess those motives, we cannot distinguish true from false friends. The difficulties power raises take somewhat different forms depending on whether one is in the advantaged position.

In the traditional, Western literature on friendship, the problem raised by power and command is generally framed in terms of the relationship between a ruler and his subjects: Can a king have friends and can one be friends of a king? In this discussion, tyrants anchor a particularly important position. The trope of the friendless tyrant appears both in the ancient and modern world. In "Hiero," for example, Xenophon notes that the despot is so hated by those who are closest to him, that it is impossible to imagine that he could be loved by anyone else (1925:3.9). The tyrant trusts no one and no one trusts him. In his "Epistle 1," Plato sends back the gold that the tyrant Dionysus paid him as an advisor by noting that "in future I shall certainly consider my own interests in less benevolent fashion, while you, being the tyrant that you are, will live in solitude" (1966:309b). In Plato's *Republic*, the tyrant's drive to secure his position ultimately leads him to do away with anyone who calls his rule into question: "until he has left neither friend nor enemy of any worth whatsoever" (1968:567b). The corresponding tyrannical soul, moreover, is one that "never has a taste of freedom or true friendship" (576a).[8]

The solitude of the tyrant appears largely to follow from the cruelty and arbitrariness associated with domination. The tyrant is a tyrant because he is willing to secure his own interests and position by doing whatever is necessary. He has little or no concern with the interests of anyone else. Friendship is literally impossible. If, however, we consider Aristotle's distinction between a monarch and tyrant, where the monarch is genuinely interested in the common good and has a right to rule, then the barriers to friendship may be ameliorated. Consistent with this line of thought, the Greek orator and philosopher, Dio Chrysostom noted, in Konstan's words, that while tyrants are friendless, "a good king inspires love and loyalty. He can be served by *philoi* and have confidence in his ministers in part because his choice is limitless" (Konstan 1997:107). Kings, or at least the right sort of king, can have friends. Konstan argues that the idea of royal friends "is a striking instance of the application of the language of friendship to distinctly hierarchical relations between people of different social stations" (97).

For those who worried about such things from the perspective of the king, the central problem that inequality posed for friendship was not that of inequality as such, but of telling the difference between friends and flatterers. Flatterers are false friends. They tell the king what they think he wants to hear. They may behave like friends, but that behavior may change as the winds of fortune change. They may act as though they are concerned with the king's welfare, but they are more than likely motivated by their own self-interest. In this case, the king is duped by a false friendship. What kings should look for in distinguishing the genuine from a faux friend is whether the advisor or counselor is willing to speak frankly. In this context, "a judicious candor is perceived as the touchstone that distinguishes the true friend from the flatterer" (Konstan 1997:104). But classical writers offered other ways to ferret out the flatterer, for example by looking for fickleness or approval of base or irrational behavior (100–101).

Moving away from the rarified world of monarchs and toward the more general problem of domination and subordination, similar obstacles to friendship arise. For example, in discussing affection between those who are positioned in a relationship of significant inequality, Howell Raines (1991) writes, "There is no trickier subject for a writer from the [American] South than that of affection between a black person and a white one in the unequal world of segregation. For the dishonesty upon which such a society is founded makes every emotion suspect, makes it impossible to know whether what flowed between two people was honest feeling or pity or pragmatism. Indeed, for the black person, the feigning of an expected emotion could be the very coinage of survival." The problem is getting an accurate assessment of the other's motivations. Preston King writes, "If then great power tends to exclude reciprocal friendship and to feed dependency, it does so by virtue of veiling one prospective friend from another. It does so by sharply diminishing common knowledge and common exposure" (2007:136). What is true of affection is also true of the other possible motives for friendship.

Consider, for example, the black maid Minny in Kathryn Stockett's (2011) novel *The Help* set in the American South of the 1960s. Minny acts in a friendly manner to her ditsy employer Celia Foote. She tries to be pleasant because she does not want to be fired and does what she can to mask her initial distain for Celia and thereby conveys the impression that she genuinely enjoys Celia's company. Minny is being forced into a nominal friendship. On the other hand, Celia may truly have affection for Minny, but because the feelings are not mutual, it is not a true friendship—at least initially. Inequalities appear to eat at the heart of friendship because they set up powerful incentives to occlude the ability to judge motivation. In Stockett's novel, friendship is not impossible, but (as Raines notes), given the legally and socially sanctioned inequalities of the Jim Crow South, it is difficult for parties to discern and reveal genuine feelings and motives of affection, respect, or care.

Inequalities of power can, of course, work to distort friendship in other ways. The king may act generously to a subject and the subject may believe that the king genuinely likes the subject when, in truth, the king was doing what any patron does for a client. Because the king has power and the subject is powerless, the action could be interpreted as a gift of grace: "Why did the king choose me? What could I possibly do for the king? It must be because the king likes me." To have genuine friends in high places is not an insignificant or unusual aspiration. Their honor reflects upon the subject. Their power may ultimately secure her against her enemies. It is the differential in power and the willingness of one party to do the things that friends do that blocks our ability to see the relationship for what it may really be—namely the king is treating the subject like a client and has every expectation that she will reciprocate in the appropriate way when the time comes. This does not mean that she cannot be friends with the king, but that it is difficult to know whether the friendship is genuine. In these sorts of cases, the problem is, once again, not so much that power erodes the voluntariness of friendship, but of identifying motives.[9]

The difficulties associated with identifying the motivations of others may be compounded if the power relationship is also one of dependence. Being friends with those upon whom one depends socially or economically could be evidence of a motive of greed (Konstan 1997:101). Alternatively, the ability to speak frankly requires far more courage in a relationship of subordination. Having much to lose, the dependent party may not be forthright. To put it in Kant's terms, a position of servility means that one cannot look one's friend boldly in the face. Finally, asymmetrical dependence may also hinder the forms of reciprocity that are part of many practices of friendship. The dependant party may simply lack the means to reciprocate. Aristotle's version of this obstacle rested on the presumption that in a friendship of unequals, the loving should be proportional to the comparative worth of the friends: the better friend should receive more. In light of this presumption, he concluded that "if friends come to be separated by some wide gap in virtue, vice, wealth, or something else; for then they are friends no more, and do not even expect to be" (1985:1159a35). For the Greeks, social or economic dependence itself could be an obstacle to friendship. Here, friendship requires equality in the sense of possessing some degree of independence.

The problem of subordination and dependence has consequences for gendered hierarchies in societies and the possibilities for friendship. As Shanley notes in her discussion of J. S. Mill, formal inequalities associated with the patriarchal control of property and a woman's body placed enormous obstacles to friendship between men and women. In particular, Mill saw these obstacles in play in the legal construction of marriage. As long as women were not seen as equal to men, friendship between men and women would always have an unstable or troubled character.[10] More strongly, as long as the domination of men over women was seen as natural, then the possibility for a full notion of friendship was seen as next to impossible, even within a marriage. The kind of openness and level of intimacy that men could have with one another could only happen with great difficulty between men and women. Hence, it is no accident that in a culture that subordinates women to men, the notion of friendship will be primarily focused on relationships between men (where, because of equality, motives may be more easily discerned). The same argument applies to situations in which class, ethnicity, and race raise questions of domination and subordination.

The language of tyranny is appropriate here. As Mary Wollstonecraft noted, men are placed in a tyrannical position vis-à-vis women, creating a relationship that serves neither men nor women. It distorts their relationship and it distorts who they are and who they could be. This was true for Wollstonecraft and, as Shanley notes, it was true for Mill. For Mill, transforming that relationship meant changing property relationships, giving women the right to vote, opening up educational and professional opportunities for women and providing women with the right to divorce their husbands.

Shanley concludes her article by noting that formal legal and civil protections have not secured equality within marriage. More is needed: maternity leave, flexible work schedules, publicly supporting day care, health care, retirement benefits for part time work.[11] While they may not prevent friendships, inequalities of power distort and occlude possibilities for friendship.

FRIENDS AND STOOL PIGEONS

These distortions and occlusions are also apparent when the state decides to use personal relationships for its own purposes. All sorts of regimes—just and unjust—have played on the relationships of friendship in order to extract information about political enemies and ordinary criminals. Getting friends to betray one another or getting individuals to befriend those who have been targeted for investigation is a widely used tactic by state prosecutors. In this regard, it can be said that the state is far more effective in producing false friends than true ones. Informants, moles, spies, agents, provocateurs, stooges, and stool pigeons have sought to create the appearance of friendships in order to serve the goals of the state. These "false friends" seek to create the impression of being true ones, but act in a manner that is inconsistent with adverbial norms of friendship and may be motivated by sentiments that are incompatible with friendship. A "Judas" may be a friend at some level, but is moved to harm (perhaps wrongfully) his or her friend. Betrayed individuals may believe that the state's agent is motivated by the appropriate feelings of friendship and be unaware of what the supposed friend is doing. Hence they may trust the state's agent, not knowing that what is said may be held against them.

One of the most famous cases of such a false friendship involves the spy, Kim Philby. For thirty years, Philby served as an agent for the Soviet Union while also serving in MI6, the British spy agency. Recruited by the Soviet spy agency (the NKVD) in the 1930s, Philby used his friendships with members of MI6 and the Central Intelligence Agency to convey information to the USSR that led to the deaths of possibly hundreds of agents and other individuals (MacIntyre 2014:249). In the course of his career, Philby "had betrayed his country, his class, and his club; he had lied to MI5 and MI6 and the FBI, his family, friends, and colleagues; he had deceived everyone, egregiously, brilliantly, for more than thirty years" (2014:248–49). Ben MacIntyre's retelling of the story emphasizes a "particular sort of friendship that played an important role in history," namely, that found between Philby and Nicholas Elliot (xi). Elliot was also a member of MI6 and had become friends with Philby at beginning of the Second World War. Philby was a role model to Elliot, introducing him to the larger fraternity of intelligence officers, and rose with him through the ranks of MI6. MacIntyre writes, "The friendship between Philby and Elliot was not just one of shared interests and professional identity, but something deeper. Nick Elliot was friendly to all but emotionally committed to few. The bond with Philby was unlike any other in his life" (26).

When Philby came under suspicion as a Soviet agent, Elliott vigorously defended him and then ultimately enabled his reinstatement into MI6. Although Elliot, like many of Philby's friends and colleagues, later contended that he knew about Philby's activities earlier than the evidence suggests, it was not until 1963 that Elliot confronted Philby while the latter was working as a British spy in Beirut. After guaranteeing Philby immunity from prosecution if he told the British government all that he knew, Philby provided a written confession to Elliot. Elliot then left for the Congo. In MacIntyre's view, Philby was allowed to escape (or do a "fade out") to Moscow because bringing him back to Great Britain would have been enormously embarrassing to an agency that had been repeatedly infiltrated by the Soviets.

For many in the West, the shock of the Philby case is inseparable from the puzzlement over how Philby could have betrayed his friends for so long despite the fact that he did not appear to be all that interested in Marxism and, during the purges under Stalin, some of his own handlers were recalled to the USSR and executed. If, however, we untangle Philby from his Cold War context, one may still be taken aback by his assertion that,

> I have always operated at two levels, a personal level and a political one. When the two have come into conflict I have had to put politics first. The conflict can be very painful. I don't like deceiving people, especially friends, and contrary to what others think, I feel very badly about it. But then decent soldiers feel badly about the necessity of killing in wartime.
> (CORERA 2013:89)

Philby appeared to think that just as a killing in a hot war would not be a murder, so using one's friends in a cold war would not be betrayal. The analogy to killing in war would, of course, be more compelling if killing in war meant intentionally killing one's own friends (although perhaps this happens more frequently than one thinks). Moreover, it is not clear why putting the political in front of the personal was a *necessity* for Philby. At the very least, it seeks to throw off any possibility of moral condemnation. At most, there is something to Philby's ranking that is deeply inhumane.

I considered whether the political should outweigh friendship in chapter 6. In that chapter I argued that the answer to that question is, "not necessarily." There may very well be situations in which one can and should support just institutions instead of supporting one's friends. On the other hand, Philby's claim regarding the necessity of always placing the political in front of the personal is an expression of the worst form of Machiavellianism. The Philby case does, however, point to other features of friendship. An adverse reaction to Philby's betrayal can be read as indicative of the value of friendship. Even for these individuals who lived in a world of deceit and prevarications, there was a tremendous value placed on being open and honest with one's friends (MacIntyre 2014:26). The fact that Philby was able to fool so many people for so long also illustrates the degree to which the relationships of friendship rest on both the mutual recognition of motivations and a set of adverbial conditions. In MacIntyre's story, it is clear that a central adverbial condition of the friendships between spies (at least at that time) was/is their ability to speak openly, freely, and confidentially. It was this last condition that Philby violated throughout the time he was friends with Nicholas Elliott. In addition, one of Philby's motivations was to simply use his friends without their knowledge or approval. Whatever feelings of affection and respect that existed between Philby and Elliott (and one does get the impression that these individuals truly had affection for one another) they were certainly poisoned by Philby's mercenary motivations.

When one looks at the friendship from Elliot's perspective, one also finds themes common to discussions of friendship and politics. Here was a friendship that distorted important functions of government because of certain epistemic biases. Philby could count on having friends in the highest places to vouch for his character. His friends gave him the benefit of the doubt, not only because he was a "gentleman" and an "Englishman," but also because they believed that they truly knew him. That knowledge was embodied in a deep friendship with people such as Elliott and James Jesus Angleton (who eventually became head of the CIA's counterintelligence group). Consequently, friendship clouded the capacity of MI6 to investigate and interrogate Philby impartially. Indeed, one wonders whether Elliott let (assuming intentionality) Philby escape to Moscow not merely out of fear of embarrassment, but out of a residual sense of friendship. Friendship can adversely affect the norms of professional conduct and lead to inequitable treatment. Elliot's tragedy is that he should have chosen politics over friendship and Philby's vice is that he should have done the opposite.[12]

At the bottom of the whole sordid story is the common assumption that states should be able to use and exploit friendships in the name of security and law enforcement. In contrast, one can argue that the use of false friends is objectionable for a number of reasons. Some have argued that the right to privacy is violated through their employment. One speaks to one's friends trustingly and confidentially, assuming they are one's friends, and the state seeks to betray that trust and confidence. American courts, however, have rejected this claim, arguing that "victims of the false friends disclose voluntarily any secret information and have no reasonable expectation of privacy in such disclosures." In response, Ethan Leib suggests, "If friends are entitled to the privilege of privacy (and the related duty of confidentiality . . .), perhaps the false-friend problem cries for a different solution in a polity properly attuned to the needs of friendships" (2007:701–2).

Whether friends are entitled to the privilege of privacy and should take on a duty of confidentiality appears to depend on both the nature of the friendship and on the relationship between more or less just institutions and our expectations associated with friendship. Given the complexities and richness of our practices of friendship, it is not always the case that friendships involve the revelation of secrets between friends, nor is it the case that friends are the only ones in whom we trust or confide. In this regard, the American courts are both right and wrong: The reasonable expectation of privacy very much depends on the sort of friendship that one has established. Moreover, protecting the confidences of friends as opposed to business partners, associates, and trusted employees very much depends on the ability to clearly distinguish between these relationships. A legally protected right to privacy or a legal obligation to protect secrets told by a friend would require the capacity of the courts to sort through these distinctions—a problem that will be considered in more detail in "The Legal Emphasis on Deficient Reasons" section that focuses on duties in the law.

In addition, the role of more or less just institutions may also complicate the question of how privileged communications between friends should be—even for those friendships in which there exists a high expectation of confidentiality. I have argued that in a more or less just state the establishment of fair procedures provides an important reason to scale-back our expectations for protecting our friends and their interests. The assumption is that in such a regime, our friends and their interests (like ourselves and our own interests) can expect to be treated fairly by a set of acceptable procedures and rules. If this assumption is correct and one becomes aware that one's friends are seeking to violate the rights of others or harm them (or those fair institutional arrangements), then friends have good reason to reconsider the claims of loyalty that may ordinarily be part of friendship. In the case of criminal conspiracy, it is not clear that claims of privacy can or should protect friendships.

A stronger objection to the state's (ab)use of friendship is not that it violates a right of privacy, but that it has consequences for our practices of friendship. In effect, the state's generation of false friends is objectionable because it can make it more difficult for individuals to recognize true ones. If there is always the risk that supposed friends are really state stool pigeons, we may call into question the ordinary ways in which we identify the motivations of others. The costs of learning about one another may become steeper. This sort of manipulation of our practices of friendship raises the costs of friendship and erodes or undermines the practices themselves. For example, consider analogous cases in which the state could be licensed to use an existing practice to advance its interests. What would be the effect on the practices of law, medicine, religion, and marriage if lawyers, doctors, ministers, and spouses could be regularly recruited or coerced into betraying the confidences of their clients, patients, congregations, and partners? Would what be lost in those practices? If the expectations and possible sorts of interactions at the heart of those practices could potentially be twisted beyond recognition, is it possible that because friendship has been so easily co-opted into law-enforcement that we have already built into our practices of friendship certain political distortions? What has been the cost of centuries of pursuing terrorists, revolutionaries, and criminals? The unreflective use of "false friends" erodes privacy and potentially erodes friendship itself.

One way to formulate this objection is by contrasting it to C. S. Lewis's comment that friendships have a subversive, revolutionary quality to them. He writes, "It is . . . easy to see why Authority frowns on Friendship. Every real Friendship is a sort of secession, even a rebellion . . . unwelcome to top people. . . . Each therefore is a pocket of potential resistance. Men who have real Friends are less easy to manage or 'get at;' harder for good Authorities to correct or for bad Authorities to corrupt" (1960:94–95). In contrast, counterfeit friendships in the service of the state have a kind of "counter-revolutionary" character. False friendships may disrupt the possibilities for conspiracies, but in so doing, they may also disrupt and devalue our practices and besmirch the quality of our institutions. If state manipulation of the practices of friendship erodes and distorts our relationships, then it also diminishes the fairness of institutions that are meant to protect our interests and associations from harm.

In response to this objection to the state generation of false friends, it could be argued that within a more or less just system, the creation of false friends would be limited enough so as not to distort the general practices of friendship or seriously diminish the fairness of criminal procedures. Putting to the side the privacy claims, should we still be disturbed by such techniques if they were used moderately? Is there something disturbing about the state's encouraging individuals to engage in insincere forms of self-disclosure and convey false sentiments and feelings toward another in the hope of revealing information? Whatever one may think of the importance of honesty, sincerity, and authenticity, there is something disturbing about cultivating dishonesty, insincerity, and inauthenticity in the false friends themselves. In addition to the harm done to the target (as covered by the privacy claim), we may also want to consider the potential harm done to the informant. Consider, for example, the case of Ernest C. Withers, "one of the most celebrated photographers of the civil rights era." In addition to having taken some of the most important images of the movement, he was also a paid informer for the Federal Bureau of Investigation. When this information was revealed after his death, it raised questions about his legacy. As reported in a *New York Times* article on September 13, 2010, "Civil rights leaders have responded to the revelation with a mixture of dismay, sadness and disbelief. 'If this is true, then Ernie abused our friendship,' said the Rev. James M. Lawson Jr., a retired minister who organized civil rights rallies throughout the South in the 1960s." Whether Withers needed the money to help support his family or believed that the information he gave did no harm, it is likely that he knew that his actions would severely trouble and disappoint his friends. Julian Bond, a founder of the Student Nonviolent Coordinating Committee noted, "We know some people in the movement were informants. I grew up in a political culture in which an informant—somebody who told on his friends—was the lowest form of life."[13]

The Withers example, it could be argued, is not a case of the moderate reliance on false friends insofar as the FBI observation of the civil rights movement's membership was inappropriate. Still, the example raises an important question regarding the effect of this technique not only on the practice itself, but also on the informant and the individuals being spied upon. The use of state power to manipulate friendship is disturbing and requires caution and oversight. It is a power that is easily abused, but given the nature of friendship, not so easily regulated. The less the state is involved in the generation of false friends, the greater the opportunity for true ones. But friendship is not the only thing of value, and not all true friendships are worthy of being protected and respected.

REMOVING BARRIERS TO FRIENDSHIP

If by setting up barriers to association, reinforcing forms of domination, or producing false friends, the state makes things more difficult for practices of friendship, then it makes sense to consider whether the state, by breaking down barriers, forms of domination, and refraining from producing false friends, may indirectly encourage friendships.[14] Given the character of friendship set out in chapter 1, the word *indirect* is important here. Individuals must act as friends and they must recognize the proper forms of motivations in each other in order for friendship to exist. To increase the space for friendship on this account may mean nothing more than removing or, at least, refusing to sanction certain obstacles that prevent individuals from associating with one another or reading their sentiments and reasons. In this regard, the indirect cultivation of friendships amounts to nothing more than removing obstacles and sometimes facilitating the ability of individuals to do what they want. For example, to the extent that forms of segregation based on race, gender, ethnicity, caste, and class can preclude or at least set up impediments to the establishment of friendships across these divides, the law can be used more or less effectively to remove barriers restricting where people live, receive an education, work, play, eat, and sleep. As such, the indirect cultivation of friendship is largely folded into laws and policies that increase the scope and value of negative freedom. Once again, such actions should not be understood as ensuring or guaranteeing that individuals who had been treated unequally will be friends.

THE VALUE AND FRAGILITY OF FRIENDSHIP

Should the state be doing more than removing barriers or hindering the hindrances to friendship? Answering this question depends, first, on whether friendship is of significant importance and, second, on whether law and policy can cultivate it in a more positive manner. The second point forms the focus of the sections that follow. Here, I want to return briefly to the first point regarding the social value of friendship. Chapter 2 broached the question of the justification of the practice of friendship. There, the claim was made that if it is a prima facie good thing for human beings to act upon their desires and feelings, then it is a good thing for friendships to exist. It was also argued that because friendships add to or intensify adverbial conditions that we already hold in high regard, our practices of friendship should also be held in high regard. This line of argument was further explored and defended in the form of a "relations view" in which friendship itself can provide reasons for action. Friendship is both intrinsically and instrumentally valuable. In addition to these arguments, friendship also falls under the interests that individuals have to associate freely with whomever they please. To the extent that joining and departing from such associations is worthy of protection, then friendship will also be worthy of protection.

From this perspective, friendship is important politically and legally because human associations in their various manifestations are understood as goods.

Others, of course, have made a stronger claim regarding the value and importance of friendship. Aristotle wrote, "Without friends no one would choose to live, though he had all other goods" (1985:1155a5). Leib follows suit endorsing Sarah Stroud's claim that friendship is an "indispensable component of a good life" (Stroud 2006:518; Leib 2007:653). Supporting this position, Leib argues that friendship is important to the development and maintenance of our sense of identity, that it confirms our "sense of social and moral worth," that it is good for our mental and physical health, that it is an important source of emotional and financial aid, and that it can "inspire innovation and creativity" (2011:38–39). These sorts of claims make friendship a universal good and hence (from this perspective) worthy of state protection and promotion.

It would be difficult to argue that friendship is not a widely valued human relationship. Nevertheless, as widely as it is shared, it is not universally seen as indispensable for the good life. Misanthropes and hermits have always appeared willing to forgo the goods of human friendship and fellowship. To say that friendship is an indispensable good is to say that they have failed to live a fully human life. Absent a demonstration that to live alone is to live necessarily a lonely, forlorn existence, the most (and it is still a lot) that can be said is that friendship is important for many, if not most people, valued for both its own sake and for the sake of other things. The value of friendship is not to be found in claims that it is indispensable to a universal conception of the good life or that it can be linked to an ideal of individuality, but that the rich set of social practices that compose friendship are important to most people. For many, friendship is not merely a means to something else, but is itself intrinsically valuable. On the face of it, this is enough to command our attention. But is it enough to support the case for political and legal promotion of friendship?

For those who have argued the case for friendship as a matter of public interest, the claim is sometimes made that not only is friendship a great good, it is, at least in the United States, on the decline (Leib 2011:46). Even as friends play an increasingly important role in our lives, friendships are becoming rare. For example, in 2006, McPherson, Smith-Loving, and Brashears compared survey data from 1985 and 2004 that allowed them to consider whether there have been any changes to the networks of confidants with whom Americans discussed matters of importance. They note that,

> The number of people saying there is no one with whom they discuss important matters nearly tripled. The mean network size decreases by about a third (one confidant), from 2.94 in 1985 to 2.08 in 2004. The modal respondent now reports having no confidant; the modal respondent in 1985 had three confidants. Both kin and non-kin confidants were lost in the past two decades, but the greater decrease of non-kin ties leads to more confidant networks centered on spouses and parents.

> (353)

On the other hand, there is some dispute over the evidence of decline (for a critique of McPherson, Smith-Loving, and Brashears, see Fischer 2009). For example, Hua Wang and Barry Wellman argue that while "panic about the decline of social connectivity is an old story. . . . [t]here has been continuing ethnographic and survey evidence of the abundance of supportive ties with friends and neighbors" (2010:1149).[15] In their study of friendship and internet use, they found that "the average number of friends contacted face-to-face and by phone was substantial early in the decade, and it continued to be substantial. The number of friendships did not decline. Rather, it increased on average between 2002 and 2007 and increased the most for heavy Internet users" (1156).

Assuming the importance of friendship and given the mixed evidence regarding friendship's decline, should the state attempt to protect and promote it more directly? One argument against the state's involvement is that, however valuable friendship may be, the cause of friendship is more likely to benefit from the state's benign neglect than from its engagement. Although she does not support such a position, Laura Rosenbury lays out this case nicely when she writes that benign neglect "creates multidimensional freedom. On one level, the state imposes no obligations on friends; therefore, any obligations arise from the parties themselves. On another level, the state does not privilege one definition of friendship over another. Many types of friendships can develop and coexist, and individual friendships can be fluid and shifting" (2007:203–4). In practice, this benign neglect means that legislators, policy-makers, and courts are generally not cognizant of relationships of friendship in formulating laws and policies and issuing decisions. In the case of the courts, whatever privileges or duties that may be part of a practice of friendship are without legal effect. The norms of a given practice of friendship fall below a threshold of legal enforceability.[16] Some may argue that it is fortunate that such neglect has occurred and thrown matters of friendship into a nonlegal, nonpolitical, private realm.

The response of writers such as Goodrich, Rosenbury, and Leib is that the notion of benign neglect is an illusion. In line with a now familiar set of claims that the state acts in a variety of ways through inaction as much as through action, Rosenbury argues that the state effectively regulates friendship by denying certain benefits to friends (medical leave to take care of friends, hospital visitation rights, certain rights of inheritance). Goodrich argues that in common law, placing friendship and domestic arrangements outside the law, "functions simply to subject amicable agreements to the default rules of equity or, when those fail, to a positive norm of nonenforcement" (2005:56). In effect, he argues that this space that is supposedly free of the law effectively deprives individuals of the "capacity to determine their own obligations" (49). Leib argues that U.S. courts have already referenced, drawn upon, and sought to regulate relationships of friends in their decisions (2011:78–79). In short, there is already an emerging law of friendship.[17] His question, in part, is whether we should rationalize existing case law and promote friendship more directly.

At this point, it is possible for the defenders of a benign neglect point of view to shift their position by arguing that the denials of legal privileges and the lack of legal enforcement of duties is a good thing. Friends should not be understood as fiduciaries; the promises of friends should not be considered contracts; and the rights and privileges associated with kin should not carry over to friends because friends are not kin. But why is it a good thing? Two possibilities will be explored in the next sections: The current state of affairs could be good for individuals who occupy the role of friends and/or it could be good for the practices of friendship. The conclusion that these explorations support is mixed. At the individual level, friendships would most likely be advantaged by the recognition of certain privileges. In contrast, the diversity and fluidity of our practices of friendship could be inhibited by laws that will require defining friendship, establishing when they begin and end, and must, inevitably, focus and elevate what are ordinarily understood as deficient reasons for acting within a friendship. In some respects, then, a law of friendship will be a good thing. In other respects, it may not be so good.

IS THE STATUS QUO GOOD FOR INDIVIDUALS?

A pretty strong case can be made that policies and laws that are purportedly friendship-blind do not serve the interests of individuals. Leib and Rosenbury argue that despite the fact that for many people their friends are more supportive and closer than the members of their family, friends do not have the same privileges as kin. In the United States, friends do not have visitation rights in hospitals, they are not covered by the Medical Leave Act, their communications are not viewed as confidential, and they cannot sue or make medical decisions on one another's behalf. In these sorts of cases, laws and policies stand in the way of the individuals' pursuit of significant interests and goods for reasons that appear either arbitrary or unclear. Far from facilitating human choices and interests, these laws and policies stand in their way.

The legal status quo can harm individuals in other ways. Because many practices of friendship engender a sense of deep trust and loyalty, they create vulnerabilities in which the betrayal of that trust can have significant harmful consequences for the betrayed individual. Leib notes that it is one thing to provide confidential information to an acquaintance with whom there is no expectation that those confidences will be maintained. It is quite another to confide in a friend with whom such expectations exist. To the extent that the courts treat friends like acquaintances or strangers or they see friendships as a relationship that should be free from legal interference, then the avenues for repairing harm that has been caused because a friend took advantage of such confidence are more limited.

Obviously, in situations where friends are advantaged by violating the norms of friendship and the law's remedies are few or difficult to obtain, then the status quo also advantages some individuals at the expense of others. Individuals who have much to gain and little to lose by harming and perhaps losing a friend are benefitted by the current system. The question, then, is not merely whether there are winners and losers, but also whether harms that arise from the betrayal of the norms of friendship should be actionable. The argument that they should not be actionable could be based on the claim that the possibility for such harm is simply part of the game of friendship. Just as we accept the risks of skiing or tennis, the possibility of not living up to the norms of friendship is built into those norms. To some degree, this does make sense. As noted in chapter 3, many practices of friendship have notions of loyalty and forgiveness that incorporate a sense of "give" in the relationship. Within these practices of friendship, the friends expect a certain amount of jostling and disappointment from their friends without undermining the relationship. When injuries occur, friends should (for some practices) be willing to forgive, simply let things slide, or end the relationship and move on.

The norms of loyalty and forgiveness, however, have their limits. While the risks of harm may be part of the game of friendship, accepting those risks does not mean accepting all forms of harm. Betrayals destroy friendships. Real and significant harms can be unforgivable. Not all harms are shielded or absorbed by the practice of friendship. In such instances, the advantages accrued by the betrayal of a friend are deeply unfair. A legal zone of purportedly friendship-blind laws that protects such advantages would also seem to be unfair. The present disposition of policies and laws that affect friendship does not necessarily serve individuals very well.

IS THE STATUS QUO GOOD FOR THE PRACTICES OF FRIENDSHIP?

It could be argued that the conclusion of the previous section is quite enough to support a more positive and conscientious approach to using the law to recognize and support friendship. It may, however, also be useful to consider the consequences of the status quo on the diversity of practices of friendship. At this level, the potential good effects of greater legislative and legal scrutiny are less clear. Although defenders of a law of friendship are well aware of the difficulties associated with recognizing friendship, those difficulties come into sharper focus when one considers not merely the diversity of practices of friendship but the possibility that our practices can change over time. In addition, although the legal recognition of certain rights and privileges can enable our practices of friendship, the legal enforcement of friendship's duties is more of a mixed bag particularly because duties are a deficient motivation for acting within a friendship. Consequently, adding the force of the law to those duties increases the chances that the law will distort our practices of friendship and raises the question of whether the law can play a positive role in protecting or repairing friendships.

What constitutes the status quo may be described as a situation in which there is no standard legal definition within American law of friendship or legal identification of the motivations and forms of self-disclosure that define the practices of friendship. In order for the law to affect friendship positively that lack of standardization would have to be remedied to some degree. The challenge here is not difficult to discern: If the idea of friendship is defined too broadly, then the law will be concerned with relationships that it need not and probably should not regulate. If the definition is too narrow, then the law will unfairly protect some friendships over others. The problem of scope, while significant, is not important enough to argue against the possibility for a law of friendship. In fact, any one of the challenges suggested here is not a conclusive argument against the possibility of greater and more explicit legal recognition of friendship. As noted earlier, the sum of the arguments is that such recognition poses difficult tradeoffs.

THE SCOPE, DIVERSITY, AND MUTABILITY OF FRIENDSHIP

The problems associated with legally defining friendship have been widely recognized. Ethan Leib writes, "We must be careful only to exact special duties and confer special privileges upon those who are friends in a meaningful sense or whose conduct implicates the very institution of friendship" (2007:707). If the law is unable to identify friendships in a clear manner and distinguish them from other sorts of relationships, then the possibility of a coherent law of friendship becomes impossible. Laura Rosenbury notes a similar problem. She writes that when discussing friendship and the law, it is not unusual for her students to argue that "friendship is too amorphous to be subjected to a functional test, because there are too many types of friends, and it is too easy for an individual to claim she is a friend when she in fact is not" (2007:206).

As we saw in the first chapter, friendship can indeed be understood as a diverse set of practices that bear no more than a family resemblance to one another. The idea that interpersonal friendships require both the mutual recognition of an appropriate set of motives plus subscription to a recognized practice of self-disclosure does not, in itself, differentiate friendship from a number of other relationships. Understanding friendship as a family resemblance concept turns on certain recognized practices and motivations that more or less hang together. It is the absence of a set of essential elements to friendship that raises the most difficult challenges to any institutional arrangements that would seek to define friendship.

In making the case for a law of friendship, Leib handles the definitional problem in several ways. He sets out ten characteristics of friendship that might be useful to courts and legislators seeking to protect and promote it. These characteristics are not meant to be "exhaustive, mutually exclusive, or necessary" (2007:642). He claims that relationships of friendship can be understood to be voluntary, intimate, trusting, exclusive, reciprocal, warm, mutually assisting, equal, durable, and able to manage conflict and tension. Recognizing that the list is meant to serve as a heuristic, it is interesting to note that Leib captures elements of friendship that include how friends interact with one another (forms of self-disclosure) and what are frequently identified as appropriate reasons or motivations. For example, intimacy (understood as a confessional tendency), trust, exclusivity, reciprocity, mutual assistance, durability, and conflict management are all forms of self-disclosure in which agents choose to act in a particular way toward one another. In contrast, the feelings of warmth, and an absence of feelings of superiority (equality) could be understood as sentiments associated with friendship, although intimacy and trust may also be included in this category as well. What must be added to Leib's discussion is that these sentiments are mutually recognized.

While he notes elsewhere that affection is "what matters so much in friendship" (2011:28), Leib's list does not include the full range of what I have called the ordinarily appropriate sentiments and motivations (e.g., desire, respect, and care). Still, there is no reason to think that his list could not include them. Such an approach would seem to be consistent with the spirit of his project and his acknowledgment of the organic character of friendship (14). The difficulty is that if friendship is a family resemblance concept, there is no core or essential feature that unites or joins the various practices of friendship. This diversity creates not only a range of motivations and reasons for friendship, but also a range of ways in which individuals can be friends to one another. In order for the law to be cognizant of friendship, it must be able to accommodate friendships that place a premium on intimacies and those that place a premium on doing things together. It must be able to acknowledge friendships in which contact occurs on a daily basis and friendships in which there is infrequent contact. There are a variety of ways to be friends, and the law would have to be flexible enough to recognize them.

In his defense of a law of friendship, Leib argues that there are limits to this sort of accommodation. For example, in his discussion of Aristotle's notion of character-based friendships that turn on the goodness or virtue of the individuals, Leib notes "we do not like our laws taking a stand on who is a good or virtuous person" (2011:33). As it is framed, this is not a claim about friendship, but about a desired characteristic of the law. The implication is that a conception of friendship in which goodness or respect for the excellence of another was the central motive for the friendship would not be legally recognized.[18] Excluding friendships based on goodness would mean that certain privileges available to other sorts of friendships (say hospital visitation rights) would not be available to these sorts of friends.

In Leib's defense it could be argued that friendships based on goodness are rare things in the modern world and hence their exclusion for consideration is not much of a problem. On other hand, it is not impossible to imagine friendships that are based on mutual respect of perceived goodness. Friendships between teachers and students, ministers and congregants or employers to employees could have such a character (and our practices of friendship could change in such a way that these sorts of relationships could come to be seen as an ideal). The fact that these roles are ones of inequality may also be seen as a strike against their qualification as being friendships.[19] Given the importance of respect, the overlay of other social roles, and the existence of inequality, it may be unlikely that these sorts of relationships would be recognized by a law of friendship, but it is not clear (at least to me) whether that would be the correct decision. The larger problem here is that if the law is unwilling or unable to recognize certain forms of friendship, then it will be promoting friendship of a certain sort.

Another example involving the narrowing of friendship can be found in Leib's own discussion of friendship and kinship. He argues, "Friendship is not kinship, and if a relationship is one of kinship, it cannot also be classified as a friendship. Friends may not be related by blood or marriage, and they may not engage in any ongoing sexual relationship (though being ex-lovers is no disqualification at all)" (2011:15–16). While recognizing that there is something "crude" and "contrived" to seeing friendship and kinship as mutually exclusive, Leib argues that not only do we distinguish between kith and kin, but understanding the contributions of friendship to society also requires a clean distinction between the two relationships. In other words, a successful law of friendship requires such a distinction. To further bolster his position, Leib argues that a law of friendship should be distinguished from family law and ongoing debates over the definition of marriage and family and that if friendships are "optimally" considered equal relationships, and familial relationships are frequently unequal, then it may be useful for the law to promote friendships that exist outside of kinship relationships (17–19).

In many respects, Leib's sharp distinction between kinship and friendship is less a matter of principle and more a matter of strategy. He notes, "Some want to use friendship and its legal recognition to disrupt our current policy focus on regulating sex and the family. But I am not optimistic about this strategy and think it threatens the agenda of promoting friendship and ties its fate to a different movement with a different ultimate goal." It is possible that there may be a more inclusive definition of friendship once the law of friendship is firmly established and we give "up on our misguided regulation of sex" (2011:19). During the interim, however, the law will be promoting some forms of friendship over others.

If a sexualized relationship (on Leib's account) would not be understood as a legal friendship, then such a relationship is transformed into a legally unrecognizable relationship: neither spouse, nor stranger, nor acquaintance, nor friend. While "friends with benefits" may mutually recognize the appropriate sentiments of friendship and continue to subscribe to a practice of friendship, Leib's exclusion recreates the very sort of category that a law of friendship was supposed to eliminate: namely a relationship that is regulated by the law by not being regulated by the law.

In addition, the legal recognition of friendships will tend to reflect the views of those with power. In a well-functioning democracy, this will frequently be the views of the majority. If the law promotes certain forms of friendship over others, it will tend to promote those that are more widely shared. In this regard, a danger of the law of friendship is that it will have a normalizing tendency. Still, one could argue, it is better to recognize and accord rights to some friends than no rights to any friends. Accepting this position, however, does not compensate for these risks. The red flags raised by unequal treatment and normalization, however, further support a degree of skepticism.

The arguments raised in the discussion of how well the law would handle the diversity of existing conceptions of friendship also apply to the challenge raised by the fact that the practices of friendship change over time. Perhaps at one time the recognition of mutual usefulness was sufficient for a friendship. That is no longer the case in the early twenty-first-century West. Alternatively, the notion of "friends with benefits" appears to be a relatively recent innovation as friendships between genders is negotiated in a heteronormative society. Can the law respond to changes in the practice of friendship? The short answer is yes. Whether it can change in a timely manner is not so clear. Depending on how well one tolerates the possibility of harms caused by time lags in the laws, the difficulties that U.S. law has had in recognizing changes within our conception of the family is, at best, a mixed message for how it will handle changes in other personal relationships. The danger here is that by directly promoting the current understandings of friendship, the law will indirectly discourage the emergence of new forms of friendship. The argument is not that a law of friendship as conceived by Leib and others would prohibit the emergence of new practices, but that it may have a chilling effect on those practices. In this case, the conservative tendencies of the law may have adverse consequences for innovation. Once again, this danger adds to a sense of caution in approaching a law of friendship.

THE LEGAL EMPHASIS ON DEFICIENT REASONS: RIGHTS AND PRIVILEGES

Assuming that the law can adequately handle the definitional questions in a manner that does not adversely affect the practices of friendship, what would be the possible effect of elevating the importance of rights and duties? Chapter 3 argued that duties play a complicated role in our practices of friendship. Unlike those who argue that they are an essential element to friendship and unlike those who argue that they have no place in friendship, I argued that duties are at best a deficient reason for acting within the relationship: If duty is the only reason why one is acting for or with one's friend, then something is awry in the relationship. Consequently, chapter 3 argued that when they are deployed within a friendship, duties can be used to signal that something is wrong. Similarly, claims can be made with regard to rights. Rights deployed on behalf of one's friends look different from rights deployed against one's friends. The complexity of the place of our duties in the practices of friendship is complicated by the possibility that even though their deployment within the relationship is problematic, they can be used to assert a certain urgency against competing claims made by third parties. If duties and rights of friendship acquire the force of law, they may have a distorting effect on our practices of friendship.

Let me expand further. As at the individual level, the legal protection of privileges against third parties could have a favorable effect on the practices of friendship. Leib, for example, proposes giving friends a number of different types of legally protected privileges: informality, caregiving, privacy, and vindicating the rights of one's friends (2007:694–705). To the extent that such privileges create obligations on the part of the friends, they raise issues considered herein. But not all of these privileges create duties between friends. If, for example a "Friends and Family Medical Leave Act" were created, then the privilege to care for a friend need not be understood as a duty to care. Such a privilege, however, would expand the available forms of self-disclosure and open up important avenues to express one's feelings of friendship for another. In this way, such a right to care for one's friends would advance both the interests of the friends and strengthen those practices of friendship in which care is central.

Could providing friends the privilege of privacy further enable the practices of friendship? One could make a strong case that the values of openness and honesty, in addition to the self-disclosive character of friendship could be enhanced through such a privilege. Obviously, extending the sorts of privacy rights found in other relationships (spousal, medical, religious) to friendships would also make law enforcement more difficult.[20] Whatever that tradeoff may entail, the rights of confidentiality would have to apply only to those sorts of friendships in which there was an expectation of confidentiality. From this perspective, the courts are mistaken in thinking that because there exists a friendship, there are no such expectations. It would also, however, be a mistake to think that all friendships entail confidentiality or even the same level of confidentiality. Even if a case can be made that friendship is benefited through the protection of privilege, not all practices of friendship have the same privileges. To be true to the particular features of friendship requires that the law offer different levels of protection to different sorts of friendship—potentially encouraging some forms of friendship and not others.

It is just as important to note that the effects of legally protecting the privileges of friendship may not all be favorable. For example, if the creation of rights of friendship also created a more general expectation that those rights would be exercised when the time comes, would that be better than the current situation? If friends have rights to take medical leave to care for friends, would the practices of friendship increasingly include the expectation that such leaves be taken? Perhaps. Alternatively, the existence of such rights of friendship may lead friends to be clearer about the sort of friendships they have. That is to say, at some point the friends would discuss the character and expectations associated with their friendship, perhaps asking what they would expect the other to do if one of them was seriously injured or ill. At one point in his discussion of legal duties of friendship (see the next section), Leib notes the value of such clarity (2011:179). In many respects, this position is admirable. In other respects, however, it forces clarification on a relationship that can change quite dramatically over time. It is possible that care-giving friends may prove to be not up to the task while less intimate friends rise to the occasion. Clarifying a friendship may be perfectly appropriate, but the existence of a legal right may also settle and solidify particular relationships that may be very fluid.[21] In addition, such a norm of clarification would undoubtedly have consequences for the adverbial conditions of many different sorts of friendships. In this society, the idea of such a conversation's being understood as an expectation of the friendship would not necessarily be entirely welcome.

THE LEGAL EMPHASIS ON DEFICIENT REASONS: DUTIES

The possibility of legally enforceable duties of friendship raises more difficult questions. One way to express these duties is in terms of a fiduciary relationship. Leib explores the possibility that close friendships could be evidence of a relationship of trust in which the parties have certain legally enforceable obligations toward one another. For example, if an individual confides to a close friend about an idea for a business which is then used by the friend to her advantage, this may be framed as a breach of a fiduciary relationship. The idea of a close friend as fiduciary captures an ordinary sense of loyalty that could be violated by a friend (Leib 2011:150). For purposes of exposition, it will be useful to rehearse briefly Leib's account of how friendships can be understood in contractual terms and then consider how the view of friendship offered in these pages can be related to that account.

To understand how friends could be seen as fiduciaries, it is important to understand a few of the key elements of fiduciary relationships. One of those elements is that the powers of the fiduciary are not used for the fiduciary's benefit, but for the benefit of her beneficiary (Leib 2011:112–13). Self-interest is put to the side and loyalty to the other is elevated to a duty. Second, the fiduciary is required to perform her duties with "reasonable diligence and prudence" (113). In addition to duties of loyalty and care, fiduciaries also have duties of candor and disclosure, confidentiality, and good faith (113–14). Central to these relationships is a very high level of trust and an understanding that the beneficiary is the vulnerable party in the relationship (116). Ordinarily, relationships such as "attorney-client, corporate director-shareholder, trustee-beneficiary, managing partner-partner, agent-principle, employee-employer, guardian-ward, and physician-patient" are viewed as fiduciary relationships. In this regard, Leib's central recommendation is that "courts take seriously claims by close friends that certain types of betrayals should be treated as breaches of fiduciary duties and remediated accordingly" (119). As he notes, to some degree this has already happened in American case law.

In the case of friendships that are not close, Leib suggests that those "somewhat weaker ties can be illuminated by the idea of the relational contract" (2011:150). Very briefly, relational contract theory argues that contractual relationships need not all be understood as between strangers, but in many cases, should be understood like a marriage: namely an arrangement that is already situated in a complex relational web that is, in many respects, both unique to the parties and governed by social expectations. Such contracts are entwined in a set of social norms that are informal, open, costly to exit, and presume a good faith and the best efforts of the parties. Even though they are contractual relationships, the law stands to the side when the relationship is working to the satisfaction of the parties. As in the case of a marriage, the ordinary motivations, norms, and expectations of the parties guide them through their day-to-day trials and tribulations. We can still talk about legal duties and rights within a marriage, but those rights and duties enter the scene only when something is going wrong. For example, the parties may turn to law "on the dissolution of the relationship or on a substantial breach of an agreement evidencing betrayal or opportunism." In such cases, "seeking remedies at law is not altogether uncommon, and the law will have to find a way to resolve such disputes" (152). Once again, it is not the threat of legal sanctions that motivates the parties as they act within a working relationship. Nevertheless, the existence of legally enforceable obligations can be of enormous significance if the relationship is falling or has fallen apart.

In employing the idea of relational contracts, Leib writes, "Friendships and relational contracts have several basic structural features in common. In both types of relationships, there is an understanding that parties contemplate a long-term endeavor to fulfill shared goals that will enhance their welfare" (2011:150). Moreover, we enter both sorts of relationships without "fully knowing what we shall be called on to do" (151). Although the analogy to relational contracts is not perfect, Leib argues that it helps us get a better sense of the difficulty of specifying our obligations within a friendship and why compliance to those underspecified and vague duties is generally left up to social norms and sanctions (153). We need not understand all friendships as contractual to understand that it is possible to see how legally enforceable duties could be consonant with very complicated, personal, socially regulated relationships. Leib argues that relational contract theory illuminates the claim that legally enforceable duties may be possible between friends.[22]

In *Friend v. Friend*, Leib responds to a wide variety of objections and potential criticisms to viewing friendship as either a fiduciary relationship or as a relational contract. Instead of reviewing those arguments and the cogency of Leib's response, the remaining sections of this chapter will consider how the perspective on friendship developed in chapter 3 informs the larger question of the legal enforcement of duties and privileges. On the one hand, the discussion of duties and (to a lesser extent) rights in that chapter reinforces the plausibility of Leib's argument in important respects. On the other hand, it suggests that if we take seriously the legal enforceability of duties of friendship, we should do so with the awareness that the law may shape and potentially constrain our practices in significant ways.

One of the lessons of chapter 3 is that there is nothing inherently inconsistent about associating rights and duties with friendship. By claiming that duties were deficient reasons for acting within a friendship, I argued that they may serve as reasons for acting within a friendship as long as they were accompanied by what are understood to be the ordinarily appropriate motivations of friendship. Similarly, claims of utility and self-interest are also deficient reasons for acting within a friendship (at least in the contemporary West). They too can serve as reasons for action within a friendship as long as they are attended by ordinarily appropriate motivations. These conclusions are consonant with a number of features of Leib's position. In particular, Leib correctly points out that friendships "routinely engage in both altruistic and selfish reasoning all the time" (2011:184). As Leib notes, the reasons associated with friendship will "sometimes compete with and sometimes complement other reasons" (185), including those reasons associated with duty. Leib's position is that the simple presence of self-interest or duty within a friendship relationship does not debase the friendship. For the most part, our practices of friendship can quite easily incorporate notions of self-interest and duty. These earlier arguments support Leib's conclusions that neither duty nor self-interest need crowd out the ordinary sentiments of friendship.

Understanding duty as a deficient reason for action is compatible with another aspect of Leib's approach. The tenor of his argument is that even if the duties of friendship are legally recognized, the social norms surrounding friendship are more likely to govern the actions of the friends than the fact that the law is present in the relationship (2011:188). Leib suggests that the heavy hand of the law, because it rests on reasons that are not the primary motives for acting within a friendship, is unlikely to be much of a concern in an ongoing friendship. In support of this claim, the deficient character of duty helps account for why the legal weight of duty would play a less intrusive role than what critics may surmise. As deficient reasons, duties (or self-interest) cannot be the central motivating factor in a friendship. In further support of Leib's arguments, the analysis of chapter 3 suggests that the ordinarily appropriate motivations of friendship plus the adverbial, self-disclosive norms of action that constitute our practices of friendship are more significant than the presence of duties.

Despite these areas of agreement, the idea that acting from duty is a deficient reason complicates Leib's argument in a few ways. First, because deficient reasons cannot bear the full weight of a friendship, the absence of the ordinarily appropriate motives of friendship signals that something is going or has gone awry with the relationship. In the extreme, it could mean that the friendship has collapsed. If John is acting solely because of his perceived fiduciary responsibility to Henry and the ordinary motivations of friendship have evaporated, then it is possible that the friendship has also collapsed. If Henry uses the language of friendship to try to get John to act a particular way (perhaps be less morose and bitter), that may have little effect on John. The practical problem here is not necessarily the difficulty of proving the existence of a friendship in the past (although this may be difficult enough), but that the acquisition of additional legally enforceable duties may require that friends be quite clear when the friendship is over—a moment that may not be easily identified by the parties themselves (unlike identifying the legal ending of a marriage). In this case, John himself may not be certain of his motivations and if John is uncertain, that may be true of Henry's perception of John.

In general, the practices of friendship do not have fully developed norms regarding the breakup of the relationship. Clearly, friendships are sometimes lost out of betrayal or some other dramatic event and in those instances one party may announce the termination of the relationship. As a gross generalization, however, it appears that in contemporary Western cultures that sort of situation is relatively rare. In most cases, friendships simply fade away or fall into a kind of limbo or suspended animation. In some cases, these moribund friendships are gone forever. In other cases, they are given new life, such as when we become reacquainted with someone we have not seen for years.

As noted earlier, Leib welcomes the possibility of friends being clear on where they stand with one another. But how often do we need to check-in with our friends and acknowledge our friendships? If we may tacitly break off our friendships, what would be signs and symbols of such a breakup? Absent such norms and expectations within our practices, the law would come to shape them, at least around the edges. If this is true, it is not clear that legally enforceable duties of friendship would be an improvement over our current, albeit amorphous, practices.

What is true of the endings of friendships is also true of their beginnings. Once again, as a gross generalization, most Western practices of friendship do not have norms in which friends signal to one another the beginning of a friendship or identify the sort of friendship that it is or has become. There is no first date, first kiss, pronouncement of love, or any of the other complicated ceremonies associated with a romance. When does a mere acquaintance become a friend? At what point have friends mutually recognized the appropriate motivations of friendship? Would the potential for legal liability eventually shape and standardize our practices of friendship such that we would announce more conclusively their beginnings? Would the beginning of the relationship also require that the parties clarify the sort of friendship they have entered? Once again, we may know a friendship when we are in one and we may understand the sort of duties associated with that kind of relationship once it is up and running, but our practices of friendship are fuzzy in their beginnings and endings, and blurry with regard to what is and what is not a friendship (assuming that it is a family resemblance concept). If there is to be a coherent law of friendship, it would have to rationalize, shape, and delineate our practices of friendship.

A second complication of according the deficient reasons of friendship with legal status is connected to the ability of duties to signal to third parties the importance of the relationship. When Greg says that he cannot keep his promise to Cuddy because he needs to attend to his friend Wilson, the deployment of the friendship-duty-card is meant to justify his actions to someone who could potentially interfere. If some duties of friendship become legally enforceable, it would add public weight to the deployment of that card. This added weight may be all to the good, but it may also have consequences for our practices of friendship. For example, once elevated to a legal duty, a requirement of friendship could come into conflict with legal requirements to employers, spouses, and offspring. Legally enforceable duties would not exist in a vacuum and would eventually have to be balanced off against other duties. This argument is not an argument against duties of friendship, but it does suggest that the process of balancing those duties becomes a legal question as opposed to merely a personal challenge. As with everything about friendship, our practices of friendship vary significantly regarding how much is owed to our friends versus how much is owed to others—family, employees, compatriots. The practices of friendship could lose their flexibility vis-à-vis these other relationships if the law must seek to settle their priority. Once again, rationalizing that variation may not necessarily be an improvement in our practices of friendship.

A third complication of establishing legally enforceable duties of friendship is that it could alter the adverbial character of our practices. Chapters 1 and 2 argued that our practices of friendship can be characterized not by specific performances but by certain expectations we have regarding *how* friends will do the things they do. Self-disclosure in friendship is primarily adverbial and not substantive. In contrast, it is not difficult to imagine the law looking toward specific actions and performances of the parties, when it seeks to enforce an obligation: for example, focusing on this or that specific action as opposed to how something was done. Such a focus would alter the tenor of friendship, creating the image of friendship as a lading-list rather than as a loosely arranged set of adverbial conditions. While we may be obliged not to do certain things to our friends, the law may require specific actions be taken. Whether good or bad, the law, once again, would affect our practices.

A final complication of giving legal weight to the duties of friendship is that the deployment of claims associated with duties could rarely serve as a *pharmacon*. Chapter 3 suggested that when one friend demands from another to provide what is owed because she has a duty to do so, it may either poison the relationship or remind the friend of what is important and repair the relationship. In this respect, the deployment of the language of duty is compatible with an ongoing practice of friendship that will either survive or go under. It is not clear that the deployment of legal duties within a troubled friendship could play a similar role. Threatening to sue a friend for breach of obligation would probably poison a friendship more effectively than the deployment of a moral duty. If moral duties have a "use in the case of emergency" character to them, legal duties have a "use when necessary to bury a friendship" character.

If it is unlikely that they could play the role of a *pharmacon*, then what is the purpose of establishing legally enforceable obligations? Leib is somewhat ambivalent about the purpose of state enforcement of the duties of friendship. On the one hand, he suggests that the state could play a positive role in knitting together a friendship that was in trouble. He writes, "Rather than seeing the law as interposing in a broken friendship that was, the law can treat parties as incomplete friends on the process of becoming. Thus unlike the posture that the law takes in divorce—a place where the law clearly steps in only upon rupture—within friendship, reconciliation could be a presumptive goal" (2007:682). On the other hand, he argues that legal intervention where friends see themselves as fiduciaries may be less a tool of reconciliation and more an indicator that the relationship has ended. Leib notes, "Indeed . . . [a] suit [involving the legal enforcement of fiduciary obligations] is pretty strong evidence that the friendship is beyond repair" (2009:731; 2011:188).[23]

In this latter case, enforcing obligations of friendship now looks more like the case of divorce. In divorce, the state's interests are driven by the interests of children (if there are any) and the entanglement of lives and property that the marriage has created. It would be a stretch to think that the point of the divorce proceeding would be to reconcile the parties and repair the marriage (although this may sometimes happen). If legally enforceable obligations are part of friendships, it is unlikely that the state's interest is that of reconciliation and the reestablishment of the relationship. In this sense, legal obligations are compatible within an ongoing friendship as long as they are not called upon. When they come to the surface and are employed by the parties against one another, then the game is over. The problem is not that legal obligations would debase or crowd out the motivations of friendship, but that their explicit use would signal the end of the relationship. In this sense, actually calling forth a legal obligation is the death knell of the friendship.

In sum, what work could the presence of legal obligations do in our various practices of friendship? In an existing friendship they are a reminder to the friends that people change, that life is complicated, and that sometimes friendships end. In such cases, getting friends to do what they would have done if their friendship had continued may be an important way to secure the interests of one or both parties. In addition, legally enforceable obligations can give greater public weight to the needs and desires of the friends vis-à-vis third party claims. But between the friends they are, at best, deficient reasons for actions—a poison that sits on the shelf when the friends are interacting as friends—that cannot repair but only signal the end of the relationship. Moreover, despite the fact that the poison sits on the shelf, it would have potential consequences for how we end or do not end our friendships. Unlike the case for enforcing privileges or rights, it is not at all clear that the enforcement of obligations would promote friendships, although it would serve to protect and remedy the harms done to individuals who have been injured by the betrayal of a friendship. This is not an argument about the law's muddying the communications of our motives, but one about the role that legal obligations can play in repairing or promoting friendships.[24]

A law of friendship would probably have a very mixed effect on the practices of friendship. In the case of granting legal friends a right to care for one another and protecting their confidences, the effect would probably be favorable for both the individual and the general practices of friendship. In the case of legal duties, the effect would be favorable for individuals but probably not for our practices. At best, the legal enforcement of duties would signal the end of a friendship, overriding whatever "give" may be part of the relationship and protecting more clearly the specific interests of the individuals concerned. Moreover, the ability of the law to capture the diversity and mutuality of friendships as well as the motives of individuals is also not so clear. At the very least, these sorts of problems suggest that the case for a law of friendship is not an unmitigated good and it would not be an unmitigated bad. To some degree, this position comes close to Wilson Cary McWilliams's claim that while governments are "too clumsy to promote friendship directly, they can at least be friendly to friendship."[25] Surely, it can do so by hindering the hindrances to friendship and carefully treading the ground of providing legally enforceable rights and obligations.

PART *three*

eight

FRIENDSHIP AND *FRIEND* IN AN INTERNATIONAL CONTEXT

The idea that nations should love one another, or that business concerns or marketing boards should love one another or that a man in Portugal should love a man in Peru of whom he has never heard—it is absurd, unreal, dangerous. . . . The fact is we can only love what we know personally. And we cannot know much.

—E. M. FORSTER, *TWO CHEERS FOR DEMOCRACY* (1938)

In thinking about international friendships, one inevitably considers the importance of personal relationships to international politics. The complex and complicated friendships of Roosevelt and Churchill, Reagan and Gorbachev, and Bush and Blair raise important questions regarding the significance of the personal to the political. In part, these questions involve standard problems of how much individual decision-makers and their relationships make a difference for the actions of states or other corporate actors (a variation of what Kenneth Waltz called first-image explanations of international relations). They also raise interesting problems of how expectations created by relationships of personal friendship are negotiated vis-à-vis a set of public, official roles as well as the transcultural understandings and misunderstandings that attend interpersonal friendship. At a conceptual level, however, the issues surrounding personal friendships in the international sphere are not unique to international affairs. Consequently, clarifying the place of personal relationships can be an important, if understudied, element of international politics, but here we shall focus on the relationship between political associations or states.[1]

As noted in the introduction, the topic of interstate friendship is warranted in part by the centuries' long use of amity and friendship in the rhetoric of international affairs (Roshchin 2006, 2014; Schwarzenbach 2009:255; Devere, Mark, and Verbitsky 2011; Devere 2014).[2] City-states, kingdoms, and nations have seen themselves and other regimes as friends (as well as neutral parties and enemies) since Thucydides. The focus of part 3, however, is not to report how these terms have been used or are being currently employed, but to explore whether international friendship (as shall be defended in chapter 9) is possible within the context of state interactions. In pursuing that question, certain generalizations will be made regarding the predominant understanding of how states are said to be friends, but that understanding will merely provide one piece of the argument. The goal is to see what is implied by that conventional understanding that points beyond itself. The concept of international friendship that will be offered, then, may turn out to be nothing more than a possibility, although I believe that there are interstate relationships that can help illustrate its character.

The heart of the argument is that if states are justified in seeking to protect themselves and their own interests, then those same reasons can carry over to the protection of other states. Paradoxically, justified national self-interest also justifies international friendship of a sort that goes beyond self-interest or utility (and vice versa as we shall see in chapter 9). Unlike the first two parts of this book, which attempted to understand the complexity of the practices of interpersonal friendship and how that complexity is related to politics, this part argues that friendship of a more robust sort is implied by the current practices of justifying state action, but may itself not be part of the actual practice of international politics.[3]

The argument proceeds along the following lines: Chapter 8 begins by setting out some assumptions and by exploring the connection between self-interest and friendship that is sometimes made in discussing international politics. It argues that although friendships of self-interest or utility are important forms of international cooperation, those uses of the terms *friend* and *friendship* imply relationships that are little more than alliances or partnerships (however complex they may be). A similar argument is made regarding Carl Schmitt's distinction between friends and enemies. The last part of this chapter uses Rawls's (1999) work in *Law of the Peoples* as a way to open up the discussion that states could have reasons to act that move beyond narrow self-interest. Where Rawls seeks to establish the reasonableness of a law of peoples, chapter 8 concludes by suggesting that reasons of self-interest can connect more or less just states in relationships of friendship.

Chapter 9 presents an account of international friendship by employing Jennifer Whiting's interpretation of friendship in Aristotle. Just as Aristotle sees character as the basis for a virtuous form of friendship, the quality of the internal institutional arrangements of another state could serve as a reason for state cooperation. The mutual recognition of such motivations can serve as the basis for what I will call "international friendships of character." Finally, chapter 10 situates this conception of international friendship in the logic of an anarchic state system that was one of self-help. It responds to a set of objections that have been and can be made to the view of international friendship presented here and concludes by employing the work of Jacques Derrida to suggest ways in which international friendship would itself generate forms of political disagreement and contestation simply because states could be friends.

SOME ASSUMPTIONS

To theorize international friendship, I will begin with a couple of assumptions. First, the phrase *international friendship* will refer solely to the relationship between states, and states will be understood as sovereign entities governing mutually recognized territories and constituted by institutions and practices.[4] Relationships between states are maintained or lost by human beings who occupy offices and positions. Although these office holders are flesh and blood individuals who have personal relationships to one another, those personal connections exist alongside their public identities as office holders. In acting on behalf of the state, their corporate roles structure and define what counts as a reason for action (Wheeler 2000:22–23). Consequently, whatever the character of friendship that existed between the former British prime minister Tony Blair and the American president George W.

Bush, our political vocabulary also includes a notion of friendship between Great Britain and the United States. Moreover, the latter sorts of relationships are not reducible to the former, although they can certainly suffer or flourish in the light of interpersonal relationships.

A second assumption is that the practices of self-enactment and sentiment-laden motives that are central to interpersonal friendship do not pertain to interstate friendship. The sorts of motives that ordinarily serve as the basis for interpersonal friendship simply do not apply insofar as entities such as states lack and cannot possess an emotional life. States do not have felt desires, affections, or care for other states in the way that individuals can and do have for each other. In other words, I will presume that E. M. Forster had it just about right in the quotation cited at the beginning of this chapter. [5]

Before proceeding, however, it is important to note that this skeptical assumption is one that a number of scholars would contest. From one perspective, Simon Keller (2009) presents a sustained critique of the idea of friendship between countries. In large part, it is based on the same sort of argument that was just presented, but concludes that because states cannot make the sorts of emotional commitments that individuals can make nor engage in the sorts of ordinary activities in which friends engage, then it is mistaken to employ the idea of friendship in an international context. In making this claim, Keller's assumption is that the language game of friendship is solely played out in the interpersonal realm. Our ordinary talk about states being friends and having friendships is not to be taken seriously. In response, I suggest that because the use of "friendship" is so broad and the practices of friendship (even at an individual level) are so diverse, we should not dismiss uses of the term at the international level. More strongly, that the notions of friend and friendship are so much a part of our talk in international relationship gives us warrant to explore the existing and possible meanings of the terms.[6]

From another perspective, Lucile Eznack and Simon Koschut state that my assumption of states not having affect is "misguided" (2014:75). They argue that affect and emotion can and do play a role in the relations between states. In their favor is the undeniable fact that we frequently talk of states being angry, hateful, satisfied, unsatisfied, hopeful, disappointed, and so on, all of which suggest that feelings of friendship could exist.[7] In addition, thinkers such as Larry May (1987), Peter French (1984), Trudy Govier (2002), and Margaret Gilbert (2000) all provide (different) accounts of how groups can be understood as responsible moral agents with reasons, desires, intentions, and perhaps the sentiments of friendship.

Despite arguments to the contrary, the discussion of these chapters will proceed on the assumption that states do not experience affect and when they are said to do so, the expression is either metaphorical, meant to signal or predict future actions, or a shorthand way for how large numbers of individuals, policymakers, or elites feel. Addressing Eznack and Koschut's criticism, however, helps clarify the argument of these chapters. To start, it is not entirely clear whether their position does reject the skeptical view that states (understood in a particular way) are incapable of experiencing emotions and affect. In other work that explores the role of affect and emotion in the relationships between allies, Eznack writes, "The argument that affect exists in close allies' relationships does not entail that states, as abstract entities, experience affect" (2011:242). If, by "abstract entities," Eznack means seeing states as a set of institutional arrangements, rules, and practices, then her own discussion does not seek to attribute affect and emotion to such entities. If affect plays a role in international politics, it must ultimately be connected back to human agents who are capable of experiencing emotion (i.e., decision-makers acting as the state). She goes on to note:

> Nor does this argument imply that affect is subject to the personal affinities of decision makers. In fact, affective attachment to specific interstate relationships is part of a given state's culture and practice of foreign policy, and it is internalized and reproduced by the individuals in charge. In this sense, when I describe a state as being affectively attached to its relationship with another one, I mean decision makers acting as the state.
>
> (242)

From Eznack's perspective, those decision-makers internalize emotional responses to other regimes via the culture and practices within which they work. International friendship becomes a matter of the right affect lining up in specific individuals in the right direction towards another state. Eznack and Koschut do not view states "only as abstract corporate actors, but also as entities represented by individuals, who act and feel as the state" (2014:73).

In considering the role of affect, they are seeking to capture forms of state behavior that other models of state behavior either ignore or do not describe very well.[8]

In contrast, the project of these chapters is more normative and speculative.[9] The goal is less a matter of explaining current state behavior and more a matter of asking what international friendship could entail to be consistent with the value (whatever that may be) we accord to the state. More important differences involve what is meant by a state and whether the idea of friendship is meaningful without some notion of affect. In the former case, even if our understanding of the state can include a reference to individuals who act and feel in certain ways (as Eznack and Koschut suggest), it is not clear that it must include such a reference. After all, we seem to be able to use the word *friendship* in international contexts absent the experience of affect and absent the recognition of such affect in others. This appears to be especially true in the case of strategic alliances. Such alliances can exist between countries even though the relevant policymakers dislike one another.

The more difficult question is whether a conception of friendship can meaningfully apply to states as "abstract entities." These chapters presume that the institutional arrangements and rules that compose states establish norms and expectations for how those who occupy the offices of state should act (offices, here, include high office as well as the office of being a citizen). These norms and expectations may be deeply internalized by decision-makers or they may be compartmentalized into a set of roles that are distinguishable from the other roles and positions an individual may occupy. In addition, states have interests apart from the specific interests of specific individuals who hold office. We talk of such interests because there are conditions which are more or less favorable for securing, maintaining, or expanding the institutional arrangements that constitute states (as well as the offices we hold). Terms such as *interest*, *self-interest*, and *reason* are the constructions of rules, procedures, practices, and institutions. States and countries are, of course, much more than these abstractions, but they are also these odd constructions that have interests, purposes, goals, and policies that they can pursue more or less rationally or more or less reasonably. In doing so, states can be said to "act"; be bound by conventions, treaties, and agreements; go to war; and sue for peace.

The idea that states, understood as abstract entities, can have interests and act in the world opens the possibility for understanding international friendship in a way that differs from interpersonal friendship. One of those differences involves the absence of affect as motivating international friendships between such entities. Another difference is that utility or material self-interest can serve as sufficient reasons for friendships between states, whereas they are deficient reasons for motivating interpersonal friendships (as was discussed in part 1). This second difference serves as the starting point for this chapter.

Before proceeding, however, it is important to note that on these matters, as with all matters of friendship, it is difficult to say anything about friendship without first mentioning Aristotle. Even in trying to understand the role of friendship in the relationship between polities, Aristotle's big feet have already trodden the ground. He writes, "For people include among friends . . . those who are friends for utility, as cities are—since alliances between cities seem to aim at expediency" (1985:1157a25–30). Without a doubt, this remains the predominant understanding of how polities or states can be friends; namely, they are useful to one another. But is this understanding of interstate friendship particularly interesting? Does it employ the notions of *friend* and *friendship* in ways that are any different from how we use the words *ally* and *partner*? If not, then a discussion of interstate friendships of utility can simply be subsumed under our current understandings of alliances and alignments. International friendship is just old wine in an old bottle. I will argue, however, that within the idea of state self-interest (in particular, as applied to more or less just states) is also the possibility for a notion of friendship that goes beyond mere utility. In other words, states, as abstract entities, can have reason to act beyond a narrow understanding of self-interest. It is this possibility that can serve as a basis for international friendship and cooperation that rests on reasons of justice.

FRIENDSHIPS OF UTILITY

For the most part, by describing an interstate relationship as a friendship of utility, the word *friendship* can easily be substituted for *alliance* or *partnership*, whether those relationships are security-related or economic. In other words, the word *friendship* is not doing much independent labor. But it is doing some work. I want to suggest that even in their self-interested forms, *friend* and *friendship* help frame (or construct) interstate relations in a couple of ways. First, as noted by Aristotle, there is something inherently unstable about friendships solely grounded in utility. In such cases, the friendship does not establish the parties' interests, rather the parties' interests establish their friendship. Consequently, if those interests change or if they can be more adequately served through some other means, then the relationship will be reassessed and sometimes abandoned. To the extent that cities or states are seen as friends of utility, this already implies that their relationship will have a potentially unstable character (in chapter 10, following Derrida, I suggest that things get more interesting when the perceptions of the parties differ over the character of their relationship). In an important sense, state actors know this to be true when they call each other friends. In other words, the predominant vision of friendship in international affairs reinforces the fluidity and ever-present possibility for realignment if not betrayal that is found in realism's account of the balance of power.

Paradoxically, the iconic expression of the fluidity found at the heart of utility-based friendships is the frequently misquoted nineteenth-century statement of British foreign policy by Lord Palmerstone: "We have no eternal allies, and we have no perpetual enemies. Our interests are eternal and perpetual, and those interests it is our duty to follow" (1848; see also Wolfers 1962:27). The misquotation usually takes the form of "We have no eternal friends." The implication of Palmerstone's quote is not merely that England will look after itself (this is its "eternal" interest), but in doing so, it will find its friends wherever it may and repel its enemies whoever they happen to be. For realists, this understanding of international friendship reinforces the idea that allies should do no more than "befriend" one another as the times require. Entangling alliances sustained by enduring, open-ended commitments are an anathema to this conception of a state-to-state friendship. A more recent example of this sort of fluidity can be found in former Secretary of Defense Robert M. Gates's account of why the embarrassing leak of thousands of confidential American diplomatic cables will make little difference to American allies: "governments deal with the United States because it's in their interest, not because they like us, not because they trust us, and not because they believe we can keep secrets. Many governments—some governments—deal with us because they fear us, some because they respect us, most because they need us. We are still essentially, as has been said before, the indispensable nation."[10] Friendships of utility already frame our attention on what, in some corners, is seen as a given, almost obvious feature of interstate cooperation, namely their fluidity.[11]

There is a second way in which the predominant use of *friend* and *friendship* as applied to states may have consequences for understanding international cooperation. Instead of reinforcing the notion of fluidity found in friendships of utility, the simple use of the words *friend* and *friendship* points to the pesky possibility of a more stable relationship. As was discussed in part I, the ordinary, interpersonal uses of these words are quite expansive. They open up the thought of other possible forms of cooperation in addition to those founded upon being mutually useful. Hence, ties of history, tradition, culture, ideology as well as past sacrifices of blood and treasure may lead states to talk about "special relationships" or enduring friendships. The rhetorical force of these words requires that we be reminded by those who are more realistically inclined that these "friends" are our friends only because of our respective self-interests. But then, how should Americans understand those states that do not fear America, but, as Gates says, respect it? Do they respect it merely because it is better able to satisfy the interests of others? Perhaps. Or, perhaps there is something in the way in which we understand self-interest that paradoxically supports a conception of friendship that goes beyond mere self-interest.

In discussing these matters, one would be remiss not to consider Carl Schmitt's friend/enemy distinction. In some ways, his distinction clarifies the account of friendships of utility but, in other ways, his distinction complicates it. The clarification comes in the form of conceptualizing a notion of a friend that departs from our ordinary interpersonal conception of friendship. For example, when Aristotle talks about the relationship of cities as being that of friends for utility it is not clear that philia loses its affective content. If it does not lose that content, then it is not clear whether and how cities can have affection for one another. Schmitt's friend/enemy distinction cuts through this problem by asserting that whatever "the friend" may mean in the political realm, it is not equivalent to our interpersonal conception of this relationship nor is it merely metaphorical. Schmitt writes, "The friend/ enemy concepts are to be understood in their concrete and existential sense, not as metaphors or symbols, not mixed and weakened by economic, moral, and other conceptions, least of all in a private-individual sense as a psychological expression of private emotions and tendencies" (1996:27–28). This idea will be discussed in more detail later. For the moment, it is important to note that even if Schmitt's notion of the friend does not ultimately get us very far, it does reinforce the theoretical possibility that many of the ordinary motivations associated with interpersonal friendship need not apply to international friendship.

Schmitt's account complicates the discussion of friendship between states in a couple of ways. First, he is much less interested in the concept of the friend than in the concept of the enemy and it could be argued that he is not interested in the concept of friendship at all.[12] Second, Schmitt's idea of the political refines the notion of state self-interest in a rather idiosyncratic way. Just as he is interested in the political or public enemy, he is interested in the political or public friend (1996:28–29). After considering these ideas, I will argue that as with other understandings that place a premium on utility and self-interest, his notion of friend carries very little weight on its own (i.e., friend means little more than ally) and hence does not advance an understanding of international friendship much beyond the traditional notions of ally or partner.

For the purposes of this chapter, I am reading Schmitt's friend/enemy distinction through the lens of international politics, where one "collectivity of people confronts a similar collectively" as opposed to seeing it as a distinction that unites a given people within a particular state. While one's compatriots can certainly qualify as one's friends, so do one's allies who are fighting against a common enemy. According to Schmitt, "it cannot be denied that nations continue to group themselves according to the friend and enemy antithesis, that the distinction still remains actual today, and that this is an ever present possibility for every people existing in the political sphere" (1996:28). The primary political sphere I will focus on is that traditionally seen as the "high politics" of international relations.[13]

As has already been mentioned, private emotions and tendencies are not at the core of Schmitt's distinction. While we may hate the enemy, it is not a necessary condition for being an enemy. The determination of some group as the enemy is a political decision that presumably rests on the sovereign's assessment that they represent a threat to one's community. It is not a function of subjective feelings. Given this understanding of the enemy, the political sense of the word *friend* is also devoid of any necessary connection to feelings. While we may love our political friends, it is not a necessary condition for political or public friendship. The public friendship of the United States to the Soviet Union during the Second World War was not based on affection. If this is a plausible reading of Schmitt's position, then political or public friends need not feel anything in particular for one another. More importantly, he asserts that "the morally good, aesthetically beautiful, and economically profitable need not necessarily become the friend in the specifically political sense of the word" (1996:27). Embedded in Schmitt's understanding of friend and enemy is the idea that both relationships are independent of moral, aesthetic, and economic considerations, although such considerations may be added to these terms to add polemical or rhetorical flourish. Still, Schmitt offers a notion of "friend" in which the ordinary sentiments of friendship as well as a host of other motivations are neither necessary nor sufficient.

The heart of Schmitt's account of the political is the sovereign's public determination of who is a friend and who is an enemy. Schmitt wishes to sustain an autonomous conception of the political, one that is not reducible to any other category. Consequently, not just any state should count as an enemy. For example, a sovereign that decided that the ugly, evil, or wealthy were the enemy would be making a category mistake unless the sovereign also believed that those groups intended "to negate his . . . way of life and therefore must be repulsed or fought in order to preserve one's own form of existence" (1996:27). The enemy is identified by the sovereign's decision based on the belief that another people or state poses an existential threat that is worth fighting against. Hence, "The friend, enemy, and combat concepts receive their real meaning precisely because they refer to the real possibility of physical killing" (33). Moreover, Schmitt presumes that in disagreements or conflicts with one's enemies, those conflicts can "neither be decided by a previously determined general norm nor by the judgment of a disinterested and therefore neutral party." The determination of a threat to

one's way of life is political in the sense that there is no algorithm or proce-
dure or stable set of indicators that will necessarily determine the existence
of an enemy. No neutral third party can confirm or disconfirm the existence of such a threat. Finally, Schmitt notes that while enemies are still
human (as opposed to moral monsters), he argues that they are "other" or
"different" or "alien" or "the stranger" (27). These descriptions, however, are
connected to the idea that the enemy is perceived as seeking to destroy one's
form of existence.[14]

We should be careful, however, not to infer too much about the concept
of the friend from Schmitt's discussion of the enemy. The reason to be cau-
tious is because the friend/enemy distinction is not comprehensive. States
can also adopt a stance of neutrality (Schmitt 1996:34–35). This suggests
that the friend/enemy categories are not exhaustive.[15] In Schmitt's system,
not to be "with us" is not the same as being "against us" if one is neutral.
But this means that there must be identifying features to being a friend
beyond not being an enemy.

Schmitt is not particularly helpful in identifying those features. He says
that those who are not enemies, that is, those who are political friends or
have adopted a position of neutrality have not been judged to be threats to
one's way of life or form of existence. But this does not distinguish friends
from neutrals. Second, as with Palmerstone, Schmitt believes that these
judgments are not permanent: It is possible for perceptions and circumstances to change such that a country judged to be a friend or neutral party
can subsequently be seen as a threat. Once again, this is of little help in
making the friend/neutral distinction. Finally, if the enemy is "other" or
"alien," friends along with neutral parties are not "other" or "alien." This
could mean that they are like oneself or the same, but it may also mean that
these are people with whom one can work, secure détente, or arrive at a
modus vivendi. Unfortunately, this also does not get us very far. As Andrew Norris notes, "friend" in Schmitt's lexicon "has a formal, almost
technical meaning" and neither depends on feelings, Aristotelian concern
with character, or even knowing one another (1998:81). At the international
level, the technical character of "friend" does not clearly distinguish between a friend and a neutral party.

At the individual level, however, things are different. Schmitt suggests that the notion of a friend implies a shared way of life which the members are willing to protect if not die for. Members of the state share this orientation, an orientation that goes beyond not being an enemy. Hence one's friends are members of a shared community. They are distinguishable from individuals who may simply be indifferent or neutral to one's own way of life and hence have no inclination to fight and die for another way of life. In other words, not to share a way of life is not the same as being opposed to a way of life. Hence, being a friend as the term applies to one's compatriots is distinguishable from being indifferent or neutral.

The problem with this solution is that what defines the members of one's community as one's friends cannot be used at the international level. Members of different states do not and cannot share that level of commitment toward the other state without collapsing the states into one another. If members of state A are willing to fight and die for state B, it is because by doing so the members of A are protecting themselves against a threat to their own way of life. To put it another way, they (members of state A) are not dying for state B for the sake of B. At the international level, the friend/neutral distinction cannot mean anything more than the following: State A is a friend of state B if they have come to the conclusion that state C is a threat to both of their ways of life. State D is a neutral party vis-à-vis states A, B, and C if state D is not a threat to any of them *and* state D has determined that none of these states represent threats to its own way of life or it has come to believe that the best way to preserve its form of existence is by avoiding war. In short, the political meaning of neutrality rests on the friend/enemy distinction.

The upshot of the friend/neutral distinction is that the notion of friend does not express a willingness to die for one's friend. One is willing to die for oneself (or, more properly, one's own way of life) and fighting alongside one's friend is the best way to ensure one's way of life (or so it may seem).[16] One does not fight and die for one's international friends (although we may *say* such things), one fights and dies for one's *own* way of life. Moreover, one provides support to one's international friends, not because they are one's friends (as if this carried independent weight) but because such support serves one's own interests. The relationship itself does not serve as a reason for action. On this reading, Schmitt's system amounts to a kind of state or sovereign-centered egoism, in which the only reasons that should count in state action are those related to the state's own interests (its way of life or form of existence). In its political manifestation, the word *friend* does not carry any independent weight but follows or tracks self-interested action. If a friend is a nation whose way of life is threatened by the same enemy (an enemy of my enemy is my friend), then a neutral party is one which seeks to preserve its form of existence by avoiding war. If one wishes to know one's international friends, one must first know one's enemies.

STATE ACTION AND REASON

So far, there is nothing in the discussion that would preclude narrow self-interest (utility) from serving as a sufficient reason for international friendship and there is much in Schmitt's account to suggest that narrow self-interest is the only reason of importance in international affairs. The problem, however, is that a relationship based purely on self-interest amounts to no more than an alliance or partnership. If the analysis stopped here, then there is not really much of interest in the idea of international friendship as a distinct idea.[17]

What is true of Schmitt's analysis would appear to be true of any international theory in which self-interest is the only reason that can count in international action. Moreover, his perspective is largely in accord with conventional realist understandings of the formation and management of interstate alliances and alignments. These also rest on strategic self-interest and instrumental rationality. From this perspective, the politics of alliance formation is largely driven by the desire of states to derive the greatest benefit out of an association at the least cost. In order to advance that end in an anarchic environment where power and information are distributed unequally, states must engage in a complex rational calculation that will yield alliances capable of balancing against threats and preserving their own independence and security. Similarly, managing those alliances requires states to deploy strategic reason in bargaining over the distribution of an association's benefits and burdens and in threading their way between the

Scylla of abandonment and the Charybdis of entanglement.[18] Forms of practical reason that go beyond what is tied to self-interest and power are what Thucydides's Athenians once described as "specious pretences," at most serving as an illusory palliative to the stark reality of power politics (Thucydides 1910:5.89.1). While its instrumental use means that reason as such is far from being merely decorative, it is largely enslaved to a desire for security defined by national self-interest.

In contrast, John Rawls argues that it is possible for regimes to be motivated by reasons other than self-interest (1999).[19] This possibility can be realized under conditions in which the internal arrangements of regimes have become what he calls, "well-ordered" (45). That is, regimes that have come to respect basic civil and political liberties. Well-ordered domestic arrangements, in turn, can transform the motivations of citizens and state actors and the sorts of reasons that they will accept for international action. In that transformation, state actors become more willing to propose and abide by fair terms of international cooperation that will advance both their own interests and the interests of peace (35). They are less aggressive and less interested in the pursuit of power. When the well-ordered domestic character of a regime transforms the motivations of citizens and policy-makers, the regime itself is transformed from being a *state* to being a *people*.

Rawls's presumption, one that he shares with realism, is that states as they have been traditionally conceived since the days of the Greek city-states are largely motivated by self-interest and the pursuit of power. "States," he writes,

are often seen as rational, anxiously concerned with their power—their capacity (military, economic, diplomatic) to influence other states—as always guided by their basic interests. . . . How far states differ from peoples rests on how rationality, the concern with power, and a state's basic interests are filled in. If *rationality* excludes the *reasonable* (that is, if a state is moved by the aims it has and ignores the criterion of reciprocity in dealing with other societies); if a state's concern with power is predominant; and if its interests include such things as converting other societies to the state's religion, enlarging its empire and winning territory, gaining dynastic or imperial or national prestige and glory, and increasing its relative economic strength—then the difference between states and peoples is enormous.

(1999:28)

Unlike what the realists claim, Rawls argues that the internal arrangements of a country make a difference to the actions of a regime: "What makes peace among liberal democratic peoples possible is the internal nature of peoples as constitutional democracies and resulting change of the motives of citizens" (29n27). Furthermore, "What distinguishes peoples from states—and this is crucial—is that just and decent peoples are fully prepared to grant the very same proper respect and recognition to other peoples as equals" (35). Peoples are motivated by reasons beyond narrow self-interest. They accept a kind of international public reason to guide their conduct and their interactions. In his vision of what he calls a realistic utopia, Rawls argues that international public reason could bring and hold together a society of peoples. In this utopia, a society of peoples governed by a law of peoples, would seek to secure general agreement to rules and principles that are perceived to be reasonable.

It is not difficult to see how a society of peoples could be said to entail a kind of friendship. In this friendship, the participants would share a vision of what they understood to be fair rules of international cooperation (or what Rawls calls the "law of peoples"). Moreover, the members of this society of peoples would be motivated by a desire for cooperation and fairness and they would interact peacefully, cooperatively, and justly. By arguing that regimes could be motivated by more than narrow self-interest, it is possible to conceive of a notion of international friendship that was based on something other than utility or Schmitt's state-centered egoism.

However attractive Rawls's society of peoples may be as a way to understand international friendship, it is important to note that Rawls did not need to turn to the concept of friendship as a way to discuss the generation or the potential consequences of his law of peoples. Clearly, the interactions of Rawls's peoples should be friendly and their motivations need to stretch beyond self-interest. What appear to be unnecessary in Rawls's account are the kinds of connections between the participants that would signal a friendship. For the most part, Rawls's account is about the transformation of motivations within states. That transformation is more or less unilateral as opposed to being relational. States become peoples because they are motivated by a sense of cooperation and fairness. They enter into a society of peoples because they would hypothetically agree to a set of rules to govern their interactions and not because they have an interest in the interests of other peoples or because they mutually recognize that other peoples are motivated by similar sorts of reasons. In this regard, the motivation of peoples looks more like the idea of civic virtue mentioned in chapter 5 than of friendship.

Still, what we can take from Rawls is the possibility that a change to the internal structure of a regime can change the sorts of reasons that could and should count when acting on the world stage. The argument of chapter 9 is that more or less just states have powerful reasons to have an interest in protecting themselves precisely because they are more or less just. In contrast to Rawls, who makes a fairly sharp distinction between self-interested motives and other motives, self-interest is moralized and enlarged for those states in a way that is not true for unjust states (i.e., states whose institutions and basic policies are depriving individuals and groups of their civil and political rights or destroying their capacities to pursue what they see as a valuable way of life). It is because of their more or less just character that certain states have reason to be concerned with the interests of other more or less just states. It is the mutual recognition of motivations based on the quality of the institutional arrangements within regimes that can serve as the basis of international friendships of character.

Friendships of utility are certainly a kind of friendship in the international realm. The ability of self-interest to be enough for friendship is another example of the flexibility of the term and differentiates an international practice of friendship from the interpersonal practices discussed in part 1. Friendships of utility, however, are not particularly interesting insofar as they are largely, although perhaps not entirely, reducible to other terms such as *partner* or *ally*. The nose of a more interesting conception of friendship can squeeze into the tent of international relationships if we see the idea of self-interest as a way to justify international cooperation. How much more of the camel can fit into that tent will depend on filling out the argument for why self-interest itself works as a reason to justify state action. In the argument that follows, self-interest should motivate state action only if a plausible case can be made for the relative justness of the state. If, however, justness is what should count, then it should also count for our relationship to other states. International friendship, then, can be understood as a relationship that depends on the character of states concerned.

nine

INTERNATIONAL FRIENDSHIPS
OF CHARACTER

Citizens have good reasons to support and promote the institutions and policies under which they are governed if those institutions and policies are more or less just. If those institutions and policies are unjust, then they have good reasons to alter or abolish them. Some have argued that if institutions and policies are just, citizens have an obligation to support and promote them. Others (e.g., Simmons) have argued that if this were the basis of our political obligations, then citizens would have obligations to any just institution and policy, not merely those of their own state. Consequently, they argue that political obligation cannot be purely based on the character or quality of the regime.

Whatever one may think of this objection to a justice-based case for political obligation, it does not affect the claim that citizens have good reason to support and promote minimally just institutions and policies. This simple claim appears to apply both internally and externally. When it applies externally, it can serve as the basis for international friendship. This chapter explores this possibility. It is divided into several sections. The first argues that just as citizens have good reasons to support minimally just institutions and policies, states have reasons to be self-interested only if they are minimally just. This view from justice presumes that not all states have good reasons to defend and promote themselves. More importantly, it suggests that for those states that do have good reasons to be self-interested, those reasons can stretch state concern beyond their own borders. International friendships of character rest on the mutual recognition of a concern for the friends' more or less just domestic institutional arrangements.

The second part of the chapter considers some objections to this view of international friendship. For example, how does self-interest in its narrower form fit into the discussion? What if citizens value their own political and social institutions because they are their own as opposed to being more or less just? In addition, this section considers why this relationship between states can be labeled a friendship. The third and fourth sections of the chapter apply part 1's framework of interpersonal friendship to the international realm. As in the case of interpersonal friendship, motivations and actions matter to international friendship. The usefulness of that framework is that it not only highlights the roles of self-interest, utility, ideology, and identity as motives for international friendship, but it also provides a way to distinguish international friendships of character from other understandings of international friendship that have been recently developed. A central concern in this discussion is the extent to which the motives of justice and character differ from ideological and identity-based motivations.

The fifth section explores the adverbial conditions that may be, in theory, associated with international friendships. Motivated by justice, character-based friends should seek to interact justly. They should also be interacting attentively to how their decisions and policies affect the flourishing of minimally just institutions in other states. The section argues that international friendships of character can take three forms: an entente cordiale, a security pact, or a special relationship. Based on contingencies of stability and closeness, these levels of friendship could generate different adverbial conditions for action. In light of these differences, the chapter concludes by considering the implications of international friendships of character for how states interact within and without the circle of friends.

JUSTIFIED SELF-INTEREST

The brief discussion of Rawls in chapter 8 concluded with the suggestion that within state self-interest might lie a concern for the just institutions of other states. In order to make that connection, it is important to discern first why the interests of states matter at all. This question, of course, is a large one, over which there is much debate. For the purposes of this argument, I will presume that the interests of states matter because states are and remain an indispensable condition of value.[1] In other words, the institutional arrangements and rules that constitute a state are necessary conditions for preserving and protecting the values and goods of individuals and groups within the state. There may be exceptions to this generalization, for example, groups that do not need the state to protect what is of value (criminal organizations, multinational corporation—groups that seek to self-insure what is of value), but these exceptions need not detain us. In many cases, such groups seek to capture the power of the state or aspire to establish the protections provided by the state.

In addition, by asserting that the state is a necessary condition of value, I am not saying that it is the origin of what is of value. If states were the source of value, in the sense of being the organic rich earth out of which all that matters arises, then it would be obvious as to why their self-interests were important. The view that I am adopting is one in which the value of the state piggybacks onto the values of individuals and groups. The state's value is a secondary or derivative concern. Moreover, the state as indispensable emerged in early modern Europe and spread globally in the nineteenth and twentieth centuries. Once upon a time, states were not indispensable conditions of value, and it is possible that they may not play this role in the future. The generalizations that follow from this presumption, then, may not extend beyond the state system as we know it.

Obviously, the slaughter bench of history shows that not all states play the role of protecting what individuals and groups value equally well. The irony is that within the history of the state system most states have protected and promoted the interests and values of the few at the expense of the many. Even though the institutional and territorial arrangements associated with the state are necessary conditions of value, those arrangements can also significantly impede the protection and realization of what individuals and groups within the state hold dear. It is liberalism's familiar attempt to tame the leviathan that provides the broad framework for the discussion that follows. This discussion begs off a number of difficulties that have occupied liberals and their critics for quite a while. Nevertheless, an enduring thread within liberalism is that governments which systematically violate the liberty, security, and welfare of the people do not deserve their respect and support. Such governments have no legitimate claim on resources to defend their abusive institutional arrangements from forces inside or outside the state. These abuses may ultimately lead to justifications for reform or revolution. They do not, however, necessarily create a right on the part of other states to intervene. The idea that the right to revolution does not warrant a right to intervention can be justified in a number of ways. The point here, however, is that states can lose the right to legitimately protect their self-interest and that can mean one thing internally (in justifying a right to revolution) and another thing externally (not justifying a blanket right to outside intervention).[2]

A more important component of the argument involves the notions of state self-interest and its legitimacy. If a government is truly protecting and promoting the values of the individuals and groups living within its domain, then they have good reason to respect, protect, and empower those state institutions. What complicates this equation is that the interests and values of individuals clash. People are *rational* (using Rawls's language) to the extent that they seek to promote their interests in a manner that connects means to ends. In this regard, the state (as an indispensable condition of value) could be understood merely as a means to protecting their interests. If, however, pluralism and the resulting conflicts of values are part of the human condition, then individuals are *reasonable* (once again using Rawls) to the extent that they are willing to abide by fair rules of cooperation that guide institutions in balancing conflicting interests, values, and rights.[3] The value of the state is not merely that it protects my interests and values, but that I see it as more or less just. That is, I understand that my conception of what is a good life may conflict with the conceptions of others and that when those conflicts happen, I am willing to abide by fair rules of cooperation if others are willing to do the same. This does not mean that all policies, laws, and decisions must meet the requirements of justice, but that judges, policy-makers, legislators, and executives are meeting, at least, some minimum standard of justice.

We have now reached a rather significant impasse. In order to proceed, it would seem that something needs to be said about justice beyond that it involves fair rules of cooperation. Obviously, this is a huge and complex problem within the tradition of political thought. As in the case of seeing the state as an indispensable condition of value, the question will be punted. For the purposes of argument, I assume that political accountability and representation (fair and free elections), respect for human rights (including political and civil liberties), and the rule of law are important elements of a just state. Moreover, I assume that, depending on the circumstances, different institutional arrangements will be more or less successful in incorporating these elements. More strongly, it is not clear that we fully understand how best to accommodate the plurality of goods and perspectives that clash within society. Even the best governments remain works in progress. Although we may have settled judgments regarding many injustices, no government has a lock on what the best institutional structure would entail or what a complete vision of justice would look like.

The more or less just institutions that serve as a condition of value and seek to embody fair rules of cooperation and the sorts of elements mentioned can now themselves be said to have a set of interests. Those interests involve securing the conditions that enable them (the institutions or the state more generally) to protect the values and interests of individuals and groups in a more or less just manner. More or less just states have good reasons to be self-interested. That is, they have good reasons to procure the resources needed to establish, enable, and secure the laws, policies, and institutions that protect and advance the interests of individuals and groups in a just manner as well as obtain the resources needed to defend themselves from internal corruption and external coercion. Unjust states do not have good reasons to be self-interested, although this claim will be modified a bit in the following discussion.

This view of "legitimate" state self-interest is not meant to deny that the word *self-interest* is frequently used to express the kind of state-egoism that Schmitt offers. For realists, legitimacy is neither here nor there: states have interests that they constantly seek to secure or pursue. Unjust states may be said to have interests in protecting themselves and securing their borders from foreign interference. In a way, however, the self-interest of such states amounts to no more than the interests of those who happen to have power. Those interests are not by themselves good reasons for others to respect them.

The self-interest of the tyrant by itself is not a good reason for citizens to support and protect the tyrant's power. Similarly, the self-interest of an unjust state is not, by itself, a good reason for foreign states to prop up its institutional arrangements.

The view of legitimate state self-interest, derivable from the justness of domestic arrangements, also does not deny that international law accords states, regardless of their character, certain legitimate interests such as territorial integrity.[4] At least in part, those interests are recognized as an attempt to control the level of international violence. They are, however, interests of the system as much as they are the interests of individual states. The international system itself has an interest in attempting to resolve disputes between states in a peaceful manner. The consequence is that the interests of unjust states that are in accord with international norms acquire a legitimacy that can moderate or restrain their actions. In part, because of those international norms, a right to revolution is not a right to intervention.

When legitimacy is based on justice, what matters for self-interest is whether a state's institutions have the right sort of character. It is the admirable or worthy quality of the institutions that justifies a concern for those institutions and for their supporting conditions (i.e., their interests). For example, the United States' self-interests should be supported and respected by its citizenry, not because they are the interests of the United States (a nationalist argument), but because those interests can ultimately be connected to supporting and promoting more or less just domestic institutional arrangements (assuming that they are). More strikingly, those same interests are worthy of support and respect by other states in the world, not because they are the interests of the remaining superpower, but because of their connection to just institutions (assuming that they are so connected).[5] It is reasonable for a state to be self-interested if its institutional arrangements are more or less just. Justice "licenses" such interest and that license is not the exclusive property of this or that state. The central implication of this view is that states should have a concern for themselves to the extent that they embody admirable characteristics that any state could embody.[6] If another state also embodies those characteristics, then the first state has reason to be concerned with those institutional arrangements as well. When two or more minimally just states mutually recognize a concern for protecting one another's more or less just basic policies and institutions and act in a manner that is consonant with those motivations, then an international friendship of character exists.

OBJECTIONS

If legitimate state self-interest is connected to the just quality of a state's institutions and international friendship is linked to the mutual recognition of the quality of those institutions, then it could be argued that friendship has been purchased at the expense of ordinary self-interest. International friendship would seem to require that more or less just states have as much regard for the interests of other just states as for their own interests. States could not prioritize their own interests above other states. Instead of friendship between states, the argument seems to move to an internationalist or cosmopolitan position. Should just states be permitted to prioritize their own self-interests, narrowly construed?

The argument in support of international friendship clearly undermines a strong priority thesis in which just states need not be concerned with the effects of their actions on the institutional arrangements of other just states. It does, however, support a weak priority thesis. Minimally just states can place the protection and promotion of their own institutions ahead of institutions of other just states largely because the state is an indispensable condition of value: Just states have strong reasons (although not indefeasible reasons) for ensuring the maintenance and advancement of their own fair policies and laws over the claims of other states. But this merely raises the question of why *this* state with *these* more or less just institutions must serve as a condition of value and not some other minimally just state.

Part of the answer is one of knowledge. Given the contingencies of history, culture, religion, and language, it is reasonable to think that state institutions will have a clearer sense of how best to match general principles of justice to the situation on the ground. Minimally just governments happen to be in a better position than foreign just governments in understanding how best to construct, maintain, and promote institutions that accord with local circumstances. Consequently, it is reasonable for minimally just states to prioritize their own self-interest over the interests of preserving foreign, just institutions. This argument supports a weak priority thesis. It is weak in the sense that occasions can arise in which it is reasonable to devote resources to the preservation of foreign just arrangements at the expense of promoting domestic just arrangements. For example, at the time of writing, the Greek sovereign debt crisis continues to simmer. Assuming that the relevant states in this crisis are minimally just, then they have good reasons to protect and promote their own just domestic institutions, but they also have reasons to protect and promote the just domestic institutions of the Greeks. They should be concerned with whether their demands for providing economic assistance may weaken or undermine Greek political and social institutions. The central point here is that the preservation of those minimally just institutions is a reason for action not only for minimally just European governments, but any minimally just government. How strong that reason is depends on the threat that the economic crisis poses to Greek democratic institutions, what foreign governments can do to shore up or promote Greek institutions as well as the potential costs to the character of foreign just governments. Obviously, there are other issues that compose this particular crisis. What is important in this line of argument, however, is that the quality or character of regimes should matter for minimally just governments, because justice itself matters. At times, advancing the vital interests of another minimally just state may outweigh the protection of domestic interests. Nowhere is this balancing act more wrenching than in a situation in which a state places the lives of its own citizens at risk in the attempt to protect the free institutions of another minimally just state.

Still, one can argue that a weak priority thesis is not good enough. It ignores the value that people place in their own institutions and ways of governing. People find *their own* institutions worthy of respect because they are *their own*, regardless of their quality. Perhaps the most common version of this argument is nationalist in character. The idea is that people hold a set of institutions as valuable merely because they value them or see them as their own. The ethnic, cultural, linguistic, and historical circumstances can form not only a set of traditions and institutional arrangements but also a bond between the people and their government. It is this particular regime that best preserves and promotes the way of life of this particular people. It is therefore rational for a people to protect their own regime and it is rational for that regime to protect itself and prioritize its interests over the interests of any other state.

As it is framed, the argument is indeed rational. It is not, however, reasonable to think that any government will perfectly mirror the way of life of everyone within its bounds. The nationalist argument is one that seeks to shrink the circumstances of justice by presupposing a monolithic culture, history, ethnicity, religion, or language. Absent that purity, states must find some way to negotiate the pluralism that it will inevitably find within its boundaries. The government needs to find a way to protect and promote the interests of individuals and groups who will have different cultures, languages, religions, and ethnicities. It must do so in a way that is understood as fair, if the state is to sustain the support of its people. Justice must reenter the equation. From a nationalist perspective, what is rational to do may not be reasonable in light of what Rawls calls the "fact of pluralism" (2005:36–39). The self-interest of a minimally just state cannot merely be found in the promotion of a national identity. It must also include an interest in establishing and sustaining more or less just institutions. If this is the case, then minimally just states with a strong sense of nationalism would still have good reason to support the just institutions of other minimally just states.

Even if all of this is conceded, what does it have to do with friendship? Why call a relationship between minimally just states in which there exists a mutually recognized motive to preserve and promote just institutions and act in accord with those motivations, a friendship at all? There are two reasons in support of this move. The first draws on Jennifer E. Whiting's Aristotelian conception of individual self-concern and friendship (1991; Digeser 2009a, 2009b). The heart of her claim is that self-concern is reasonable when it is connected to attributes of one's character that are valuable. From this position she argues that those valuable characteristics give us reasons to be concerned for ourselves and they provide reasons to be concerned for others who share those characteristics. All people of good character compose a pool of what Whiting calls "impersonal friends" (7). Specific friendships grow out of a sense of good will and affection toward those who possess the characteristics that are valued.

Whatever its virtues as an ideal of interpersonal friendship or as an exposition of Aristotle's character-based friendship, Whiting's notion of friendship can be transposed (or so I argued) to the language of interstate relations. Although the transposition requires certain modifications to her argument (e.g., countries do not have emotional states, the character that is valued in states is more easily identified in terms of justice, the defense of state self-concern is not exactly parallel to the defense of individual self-concern), it suggested a way to understand how states could have analogous relationships based on character. In certain respects, some of the difficulties of applying her ideal of friendship to individuals become less troubling at the interstate level. For example, our practices of interpersonal friendship rarely draw on character as a motivation. In contrast, to talk of the character of institutions or regimes as a basis for motivating international cooperation may be less of a stretch.

A second reason to call such relationships *friendships* is that there exists an international rhetoric of cooperation that draws on the idea of friendship. Even if there does not currently exist a full-blown practice of international friendship that rests on character, state actors deploy the notion of friendship as a way to signal an association between democratic regimes. Of course, *friendship* and *friend* are used in a number of ways, as discussed in the introduction and in chapter 8. Nevertheless, implied in certain statements, pronouncements, and analyses, friendship is a way to indicate that both rational self-interest and state character matter in the quality of interstate relationships. International friendships are useful, but they are more than just useful. The possibility is that the idea of international friendship may be imminent to ongoing forms of cooperation. This point will become clearer in chapter 10's discussion of the potential politics associated with such friendships.

IDEOLOGY AND THE MOTIVES FOR INTERNATIONAL FRIENDSHIP

If one is willing to entertain the possibility of applying the idea of *friendship* to interstate relationships based on character, do the general features of friendship discussed in part 1 apply? More specifically, do the formal motivational and action conditions associated with our contemporary practices of interpersonal friendship make sense when talking about international friendship? This section applies that framework to the discussion of international friendship by first looking at what may motivate such relationships and then turning to the issue of whether there are adverbial conditions that could govern them.

In considering motivations, it will be important to keep in mind important differences between the interpersonal and the international. As discussed in chapter 8, one of those differences is that the motives of sentiment that drive many interpersonal friendships simply cannot be had by states as abstract entities. Nevertheless, states can still have motives in the sense of having reasons to act one way or the other. Those reasons are, of course, had by flesh and blood individuals who are acting in their official roles. Another difference, that also has been mentioned in the previous chapter, concerns the role of self-interest and utility. While interpersonal friendships tend to view utility as a deficient reason for friendship, that is not the case in international affairs. Unlike interpersonal friendships, narrow self-interest (usually military or economic) serves as a sufficient basis for international cooperation and friendship or what Oelsner and Koschut call "strategic international friendships" (2014b:14). As Aristotle noted long ago, much of interstate cooperation rests on utility.

The general idea of friendship in international affairs raises the question of whether additional motives, beyond self-interest, can drive international relations. As in the case of interpersonal friendships, is there a repertoire of "ordinarily appropriate" motives for international friendships? Stephen Walt, for example, talks about alliances based on ideology and constructivists note the importance of identity to international collaboration.[7] If these are plausible motives that compose a kind of repertoire, then perhaps there already exist multiple practices of international friendship. These motives, however, also raise the question of whether international friendships of character are adding anything new to the subject of international cooperation. Do the motives of character and justice differ from motives of ideology and identity?

The answer depends on how one understands the terms involved. Taking *ideology* as broadly as possible, it could be argued that character and justice involve systems of ideas and hence qualify as ideologies. For example, Walt seems to provide a concise account of ideologically based alignments that would appear to include international friendships of character. He writes that "alignment with similar states may be viewed as a way of defending one's own political principles. After all, if statesmen believe their own system of government is inherently good, then protecting states with similar systems must be considered good as well" (1987:34). In what he calls a "unifying ideology" there need not be an international leader or a monolithic interpreter of its meaning (35–37). This understanding of ideology accommodates alignments of states that are motivated by an idea of being "minimally just."

Ideology, however, is frequently used to refer to a set of economic arrangements, political institutions, or cultural practices or it is sometimes used to refer to a set of ideas that mask reality and legitimize exploitative social relationships. In the first case, it is usually cashed-out in terms of a set of "isms" (capitalism, socialism, liberalism, etc.). In the latter case, it is used to identify and critique a false and harmful worldview. In both cases, ideologies are understood as resting on presumptions that are either not ordinarily called into question or cannot be called into question without questioning the worldview that they support. Motivations could be deemed ideological in this narrower sense if they support or legitimize a worldview as opposed to calling into question assumptions of that worldview.[8]

Is the motive of justice ideological in these narrower terms? If a state is motivated to act because of the character of another regime, is that character-based motivation ideological? The answer is yes and no. To the extent that the motive of justice is held by states that are presumed to be indispensable conditions of value, then it is ideological. This presumption of the state's role is being accepted as given and not questioned in the analysis. In addition, the idea of justice used here is presumed to include the protection of basic civil and political liberties, the rule of law, respect for human rights, and a competitive political process. If left there, the discussion of justice is ideological because it has proceeded in a manner that has taken certain claims as given. The theory of international friendships of character presumes a certain view of the world without attempting to defend key elements of that view (a view that most readers would recognize as some kind of liberalism).

The motivations associated with international friendship would not be ideological if they were based on a correct view of the world (e.g., the state is indeed an indispensable condition of value, the fact of pluralism is a fact in the most defensible sense of that word) and a correct view of justice (e.g., that justice matters, that it involves balancing the claims of individuals in a fair manner, that certain institution are better able to perform that function, etc.). Instead of making these stronger claims, I will claim that the motivations of justice and character are different from ideological motivations because there is a questioning attitude built into them. The theory of international friendship offered here is provisional. In the future, states may not serve as indispensable conditions of value. It argues that how best to preserve the values of individuals and groups within a given territory and resolve their disputes in a fair manner are questions whose answers may take a variety of forms depending on the circumstances. The notion of what constitutes "minimally just" may always give rise to differences of opinion. What is understood to be a defensible set of just principles need not be understood as complete, entirely adequate, or the only game in town. States need not interpret "minimally just" to mean similarity in political or economic institutions. As we shall see in chapter 10, the challenges of understanding justice will create questions regarding how to identify who is in the circle of friends. While international friendships of character are ideological in the original sense of being based on a set of ideas that hang together, they are not ideological in the less nuanced sense of closing off deliberation and debate over fundamental matters.

IDENTITY, CARE, AND THE MOTIVES OF INTERNATIONAL FRIENDSHIP

If the motivations of international friendship are distinguishable from narrower conceptions of ideological motivations, are they different from the sorts of motivations associated with identity? For constructivists, ideas matter and identity matters in international relationships. States may be motivated by narrow self-interest, but that notion of self-interest is a function of the construction of a state's identity which, in turn, is connected to how a state patrols the ways in which it differs from and perceives other entities. To the extent that states come to acquire "an identification with the fate of the other" (Wendt 1994:386), the identity, interests and motives for action may also change. In situations of what Andrea Oelsner calls, "positive peace," states "do not prepare for war, nor do they expect other states in the zone to do so" (2007:264). These attitudes are most fully developed in a pluralistic security community in which war becomes unthinkable and "the societies involved have developed links, mutual sympathies, and some sort of common identification that makes them perceive each other as members of the same community" (264–65). In such a community, there is the development of a "we-feeling" (267) or perhaps a collective sense of identity that transcends the identities of the participants to the relationship (Adler and Barnett 1998:31; Tusicisny 2007:429). Not only do such communities abide by rules of nonviolence and mutual aid, but their actions are not "narrowly self-interested." As a result of these domestic and regional developments, states may be motivated by an enlarged sense of identity.

Within the security community literature, friendship has become a useful concept for capturing especially close forms of regional and state-to-state relationships. In theorizing those connections, Andrea Oelsner has defined international friendship as

> both a relational and dynamic process made up of regular manifestations of mutual trust, shared affinities, and cooperation that will allow it to reproduce and maintain itself. Elsewhere, Vion and I referred to it as a cumulative process of speech acts and institutional facts representing signs of engagement in, and proofs of, friendship.
>
> (2014:148)[9]

Those speech acts and institutional facts can result in a distinction between strategic and normative international friendships. As mentioned earlier, the former is an instrumental relationship wholly based on the rational self-interest of parties where the friends rely on one another as opposed to trusting each other. In contrast, a normative international friendship is one in which the parties "genuinely trust each other because their relationship is not based on an instrumental rational thought process (trust-as-predictability or reliance) and utility-based cost-benefit calculations but is manifested as an emotional and moral disposition (trust-as-bond)" (Oelsner and Koschut 2014b:14).

Although they contribute to and draw on the security community literature, Oelsner and Koschut argue that normative international friendships are distinguishable from zones of stable peace and from security communities: "zones of stable peace and security communities are conducive sites for friendship relations rather than its result. Furthermore, they are neither synonymous to friendship nor a sufficient condition for international friendship" (9). They argue the distinction between a security community per se and an international friendship is "the degree of closeness and extension of trust to others" (19). Friends in normative international friendships care for one another, experience deeper, more intimate bonds, and are at least partly motivated by the friendship itself to engage in shared activities (14–15). In addition, while security communities have a regional character to them, normative international friendships can "also develop out of strategic alliances and close partnerships not sharing geographical regions," as in the case of the U.S.-Israeli relationship (21). Normative international friendships will exhibit frequent interactions and transactions (or what Oelsner and Koschut call symbolic interaction), they will contain an affective dimension that is conveyed through speech acts and institutional facts, they will be more disposed to reveal information to one another (what they call self-disclosure), and they will be committed to one another's security (20–21).

The terminology is still very much in flux. Nevertheless, Oelsner and Koschut's key distinction is between normative international friendships and strategic friendships. Although they do not identify regional security communities as forms of friendship, it is not clear why this is the case (perhaps they can be assimilated to strategic friendships or perhaps they form a third kind of friendship). I argue that if a strong notion of identity does motivate the members of a security community, then it may not qualify as a relation of friendship. For the moment, however, it is important to note that these three forms of cooperation draw on very different motives. Strategic friendships are motivated by reasons of utility and narrow self-interest. Regional security communities appear to be motivated by a shared identity and normative international friendships are motivated by care, deep emotional bonds, and the friendship itself.

The question at hand, however, is whether the motive of justice that drives international friendships of character differs from the motives behind these other relationships. As discussed already, the motive of justice does not drive strategic friendships. In the case of regional security communities that are driven by a shared sense of identity, the motive may itself move the relationship beyond that of friendship. It could be argued that such communities are driven by self-interest, but that their sense of "self" encompasses more than one state. To the extent that they acquire an identity that transcends their individual identities, they would view themselves more as one body than as independent agents with competing interests and goals. If this description is correct and security communities require a melding of identity or an identity that transcends the identities of the participants, then they are incompatible with friendship. As a relational term, *friendship* requires distance between the parties. In order to remain friends, it is conceptually necessary that states remain independent of one another. Unlike individuals, states can actually meld into one another.[10] In chapter 10, I will argue that those pressures generate a politics of amalgamation in which friends must engage if they are to preserve their independence and their friendship. In an alignment of minimally just states, the members must be able to distinguish themselves and preserve their independence from other minimally just states if they are to remain friends.

Regional security communities, if they truly are pluralistic, could be motivated in a way that preserves their independence (and the possibility for friendship). In this case, does the motive of justice differ from the motive of identity? As in the case of ideology, much depends on what goes into understanding the idea of identity. At the very least, the motive of identity does not necessarily mean that the states within the community will be motivated by a sense of justice toward one another. The "we" of the identity could be centered on a shared sense of the past or on common cultural and ethnic heritage and have little do with preserving fair rules of cooperation. Alternatively, justice could itself be built into the shared identity of the community. The motives can overlap, but they are also distinguishable.

Behind identity as a motive lies the problem of the subjects of international friendship. Clearly, Oelsner and Koschut's idea of normative international friendship does not turn on a view of the state as an abstract entity. In their conception, friends trust one another as the result of their "high levels of ideational and emotional bonds" (2014b:14). Such friendships place less emphasis on regime-type and more emphasis on feelings of confidence that may be the result of either domestic or regional developments (Oelsner 2007:260, 268, 277). At least some of the motives behind this sort of international friendship are sentiments and emotions. From this perspective, the bonds between the United States and Israel are, in part, emotional and those emotions move the parties to act. From this perspective, international friendship begins to look much like interpersonal friendship.

The analogy to interpersonal friendship would be strengthened if the existence of the relationship depended on the mutual recognition of those motives. Such recognition could be evidenced in official statements of trust and care by the parties. As with both ideology and identity, the motives of justice need not be included in the feelings of confidence and trust that the policy-makers consistently feel for one another. Alternatively, it is possible that those state actors have those feelings because they recognize in the other regime institutional qualities that are admirable and worthy of respect. That is, they have confidence in and trust their friends because their friends are composed of more or less just institutions. From this perspective, a number of differences between their notion of normative international friendships and international friendships of character can now be highlighted. First, there is the difference in motivation already mentioned. Second, international friendships of character are not themselves based on trust, but on the belief that the states have interests in the interests of other states because of the quality of their institutions and basic policies. Trust may then follow from the perceived justice of one's friends. The driver is not a feeling of trust or intimacy, but an understanding of how a set of internal institutions and policies may motivate states to interact in a particular way.

A third difference has to do with approach. Normative international friendships are attempting to capture "aspects of international politics" that have not been considered in the predominate paradigm of international relations (Oelsner and Koschut 2014b:21). This descriptive perspective is consistent with the security community literature more generally in that one of its goals is to establish the inadequacy of the realist/neorealist description of the world. By talking about friendship in international politics, Oelsner and Koschut are arguing that the world does not function in the way the realists claim that it does.

In contrast, the idea of international friendships of character is less about capturing how the world works and more about what reasons could and should count for when states decide to cooperate. In the extreme, the realist description of the world could be correct, but that would not defeat the idea that friendships of character could and should count as a reason for state action. To put this point another way, the "normative" in Oelsner and Koschut's "normative international friendship" is more one of regularity (a norm) or prediction. In other words, a given combination of feelings and ideological similarity should (as in "will") drive states closer together. This interpretation does not deny that Oelsner and Koschut have captured a practice of international friendship that can be differentiated from the qualities associated with international friendships of character. Moreover, it does suggest that part of the difference lies in differences in motives that support the two understandings of friendship.

THE ADVERBIAL CONDITIONS OF FRIENDSHIP

Interpersonal friendships are identified not only by a set of mutually recognized motives, but also by the mutual subscription to a set of adverbial conditions that govern their actions. Part 1 distinguished practices of interpersonal friendship from other interpersonal practices (psychiatry, parenting, policing, and so forth), not so much by what is done with or for friends, but how they go about doing the things they do. The appeal of adverbial conditions as opposed to setting out a list of substantive actions is largely because the things we do with friends can be done with those who are not friends.

When we turn to potential practices of international friendship of character our discussion becomes more speculative than the discussion of motives. Nevertheless, if friendships of character are to have an identifiable place in the world, then it is reasonable to think that either the manner of cooperation or specific kinds of performances would accompany them. If we think in adverbial terms, then the way that international friends of character will interact should not be difficult to specify. Motivated by the justness of their friends' domestic institutions, they would seek to act justly toward one another: they would abide by fair rules of cooperation to advance of their own interests and use those rules to resolve disputes between one another. Such states should see the use of force as an unreasonable way to solve their problems. Moreover, they would act attentively to how their political, legal, or economic policies could undermine or adversely affect the basic structure of other minimally just states. The monetary policies, trade imbalances, import restrictions, drug policies, patent requirements, judicial procedures, and forms of punishment of one state can have implications for another state's ability to enact policies of distributive justice, property protection, health care, or criminal law. The familiar litany of effects of globalization and interdependency create responsibilities to be attentive to the significance of those effects upon the minimally just institutions of one's friends. For one state to establish policies that threaten to undermine the pursuit of justice by another state should be cause for concern and consultation.

Stronger still, they would have reason to act supportively vis-à-vis those institutional arrangements. This may entail providing expertise in establishing an impartial system of justice, economic aid in supporting a burdened financial system, educational resources for expanding a school system to include women. All states that appear to have admirable characters have reason to protect and promote the minimally just domestic institutions that they are all trying to maintain. In so doing, all states that appear to be minimally just have a reason to consult, cooperate, and even learn from one another. That is, they would have reason to enter into an entente cordiale. The adverbial conditions associated with such an entente could entail states acting justly, attentively, cooperatively, honestly, and consultatively.

Within the pool of international friends of character, contingencies involving institutional stability and the nature of international threats may draw some minimally just states closer together than others. Through reform or revolution a state may formally establish free and fair elections, impartial courts, the protection of basic civil and political liberties, but those institutions may not be well entrenched. These changes may be enough for the entente cordiale, but as in the case of persons, the character of regimes takes time to determine. In regimes whose institutional structures appear to be more durable, the identification of the regime as minimally just may be more confident. Stable, minimally just states have reason to share more information, engage in frank communication, heighten the level of consultation, and commit resources in the name of mutual defense. The preservation of their minimally just domestic arrangements may take the shape of security pacts as opposed to a weaker entente cordiale. In additional to the adverbial conditions already mentioned, these friends may interact jointly, loyally, frankly, protectively, and defensively. In both forms of international friendships of character the states are also acting usefully toward one another. In the case of an entente cordiale, the utility may primarily take the form of doing no harm and providing political and economic support to nascent or wobbly institutional arrangements. Such an association is closer to an informal alignment of states than to an alliance.[11] In the case of security pacts, the relationship is not merely formalized into an alliance but that alliance includes the provision of military assistance.

A third form of international friendship goes beyond a security pact or entente cordiale. Minimally just regimes that have a shared history of sacrifice or shared legal, religious, or cultural heritage may find that the ways in which they have attempted to instantiate broad principles of justice are also shared. One could call these sorts of friendships of character "special relationships" because of the closeness of the bond. The relationship is special in that the friends believe that they understand their institutional arrangements in a way that few states may. The interests of a friend in a special relationship are accorded a higher priority. The expectations for consultation are greater. The willingness to defend one another's interests are stronger. In a special relationship, states may go so far as to seek to protect one's friend from internal threats. The autonomy of one's friends is not an insurmountable barrier to providing such protection.

The adverbial conditions associated with special relationships include interacting confidently, trustingly, closely but also, perhaps, presumptuously, boldly, and immodestly. In a special relationship, the friend is very much like another self in a way that can potentially threaten the independence of one party or the other. This closeness poses one of the risks of special relationships. As noted earlier, friends must preserve their autonomy and independence if they are to remain friends. In a special relationship, their closeness may be understood as giving one state a license to intervene in order to preserve or restore just institutions of a friend. The risk in this course of action is that intervening in a friend's internal affairs increases the chance of conflict, misunderstanding, and the dissolution of the friendship. In chapter 10, these risks create the prospect for another kind of politics of friendship.

The possibility that justice and character can serve as a motivation for international friendship expands the repertoire of ordinarily appropriate motives. These motives are distinguishable from motives of self-interest, utility, ideology, and identity. In addition, it is possible that there are different adverbial conditions that could govern international friendships of character. These differences suggest that even within friendships of character there could be multiple practices of friendship that take the shape of an entente cordiale, a security pact, or a special relationship.

THE CIRCLE OF FRIENDS

What, if anything, does the discussion of international friendship of character tell us about the relationships between friends and between friends and others? First, just as in the case of interpersonal friendship, friendly actions are not sufficient for a relationship of friendship. That a state provides disaster relief to another regime does not a friendship make. In addition, given the existence of different practices of international friendship, states can align, ally, cooperate, and defend one another without the existence of a friendship of character. As realists have long noted, utility and self-interest can go some distance in motivating cooperative behavior between all kinds of regimes. The significance of this claim is that states that fall outside of the circle of friends of character need not be considered enemies.

Second, the reasons that support international friendships of character do not necessarily trump all other reasons. There is nothing in the discussion of international friendship that requires states to put the interests of other minimally just states necessarily above their own or that denies the importance of norms as found in international law or in cosmopolitanism. The claim is merely that friendship counts as a reason for action that may prioritize the claims of one's friend over the claims of nonfriends, all other things being equal. Its strength depends much on the circumstances in which states are balancing a number of different sorts of claims and reasons. For example, it may well be the case that the reasons for providing humanitarian aid to a corrupt, but destitute regime outweigh the reasons for using those funds to support one's friends. These types of reasons may not be commensurable or easily reconcilable.

Third, the reasons supporting international friendship do not create obligations, although it is possible for states to formalize their relationships and generate obligations. All minimally just states have good reasons to form an entente cordiale, but they do not have an obligation to do so. Alternatively, states that form a security pact may establish a set of mutual obligations for when they can call on one another's aid. As in the case of interpersonal friendship, obligations can motivate action within a friendship, but it cannot be the basis of a friendship. Along these lines, there is no obligation to create friends. In the international realm, the notion of creation can be taken literally to mean intervening into states to establish minimally just institutions. The notion of what is sometimes called "reform intervention" is not part of international friendship as it is understood here. This view does not deny that intervention may be justified in instances of massive violations of human rights or in aiding the self-defense of another state, but these matters find their source in other principles associated with internationalism or international law and not in international friendships of character.

Fourth, the reasons for international friendships alter the perception of gains that may advantage one's friends. In practices of interpersonal friendships, it is frequently the case that the gain of a friend is like a gain to oneself. In the case of states, the gains of the individual friends within the entente should not necessarily be seen as an existential threat. Such states already recognize reasons not to harm one another's basic institutions and policies. But, it could be argued, as realists do, "that today's friend may be tomorrow's enemy in war" (Grieco 1988:487; see also Waltz 1979:105). From this perspective, the relative gains of one's friends matter a great deal because present friends can always be future enemies.

On the face of it, the realist's logic would also seem to apply to friendships of character. After all, there is no guarantee against the corruption of any state institution, no matter how just. If all state institutions are corruptible, then all minimally just states need to be concerned with the relative gains of their friends. On the other hand, the sort of friendship with which we are concerned is focused on character, and reasonable distinctions can be made between institutional arrangements that are more or less stable. The more stable the minimally just internal arrangements become, the less friends have to worry about their respective relative gains. As the perception of that stability increases, states have more reason to strengthen their friendship, say moving from an entente cordiale to a security pact. Confident in the character of their friends and joined by a motivation to support just institutions and to settle their differences according to fair rules of cooperation, these sorts of countries should not see the gains made by a friend as a threat to their own security.

Finally, in a world composed of states of all stripes, just and unjust, the solidarity of international friendships of character is partial. Within the circle of friends, states are motivated in a way that would have consequences for how they treat their own citizens and one another. Even though friendship does not preclude states from acting friendly with unjust states, the question arises of whether such solidarity generates a bipolar moral world, a world in which states fall either inside or outside the circle of friends. What would partial solidarity mean in a world in which self-help remains the primary mechanism for states to preserve and protect their interests? This question will be considered in chapter 10.

Friendship has been used to describe relationships between all sorts of regimes, just and unjust. Unjust states lack good reason to advance their self-interest; hence they seek allies to advance the self-interests of the individuals, elites, classes, or groups governing the state. They can form no more than alliances, partnerships, and friendships of utility, ideology, or identity. They cannot form international friendships of character. Minimally just states can enter into friendships of a different sort. The motivations for these friendships hinge on reasons to promote and protect more or less just institutional arrangements, do not depend upon the sentiments or feelings of the individuals involved, and need not be free from concerns of self-interest or obligation. These friendships can take at least three different forms and the motive behind each of these forms of friendship is largely the same: the preservation and promotion of just institutions. They differ in terms of how the friends interact and those differences depend in part on the perceived stability of their respective domestic institutional arrangements.

Following the discussion of part 1, international friendships of character may be distinguished by the motives and ways the friends interact. The difficulties that may arise in recognizing forms of international friendship combined with the role that self-interest can play as a motivation, opens the possibility that states may have differing motivations and goals in pursuing international friendship. As is argued in the next chapter, these difficulties will be a potential source of political difference and disagreement within this conception of international friendship.

ten

THE POLITICS OF INTERNATIONAL FRIENDSHIP

What difference would international friendships of character make to international politics? Even if one was convinced by the idea that minimally just states have other-regarding reasons to protect and advance the interests and institutions of other minimally just states, it could be argued that taking such reasons seriously would not be a welcome development. International friendships could have unfortunate systemic consequences even though individual states may have good reason to align in a particular way. It could be argued that not only do states fail to act on such other-regarding reasons, but that it is a good thing that they do not.

Much of this chapter addresses this possibility by exploring how the idea of international friendship would fit into the logic of an anarchic state system that, in significant ways, remains one of self-help. The primary challenge to international friendships of character is that they would create a bipolar moral world, reifying a "with us" or "against us" mentality. From this critical perspective, taking international friendship seriously would moralize and harden a sharp distinction between friends and enemies so much that it would close down the possibility of political engagement with those outside the club of friends. In response to this challenge, I argue that the different forms of international friendships of character discussed in chapter 9 would moderate the distinction between friends and enemies and itself generate different kinds of politics. Depending on the type of friendship, one could imagine at least four kinds of politics: a politics of exclusion/inclusion, a politics of penetration, a politics of entrapment, and a politics of amalgamation. This chapter considers each of these possibilities. Before doing so, however, it imagines what friendships of character could means in an anarchic realm of self-help as well as addresses both realist and cosmopolitan objections.

TAKING INTERNATIONAL FRIENDSHIP SERIOUSLY

It is not unreasonable to think that if international friendships were taken seriously by a sufficient number of states in an anarchical system, then minimally just states would form an alignment or bloc of states. If the international system was composed of some mixture of unjust and minimally just states, then international friendship could result in a bipolar structure, not based on the distribution of power, but based on whether states had other-regarding reasons to protect and promote the basic institutions and policies of other states. States that saw themselves as minimally just would be in one corner and that corner would exclude unjust regimes.

To go further, it would be plausible to think that those regimes that were excluded, or believed themselves to be excluded would create a competing alignment of states. Such a counteralignment could happen even if an alignment of minimally just states would not be oriented toward expansion or conversion of the rest of the world. Assuming the anarchic character of the system and the self-interested character of all states, unjust states would come to view an alignment of friends as a potential threat to themselves. What Snyder says about the effect of alliances would also apply to such an alignment: "Those left out will perceive themselves as possible targets of the alliance, they will feel threatened by it and begin to take measures against it, and that will sharpen the allies' initial image of them as potential adversaries" (1997:24–25).[1]

To some degree, however, this logic would be disrupted by the existence of international friendships of character. The most important disruption is that the bipolar moral world would operate independently of the distribution of power in the system. In other words, in a world in which international friendship was taken seriously, the distribution of power would not itself

generate or prohibit an alignment of more or less just regimes and that alignment would not be determined by whether power was concentrated in one,
a few, or dispersed among many states. As Raymond Dawson and Richard
Rosecrance once observed in another context, "between friends the balance
of power does not mean much" (1966:51). Consequently, in a unipolar power
system, if the single great power was minimally just, then all other minimally just states would have reason to align with it, not because of a desire
to bandwagon, but for reasons of friendship.[2] Alternatively if a singular
superpower was the moral equivalent of an aggressive, unjust hegemonic
power and if the rest of the world was composed of minimally just states,
they would have reason to align together not merely because of the need
to respond to a hegemonic threat, but because they were minimally just
(contrary to the balancing thesis of realism).

If we consider international friendship in a bipolar system, then one,
both, or none of the two great powers could be part of the club of friends.
It is conceivable that if the reasons for friendship were taken seriously, then
the two great powers (if minimally just) could find themselves aligned with
one another (once again, contrary to the balancing thesis of realism). Finally,
in a multipolar system, the club of friends would hold together even if the
alignment of any particular state was not necessary to balance against an
opposing alignment. From the perspective of looking at international politics,
the most interesting case is the one in which this bipolar moral world is associated with a multipolar power structure. For the most part, the discussion
that follows assumes that configuration.

COSMOPOLITAN OBJECTIONS

For very different reasons, both cosmopolitans and realists would find troubling the kind of world that could result from taking seriously international
friendship. Turning to the cosmopolitan objection first, it has been argued
that character-based international friendships entail an incomplete ethical
system that would engender a disturbing form of clubbiness. For example,
Catherine Lu (2009) argues that the idea of international friendship does
not itself engender a critical examination of the more encompassing context
within which these relationships are being formed and enacted. International

friendship offers an incomplete ethic because it does not require states within the club to look outward. Lu considers a case in which two minimally just states are willing to assist one another by providing favorable trading terms in part because it will advantage each one and because each one sees that the terms will advantage the other. Lu writes,

> Can they claim that their special relationship justifies their devotion to projects of mutual advantage, at the expense of their commitment to projects of assistance to burdened societies? Or put another way, how should claims of particular friendships of this kind be reconciled with the claims of burdened societies? Digeser is right that this conflict need not be characterized as one between impartial morality and narrow self-interest. At the same time, however, it would seem that claims of special duties arising from special relationships, especially in the distribution of goods, are difficult to sustain ethically if pursued in a wider context of pervasive injustice or deprivation.
>
> (53)

In response to this objection, nothing in the concept of international friendships rules out larger legal or ethical requirements nor is there anything in the theory of international friendship that precludes consideration of a more encompassing context. As suggested in chapter 9, the idea that international friendships of character serve as reasons for state action is not the same as arguing that those reasons preempt or exclude all others. By themselves, international friendships provide reasons (sometimes compelling, sometimes not) for acting in a way to protect and promote the just institutions and policies of another minimally just state. In some cases, where an international friendship has been formalized into an alliance, there may be duties associated with the friendship. In other instances, the reasons of friendship need not rise to the level of creating obligations. It may very well be that if the special trade arrangements between minimally just states are harming individuals elsewhere then the justness of those arrangements should be questioned. The hope here is that because minimally just countries are minimally just, they would be willing to engage in such a reconsideration of their arrangements. In this sense, Lu is correct that the notion of international friendship is ethically incomplete, if by *complete* one means that a principled scale will always be available to weigh these reasons.

Still, one of the features of interpersonal friendships is that friends tend to overvalue the perspective of one another and undervalue the perspective of those outside the relationship. In addition, as was discussed in chapter 7, Keller and Stroud argue there is an epistemic bias built into our norms of interpersonal friendship that can place the welfare and approval of our friends over what the evidence may indicate. In the case of international friendships, perhaps an analogous bias leads states into foreign engagements that they might otherwise have avoided. This sort of bias may be at the heart of a tension that Felix Berenskoetter points out between friendship and maintaining the norms of international society. As an example of that tension, Berenskoetter considers the U.S.-British relationship and the 2003 decision to invade Iraq (2014:66–67). That relationship, he argues, led the parties down a path that violated norms of nonintervention. The presumption is that without that special relationship, one or both of these states would have been less likely to participate in the invasion.

The clubbiness that concerns Lu, the bias that concerns Keller and Stroud, and the tension that concerns Berenskoetter suggests very real risks to international friendships of character. The fear is that a state becomes trapped into a perspective or even into a course of action that violates other important values. Furthermore, it may not be enough to say that if the parties understand the existence of those risks, then they will also understand that in order to preserve their independence of perspective and ability to act, they must also sometimes resist what their friends are saying or urging them to do. It may not be enough to say this in part because of what Snyder calls the alliance security dilemma.

The alliance security dilemma entails managing the tradeoff between security and autonomy—a form of management that has been expressed in two fears: the fear of abandonment and the fear of entrapment. The fear of abandonment is that a state may depart from an alliance, failing to live up to its commitments or the expectations of its partners, and leaving them in the lurch (Snyder 1984:467; 1997:181; Cha 2000:265). The danger of abandonment is that by being left in the lurch one's security will be diminished. The fear of entrapment or entanglement is that partners can be drawn into con-flicts that do not serve their interests (Liska 1962:74; Kahn 1976:620; Morrow 1994:209; Cha 2000:265; Snyder 1997:181). One of the dangers of entrapment is that a state's autonomy is diminished. According to Snyder, "The risks of abandonment and entrapment tend to vary inversely—hence the dilemma" (1997:181). Responses to one horn of the dilemma therefore exacerbate the dangers posed by the other. In order to diminish the risks of abandon-ment, a state may seek closer ties to its allies. Unfortunately, by tying itself closer, it will also increase the risks of entrapment. This balancing act, of course, is also affected by the responses (perceived and actual) of one's ad-versaries. All of these elements of the alliance security dilemma suggest a location for negotiation and contestation—that is, a location for politics.[3]

In the following, I suggest that the idea of character-based international friendships may diminish the risks of abandonment and thereby open the possibility for political disagreement surrounding the questions of entrap-ment. On the other hand, because there are different levels of international friendship, the fears of abandonment do not entirely disappear. Hence the politics associated with entrapment will differ depending on how close the friends believe themselves to be to one another. Alternatively, when the friendships rise to the level of a special relationship, the risk becomes not merely entrapment but the amalgamation of political identities. The existence of an international friendship of character between independent states must itself generate political differences if the friendship and identity of the friends is to survive. As we shall see in the following section, this feature of international friendship may also serve to respond to possible realist objections to international friendship.

REALIST OBJECTIONS

From a realist perspective, the problem with the bipolar moral world cre-ated by international friendship is easily discerned: Basing alignments on the character of regimes would distort the capacity for states to realign in a multipolar system in order to balance against emerging hegemonic powers. In a multipolar system, as long as states possess a kind of freedom or indeterminacy in their ability to align, they are able to balance against a threat from any direction.[4] If one of the unintended consequences of such a balancing system is that it can preserve the independence and existence of its members through the unintentional creation of an equilibrium, then taking the reasons of international friendship seriously would jeopardize that systemic outcome: If unjust states could not be admitted into the club of friends, or the members of the club of friends would not align against other minimally just states, then it would be impossible to balance against a threat that called for such flexibility.

More troubling is the charge that a bipolar moral world could generate an imperative to destroy as opposed to defeat one's enemies. This imperative could follow from an intensified form of the security dilemma (as opposed to the alliance security dilemma discussed earlier). From the unjust side, the alignment of regimes that call themselves minimally just would be seen as a threat that could be remedied only if that kind of a regime was destroyed. From the minimally just side, the generation of an opposing alignment that was now bent on their obliteration, could lead to the idea that a semblance of peace could exist if only all states were minimally just. Unjust states, then, must be destroyed and remade. The logic of the formation of international friendships appears to lead to a system of inflexible alignments which calls for the destruction of state actors. It would be a world in which the now all too familiar doctrine that you were either "with us" or "against us" would be held by all.

A bipolar moral world would not only distort the capacity to balance against threats, it could also destroy the possibility for international politics. Schmitt argued that the political exists precisely because of the fluidity of the international system in identifying friends and enemies. The indeterminacy of alignments that the neorealists identify as part and parcel of a multipolar system is where the political is located. Accordingly, the decision of who is one's enemy and who is one's friend is a political decision (1966:26). If we impose ethical, aesthetic, economic, religious, or cultural criteria upon that decision, the possibility for politics dissipates. In effect, these nonpolitical criteria *determine* an outcome. They settle and harden what must be unsettled and fluid if politics is to exist. From a Schmittean perspective, because international friendship would be based on a set of ethical reasons for states to align, it paradoxically destroys the friend/enemy distinction that constitutes the political.

For Schmitt and for realists who resist the importation of "moralisms" into international politics, a world divided by moral judgments is one in which the ferocity of modern warfare would be exponentially increased. As states fight for some larger moral stake—be in humanity, human rights, or justice—the opponent moves from merely being an enemy to being a monster (1966:36, 54). Once this demonization has happened, it is virtually impossible to realign in a manner that could admit such evil characters into one's club. The presence of international friendships would be something to be deeply regretted, assuming the desirability of state independence, of limits to interstate violence, and of the political.

POLITICS AND THE FORMATION OF INTERNATIONAL FRIENDSHIP

The realist critique points to the undesirability of international friendships of character from a systemic perspective. To respond to these challenges, it is necessary to say a few more things about the logic of international friendship and the possible sites or locations for politics that would be created by such friendships. I will begin by assuming the conditions noted herein (the international system is anarchic, multipolar, composed of a mixture of states, and that minimally just states are acting on the reasons for international friendship) and accepting the claim that international friendship would generate an alignment of states that perceive themselves as minimally just. The creation of an inflexible bipolar moral world, however, assumes not only that minimally just states will align with one another but also that they cannot associate, partner, or ally with unjust states. As chapter 9 noted, this assumption does not necessarily hold. Although minimally just states have good reasons to align with one another (and hence good reasons not to align against one another), they may also (on occasion) have good reasons— say security—to ally with unjust regimes.

International friendships of character are not the same thing as alliances/ alignments/friendships based on economic gain or military security, but they do not preclude such partnerships. In fact, to the extent that states have good reason to preserve themselves because of the quality of their own institutions that same reason can also serve as a justification for partnerships with states that advance that goal, but are not minimally just. Alternatively, international economic and political engagements with autocracies can be supported in terms of their possible effects on promoting international peace and cooperation and generating the conditions necessary for political reform. In making these claims, I am holding in abeyance other kinds of reasons that could discourage partnering with unjust governments—particularly those from a human rights perspective. The importance of this claim is that even though international friendship would generate a bipolar moral world, it would not preclude what Count de St. Aulaire in the early twentieth century called the penetration of alliances.[5] If minimally just states can ally with unjust states for reasons of security or utility, then the bipolar moral world need not find expression in a bipolar political world.

Two implications can be drawn from this possibility of the penetration of alignments. The first is that international friendships would be sticky, but only in one direction. Minimally just states that were motivated by friendship would hang together for reasons that alliances to and between unjust states could not. Because minimally just states have good reasons to support and promote the internal institutions of other minimally just states, they would not see one another as ever posing a threat to their own survival.[6] Such is not the case between minimally just and unjust states, although there is no reason to see themselves as posing existential threats to one another. This asymmetry means that minimally just and unjust states live in two different worlds that can overlap. If minimally just states are willing to ally with unjust states, then unjust states will not necessarily form a counteralignment to an entente of international friendship. Nor will unjust states stick together unless their alignment is seen as necessary for their security. Consequently, if an unjust state must leave an alliance of unjust states in order to balance against a threat, then it will not have the same kinds of reasons available to stay within the unjust alliance (bracketing reasons of bandwagoning, ideology, ethnicity, culture, religion, and so on). In other words, the bipolar moral world of international friendship would be more complicated than what would be suggested by a Schmittean analysis.

A second implication is that the penetration of alignments could itself generate political disagreements or what I will call a "politics of exclusion/ inclusion" and a "politics of penetration." The political would not, as the Schmittean analysis suggests, go away in the formation of international friendships, rather it would be transformed. The politics of exclusion/inclusion entails establishing which states are within and which states are outside the club of friends. The politics of penetration concerns the dynamics generated when minimally just states are allied with unjust regimes. The following sections expand on the character of those forms of politics.

THE POLITICS OF EXCLUSION/INCLUSION

The politics of exclusion/inclusion can be conducted both within and between minimally just states as governments decide whether to admit previously unjust regimes into an entente cordiale. Practical reason is the basis for this politics insofar as states take seriously and act on the reasons for international friendship. Taking these reasons seriously, however, does not mean that they should be applied in a dogmatic or algorithmic fashion. Obviously, while various dogmatic conceptions of justice may be advanced and hardened into ideologies, practical reason requires an openness to different perspectives, understanding those perspectives on their own terms, and then critically engaging them. The common opinion of humankind or various monitoring organizations may come to identify certain governments as oppressive and other governments as more or less responsive to and protective of their people, but such judgments and conclusions have to be open to assessment in the political realm. Even when a general sense of justice is discerned and agreed upon, the constitutive elements of that sense may receive different weight by different parties. Some may weigh individual freedom more highly than equality. Some may argue that security can trump civil liberties more easily than others and so on. These differences suggest that there may be more than one way to understand when a state is minimally just.

Finally, the application of a shared sense of justice can also yield different perspectives. For example, institutional changes may have occurred in a revolution, but the new boss may be the same as the old boss. Alternatively, a coup may result in the accession of a benevolent ruler who is working toward the establishment of a just set of arrangements, but has yet to achieve them. Consequently, while such a leader may establish greater civil and economic liberties, he or she retains autocratic power. In addition, regimes may backslide. Countries that have been identified as being minimally just one day can slip back into autocracy the next. These difficulties in identifying and applying the idea of what constitutes a *minimally just* regime do not mean that the term is meaningless or entirely up for grabs. They do suggest that while the question of what it means to be *minimally just* can be informed by thoughtful philosophers and theoreticians, it is ultimately a political decision that unavoidably calls upon the imperfect judgments of policy-makers. In short, the politics of international friendship is a politics of identity.

For example, the logic of international friendships suggests that we should not be surprised that the character of a state (e.g., Russia, Ukraine, Egypt, Tunisia) is important to the level and kind of relationship that minimally just states will have to it. The ouster of the Ukrainian president Viktor Yanukovych from office, for example, has been taken by some as a sign that a less corrupt government is in the offing and hence the regime is deserving of greater support and cooperation, just as, in the 1990s, the ouster of the communist leadership in the Soviet Union was read as a movement toward a more accountable regime. The question of whether a regime is in or out of the circle of friends becomes a political question that may be continually negotiated and renegotiated. All of this may happen alongside whatever political and economic interests are at play. These are the sorts of questions that compose a politics of inclusion/exclusion.

THE POLITICS OF PENETRATION

The politics of penetration is somewhat different, insofar as it emerges in cases in which unjust states are allied with minimally just states. The terrain for this politics is created because the parties to such arrangements as well as political actors within each country can have different understandings of the same relationship. From the perspective of the minimally just state it is politically easier to maintain the relationship if it is a "real friendship" (as opposed to merely a friendship of utility) with a regime whose character is on the upswing. One may be allied with a tyrant, but at least it is a benevolent dictator whose policies are moving in the right direction. In contrast, for realists it is more important to see the relationship solely in terms of utility and the effects of the relationship on the balance of power or threat (simply because realists will view all international relationships in these terms). As Derrida notes, between these perspectives a politics can be generated through different understandings of the relationship. The one party sees the relationship solely in terms of utility. The other party sees it as more than a relationship of utility in that the internal character of autocratic regime matters. If either the utility of the alliance changes or the quality of the unjust regime changes (i.e., improves or becomes more brutal), this difference in understanding can give rise to political negotiation and contestation.

An illustration (however imperfect) may be helpful. Before the Shah of Iran was deposed by a revolution in 1979, the Carter administration in the United States was deeply divided over how to understand the relationship (Schmitz 2006). In 1978, Zbigniew Brzezinski, Carter's national security adviser, vigorously argued for U.S. intervention on the Shah's behalf and called for U.S. support for his crackdown on internal dissent. These tactics, he believed, were essential for maintaining the stability of the region, preventing Soviet dominance, and maintaining American international credibility with its allies. In contrast, Secretary of State Cyrus Vance argued that Brzezinski's "iron fist" approach was inconsistent with the human rights orientation that the Carter administration wished to advance in foreign policy. Consequently, Vance argued that the United States should push the Shah to engage in a political solution which advanced the cause of democratization. In effect, Vance and Brzezinski had very different understandings of the United States' partnership with Iran. Brzezinski saw the relationship in purely strategic terms and Vance saw it as a strategic relationship in which the character of the partner mattered a great deal. For the former it was a partnership of utility and for the latter it was something that could, under the right sorts of reforms in Iran, resemble what I have called an international friendship of character. It is of course true that even if a common understanding of the relationship existed between all parties, difficult decisions would still have to be negotiated. Moreover, this brief illustration truncates a larger context and history that is a necessary part of understanding the partnership. The point here is merely to illustrate how the absence of a shared understanding of the nature of the relationship generated a political dispute that ultimately was settled by Carter's decision not to continue to support the Shah's position in Iran.

The sort of dispute between Vance and Brzezinski can also find expression in the states themselves. From the perspective of the autocratic state, the alliance could simply be one of utility in which both parties receive significant economic and strategic benefits. Moreover, that assessment may be correct. From the perspective of the minimally just state, however, the relationship may not be viewed solely in those terms, but may include the expectation of pressing for internal changes in the name of human rights or democratization. Once again, these differences in understanding the nature of the relationship give rise to different expectations. As Aristotle wrote, "Friends are most at odds when they are not friends in the way they think they are" (1985:1165b). This observation, which Derrida makes much of in his work on friendship, may be even more appropriate in the case of interstate friendships insofar as the understandings of just and unjust states may be significantly different when it comes to their partnerships. These sorts of surprises were particularly acute in the Carter administration, but periodically arise in American negotiations with China and, perhaps, with its relationship to Russia for the past twenty years.[7]

THE POLITICS OF ENTRAPMENT AND ABANDONMENT IN INTERNATIONAL FRIENDSHIPS

There may be other arenas in which international friendships would generate political contestations. In the literature of managing alliances, for example, a distinction is frequently made between short- and long-term interests and how these types of interests can be sources of political dispute. The central short-term issues involve the distribution of costs and benefits. While states come together to form alliances in order to satisfy convergent interests, the management question arises because allies can have divergent interests that can pull them apart. As Snyder writes, "The interests at stake in intra-alliance bargaining typically are conflicting interests in how to implement the allies' common interests *vis-à-vis* an adversary." As he notes, these conflicts may involve military contributions, diplomatic positions, and strategies to adopt toward an adversary and whether to admit a new ally (1997:171). The results of intra-alliance negotiations are dependent on the participants' bargaining power which, in turn, is contingent on a state's level of independence and its degree of commitment to the alliance. To the extent that the states joined in the alignments of international friendship will have divergent interests (and there is no reason to think that they will not), then the realist analysis of these traditional short-term concerns will also apply to the management of international friendships. What international friendship adds to these negotiations is a sensitivity to how their political decisions could adversely affect or promote their respective minimally just institutions and basic policies.

Things are somewhat different when considering the conventional analysis of the long-term health of an alliance relationship. A key challenge here involves how states manage the alliance security dilemma. This dilemma had come up earlier in the discussion of cosmopolitan objections to international friendship. In that discussion, the problem was how to deal with the risks of entrapment, i.e., states being brought into international engagements that they would not otherwise do because of their friendship. The problem was compounded if lowering the risks of entrapment meant raising the risks of abandonment. The logic of international friendship, however, may disrupt or dissolve the alliance security dilemma. Unlike partnerships of utility or security, international friendships may significantly lower the risks of abandonment. They do so because international friendships turn on the perceived internal character of the regimes. As long as the perception remained that the states were minimally just, and they were motivated by the reasons of friendship, then the problem of abandonment would be mitigated if not eliminated altogether. If the fear of abandonment disappears, then so does the alliance security dilemma. In other words, states need not risk abandonment by trying to avoid entrapment.

If aligned minimally just states should have no fear of abandonment, then international friendships are similar to formal alliances insofar as they provide a fair degree of freedom of action for the participants. In addition, international friendships of character may include the norms of consultation and frank speech, of cooperation and bounded disagreement that regulate the conduct of their negotiations. In a way, the disappearance of the alliance security dilemmas enables the appearance of politics. States can disagree and still expect to remain friends. Consequently, entrapment remains a risk, but it is a risk that can be negotiated without the fear of abandonment.

While this general logic regarding international friendship is in some respects correct, it needs to be fine-tuned. Because different levels of friendship exist, the fear of abandonment may not be entirely dissipated at every level. Freshly minted, minimally just regimes will find themselves at the outer edges of international friendship. Their admission to an entente cordiale is provisional insofar as their just character has not been fully formed and tested: Has power been peacefully transferred? Have arbitrary rulings and corrupt officials been rooted out? Are the basic rights of minorities and individuals respected? In order to respond to the risks of abandonment, new regimes may desire to move up the ladder of friendship and into the tighter circle of mutual security. The difficulty here, however, mirrors the difficulty of crossing the threshold of being identified as a minimally just state. How stable must a minimally just regime be if it is to be admitted into the higher circle of friendship? How much corruption needs to be eliminated? How many fair and free elections need to be held? As in the earlier questions of meeting a threshold of being minimally just, these decisions may be informed by scholars and observers of the international scene, but they are still political decisions informed by practical reason.

A state at the edge of the circle of friends may have incentives to elide the difference between a friendship understood as an entente cordiale and a friendship understood as a mutual security pact. It may try to pull other minimally just states into outside conflicts in order to generate expectations of collective security. From the perspective of the inner circle, a blurring of expectations may be driven by claims of military necessity and the importance of the state's resources to an alliance. Alternatively, it may be driven by a sense that if the security demands of this fledgling democracy are assuaged, then it will be less reckless. Or the inner circle may push a minimally just state down the ladder of friendship if there is a fear that it will entrap the circle of friends in unwanted conflicts. These first two responses, of course, are familiar to realist analyses of state behavior. Pushing a state down the ladder of friendship (say from inclusion in a mutual security pact to a member of an entente cordiale) becomes a possible option within the practices of international friendship. It entails calling into question the domestic character of the regime in order to signal some distance from that government.

To illustrate, consider another imperfect example: Prior to and immediately following the 2008 Russo-Georgian war, there was a question as to how far the West would go in supporting Georgia's attempt to recapture South Ossetia and defend it against the Russian invasion. To the extent that Georgia was aligned with the United States and there were serious discussions of bringing Georgia into NATO, it could play up its democratic credentials. To the extent that it desired not to be entrapped by Georgia's dealings with Russia, the West could play down those credentials. As Nicholas D. Kristof wrote in an op-ed piece arguing that NATO distance itself from Georgia, "Look carefully and you see that Georgia isn't quite the shining beacon of democracy that Americans sometimes believe" (2008). Within the politics of friendship, if a state is seen as something less than democratic, then other minimally just states may have less reason to aid or assist in the protection of the regime.

An important complicating factor in the different levels of friendships of character is that friends can be useful to one another. While utility is not the basis of an international friendship of character it can create certain confusions within the circle of friends. International friends at the level of an entente may view one another as useful, but, as friends of character, see utility as a deficient basis for their relationship. Without reassurances, they may believe that they are *merely* useful to the circle of friends and not part of the circle of friends. Because both justice and utility are in the mix within the circle of friends, the motivations of one's friends becomes a political issue. Within the logic of an international friendship of character, once the parties to the relationship can no longer be assured that they are acting out of a character-based friendship, the relationship may slip into a relationship based on narrow self-interest. Reconsideration, repair, and renovation of the relationship would be possible, raising once again the politics of exclusion/inclusion.

As discussed in chapter 9, the inner sanctum of international friendships of character is the special relationship. It is a relationship in which states have expectations of an extremely close association—even closer than what is found in a collective security arrangement. In this kind of relationship, states are drawn together not merely because they are stable, minimally just regimes, but because they also share some deeper tie of culture, ethnicity, or historical sacrifice. Within this relationship, states may believe that they have reason to protect one another from both external and internal threats. Even if the alliance security dilemma no longer applies, special relationships raise their own risks and potential political terrain. The primary risk in this kind of friendship is losing one's autonomy. Preserving one's independence requires a certain respect for the independent actions of one's friend. It may go so far as not preventing states from making serious mistakes. The risk of a special relationship is that distance can be so diminished that the friendship is transformed into something like a transnational self. In foreign affairs this may happen when one state begins to look like a mere extension of another state. One could call this an empire of friendship, where the imperial proclivities of the more powerful friend, as expressed in its own identity, extinguish the autonomy of the friend.

The politics of special relationships clearly include the ordinary differences associated with conflicting interests. They also include, however, negotiations and contestations over the friend's autonomy or what could be called the politics of amalgamation. On the one hand, a friend's assertion of too much independence could challenge the existence of the special relationship. In the extreme, it could generate a charge of betrayal. On the other hand, a failure to assert such independence could generate claims of toadyism or of being a lapdog (as the British prime minister Tony Blair faced in his relationship to the United States during and after the 2003 invasion of Iraq). The political terrain of a special relationship is generated by the possibility that when the fear of abandonment is completely gone, it can be replaced by an overwhelming risk to one's separate identity and a more complete entrapment.

One way in which the amalgamation politics of special relationships can be played out is through discussion of reconfiguring the relationship. Reasserting one's autonomy may entail denying solidarity between the two countries: extraordinary past sacrifices of blood and treasure may be recognized as an ordinary quid quo pro; a shared cultural heritage may be understood as an appendage of imperialism; the commonality of ethnicity may be broken apart by rethinking the importance of difference in local ways of life. Alternatively, a special relationship can be contested by calling into question the minimally just credentials of one's friend.

An illustration of this kind of contestation appears in John J. Mearsheimer and Stephen M. Walt's analysis of the U.S.-Israel relationship. Assuming, for the sake of argument, that this relationship is a special one of the sort considered here, Mearsheimer and Walt can be seen as engaging in a politics of friendship. From this perspective, such a politics seeks to pry apart the forces of amalgamation that appear to hobble the independence of both actors. Of the six moral arguments that Mearsheimer and Walt see as the contestable basis for American solidarity with Israel, they argue that Israeli political practices and legal institutions are "at odds with the core American values." They feel it is important to make this case, even though the prior paragraph argues that "being democratic neither justifies nor fully explains the extent of American support for Israel" (2007:87). On their view, whatever special relationship is alleged to exist is really an artifact of the Israel lobby. The core of their argument is that American ability to advance its own interests has been compromised and Israeli policy distorted. The parties cannot, in short, speak frankly to one another about the differences that they have. The politics of international friendship requires disagreement in order to preserve the friendship and prevent it from shifting into something else (i.e., a transnational self).

THE POLITICS OF FRIENDSHIP

I have argued that international friendships need not be based solely on economic or security concerns. It is conceivable for international friendship to be based on the character of the regimes in question. But even within these international friendships of character there are different degrees of proximity and there are issues surrounding who is in and who is outside the club of friends. Some newly minted regimes may be minimally just, but more or less stable. Among the more stable just regimes, some relationships are understood by the parties as sufficiently close to establish collective security arrangements and other relationships can be characterized as "special" because the ties of history and culture have created heightened expectations for consultation and loyalty. These differences in kinds of alliances and levels of closeness present the possibility to generate a politics of international friendship.

The idea that there is a politics associated with friendship is indebted to Derrida's (1997) discussion of the history of philosophical attempts to understand friendship. In that work, Derrida uses Aristotle's distinction between three kinds of interpersonal friendship to point to various aporiae and sources of misperception that are built into the relationship. He argues that Aristotle's distinctions between friendships of virtue, friendships of utility or usefulness, and friendships of pleasure are further multiplied by additional subcategories within these forms of friendship. Each of these categories of friendship comes with its own set of expectations regarding how the friends should treat one another and ultimately what just treatment entails. Derrida believes that these various distinctions raise a difficulty because, despite our insistence on their separateness, we have a tendency to "smuggle" one form of friendship into another. Business friendships based on utility can acquire a more virtuous cast when the parties begin to trust one another and move away from the language of contract and toward the language of good faith. This movement is not at all unusual, but even when it happens, Derrida notes the friendships try to occupy a middle ground in which both types of friendship operate simultaneously. This kind of "trust, but verify" attitude is one in which the friends see themselves as more than partners, but never abandon the formal, legal protections that more impersonal forms of business rely upon.

Alternatively, Derrida suggests that the desire to move from a friendship of utility to a friendship of virtue and portray it as such, need not arise simultaneously for each party, and so one friend may come to believe that the relationship has moved to the ground of good faith and trust while the other party sees the relationship solely in terms of its usefulness. In both of these cases, enormous differences in expectations can be created. According to Derrida, these differences make it impossible to "'judge the just' in friendship" and consequently a grievance arises, "not between enemies but between friends who, as it were, have been misled, and have misled each other because they have first mistaken friendships, confusing in one case friendship based on virtue with friendship based on usefulness, in another, legal and ethical friendship, etc." (1997:206). On Bonnie Honig's reading, this slippage between forms of friendship is a place of politics (Honig 2001:78). It is a place where contestation and negotiation can occur precisely because the misperception forces the parties to talk to one to another and think about the character of the relationship. At an interpersonal level, a politics of friendship exists (at least in part) because of the difficulties, and for Derrida the impossibility, of properly calibrating where one is in a particular relationship. These negotiations over the character of the relationship are never ultimately resolved in a manner that the same kinds of discussions cannot recur.

My argument is that Derrida's portrayal of a politics of friendship can be usefully applied to international friendship. In chapter 3, I argued that Derrida's position was not particularly compelling at the interpersonal level, in part because the role of utility has been reduced to a deficient reason for most of our contemporary practices of friendship. In addition, the presence of a repertoire of ordinarily appropriate motivations provides more give to our relationships. However plausible those arguments may be, it seems that if international friendships of character were taken seriously, then Derrida's argument would be more applicable. At the international level, utility as a basis for friendship will remain compelling and the possible motivations for friendships of character are narrower. What may be the case at the international level may not be true at the interpersonal level and vice versa. More importantly, the possibility of a politics of international friendship responds to the critique that a practice of international friendship would not necessarily preclude the emergence of political differences.

THE POLITICS OF INTERNATIONAL FRIENDSHIP

Much of part 3 has explored how the idea of international friendship could fit into an ongoing system of independent states, some of which have good reasons to be self-interested and others of which may not. Those states that have good reasons to be self-interested are minimally just. Those states that are minimally just also have good reasons to protect the basic institutional arrangements and policies of other minimally just states. States that are moved by such reasons and mutually recognize such motivations in other states can compose an international friendship of character. As I have argued, for a variety of reasons, these international friendships of character can take different forms.

Not surprisingly, this perspective is "state-centric." As set out in chapter 9, it rests on the assumptions that states are indispensable conditions of value. If that assumption is incorrect or if it proves to be incorrect in the future, then the logic that supports the idea of international friendships of character would no longer apply. If, however, states continue to condition value and exist in a system in which self-help remains an important way to protect their interests, then the possibility for international friendship is embedded in the reasons for advancing the self-interest of minimally just states. Realizing that possibility may not be the best of all worlds, but neither would it result in a frozen, divided system between friends and enemies in which all differences along with politics would disappear.

This chapter has argued that international friendships would themselves generate political divisions. In part, this is the case because international friendships that were formalized into alliances would still have to make the kinds of decisions that other alliances have to make. States, even states that share a common character of being minimally just, will have different perspectives on security and economic advantage as well as ideological and cultural differences. These differences may be based on differences in resources, geopolitical position, level of development, historical circumstance, and so on and can themselves generate political disputes, coalitions, and negotiations. In addition, the politics of alliances emerges in deciding how to divide up burdens and benefits, how to sell an alliance to a domestic audience (two-level bargaining) and how to manage the partners once they are in an alliance. Whether minimally just states handle these kinds of political disputes any differently from other kinds of states, they always have reason to act in manner that protects and promotes one another's just institutions and policies. They have reason to subscribe to certain adverbial conditions that will guide their interactions. In addition to these usual sources of political engagement, this chapter has argued that partnerships between just and unjust regimes as well as friendships between just states could generate their own political disagreements and different forms of politics. These include a politics of inclusion/exclusion, a politics of penetration, a politics of entrapment and a politics of amalgamation. Within the logic of international friendship there exists a great deal of room for the sort of slippage that Derrida discusses in his analysis of the politics of friendship.

International friendships of character need not mean the end of politics nor need it lead to a bipolar moralized world that intensified the level of international violence and threatened the state system itself. Instead, this chapter has suggested that international friendships can themselves generate political disagreements within a normative structure that sought to maintain the just institutions and policies of the participants. If the reasons for international friendship were acted upon, it is unlikely that in an anarchic system composed of states we could ever evade or overcome politics. Even if Kantian islands of perpetual peace could emerge in the anarchic waters of international relations, they would not be entirely conflict-free precisely because states could be friends.

SOME CONCLUDING THOUGHTS

These chapters have offered a consideration of friendship that is also a reconsideration of the idea's role in political thought. In the past couple of decades there has been something of a revival of interest in friendship by political theorists. This book is part of a larger conversation rethinking a concept that had fallen out of favor of Western political philosophy for quite some time. With a few exceptions, however, much of that revival has been one in which friendship is seen as a way to revitalize or recover something that is dying or lost in our contemporary political life. It is sometimes portrayed as an important part of the puzzle of politics that connects disparate pieces that appear otherwise unrelated.

This book is a reconsideration of friendship in a second sense insofar as it has taken issue with some of the more optimistic hopes attached to friendship. International friendships of character are a limited ideal that apply to regimes of a certain sort, motivated by certain reasons to interact in certain ways. At an interpersonal level, the state can encourage friendship by removing significant barriers (many of which governments themselves set up), but there are significant risks in using the law to foster friendship directly.

Friendship in a delegitimized political environment may help keep the opposition alive, but it is an extraordinarily challenging ideal with no guaranteed outcome. Civic friendship is not a scalable ideal in contemporary, complex, large societies, but a way for smaller groups of individuals to join the coolness of their civic duties to the warmth of friendship. Bridging/ bonding friendship is not the only ideal in town, but it is one that expresses the values of individuality and choice implicit in many of our practices of friendship.

Finally, this book has reconsidered friendship not as a relationship in which we can set out its necessary and sufficient conditions, but as a family of practices that are loosely joined by a changing repertoire of motivations and adverbial conditions. In our current practices of friendship, material self-interest, utility, and obligation play no more than deficient roles. At the individual level, pleasure, desire, affection, respect, appreciative love, and care can play larger parts in motivating individuals to initiate and sustain their friendships. At the international level, friendship may be motivated by self-interest, utility, ideology, identity, and perhaps justice. The point is that friendship is not just one thing. One of the great temptations in thinking about friendship is to believe that one's particular ideal of friendship is the only way to understand it. There is no one true friendship. There are, however, true friendships.

NOTES

INTRODUCTION

1. Recent thinkers who have taken up the question of politics and friendship include Allen (2004), Arendt (1968), Derrida (1997), Frank (2005), Friedman (1993), King (2007), May (2012), Nixon (2015), Schwarzenbach (2009), Scorza (2004), Smith (2011a), and Vernon (2010). Some of the prominent legal thinkers to have taken up the issue of friendship and the law include Goodrich (2005), Leib (2011), and Rosenbury (2007). Writers who have considered the connection between friendship and international politics include Koschut and Oelsner (2014), Oelsner (2007), and Lu (2009). In the realm of political science, some attention has been paid to the role of friendship in legislative politics; for example, Arnold, Deen, and Patterson (2000), Baker (1999), Caldeira and Patterson (1987), Childs (2013), Patterson (1959), Wahlke et al. (1962). The renewed interest in friendship and politics does not mean that previous thinkers, politicians, and commentators had entirely ignored the ideas of friend and friendship. However, at least in the West, early modern and modern political thinkers have largely been uninterested in offering sustained theoretical accounts of politics and friendship of the sort encountered in Aristotle (Smith 2011b:15). It is not infrequently claimed that liberalism is responsible for this exile, having relegated friendship to the private realm (see, for example, Ludwig 2010:134–35), although nonliberal modern ideologies such as nationalism, Marxism, and fascism have also paid little attention to the idea of friendship. The exception may be found in eighteenth- and nineteenth-century republican ideology (Godbeer 2009; Schweitzer 2006). In any case, there is a modern theoretical neglect of friendship

in the West and this neglect was probably overdetermined by such factors as the emergence of the large, impersonal state, industrialization, Weberian rationalism, a culture of rights, the increased mobility of individuals, and nationalism.

2. "Facebook Users Average 3.74 Degrees of Separation," *BBC News*, November 23, 2011. Accessed July 15, 2012. http://www.bbc.co.uk/news/technology-15844230.

3. For a useful, but dated, discussion of the various ways that friends have gotten American presidents into trouble, see Baker (1999:34–35).

4. Skeptics of the usefulness of friendship in politics include Bickford (1996), Jeske (2008), Keller (2009), and King (2007).

5. The reference to the kaleidoscopic character of friendship comes from Cicero. The awareness of the inherent diversity of friendship comes from Sandra Lynch (2005).

6. The Greek word that is commonly translated as friendship (*philia*) appears in Thucydides's *Peloponnesian Wars* when the Mytliteneans disparage their fear-based alliance with Athens by pleading to the Spartans: "How could we feel any genuine friendship or any confidence in our liberty when we were in a situation like this?" See Thucydides 3.12.1. See also Konstan (1997:83) for a fuller discussion of ancient uses of friendship in interstate affairs and Devere, Mark, and Verbitsky (2011), Devere (2014), and Roshchin (2011, 2014) for a discussion of the history and role of friendship in international treaties.

7. Schwarzenbach argues that *friendship* appears as far back as Thomas More's *Utopia* in 1516 (2009:255, 2011:32–33; see also Roshchin 2006 and Devere, Mark, and Verbitsky 2011).

8. For example, since Winston Churchill's "Sinews of Peace" address of March 5, 1946, at Westminster College, Fulton, Missouri, politicians, analysts, and journalists have considered the plausibility, nature, and implications of the "special relationship" between the British Commonwealth and Empire and the United States. Commentators have also explored the nature of the friendship between Israel and the United States. Since the Johnson administration, critics and defenders have sought to make sense of the origins and nature of this "special" relationship.

9. See, for example, Berenskoetter (2007), Constantin (2011), Devere, Mark, and Verbitsky (2011), Koschut and Oelsner (2014), Lu (2009), Oelsner (2007, 2014), Oelsner and Vion (2011), Patsias and Deschenes (2011), Roshchin (2006, 2011), Schwarzenbach (2011), Slomp (2007), Smith (2011b, 2014), and Vion (2007).

1. FRIENDSHIP AS A FAMILY OF PRACTICES

1. The Epicureans also saw the relationship between utility and friendship in this way. Epicurus wrote, "One who is always looking for help is not a friend, nor is one who never associates help with friendship. For the former trades sentiment for

recompense, while the latter cuts off confident expectation in regard to the future." He then continued with one of the most delightful expressions of friendship: "Friendship dances round the world announcing to us all that we should wake up and felicitate one another" (Long and Sedley 1987:126).

2. In making this assertion, I do not deny those positions (such as Kierkegaard's) that largely dismiss the value of friendship (see Kierkegaard 1991; Smith 2011a). There are important reasons to value friendship, but friendship need not be a value for everyone.

3. Those who see friendship as a much broader concept may also find this focus excessively narrow. For example, Mark Vernon (2010) and Graham M. Smith (2011a) use it in a much more expansive way. In Smith's analysis, friendship is an idea that connects "a wide-range of bonds from the immediate family, to the familial, to the pleasurable, to the useful, to the virtuous" (2011a:3). Smith sees his work as adopting a functional as opposed to a definitional approach to friendship (2014:37, 42–43). From this perspective, friendship in Western political thought "has come to take on a wide variety of forms: *eros*, *philia*, *agape*, amity, dynasty, citizenship, concord, loyalty, community, solidarity, neighbourliness, fraternity, compatriotism, and comradeship" (Smith 2011a:15). In contrast, the ordinary, commonsensical view is identified by Smith as mysterious, ambiguous, culturally and historically relative, and "not exceptionally coherent" (9). In response, this book seeks to abate that mystery to some degree. I depart from Smith's claim that the commonsense view "hides a host of questions and ambiguities" (9). Instead of saying that they are hidden from view, the sorts of questions and ambiguities that Smith raises of and about friendship are infrequently attended to. They are simply waiting to be explored.

4. The nature of these differences has been of concern for sociologists. For example, Ray Pahl writes that "It is surely the case that any attempt to tie a particular form or style of friendship to men or women in general is a singularly fruitless exercise" (2000:126). While women may be "more touchy-feely" and men more "inarticulate," the styles of friendship for the genders, according to Pahl, are very much connected to context that override expectations of gender. In his view, a rigid distinction between the genders is more a cliché than an empirical fact. Along these lines, he argues that economic circumstances can have enormous consequences for the quality and number of friends. Nevertheless, hard and fast distinctions in types of friendship are also not a simple function of class. He concludes that sociologists are "now much more wary about playing their traditionally strongest cards of class and gender and are coming to acknowledge the fluidity, if not the slipperiness of contemporary styles of friendship and the need to place these styles in context" (142).

5. As the anthropologist Fernando Santos-Granero notes, "relations of friendship can be found in almost all human societies, models of friendship vary substantially, making it difficult to offer a single, all-encompassing definition of

Friendship with a capital F" (2007:9). See also Bell and Coleman (1999:4) and Guichard, Heady, and Tadesse (2003:10).

6. This brief summary of the "Lysis" is not meant to deny the complexity of the dialogue, which has been discussed more thoroughly by a number of different commentators. As with all of the Platonic dialogues, there are a variety of ways to read it. See, for example, Bolotin (1979), Vlastos (1981), Pangle (2003), Penner and Rowe (2005), Fuller (2008), Nichols (2009), and Smith (2011a). At the conclusion of the dialogue, Socrates says that none of the accounts that he discusses tells us what a friend is (Plato 1991:222e). Others are more willing to see Socrates as holding onto the utility claims associated with friendship (see, for example, Ludwig 2010).

7. For a variety of reasons, the "Lysis" is a particularly strange dialogue. Paul W. Ludwig's supple reading of it argues that Socrates, by entertaining the extreme view that all beings are evil, provides "a model for how to keep foundations-level analysis relevant to social and political problems" (2010:146). By getting the participants to the dialogue to see their friendships skeptically, they can be nudged toward the philosophic life. According to Ludwig, Socrates's negative ontology is a way of "privileging philosophy over friendship" (149). In other words, in this dialogue, Socrates may be showing us how the "philosophic way of life inevitably becomes philosophy's highest theme" (147). In contrast, I am suggesting that if we take seriously the inability of philosophy to nail down the meaning of friendship—after all, Socrates states at the dialogue's conclusion that none of the accounts of friendship succeed—and we keep in mind that Socrates and Lysis agree at the end of the dialogue that they are friends, then the engagement of philosophy yields a friendship. From within the text of this dialogue (bracketing Plato's other work), philosophy, with its outlandish claims and, at least in this dialogue, its empty conclusions, appears to be instrumental to the creation of a friendship (whether friendship is the greatest good is never asserted or entertained). All readers of "Lysis" need to take seriously (even if they deeply disagree with) the possibility that philosophy is merely the handmaiden to friendship (for the opposite conclusion see Ludwig 2010 and Pangle 2003) and that it may be impossible to capture the essence (if there is one) of friendship.

8. Despite defending friendship as a family resemblance concept, Lynch also argues that there are "crucial structural features constitutive of friendship: affection, enjoyment as a byproduct rather than an end of friendship, the role of choice, and friendship's contribution to self-knowledge," none of which are sufficiently recognized by Aristotle (2005:31). For Lynch, the etymology of friendship involves an emotional bond and voluntary choice (4–5). In contrast, what I see as "structural features" of friendship are contingent but include certain motivations, their mutual recognition, and adverbial self-disclosure.

Jeske explores another interesting possible understanding of the complexity of friendship. Even if friendship is not a family resemblance concept, it may be that "we are unable to articulate or to represent the determinate features of the world that make it the case that a relationship is a friendship or is some particular type of friendship." We can determine that a relationship is a friendship and we may be able to determine that it is a friendship of a particular kind. The problem with friendship, as with concepts of blue or beauty, is that "we may not have concepts sufficient for stating or representing what it is in virtue of which the relationship is friendship." We simply cannot "grasp all of forms that friendship can take, and we cannot give an enumeration of all the determinate features of the world that may be constituents of friendships" (Jeske 2008:98). As I understand it, the source of this difficulty is that we cannot "articulate all of the distinctions that we can grasp . . . or we may not be able to grasp all of the distinctions in the world" (89). If we understand friendship as a practice, perhaps it is possible (despite its conventional nature) that we can generate distinctions that we cannot grasp nor fully articulate the distinctions that we can grasp. Consequently, even if we see friendship as a social practice and reject the idea that our understandings of friendship bear a family resemblance to one another, we may not be able to articulate why this relationship is a friendship or a friendship of a particular type "because the determinates may be extraordinarily complex" (98). How one would decide between a family resemblance account and this alternative is a difficult question to answer. For purposes of argument, I suggest that a vision of friendship as a practice and hence a social convention seems more in accord with the kind of account offered by the family resemblance account.

9. For example, do you do certain sorts of things with your friends that you never do with acquaintances, lovers, colleagues, and associates? Do you assist only your friends? Have you ever had enjoyable experiences with strangers? Have mere acquaintances been useful to you? Have you benefited strangers? Told secrets to a priest, a doctor, an officer of the court? Are all of your friendships conditioned by affection or are some motivated by other sentiments and feelings, such as care and respect?

10. The literature on friendship is replete in references to friendship as a practice. In many cases, however, when the word *practice* is associated with friendship, it is meant as a contrast to the *theory* of friendship. The application of the word practice as it used here to friendship makes a brief appearance in Allan (1989:66), Allen (2004:156), King (2007:142), Lynch (2005:100), and Nixon (2015:160). Jordan Joel Copeland turns to Alasdair MacIntyre's conception of practice to talk about friendship (2007:170).

11. The idea that the practices of friendship condition the actions of friends also appears to be in accord in Graham Alan's view that "friendship is not just a voluntary or freely chosen relationship. It is one which is patterned and structured in a variety of ways by factors which can be recognized, at least to some degree, as genuinely social and lying outside the individual's immediate control" (Allan 1989:152). While the rules of the practices of friendship may be outside the individual's immediate control, they are not totally beyond control. Practices of friendship vary within cultures, over time, and between cultures. As we shall see, these variations further support the view of friendship as a family resemblance concept.

12. As Jeske writes, "It is true that in friendship we sometimes have a sudden realization that we are now friends with some person, a fact that appears more like a discovery than a choice. But what is being discovered in such cases is what we have in fact chosen through acts that we have voluntarily chosen to engage in" (2008:129).

13. Chapter 3 considers how a practice of friendship can be rendered compatible with the sort of individuality prized by Montaigne and others.

14. It should be noted that Blum's specific concern here is to defeat any kind of impartialist vindication of friendship, such as that associated with rule utilitarianism. For example, he rejects vindicating friendship on the rule utilitarian claim that the practice of friendship promotes the general welfare. In rejecting this sort of position, he writes, "what friendship requires is acting for the sake of the friend as such, rather than because, as it (contingently) turns out, such a practice serves the general interest" (Blum 1980:60). As I understand it, this position is less an argument against seeing friendship as a practice, than it is against a form of impartiality (such as Kant's) that requires we must act out of impartial motives if we are to be moral. One could reject this view of morality and still claim that friendship is a practice. A similar perspective is provided by Friedman when she writes, "Partiality for a friend involves being motivated by the friend as an individual by who she is and not by the principled commitments of one's own which her circumstances happen to instantiate" (1993:192; see also Keller 2013).

15. Ludwig argues that "Philosophy can do without foundations in goodness or nature, but friendship cannot. Friendship lays a serious claim to being the greatest human good" (2010:149).

16. Pangle goes on to argue that while friendship is an important element of human happiness, it is not "at the very center of the best life" (2003:197). That position is accorded to philosophy.

17. For a very different view that a focus on friendship reinvigorates foundational explorations and the connections between those foundations and political theory, see Ludwig (2010).

18. This formal analysis of friendship differs from the sort of formal understanding offered by Martha Nussbaum and modified by James O. Grunebaum. In her

account of Aristotle's conception of philia, Nussbaum argues that we can make a distinction between the basis, the object, and the end of the relationship. The basis of a friendship is that which brought the individuals together and rests on the kinds of things that different people tend to love (philia)—be it pleasure, utility, or (for a few?) virtue. The object of a friendship is the other person as seen in the light of the basis: "as someone who is pleasant to be with, as a person well-placed for useful dealings, as a person of good character" (Nussbaum1986:n.355). The goal of friendship is mutual benefit.

As useful as Nussbaum's account is for understanding Aristotle's conception of friendship, it may not capture and accommodate the rich diversity of understandings. For example, Grunebaum is correct in noting that her third category (that of the goal) runs the risks of instrumentalizing the relationship and hence precluding friendships that are seen as intrinsically valuable. Her second category of the object would appear useful and hence necessary only if we were interested in distinguishing friendship between human and nonhuman entities (gods and animals) or if we wanted to distinguish between friendships that took in the whole person or simply that person in a particular light (a question that will arise in chapter 2). Her first category, the basis of friendship, does point to a more or less stable element of friendship, which Grunebaum refers to as the reasons for the friendship. In the account given here, the motivation or reasons for the friendship are meant to accommodate explanations (that would be given by the friends themselves) for why a friendship may have started as well as why it may be maintained (even though in any given friendship, these need not be the same). In addition, I will use motivations and reasons more or less interchangeably. The affection that Alan feels for Denny and Denny feels for Alan are reasons for the relationship. If asked why they were friends, they could point to the deep affection they have for one another.

2. MOTIVATIONS, ACTIONS, AND THE VALUE OF FRIENDSHIP

1. This chapter's focus is on the work of Elizabeth Telfer, but Marilyn Friedman provides another such example when she writes, "The relationship of friendship is motivated by mutual affection and positive regard. Without such a mutual interest, a relationship would simply not constitute a friendship" (1993:224). For an ancient and concise definition of friendship, one may turn to Cicero's statement: "Now friendship is just this and nothing else: complete sympathy in all matters of importance, plus goodwill and affection and I am inclined to think that with the exception of wisdom, the gods have given nothing finer to men than this" (1991:80). Fernando Santos-Granero suggests that Montaigne's view of

friendship has become enshrined as the ideal Western conception of friendship (2007:8). In response to that ideal, Santos-Granero argues every one of the aspects that Montaigne sees as central to friendship (that it is voluntary, unselfish, intimate, informal, between equals) "has been attacked by anthropologists on the basis of cross-cultural analyses" (9).

2. For Marilyn Friedman, "Affection encompasses the fond and tender feelings of liking and love with which we respond to (some) other persons. Affection need not involve any judgmental or evaluative component" (1993:193).

3. In the "Lysis," Socrates explicitly rejects the idea that mutual liking (and hence mutual recognition of the sentiments of friendship) is necessary. As Julia Annas, notes, however, this is an artifact of the notion of philia in that its "non-mutual" senses could apply to quail, wine, and philosophy—all things that could be liked without liking in return (1977:533). In contrast, she argues that Aristotle takes those nonmutual senses of philia as secondary. Aristotle writes, "Love for a soulless thing is not called friendship, since there is no mutual loving, and you do not wish good to it" (1985:1155b25–30). The mutuality condition means that for Aristotle friendship is not the same as simple benevolence or wishing someone well. Aquinas also talks of the necessity of mutual recognition when he writes, "neither does well-wishing suffice for friendship, for a certain mutual love is requisite, since friendship is between friend and friend: and this well-wishing is founded on some kind of communication" (quoted in Schwartz 2007:172). The political significance of the mutual recognition of the appropriate sentiments of friendship will be discussed in chapter 4.

4. For Aristotle, friendship "is said to be reciprocated goodwill" (1985:1155b34). Toward one's friend, one must "wish good for his own sake" (1155b30), and this attitude needs to be recognized by both individuals. According to Grunebaum, this attitude is encompassed by the notion of caring for another, which is not necessarily the same thing as fondness or affection (Smith also notes that "Aristotle does not focus on this sharing of an emotional life" [2011a:73]). Feelings are not as important to Aristotle as the motivation of goodwill. Despite this absence, Grunebaum notes that "it is almost impossible to imagine friends, as Aristotle understands them, wanting to spend all of their lives together engaging in joint virtuous activities and failing to like each other or without growing in affection for each other" (2003:39). In this case, affection is not a necessary condition for friendship but a likely result of it. In contrast, Konstan notes that *philia* "means affection in Aristotle and in Greek generally" (1997:73).

5. See also Schall (1996:131–32).

6. This sort of move in which a thinker sets out what is understood as a complete or true or more worthy conception of friendship is frequently accompanied by an addendum or sidebar in which there are other incomplete, degraded, or merely common understandings of friendship. Nevertheless, it is rare for a thinker who makes this sort of a claim to argue that the latter do not qualify as

friendships. Jeske comes close to doing so when she suggests that for Aristotle "friendships for utility or pleasure are friendships in something like the sense that rubber ducks are ducks" (2008:44). For a contrasting view, see Annas (1977:546).

7. In his development of an Arendtian conception of friendship, Jon Nixon argues that Arendt saw her friendships as based on mutuality of respect. He then goes on to conclude that it was therefore based on equality (2015:8). It is not clear, however, whether equality necessarily follows from that motivation. If, as Nixon suggests, Arendt and Heidegger negotiated a friendship in the postwar period and if one of the motives of that friendship was respect, it is not clear that Heidegger's respect for his former pupil was at the same level as Arendt's respect for him.

8. Lynch notes that "modern friends do not necessarily develop friendships with those whose goodness they admire or esteem. Such admiration and esteem are not sufficient on their own to ensure the development of a friendship" (2005:31). Lynch is correct if she means that admiration or esteem by themselves need to be supplemented by mutual recognition and certain actions.

9. On Blum's account, "not everyone does have friends in the same way" (1980:71). For Blum, however, the difference is in how they care or in the level of caring, where care entails a willingness to work through trouble. Can one have a friend and not care for her (in this sense of care)? A friendship, say, between selfish persons may be largely based on their enjoyment of one another's company—they are fun to be with. It may not be a very valuable or deep friendship, but it can be a friendship nonetheless. In contrast, the idea here is that in addition to levels or kinds of care, friendship can be motivated by a range of other reasons and feelings.

10. For Kant, the roles of need and confidence place friends in a bind. He argues that a true friend is one in whom I have confidence that she will help me at the drop of a hat. But if I am a true friend of hers, then "I ought not" expect such help from her or place her "in any quandary." Kant notes, that "I must have confidence only; rather than make demands, I ought to bear my own troubles" (1991:213). Similarly, my friend should feel the same toward me. In this form of friendship, there exists a benevolent disposition to aid combined with a disposition to abstain from calling on such aid: "The finest sweets of friendship are its dispositions of good-will; and on these we must avoid encroaching." This bind, however, may be the result of seeing friendship as incompatible with notions of self-interest and utility—a view that will be challenged in chapter 3.

11. This understanding of our practices of friendship illuminates the character of online friendships. In cases where the individuals do not mutually recognize the motivations for their interactions, they may acknowledge one another as "friends" and even "unfriend" one another, but more is needed for a friendship. In these cases, the "friend" is more like a "befriend" in which what exists is a

friendly relationship and not a friendship. On the other hand, online friends may quickly form the belief that they enjoy one another's interactions and simply desire to share their posts, pictures, etc. When this mutual recognition of motivation happens and is accompanied by a mutual subscription to a set of adverbial conditions for how they should interact, then an online friendship has begun. Although it is arrived at in a somewhat different way, this conclusion is no different than Ethan Leib's conclusion that some online friendships will qualify as friendships and some will not (2011, 25). The difference is that for Leib, "Affection is what matters so much in friendship, and online 'friendships' do not easily translate or transmit warmth" (28), whereas affection (and the account offered here) is merely one motivation in a larger repertoire that can drive friendship.

12. In her biography of Hannah Arendt, Elizabeth Young-Bruehl notes that Arendt described Rahel Varnhagen as "my closest friend, though she has been dead for some one hundred years" (1982:56). Varnhagen, the subject of Arendt's first book, of course, could not say the same about Arendt. Given the impossibility of mutuality, it would seem strange or metaphorical for a third party to discuss the Arendt-Varnhagen friendship.

13. A "secrets" view versus a "mirror" view of friendship is found in a discussion by Dean Cocking and Jeanette Kennett.

14. At least in quantitative analyses of friendship, Pahl notes "The fact that there are different kinds of friends is rarely considered" (2000:7).

15. While he does not say anything about the nature of the considerations associated with friendship in *On Human Conduct*, Oakeshott himself notes that the intercourse of friends is itself qualified by such adverbial conditions (1975:57).

16. Andrew Sullivan writes,

> I think the primary distinction between homosexuals and heterosexuals in our society is not that they are attracted to different genders, and certainly not that their sexual lives and needs are radically different from each other. It is that homosexuals, by default as much as anything else, have managed to sustain a society of friendship that is, for the most part, unequaled by almost any other part of the society. Heterosexual women have long sustained it, of course, when their familial responsibilities have not overwhelmed them. But heterosexual men, to their great spiritual and emotional impoverishment have far too long let it pass them by.
>
> (1999:231)

For Sullivan, the basis for this friendship is the revelation to another of one's "deepest self" that one is gay. This would seem to suggest that gay friendships are less about how one relates to another (as suggested here) and more about a very specific revelation (that one is gay). In contrast, one could argue that the adverbial conditions associated with gay friendships (acting intimately and supportively) are extremely difficult to meet in a homophobic environment, but when met they are highly valued. The sociological question is the degree to which similarly adverbial conditions define friendship among heterosexual men and the degree to which male friendships are more constricted in this regard (particularly, as Sullivan notes, given the fear that acting intimately may be driven by a fear of homosexuality).

17. For an alternative perspective that sees gendered distinctions as connected to other variables, see Pahl (2000). The questions surrounding how friends interact are also cultural and historical. Employing Alan Bray's work on medieval friendship, Vernon notes that the physical aspects of how to be friends changed significantly in Europe. The practices of medieval friendship included a bodily intimacy that was ultimately confined to a heterosexual marital space in the West (2010:175).

18. In the ancient world, "The term *amica* or 'girlfriend' had pejorative connotations and husband and wife were no more likely to be described as friends in Latin than in Greek" (Konstan 1997:146).

19. Within psychology, much has been written about the relationship between self-disclosure and friendship. See Cozby (1973) and Schubertwalker and Wright (1976).

20. As Konstan notes, this conception of friendship is very old. St. Ambrose wrote, "Therefore a friend hides nothing, if he is true: he pours forth his mind, just as Lord Jesus poured forth the mysteries of his father" (quoted in Konstan 1997:150).

21. Cocking and Kennett call this the "secrets view" of friendship (1998:514). Although she does not use the language of self-disclosure, Lynch also sees friends as having or aspiring to have "an intimate knowledge of one another" (2005:4). She argues that "the possibility of friendship rests on our acceptance of a fiction—or what Derrida argues is an illusion—of connection, despite the impossibility of any complete or sustained connection between friends" (95).

22. This difficulty also plagues what they call the *mirror conception* of friendship in which one's closest friends reflects one's own traits (Cocking and Kennett 1998:505). For a psychoanalytic account of mirroring and its relationship to friendship see Lynch (2005:171–75).

23. The possibility that there are no essential motivations or adverbial conditions for friendship and that the relationship is both interpretative and willful may go some distance in accounting for the difficulties that social scientific explanations of friendship have had. Pahl notes, "Friendships, more perhaps than any other aspect of our social lives, have eluded the attempts of social scientists to be classified and codified" (2000:142). This problem comes again in chapter 6 when considering whether the law should attempt to foster and protect interpersonal friendships.

24. In Scheffler's view, valuing relationships noninstrumentally also yields special responsibilities or special duties (2001:97). Agreeing with Keller, I do not
believe that such relationships necessarily yield duties (Keller 2013:51, 65). The
relationship between duties and friendship is considered in chapter 3.

25. Blum argues that friendship tends to raise difficulties for any ethical theory that
stresses impartiality, such as Kantianism or utilitarianism. In contrast, virtue-
theorists are less puzzled by the weight accorded to friendship insofar as friendship is understood as an exhibition of human excellence. However these ethical
theories deal with conflicts between our responsibilities toward our friends versus
the responsibilities to others, a discussion of the practices of friendship is unlikely
to provide a comprehensive solution to those conflicts. More generally, I am inclined toward Keller's view on this matter that it may be impossible to deduce the
moral value of a partial relationship such as friendship from moral standards of
impartiality, such as those found in consequentialism (Keller 2013:150). For me,
this appears to indicate a deep form of pluralism within our morality.

3. SELF-INTEREST, DUTY, AND FRIENDSHIP

1. See, for example, Epstein (2006:69), Friedman (1993:212), Grunebaum (2003),
Jeske (2008:129–34), Leib (2011:20), Nixon (2015:49–50), Raz (1989), and
Schwarzenbach (2009:xi, 212).

2. See Lynch (2005:8–10). According to Julia Annas, in Homeric Greece, *"philia*
was very largely a matter of inherited guest-friendships depending little if at all
on the individual's personal preferences" (1977:552). The view that the Greeks
could see utility-based friendships as friendships is different from a view that
argues that all friendships must be utility-based. In ancient Greece, the latter
position was apparently held by the Cyrenaics, who followed the teachings of
Aristippus. As Annas notes, for the Cyrenaics, "friendship has merely instrumental value" (1993:231).

3. Martine Guichard, Patrick Heady, and Wolde Gossa Tadesse write, "These
institutionalised friendships include such phenomena as best-friendship,
blood-brotherhood, bond-friendship, trading-partnership and co-parenthood,
especially those forms of spiritual kinship established through baptismal rites
of the Roman Catholic Church" (2003:8). The anthropological study of friendship suggests that at other times and in other places, some cultures give more
weight to action, ritual, or ceremony than we do. Can it remove all the weight
from sentiment? In his account, Wolf argues that even in an instrumental
friendship, "a minimal element of affect remains an important ingredient in
the relation. If it is not present, it must be feigned" (1977:173).

An alternative perspective is offered by the anthropologist James G. Carrier
who asserts that "To speak of friendship, then, is to speak of people as respond-

ing to an internal spring of motive, their sentiments. Without the presence of people construed in this way, the sort of people who are capable of friendship, we must speak of co-workers who get together, of kin who feel the bonds of their relationships and the like. Without people who can be friends, in other words, we can not speak of friendship" (1999:21). For Carrier, the sort of "self" associated with friendship is "a recent phenomenon" (23). The difficulty with Carrier's language here is that "we" *do* speak of people as friends (coworkers, associates, even strangers) even though they do not necessarily have or recognize the appropriate sentiments. This flexibility in our language should give us pause. I am suggesting that it is possible that for some cultures, friendship emphasizes the situational or doing-component and de-emphasizes the motivational component. In contrast, Carrier is wedded to Western practices of friendship (that emphasize affect) in order to establish *the* meaning of the term. Lost in Carrier's account, however, is the variation in Western uses of *friend*. Still, Carrier may be quite correct in arguing that some cultures lack not only the motivational understanding of friendship, but also any concept of friendship. It is simply not part of their reflective understandings (31).

4. The distinction between someone who is a mere friend (she acts friendly, but lacks the motivational component associated with friendship) and a friend with whom one has a friendship may also go some distance in clarifying the sorts of interpersonal relationships that Ross K. Baker observed in the U.S. Senate. On the one hand, Baker identifies different types of friendship between senators depending on the level of intimacy (1999:22). On the other hand, he writes, "It seems clear that the very frequency with which the term 'friend' is now used [in the Senate] has hopelessly confounded and debased its meaning" (36). For Baker, the problem is that senators describe one another as good friends, even though their relationships are largely self-interested and utilitarian. But if we make the distinction between mere friends and friendships, the senatorial use of term *friend* neither means that the term has been confounded, nor that all such friends point to the existence of friendships. They may be friends in the sense that they act friendly toward one another, but they do not mutually recognize the sorts of motives ordinarily associated with friendship. This ambiguity in the meaning of *friend* may also exist in Arnold, Deen, and Patterson's study of the effect of friendship in the Ohio House of Representatives where they asked lawmakers to identify their legislative friends (2000:142). In identifying the friendship variable, they assign a 0 "when neither legislator names the other as a friend; 1 when one legislator in the pair names the other as a friend; and 2 when both legislators name one another as a friend" (145). Obviously, there can be no friendship in the case of 0 and 1 and it is not at all clear that even when two individuals identify one another as friends, that they also have a friendship.

In Baker's study, this ambiguity raises the question of whether what he identifies as the most prominent and least intimate form of friendship within the U.S. Senate qualifies as a friendship. He calls this friendship, "institutional kinship" because it is not driven by the ordinary intimacies of many friendships and may not be found outside the Senate. Baker writes, "Institutional kinship can be considered a modality of senatorial friendship because that is what senators say it is" (1999:68). But it is also not a simple ipse dixit. Baker argues that an institutional kinship emerges when senators mutually recognize the qualities of empathy, integrity, diligence, and restraint in one another (66). Moreover, he notes that "the emotional commitment inherent in institutional kinship is not great, but neither is it insignificant" (69).

Baker's description of institutional kinship does suggest that senators subscribe to a set of adverbial conditions to act empathetically, honestly, diligently, and temperately toward one another. However, this relationship may lie in the blurry edges of our practices of friendship because it is not clear what motivates the relationship or whether those motivations are mutually recognized. For example, if senators are primarily or solely motivated by self-interest, then Baker's description of institutional kinship is closer to the anthropological idea of an instrumental friendship as found in other cultures. Alternatively, if senators mutually recognize an ordinarily appropriate motivation of friendship then that is something else. In this regard, Baker does mention that "the term used most frequently to describe the possessors of the most desirable traits was 'respect'" (62). If, in addition to self-interest, senators are motivated by respect toward one another, then Baker's notion of institutional kinship is more clearly part of the family of practices of friendship.

5. In contrast, following John Cooper (1993), Schwarzenbach argues that a purely self-interested relationship based on pleasure could not qualify as a friendship for Aristotle (2009:44). However one interprets Aristotle, I will assert that it is not unusual for friendships of a sort to be motivated by self-interested pleasure and the enjoyment of the company of another. Such relationships may be more common for the young and more unstable, but, once again, they are still friendships.

6. As noted earlier, by nonmaterial desire, I am referring to friendships based on pleasure. One could argue that nonmaterial desire could include a form of self-interest rightly understood. According to Schwartz, for Aquinas, "The virtuous friend has, as Aristotle would put it, self-love based on a correct understanding of his self, and therefore of what goods are truly beneficial to himself. He also has a correct understanding of the friends' self and so, of the goods that truly benefit him" (2007:15).

7. In his account of utility-based friendship, Aristotle notes that the philia of the friends is generated by their mutual love of utility. Konstan's interpretation of

this view is that Aristotle "never suggests that two people who are useful to one another are automatically and on that basis alone friends. But it does often happen that two people who have a mutually advantageous association become friends. In such a case, the origin of the *philia* is in utility, but their affection is not reducible to the mutual appreciation of one another's serviceability" (1997:72). Lynch and Vernon make a somewhat stronger claim. Lynch argues that utility cannot be an explicit objective of the relationship if it is to be a friendship, hence the emphasis she places on "indirection of intention" (2005:183). This idea will be discussed later. Vernon sees the notion of utility as applied in the world of work as a threat to friendship. It is only when people can be valued for who they are as opposed to what they do that friendship is possible (2010:152). I am arguing that utility can be an explicit objective and need not be seen as a threat to friendship, but it is not sufficient and is, for us, a deficient motive for friendship.

8. David Konstan argues that for the Romans, actions motivated by the hope for reciprocity in benefits were distinguishable from actions motivated by generosity. He writes, "Mutual support is the point at which the vocabularies of friendship and exchange of benefits intersect" (1997:128). This reading suggests that even for Romans self-interest could be a deficient reason.

9. Another example of contemporary motivational mismatch is that of love and friendship, where one party just wants to be friends, while the other party wants to be lovers. For the most part, this is a distinction between social practices (although not entirely so). Vernon argues that the "urges of erotic love" can compete with the gentler affections of friendship (2010:43–72).

10. At the end of chapter 10, in the discussion of the friendship between states, I argue that the sorts of differences in perception plus certain temptations to misrepresent one's motives can lead to a more robust politics of friendship of the sort that Derrida suggests.

11. King makes an even stronger claim regarding such divergences. He writes, "It is never the case that what attracts A to B is exactly identical to what attracts B to A" (2007:139). These differences, divergences, and forms of separateness are part and parcel of friendship.

12. The hospital visit example comes from Michael Stocker (1976:462). Stocker's goal, however, is not to deny that there are duties of friendship, but that there is something wrong with impartial moral theories that cannot successfully motivate our actions. This latter problem, in which some motives for friendship have a self-effacing character, is considered later. The idea that friendship entails acting for the sake of our friends appears to be a necessary condition for Aristotle's conception of friendship. In the *Rhetoric*, he argues, "Things that cause friendship are: doing kindnesses; doing them unasked; and not proclaiming the fact when they are done, which shows that they were done for our [the friend's] own sake and not for some other reason" (1985:1381b35–37). In

chapter 2, I have argued that the relationship of friendship can itself provide a reason for action.

13. Wellman is certainly on to something in arguing that many of our judgments and assessments of friends' favorable and unfavorable actions are linked to an assessment of character. I am less inclined, however, to agree with Wellman's claim that the use of duty- or rights-talk is a matter of misspeaking. In addition, it may very well be the case that his virtue-based analysis is not entirely up to the task. The example that Wellman uses to illuminate this part of his argument involves a decision of the narrator not to pick up the phone when Eric, a close friend, calls. The reason he does not pick up the phone is because he would rather watch an episode of *Seinfeld* than talk to Eric who has just had a major fight with his partner. This decision reveals the narrator to be self-centered and insensitive, as opposed to violating a duty. But these judgments of character ("self-centered" and "insensitive") seem rather rushed. Perhaps it would be more judicious to say that the narrator is not a very good or close friend to Eric or that his understanding of what it means to be a close friend is flawed. If friendship involves practices that require not only the right motivations, but also a subscription to certain conventions of self-disclosure, then the disappointments (and achievements) associated with a friendship are a function of the relationship between the actions taken and standards that the friends believe to be in operation. For the friends themselves, the failure to live up to those standards is not a violation of duty and it need not be indicative of a general failure of character. The narrator may not be a good friend to Eric, but he may be a great friend to Susan (suggesting that it is not a character flaw as such). Alternatively, his decision not to pick up the phone may be a one-shot deal. In either case, his interaction with Eric does not necessarily signal a failure of character.

14. Badhwar notes that most writers on friendship see it as antithetical to justice. In contrast, he argues that "in real life justice *is* central to friendship: the commonest complaint of friends when they break up is that they were manipulated, used, misjudged, or wrongly neglected—in short that they were unjustly treated" (1993:26). If, however, these sorts of actions indicate that the "friend" is not motivated by the appropriate sentiments of friendship or that she is not acting in accord with the appropriate adverbial conditions, it is not clear that the notion of justice is needed. The "friend" is not a very good friend. In addition, many practices of friendship are incompatible with the sorts of calculations that are associated with justice.

15. In response, it could be argued that it is precisely this voluntary quality of friendship that creates a special obligation. While this may explain how we are able to deploy the language of obligation against others who are preventing us from living up to the expectations of a practice of friendship, it cuts against a sense of voluntarism that pervades the relationship from within.

16. The idea that there may be a set of reasons for acting that should not move us to action is one that is sometimes used by defenders of theories that place a premium on impartiality in justifying partial relationships. For a useful discussion of some of the problems associated with self-effacing theories of morality see Keller (2013:82).

17. The distinction between acting for the sake of friendship and acting out of friendship may be usefully deployed here (Stocker 1993:252–53). In the case of acting for the sake of friendship, the goal of the act is intimately connected to sustaining or maintaining the relationship itself. The language of obligation or duty may make sense when acting for the sake of friendship, but not when acting out of friendship.

18. A similar analysis may apply to rights, whose role is also contested in discussions of friendship. As noted earlier, Wellman is critical of the language of rights within friendships, arguing that they are subject to a reductio and imply a kind of demand that is incompatible with friendship. In contrast, Badhwar argues that rights are compatible with friendship in the sense that they entail something other than a mere demand. For example, "I have a right to expect that my friend gives me more of her time than she give[s] mere acquaintances, but to get this time as the result of a demand would be self-defeating" (1993:27). The right, in this case, may be a marker of legitimate expectations and entitlement.

A third view can be found in Meyer, who concludes that "close friends will spontaneously go to great lengths for one another and they will do so without either claiming rights or giving any thought to the existence of rights" (1992:483). Nevertheless, he still argues that close friends have the right to be treated openly, respectfully, noninstrumentally, and with the benefit of the doubt (481–83). On this account, "the adversarial use of rights is not an inevitable consequence of having rights, [and] neither is an adversarial position somehow inherent in the idea of rights" (479).

Suppose within friendship, that rights are also deficient reasons for actions. If so, we can reframe both Badhwar's and Meyer's arguments. In Badhwar's case, where rights serve as a reminder, it could be argued that it is a reminder that could be self-defeating. As in the case of obligations, this deployment of rights in many practices of friendship could be used to jolt the relationship. We may ask Meyer why close friends do not give thought to the use of rights and claim them when seeking to receive benefits from each other. The answer could only be the one that Meyer notes and rejects, namely that there is something adversarial about rights that is incompatible with friendship. As with obligations, we may deploy the language of rights against others who are seeking to prevent us from living up to the adverbial conditions of a practice of friendship (e.g., acting openly, respectfully, noninstrumentally), but the deployment of rights within a friendship suggests that something has changed or is changing within the relationship.

4. FRIENDSHIP AND INDIVIDUALITY

1. The expression "bridging/bonding friendship" was inspired by Robert Putnam's distinction between bridging and bonding forms of social capital. Obviously, its use here does not refer to groups or in-group and out-group relationships. Combining the terms is meant to express the sorts of tensions that may arise and the adjustments that may need to be made by friends who are joined together by the pursuit of their own individuality (bonding) but whose pursuit may lead them in very different directions (bridging).

2. For a position that would be skeptical of a project celebrating both individuality and friendship, see Smith (2011a). Smith writes, "Whilst individuation and even individuality might be promoted as an ideal, such an ideal can only be considered a partial abstraction from reality. Indeed, from the perspective offered by this [Smith's] view we might question whether 'individuality' as it is understood in modernity is either a realistic or desirable goal at all" (184).

3. Perhaps this sort of experience captures something of the friendship described by Andrew Sullivan in his essay discussing his relationship to his friend Patrick, who died of AIDS. Sullivan writes, "There were many parts of Patrick that rankled, puzzled me, infuriated me" (1998:235). Some of these were insignificant and others were quite important—such as Patrick's attitude to deal with AIDS "more aggressively" (238). In these matters, Sullivan refers to his own attitudes to his friend as a matter of learning to accept a friend (235). The notion of bridging/bonding friendship, for which I am reaching, is an attempt to unpack that notion of acceptance. It is an attempt to consider how one deals with oneself when one is infuriated with a friend's idiosyncratic take on the world. In words that echo Montaigne, Sullivan notes that Patrick "was himself to the end. He never compromised his character or his idiosyncrasy or his freedom for a second. This was why, of course, I loved him. Because he was him" (240).

4. Strictly speaking, the ideal of individuality rests less on the existence of difference than on how one approaches one's life. The result of that approach could mean that the friends are very much like one another in terms of their interests and activities or not. To put this issue another way, one may ask of this ideal of friendship whether "birds of a feather flock together, or are friends chosen for characteristics considered lacking in the self? Are friends homophilic or heterophilic?" (Du Bois 1974:27). The short answer is that in a bridging/bonding friendship the friends share a pursuit of individuality, but they could differ in terms of where that pursuit takes them. Hence the bridging/bonding label.

5. In Oakeshott's view, self-enactment is a demand that an agent make on himself, "in which he requires of himself a *délicatesse* of conduct which cannot be required of him by another, which he may not make a show of requiring of others, but which are not merely his good opinion of himself" (1975:77). It is not merely the good opinion of himself insofar as we possess a shared sense of what constitutes virtuous self-enactment. In stating that others cannot require it of us or we of them, Oakeshott is arguing that the decision to be virtuous is ours alone to make. And we only make it when we perform the difficult task of choosing certain motivations over others. When we fail in this choice and find ourselves acting out of spite instead of generosity, the conduct is less a matter a guilt and more a matter of shame at failing to live up to our own project.

6. One of the more troubling discussions of the relationship between friendship and individuality can be found in Nietzsche's work. As discussed by Smith, the arc of that discussion is one in which Nietzsche is torn between seeing friendship as a "mechanism of self discovery" versus an agonistic relationship that must ultimately be overcome (2011a:156). At best, the friend becomes "a kind of 'camp-bed': a temporary and hard place of rest for the purposes of recommencing a journey" (173). Smith argues that by the time Nietzsche writes *Zarathusthra*, "friendship is cast as a resistance to the other with the supreme achievement of friendship being able to break free of the relationship" (176).

7. Of course, bridging/bonding friendship is not Aristotle's ideal. Nor is the notion of self-enactment, Aristotle's conception of character. In the case of self-enactment, *character* refers to the willingness of an individual to take on the task of self-enactment and self-care. Bridging/bonding friendship is one in which that engagement is mutually acknowledged and encouraged.

8. It would, however, be a mistake to think that the importance of individuality (in some form) for friendship was denied by ancient thinkers. As Sandra Lynch notes, "Aristotle's prescription that a good friend is one who wishes his friend well for that friend's own sake, then we recognize that friend's separateness from us, we admire his qualities and we give him room to develop them" (2005:112). See also Rhodes's response to Vlastos's argument that Socrates's love is not focused on a person's individuality (Rhodes 2008, 45). Moreover, the very old theme of friends being irreplaceable taps into a notion that it is the individual's uniqueness that can draw and hold friends together.

9. Finally, he argues that self-enactment contributes to the development of social pluralities that enhance the stability and durability of the interactions between individuals (2005:129). It performs this function, he suggests, because both self-disclosure and self-enactment entail subscription to a set of social norms and expectations. Expectations for cooperation or forbearance can be developed and met because individuals in the pursuit of their wished-for satisfaction do so in certain ways and not others. Individuality is not a function of doing anything or always doing the unexpected thing. Flathman emphasizes Oakeshott's idea

that in the engagement of self-enactment, the success (however limited) of cultivating one's character can be gracefully enjoyed by the agent herself—establishing a kind of balance and equanimity. In his interpretation of Oakeshott, Flathman writes, "At a minimum we can say that a *respublica* blessed by the presence of persons enjoying this degree of equanimity will be less fractious, rancorous, certainly a less brutal place" (2005:130). While this is not Flathman's description of his own position, there is no reason to think that he does not endorse this view of self-enactment.

10. A relevant contrast here is to the Platonic view of self-improvement in which the self becomes an enemy to be conquered (Ludwig 2010:140). The enemy is oneself, and the victory of oneself over oneself is the "first and best of all victories" (Plato 1980, 626e). If, on Flathman's view, we forego the idea of an internal sovereign or master, then the metaphor of conquest does not capture the sort of self-overcoming implied by self-enacted individuality. For such self-overcoming is less a form of conquest than an ongoing engagement (and sometimes struggle) with oneself in which the victories (if they can be considered as such) are always tempered by an agonal respect for that within oneself against which one is resisting and pushing.

11. Another way to frame this question is whether individuality requires the kind of self-sufficiency that is incompatible with friendship.

12. Lorraine Pangle offers a very different account of Montaigne's understanding of the relationship of individuality and friendship. In her view, the very possibility of separate selves may undermine the sort of perfect devotion that Montaigne talks about (2003:75).

13. As Smith notes, Nietzsche recognized this risk when he wrote, "You should honour even the enemy in your friend. Can you go near to your friend without going over to him?" (quoted in Smith 2011a:176).

14. One could read Flathman as saying that the risk of friendship is a loss of the pathos of distance (which, I think, is true in the case of Montaigne's ideal). Alternatively, it may be possible to preserve a pathos of distance even when one seeks a shape for life through and with one's friends. I think some sense of distance is necessary for this ideal of friendship—hence the idea of bridging presupposes the creation of difference. When that distance collapses (as may happen when the bonding becomes too strong) one may have a different kind of relationship.

15. This "standing on its own" creates the potential for friendship to have "socially disruptive possibilities" (Friedman 1993:248).

16. The metaphor of a friend as "another self" or as a "mirror of the soul" can function in a number of ways. At one level, the mirroring metaphor is causal: the image in the mirror is caused by the object. For those who see the self as fundamentally shaped through friendship, this is a particularly useful metaphor. Of course, in a mirror, what is created is an exact image. At this level, friendship

is a replication of oneself. You have been made in my image. In this sense, I can see myself in you. What is seen, however, may be more or less identical or conformist, depending on whether the image is understood formally. From the perspective of bridging/bonding friendship, the metaphor of a mirror becomes troubling when it is turned into an expectation that the friend's wants and actions will conform to one's own desires. The metaphor is less troubling if the image is taken to mean that one's friend, like oneself, is trying to establish her own sense of individuality.

17. In contrast, Keller argues that because of the point of friendship and other relationships of partiality is to serve the good of the individuals involved, one should never choose the good of the friendship over the good of the friend. Saving a friend from self-destructive behavior even if it means destroying the friendship makes the most sense for Keller (2013:98). This is a plausible response. But it also seems plausible that in a bridging/bonding friendship, one would be deeply torn by those alternatives because of the value of and respect for individuality.

18. The sociological version of this argument can be found in the theory of weak ties. Drawing on the work of Mark Granovetter, Leib writes, "Close friends, precisely because of the dynamics of homophily, will already have all the same information and opportunities at their disposal: close friendships create closed systems, but weak ties (generally something less than friendship) can more easily expand our exposure to new things" (2011:55). From one perspective, the idea of weak ties suggests that the realization of an ideal of individuality is more likely in a context that engenders such ties. From another perspective, the theory of weak ties suggests the challenging nature of an ideal of bridging/bonding friendship.

19. Others have also noted a connection between a pathos of distance and friendship. For example, Susan Shell writes, "The insistence on a certain 'pathos of distance'—even, and perhaps especially within the bonds of friendship— provides certain anticipatory democratic answer to Nietzsche's later animadversions against the 'last men' who like 'to rub against one another for warmth.' Indeed there is in Kant's and Nietzsche's common fastidiousness a curious aesthetic convergence; both are nauseously repelled by common intimacies— Nietzsche in the name of aristocracy, Kant in the name of nobility consistent with equality" (quoted in Salkever 2008:71). Whatever Nietzsche's views may be, it is not clear that Kant, especially in his writings on friendship, was so repelled by common intimacies (see Kant's discussion of the importance of self-disclosure in 1991:214–15).

20. King talks about the importance of tolerance to friendship (2007:140). In the case of the bridging/bonding friendship offered here, tolerance is not quite the right stance insofar as the friends work on themselves to overcome their objections and disclose a more supportive attitude. That tolerance falls short of this ideal of friendship does not mean that it is inappropriate in other ideals or ideas of friendship. There are also elements of Nixon's Arendtian ideal of friendship

that resemble bridging/bonding friendship. This is particularly true when he emphasizes friendship forged by differences in perspective (2015:91).

21. Perhaps this possibility illuminates Emerson's ideal of the friend as a "sort of beautiful enemy, untamable, devoutly revered, and not a trivial conveniency to be soon outgrown and cast aside" (1991:229).

22. Focusing on the adverbial character of bridging/bonding friendship may also provide a way to address the paradoxical character of what Paul Ludwig calls the "philosophic friend." He writes, "Friendship is about others who are one's own, while philosophy cannot let preference for one's own elide the otherness of the other. Finding a philosophic friend begins to look like squaring the circle" (2010:143). Accepting for a moment this characterization of friendship and philosophy, perhaps the tension emerges because both terms are being understood as substantive endpoints. In contrast, suppose that philosophy is understood not in terms of possessing "the good," but as a way of thinking about the world that is good. In addition, suppose that friendship could be understood as an attachment to *how* a friend does something and not, specifically *what* that friend does. On this reading, one could see "one's own" (to use Ludwig's language) as an attachment to a person whose philosophical disposition is expressed in the sometimes thrilling, sometimes irritating, sometimes overbearing willingness to go wherever an argument takes her. This is the challenge of a philosophic friend. The circle may not be squared, but one can understand better that one can love a philosophic friend because she is a philosopher. When seen in these terms, this sort of tension is not peculiar to philosophy but to the "otherness" that must be implied by any conception of individuality.

23. Not to mention that Simmel's ideal friendship looks more like the construction of nineteenth-century romanticism than of the ancient world.

24. This is certainly the case for Oakeshott as he notes in his essay "The Rule of Law" (1999).

5. CIVIC FRIENDSHIP

1. Although neglected, that view persisted: civic friendship may play an important role in eighteenth- and nineteenth-century republican ideology (Schweitzer 2006; Schwarzenbach 2009; Godbeer 2009). For example, Schwarzenbach argues that "beneath the surface of the American constitutional tradition and alongside the explicit values of liberty and equality, there lurks the necessary requirement of a minimal civic friendship between citizens as well" (197). On the other hand, republican theorists such as Montesquieu, Rousseau, Tocqueville, and Barber do not spend much, if any, time discussing the importance of friendship (e.g., see Mitchell on Tocqueville 2008:280). In the case of liberal theory, civic friendship is moribund, as many thinkers have noted (e.g., Schwarzen-

bach 2009:xii). Similarly, philia does not play much of a role in Marx. Although Richard Miller (1981) uses Aristotle and his conception of friendship as a way to illuminate Marx's nonutilitarian form of consequentialism, Schwarzenbach offers a compelling argument that Marx "has not an adequate account of *philia*, or friendship (personal or otherwise)" (2009:132).

2. Beyond the idea of civic friendship a few political theorists have seen interpersonal friendships as a way to acquire important political virtues (e.g., MacIntrye 1999; Scorza 2004). Fewer, however, have focused on the question of whether ordinary friendships make a positive difference to the functioning of political institutions. American political scientists, however, have explored this question particularly as it relates to the functioning of legislative bodies (see, for example, Arnold, Deen, and Patterson 2000; Baker 1999; and Caldeira and Patterson 1987). As noted earlier, one challenge raised by these studies is whether they are capturing friendship or merely friendly relationships. The next two chapters explore normative issues raised by possible relationships between ordinary friendships and political institutions.

3. I am sympathetic to the sorts of objections implied by various liberalisms that see friendship in tension with the attempt to secure a degree of impartiality and equal treatment. As Judith Shklar notes in her essay on the friendship of Thomas Jefferson and John Adams, "it is not at all clear that friendship and politics mix all that well" (1998:14). Yack goes farther and, drawing on Aristotle, notes the dangers of establishing an ideal of political friendship that rests on intimacy or revolutionary comradeship (1993:118–22). On the other hand, as discussed in this chapter, I do not find those reasons strong enough to preclude friendship as an ideal in politics. The clash between friendship and impartial institutions is discussed in further detail in chapter 7.

4. Nixon presents what could be called an Arendtian conception of friendship, in which friendship is a precondition for democratic politics. He writes, "Friendship is what lies between the private world of familial, tribal, and religious affiliation, and the political world of institutional and associative affiliation based not on family, tribe or religion but on equality" (2015:7, 194).

5. In many respects, I agree with Diane Jeske's claim that

in recent years, philosophers have appealed to intimate relationships, particularly those between friends and those between parents and children, to model political obligations and even all of morality. These projects have gained even a minimal plausibility that they have by selective focus on certain aspects of intimate relationships in conjunction with a complete disregard of other aspects and of the ways in which all of these aspects work together. So, while friendships satisfy the mutuality requirement, it seems quite clear that relationship between, for example, compatriots do not.

(2008:49)

As noted earlier, Bickford (1996) is skeptical that friendship can serve as a model for political action largely because she sees disagreement as endemic. I disagree with Jeske and Bickford, however, if their assessments are meant to close down thinking about other possible connections between friendship and the relationships of compatriots.

6. Awareness of this problem goes back to Aristotle and the question of how many friends one can have. If friendship is dependent on the mutual recognition of motivations (and not all conceptions may be so dependent), then the upper limit rests on our abilities to judge the nature of our own and others' motivations. See also King (2007:132).

7. Hannah Arendt makes a similar claim in *On Revolution* when she writes, "When we say that nobody but God can see . . . the nakedness of a human heart, 'nobody' includes one's own self" (1963:96). The difficulty of discerning motivations is also part of Judith Shklar's account of hypocrisy in *Ordinary Vices* (1984).

8. The idea of civic virtue is also floating around in this discussion. Civic virtue requires not merely doing the right thing, but doing it for the right reason. Like friendship, civic virtue requires attention to motive. Unlike friendship, however, civic virtue can exist without the *mutual recognition* of motives. The usual motives associated with civic virtue (love of liberty, love of country, concern for the good common) are also directed to an idea or ideal. One may love liberty and be willing to fight and die for it without necessarily loving one's fellow citizens.

9. The attraction of this perspective was explored in some depth in offering a political conception of forgiveness. See my *Political Forgiveness* (2001).

10. Bernard Yack notes that Aristotle "recommends something like friendliness as a general virtue (Aristotle 1985:1108a27, 1126b15). But friendly individuals, he argues, should behave in different ways towards different people, depending on the kind of things that they share with others" (Yack 1993:110). The difficulty here is that philia may not embrace the distinction between a friendly relationship and a friendship.

11. Scorza uses Emerson's ideal of friendship to develop and support individuality and democratic connectedness without emphasizing nationalism or unity. For Scorza, friendship is not the basis for politics. Rather, he argues "certain communicative norms based on the norms of friendship may also serve, effectively, as constraints on disagreements between members of modern societies who often have different values, competing interests and conflicting understandings of the good" (2004:92). Building on discourse ethics, Scorza argues that the ordinary relationships of friendship teach us how we can talk to one another as citizens. Because we are so familiar with what it means to be friends and to interact with our friends, we can understand what it means to interact with one another as citizens. Out of Emerson's work we can draw certain norms of communication: frankness or truth-telling (we call it sincerity), and kindness or

gentleness (Emerson calls it tenderness). Scorza appears to be reaching for an ethos or attitude that anyone can bring into political deliberation regardless of the orientation of the other. That such an ethos can be acquired through experiences of friendship does not mean that it is itself friendship.

12. Baker's notion of "pure friendships" between U.S. senators captures this sort of relationship insofar as the affection felt for the colleague involves an emotional commitment and concern for the welfare of the colleague as a person (1999:22). In Baker's view, these sorts of relationships are relatively rare, but they do "exist even among competitive people doomed by their own ambitions to live in a world of favor-seeking, backslapping, and trading of positions and associations" (45).

13. It also rests on the presumption that we are capable of acting one way (e.g., civilly) even though we feel another way (e.g., distain). Here, our capacity for hypocrisy works in favor of our ability to be citizens.

14. As I shall argue in chapter 6, this does not necessarily mean that friendship becomes impossible with those who have betrayed their country, but it does mean that civic friendship is impossible.

15. Insofar as this phrase indicates the institutionally circumscribed character of friendship it is useful. The problem with *kinship*, however, is that it suggests that the relationships are unchosen and involuntary.

16. Caldeira and Patterson make a larger claim that "it is ultimately inconceivable that legislative decision making could properly be understood without an accounting of the bonds of political friendship in the legislature" (1987:954). Justin Kirkland offers a different view. He argues that if we are interested in understanding legislative success, then we should not focus on "strong ties" (defined by frequent interaction and collaboration). These ties exist between lawmakers who are already disposed to support one another's positions. In contrast, "weak ties" (those between acquaintances who rarely interact) "are critical for legislative success precisely because they form between legislators who do not share many other similarities.... Establishing relationships with those less similar to themselves allows legislators to expand their potential sphere of influence beyond those who are already predisposed to support them because of some set of shared characteristics" (2011:889). Although this may not affect Kirkland's larger argument, it is not clear how well the weak tie/strong tie distinction maps onto the notion of civic or political friendship. Clearly, disdain between legislators may exist even though their relationship could be identified as a strong tie. As Baker notes, deep animosities have existed between members of the Senate from the same state who shared a similar ideology (1999:94–95). Alternatively, civic friendships may exist between legislators who could be seen as possessing weak ties. For example, Kirkland uses the example of the Kennedy-Hatch relationship as a weak tie. Later, I use it as an example of civic friendship. What Kirkland's position does reinforce is the value of reaching across the aisle for legislative

success, a point that is not inconsistent with Caldeira and Patterson or with the potential value of civic friendship.

17. See also Baker for a brief discussion of the Kennedy-Hatch friendship and for other examples of senatorial friendships (1999:7–11).

18. Baker argues that the Kennedy-Hatch friendship was something more than an "institutional kinship" but something less than a "pure friendship." On his account, the relationship was a kind of political friendship that he calls an alliance (1999:10). In Baker's nomenclature, alliances are friendships in that they are associations "based on agreement on an issue or complex of issues and solidified by the development of personal ties" (79). Elsewhere he says that they create "important personal bonds and feelings of human as well as political solidarity" (21).

19. See also Canellos (2009:264).

20. She also explains that her notion of care differs significantly from feminist theories of care that stress its naturalness and nonrational character (2009:112). Later, she argues that genuine friendship, unlike care, "has the reciprocal aim of equality at its heart" (243).

21. She writes, "My argument runs that the traditional, ethical reproductive practice of women not only embodies and consciously aims at *philia* in the best case (something Aristotle already recognized) but also contributes greatly toward binding even the modern state together" (2009:5).

22. This, of course, is not surprising insofar as both thinkers draw on Aristotle. However, Aristotle goes on to argue that friendship is a function of good will that is reciprocated. Moreover (and more importantly), he notes, friendship requires an *awareness* of the reciprocated good will (Aristotle 1985:1155b35–56a5).

23. The notion that motive is essential to Schwarzenbach's position is also evidenced by her claim that "unlike in market production where the goal is the product and the motives of the individual person are largely irrelevant (the motive can even be pure greed), in reproductive *praxis* the aim is constitutive of the action, and this action itself is worth doing for its own sake" (2009:282). In reproductive labor, the motive is not irrelevant.

24. Allen may be offering a third way, although it is not clear what it entails. She notes that "in utility friendships trust is impermanent" (2004:136) and that for Aristotle "goodwill does not arise in 'friendships of utility and pleasure,'" yet "citizens are, in fact, utility friends by his own account" (156). As I understand it, her answer to this conundrum is that "political friendship consists finally of trying to be *like* friends" (157). Citizens should act as if they are friends. It is not clear that this gets Aristotle out of the bind insofar as he does not associate political friendship with the best kind of friendship, but with friendships of utility. Putting Aristotle to the side, Allen's argument rests on a hope that our expressions of friendship will be reciprocated with strangers, even though rivalrous self-interest never disappears.

25. For both Frank and Schwarzenbach (2009:202, 230), friendship is a precondition for justice.

26. Although she does not define her own position in these terms, Allen does see Aristotle as arguing that bargaining "is not fundamentally different from the ethical act of coming to agreement" (2004:132).

27 As I read them, Frank's position is very close to Yack's. Yack sees Frank as offering a version of political friendship much closer to virtue friendship than his own (2006:436). While Frank certainly turns to a notion of virtue, that turn may be less important than her appeal (which is also in Yack) to something that is shared. From this perspective, perhaps the central difference (if it is one) comes down to Yack's belief that political friendship grows out of practices of justice, while Frank believes that it grows out of a commitment to the constitution.

28. To some degree, once civic friendship is shorn of mutual concern and well-wishing as its basis, the position begins to look more compatible with Bickford's (1996). She argues that shared practices of decision making perceived to be just are all that hold an adversarial, deliberative democracy together.

29. A few pages later, Schwarzenbach offers a fairly strong view of the role of civic friendship. She writes, "Beneath the surface of the American constitutional tradition and alongside the explicit values of liberty and equality, there lurks the necessary requirement of a minimal civic friendship between citizens as well" (2009:197).

6. FRIENDSHIP DURING DARK TIMES

1. Part 3 takes up Schmitt's friend/enemy distinction as it applies to understanding friendship among states.

2. Shklar argues that in a free society, the claims of friendship are more politically ambiguous (1998:14). In such a society, one's political obligations are less likely to be morally problematic, hence it is less likely that claims of friendship will have greater weight. Paradoxically, in a free society what tears friendships apart are "incompatible beliefs sincerely held" (15).

3. Undoubtedly, there is a range of possibilities here as well. In extreme situations of starvation, even these social bonds are fractured and desiccated.

4. In *Hannah Arendt and the Politics of Friendship* (2015), Jon Nixon offers an Arendtian theory of friendship built on her political thought and her lived friendships. In contrast, my concern here is with Arendt's discussion of the role of friendship under conditions in which political legitimacy is at issue. For a wonderful discussion of friendship in general and of Arendt's friendship with Mary McCarthy in particular see Svetlana Boym (2009/10).

5. I would like to thank Andrew Norris for pointing me to this possibility.

6. She also mentions the Roman notion of *humanitas* as corresponding to the Greek idea of *philanthropia*, expressed in a "readiness to share the world with other men" (Arendt 1968:25).

7. In *The Human Condition*, Arendt sees respect as akin to Aristotelian *philia politike*, "a kind of friendship without intimacy and without closeness; it is a regard for the person from the distance which the space of the world puts between us" (1958:243).

8. In addition to compassion, fraternity, truth, and scientific right, one can add her conception of "the social" to the list of such forces. In particular, see her discussion in *On Revolution* (1963).

9. A point that Canovan (1988) emphasizes.

10. Despite what she says in this last quotation, it is clear, given her example of scientifically demonstrating that there exists a superior race, that she is not merely concerned with men uniting into a single opinion, but also in the possibility that truth may set one individual against another and destroy the possibility of friendship. In other words, truth resembles compassion and fraternity in collapsing the space needed for politics, but it can also preclude the joining together that is most conducive to talk. Friendship, then, is linked to plurality.

11. Alternatively, while she notes that compassion can join together individuals who are the subject of violence, the fear that that compassionate unity may somehow carry over into the politics of a free state leads her to be suspicious of such emotional attachments.

12. The friendship between Atticus and Marcus Cicero is particularly well documented in the hundreds of letters that Atticus saved from Cicero. See the four volumes of Cicero's *Letters to Atticus*.

13. The praetor is a governor. According to Rolfe, prefectures were "positions of the third rank under governors of provinces, the second rank being that of the *legatus*. They were commonly held by Roman knights [Atticus was a member of the equestrian class] and offered numerous opportunities for personal profit" (*Cornelius Nepos* 1929:296–97n4).

14. This is not to say that he was not an Epicurean. In Miriam Griffin's view, his suicide "may explain why philosophy was not explicitly invoked by Atticus, though editing by his biographer, who disliked philosophy, cannot be ruled out" (1986:67). Nepos, she notes, had "no use for philosophy . . . because of the hypocrisy of its adherents." (76n6). If anything, Nepos appears to stress the Stoic quality of *constantia* (76n7) or constancy.

15. In Millar's view while one could take Atticus's inaction as evidence of placing private duties above public action, it is also true that for an individual with Atticus's wealth the division could never be firmly set. Millar notes that "if we go back over Nepos' biography of him, though he would never join any *factio* or *coitio*, he did in fact deploy his wealth repeatedly to assist individuals in public life who needed it" (1988:45).

16. Nepos goes so far as to write, "Once he escaped from those evils [of political instability], Atticus' sole effort was to help as many as possible in whatever manner he could. At a time when the rewards offered by the triumvirs caused a general hounding of the proscribed, no one came to Epirus who did not get everything that he needed, no one was not given the opportunity of living there permanently" (*Atticus* 11).

17. Alternatively, Welch's claim that self-interest provides a satisfactory answer is itself not particularly satisfying. It is true that capital tends to hedge its bets. In American politics, one can find the same corporations providing support to both of the major parties. That strategy makes sense in a particular environment in which support for the loser is not particularly costly. On Nepos's portrayal, that does not describe Atticus's situation. Assisting the defeated and, in a number of cases, those who were proscribed is not a risk-free action, particularly if under Roman law, one's property could be confiscated and sold off.

18. As a number of commentators have noted, this is a wonderful mirroring of Lucretius's Epicurean account of a kind of pleasure:

> When winds are troubling the waters on a great sea, it is a pleasure to view from the land another man's great struggles; not because it is a joy to delight that anyone should be storm-tossed, but because it is a pleasure to observe troubles from which you yourself are free. It is a pleasure too to gaze on great contests of war deployed over the plains when you yourself have no part in the danger. But pleasantest of all is to be master of those tranquil regions well fortified on high by the teaching of the wise.

(LONG AND SEDLEY 1987:119)

19. Atticus's Epicureanism also adds weight to the importance of friendship. Epicurus wrote, "All friendship is an intrinsic virtue, but it originates from benefiting" and "it is also necessary to take risks for the sake of friendship." (Long and Sedley 1987, 126). In his *Against Epicurean Happiness*, Plutarch wrote that the Epicureans "in fact say that it is more pleasurable to confer a benefit than to receive one" (Long and Sedley 1987:126). From Diogenes Laertius, we also learn that the Epicurean "never give[s] up a friend" and "will on occasion die for a friend" (133). The extraordinarily high value that the Epicureans place on friendship ("Of the things wisdom acquires for the blessedness of life as a whole, [by] far the greatest is the possession of friendship" [126]) may go some distance in accounting for Atticus's motivations in helping his friends in times of trouble. As it stands, friendship is a value that simply trumps politics. One gets involved in politics, if one must, only when one's friends are in trouble. The appeal to Epicurean philosophy offers a useful way to understand Nepos's Atticus. As noted previously, the puzzle, of course, is that Nepos does not draw on such an account. Perhaps Nepos believed that these connections were so obvious

312 · 6. FRIENDSHIP DURING DARK TIMES

that he need not mention them. Alternatively, this omission may signal that Atticus's interventions were meant to be seen as more than an expression of Epicureanism.

20. One is reminded of Antigone's response to Creon's edict that Polynices (the enemy of the state) not be buried. He is not an animal.

21. One response to this view is to argue that political turmoil is never truly a realm of necessity. To use Michael Walzer's critique, what is really meant by necessity is not causal determination but indispensability (1977:8). To argue that a course of action is necessary is really to say that it is indispensable for achieving certain ends or purposes. Once one sees necessity as indispensability and not causal inevitability, agency and choice are restored. The idea of indispensability allows us to ask about the importance of the ends in question and whether the means that are being used are commensurate or proportional. On this reading of necessity, Atticus is mistaken: Political turmoil is never like the ocean. Political actors remain agents as long as they have the capacity to judge the value of their ends and understand the relationship between means and ends. Atticus's position, like that of the Machiavellian realist's is a form of misunderstanding, perhaps even self-deception.

It is not clear, however, whether Walzer's position entirely settles the matter. Political turmoil is a realm dominated by necessity and fortune (which are now joined at the hip) because it is chaotic. The very notion of "indispensability" that draws together means and ends in some sort of expected fashion is radically disturbed. Brutus may have believed that Caesar's death was indispensable for the preservation of the republic. But what precisely does indispensable mean here other than a presumption of a causal relationship between Caesar's death and a desirable end? Perhaps he thought it was a necessary condition (albeit not sufficient) for protecting the republic. Unfortunately, in this environment, the linkages that connect means to ends are easily broken or occluded. From Atticus's perspective (or, at least, the perspective which I am attributing to him), it is sheer self-deception to believe that one can fully understand and control the relevant events and individuals during dark times. If that analysis is plausible, then once again there is a fair amount of hubris in thinking that individuals can control a situation in the same manner as when our moral and political practices and institutions have a degree of stability.

22. The view that I am attributing to Nepos is not quite the same as the sort of position that Ludwig attributes to Derrida. On Ludwig's interpretation, Derrida believed that "because enemies are constitutive [of one's identity], they are no longer 'other' to us, but intimately part of the self. Insiders cannot in good conscience attack outsiders once they have come to realize that the outsiders helped constitute them as what they are (cf. Derrida 1997:139). We must

embrace the Other who constituted us" (136). Part of the difficulty with this position is that it is not clear that the oppositions that result from pursuing power and position constitute identity in the relevant way. More importantly, the question raised by Nepos's biography is whether friendship should survive deep and violent political divisions. In contrast, the question raised by Derrida is whether deep and violent political divisions presuppose a sort of debt to the other. In response, Derrida's question could raise the question of friendship, but it need not. It need not because one could acknowledge the constitutive role of one's enemy to one's identity without acquiring the motivations of friendship and subscribing to its adverbial conditions. To frame this in terms of concerns that drive Ludwig's analysis of friendship, the metaphysics surrounding these deeper questions of identity formation do not direct answers regarding with whom one should or should not be friends.

23. This reaffirms one of the points made in chapter 4 rejecting a moral test of character for friendship.

24. More disturbingly, it runs counter to the view that maintaining an association with thugs and tyrants is a despicable form of collaboration and toadyism.

25. Ludwig's essay presents an alternative thesis regarding the relationship between friendship and the liberal, procedural republic. Ludwig suggests that the problem with friendship, even civic friendship, from a classical, Socratic position is that it violates the self-interested assumptions of modern liberal theory. On his account, it is not rules and procedures pushing out friendship, it is the exhortation to be a fully self-interested rational actor à la Hobbes. From the Hobbesian perspective, "citizens [who are] willing to sacrifice themselves for their friends introduce an irrational element into politics" (Ludwig 2010:149). In contrast, I am suggesting that it is precisely because the protection of our friends can be understood as rational that civil procedures and rules need rely so heavily on a notion of fairness. Fairness provides a reason for individuals to subsume (on occasion) their own self-interest as well as the interests of their family members and friends to the procedures and laws of the state. This is no easy or slam-dunk decision either for oneself or for one's friends and the support of one's friends is no more or less rational than the support for oneself and one's family.

7. INSTITUTIONS FOR AND AGAINST FRIENDSHIP

1. These generalizations are not meant to deny the fact that historically (and culturally), there exists a long tradition of using one's office and its spoils to help friends and punish enemies. Indeed, the idea of justice as helping one's friends and harming one's enemies is old and has never been entirely abandoned. To the extent that friendship is a relationship in which one seeks to be attentive to

the interests of the other, it has been the case that the distribution of the goods of office to one's friends is frequently understood as an expression of good friendship (Hyatte 1997; Langer 1994). Patronage systems, however, are not always compatible with the expectations of friendship. For one thing, not all patron-client relationships are friendships. On the other hand, the existence of a patron-client relationship and its attendant inequality does not preclude friendships. For another, rewarding allies may be at the expense of rewarding friendships (as well as one's family). Obviously, partiality comes in many forms.

2. One could argue that the very idea of the impartial application of the law is a charade given that it is virtually impossible to adopt an impartial point of view. All points of view are informed by subjective biases, unconscious quirks, and structural distortions. Consequently to criticize friendship from such a perspective is no criticism at all. In response, unlike biases based on such things as race, gender, sexual orientation, and class, the problems raised by friends and family can be identified and handled relatively easily. In cases of kith and kin, we need not think of the impartial application of the law as requiring a view from nowhere. Rather, it simply means abstaining from the application of laws and policies in matters of one's friends and family.

3. Baker carries the critique in a somewhat different direction by arguing that if we imagined a legislative body, such as a senate, based on friendship cliques it "would be an oppressive and suffocating institution which would induce the most stifling forms of conformity. Cohesion based on personal attachment and carried to an extreme would cause every issue to be decided on the basis of like and dislike, every vote to turn on personality and every outcome on favoritism" (1999:321).

4. A version of this challenge will reappear in the discussion of friendship between states in chapter 9. In the case of states, the importance of friendship and the possible erosion of an independent perspective can lead countries into foreign engagements that they would not otherwise undertake or what is sometimes called entrapment.

5. The difficulty of distinguishing a flatterer from a friend is considered in more detail in the "Chilling Effect of Legal and Political Institutions" section and is part of a larger problem of distinguishing false friends from true friends in an environment in which states sometimes seek to produce false friends.

6. In this regard one may think of legal forms of segregation such as Jim Crow laws in the United States or laws that sought to divide and isolate individuals. Writing about the Soviet Union before the end of Stalinism, Barrington Moore asserted that "the regime deliberately seeks to sow suspicion among the population, which to a marked extent results in the breakup of friendship groupings, in the work situation and elsewhere, and the isolation of the individual" (1954:158).

7. Pahl writes, "One of the strongest barriers to pure friendship is structurally conditioned inequality" (2000:162). Pahl's use of the term *pure* friendship is not fully elucidated, although it could be read in terms of making a distinction between true and false friends. See also King (2007:136–37).

8. A similar view of tyrants was held by Montaigne's close friend, Étienne de La Boétie, who wrote that

> There is no doubt that the tyrant is never loved, and loves nobody. Friendship is a sacred word, it is a holy thing, and it exists only between good people, it is kindled by mutual esteem. . . . Now even if [fear of the cruelty of a tyrant] . . . were not an obstacle, it would still be difficult to establish solid friendship with a tyrant. The reason is that he is above all other men, and has no peer, and so he is necessarily beyond the bounds of friendship, which is all about equality: you do not want a relationship which limps.
>
> (CA. 1548)

9. The extreme case of a power differential is that between a human and a god. Discussions of friendship have occasionally taken on the question of whether such friendship is possible. If that divine being is believed to be both omniscient and good, these obstacles are effectively removed. On the one hand, a god's ability to see into the human heart disposes of the problem of the flatterer. You cannot dupe such a god in those matters. On the other hand, if the god's motives are not in question and her grace truly comes without strings attached, then the relationship is not one of patron to client. In Exodus (33:11), Moses is described as a friend of God. In the New Testament, John 15:14 acknowledges that Jesus issues commands to be followed, but that is not an obstacle to friendship. David Konstan (1997) argues that while the Greeks believed that humans could be favored by the gods, they could not be their friends. For example, Aristotle denied this possibility (1985:1158b33–36).

For the Stoics, however, the sage can be a friend of the gods. As Konstan notes, the reason is that the sage is truly free and hence is equal to the gods. Within the Christian tradition, this kind of equality with God is never asserted and hence John's notion of friendship is a significant departure from the classical Greek conception. The practice of friendship with God, if one can call it that, is very much a relationship of dependence.

10. It is important to note that what Mill and Shanley are considering is a particular kind of friendship that places equality at the center. Under the common law of England, there was an older tradition that saw marriage as a very different sort of friendship compatible with inequality. Peter Goodrich notes that "the early modern meaning of amity was often illustrated by the relationship between husband and wife. The wife was a friend, the queen of friends, according to the treatises on amity, and marriage was friendship" (2005:48). In this tradition,

amity was not only compatible with but reinforced the rights and powers of the husband over the wife. Goodrich's historical observations are an important reminder of the historically situated character of our practices of friendship.

11. Rosenbury makes a similar point by arguing that inequalities continue to exist within marriage (2007:216). The law encourages domestic couplings that continue norms of inequality and dependence. In effect, the state maintains gender inequality by glorifying marriage and not recognizing friendship.

One can argue that equality in the form of social and economic independence (or perhaps even in terms of equal economic and social vulnerability) is a necessary feature of certain practices of friendship. In addition, one could argue that the absence of domination or subordination can make it easier to discern the motivations of friendship. The law may not be able to generate friendships by being attentive in inequalities, but it may create greater opportunities for friendship, and by advancing the cause of social and economic independence, it can foster a particular kind of friendship, one consonant with an ideal of individuality discussed in chapter 4.

12. When those norms of friendship are further layered with the privileges of class, as was true for both Elliott and Philby, the distortions can be intensified. When John le Carré asked Elliott whether he or MI6 considered assassinating Philby, Elliott replied, "My dear chap. One of us" (MacIntyre 2014:300). The expectations associated with a certain class position enabled Philby and Elliott to acquire their positions and ultimately protected Philby from the investigations of MI5.

13. *Washington Post*, September 14, 2010.

14. The relationship between negative freedom and friendship is not solely a political concern. The question of promoting or impeding friendship can also be raised of the economic and property systems. For example, consider the argument that historical sociologists make that, with the rise of commercialism and the "commodification of social relationship," the possibilities for close friendships found in traditional societies were replaced by cool, mobile, exchange relationships of modern capitalism. Simmel's idea of the impossibility of complete intimacy in modernity could be read as an example of this idea, but it also informs the work of Marx and Tönnies. On the other hand, Ray Pahl argues that "far from the traditional society being suffused with brotherly *Gemeinschaft* virtues, the reverse appears to be the case. Counter to what the classical sociological tradition appears to suggest, Aristotelian styles of friendship reemerge with the coming of commercial-industrial society in the eighteenth century" (2000:53–54). Drawing on the work of Allan Silver and informed by the ideas of the Scottish Enlightenment, Pahl argues that "the great virtue of commercial society was to allow a clear distinction to be made between those relationships based on interest and those relationships based on sympathy and

affection" (2000:58). With the emergence of a realm of market relationships, it is possible to develop a parallel system of personal relationships that, in the words of Silver "excludes exchange and utility" (quoted in Pahl 2000:60).

The story that Hume, Adams, Pahl, and Silver tell is one of the indirect cultivation of friendship, or, at least a certain sort of friendship. The ideas that friendships must exclude utility (hence excluding precommercial conceptions of friendship in which utility may have been seen as an ordinarily appropriate reason for friendship) and whether contemporary accounts of friendship do preclude exchange relationships (which suggests that exchange and utility play no role in contemporary friendships) was contested in chapter 2. At this point, however, what is more important than the details of the argument and even more important than the question of whether the classical sociologists are right is the presumption that the effect of markets, commerce, and property relationships on friendship is an important concern. It is not, of course, the only concern in assessing economic systems, as the issues of distributive justice, freedom, equality, and efficiency remain central. If, like political regimes, economic regimes have some effect on the ability of individuals to form friendships, then the quality of those regimes should be, in part, judged by those effects.

15. As we saw in chapter 3, George Simmel made a rather sweeping assertion about the infrequency, if not impossibility for what he called complete intimacy in modernity.

16. Goodrich (2005) explores the story of why friendship currently has this status. He argues that in English common law, the neglect of the law courts in matters of amity and love is an historical artifact. At one point, such matters would have been the provenance of ecclesiastical courts that ran parallel to the secular legal system. Since the disappearance of ecclesiastical regulation, secular courts have been reluctant to see amity and love as civil interests.

17. At the very least, there is an emerging literature on the connection between law and friendship. In 2011, Leib published a major book on the topic (*Friend v. Friend*). See also Chambers (2001), Friedman (1993:248), Goodrich (2004, 2005), Karst (1980), and Rosenbury (2007).

18. More generally, Leib writes, "Contrary to Aristotle's account, my account here excludes from consideration spousal friendship, familial friendship, erotic friendship, and a generalized civic friendship" (2011:35).

19. In the case of equality, Leib writes, "Although friends are rarely equal in all ways, true friends treat one another as if they are. Friends give and take equally, or risk rupturing the bond of friendship. We cannot assume a sense of superiority over a friend without undermining a core attribute of friendship" (2011:23). This is not an implausible account of many, perhaps most friendships, but it need not be an ideal for everyone.

20. Presumably, a law of friendship would have other sorts of costs as well. For example, what would be the financial costs and benefits of bringing friends into the benefits of medical leave? Public policies that were cognizant of friendship would have certain costs that are borne more heavily by some parties and not by others. More generally, is the urgency of protecting and promoting friendship through the law more compelling than whatever those costs may be?

21. Leib offers a version of this argument in discussing duties of care when he notes that "the duties of friendship are always underspecified and can always shift from under our feet. Friendships themselves are always organic, always in motion, and always responsive to shifting realties. It is impossible to be too exacting about what would count as meeting or violating a relevant duty of care; the discretion friends need recommends deferring to the judgment of friends unless departures from good behavior are manifest" (Leib 2009, 710). The morality of friendship is "blurry." Consequently, Leib notes that it is difficult to precisely delineate how far friends should go in pursuing the self-interest of their friends (710).

22. It may be useful to note that Leib not only sees relational contract theory as illuminating friendship, but also the idea of friendship as helping to illuminate relational contract theory. In the latter case, his goal is to decenter marriage as the paradigmatic case of a relational contract and argue that such contracts are better understood as friendships (2011:159–66). The degree to which our understanding of the law of contracts is improved by making this move lies far beyond my limited understanding of the law.

23. Similarly, Leib considers the argument that the problem with a law of friendship is that it would step in once a friendship has dissolved and "in such cases it would be hard to justify enforcing friendship's norms upon parties who do not want to be bound by them; as many suggest, the norms of friendship are often defined in contradistinction to nonvoluntary norms that the law imposes" (Leib 2007:680–81). If the friends themselves do not voluntarily act like friends, why should the law try to coerce them to do so through the operation of obligations?

24. At times, the thrust of Leib's project appears to be one of using the law to protect and promote friendship. At other times, he notes that "it is not obvious that legal recognition will lead to an increase in the actual number or quality of friendships within society" (2011:46). In the latter mode, his project becomes one of being mindful of the law's effect on friendship (45).

25. Quoted in Deneen and McWilliams (2011:13).

8. *FRIENDSHIP* AND *FRIEND*
IN AN INTERNATIONAL CONTEXT

1. For a contrasting position, see Oelsner and Koschut, who argue that international friendship operates at both an official level and is a matter of people-to-people ties (2014a:203–4; see also Eznack and Koschut 2014).

2. That such a warrant is needed to discuss friendship may well be due to the predominance of realist approaches to international relations (Oelsner 2007:257). In this chapter, I will suggest how the predominant conception of friendship has reinforced certain features of realism.

3. Although the idea of practice played an important role in earlier chapters, it plays a less significant role in this discussion. In considering international friendship, I am less concerned with what practitioners do than with eliciting forms of cooperation implied by self-interested justifications for state action.

4. I will use the words *state* and *country* interchangeably.

5. Along similar lines, Preston King writes, "If reciprocal friendship is always dual and intimate, then though there may be friendship within groups, there is no friendship of groups. On the reciprocal view, there may be friendship within, but not of, the mass. Reciprocal friendship does not come en masse. There is no dyadic friendship as of all citizens, or of all nationals, or of any group too large to accommodate reciprocity. The state, nation, region, city can never enjoy friendship of this type" (2007:134). The qualification, however, at the end of the quote ("of this type") may be enough to squeeze the nose of international friendship under the tent of forms of international cooperation. A more sustained skeptical account can be found in Simon Keller's "Against Friendship Between Countries" (2009). Keller's position is discussed below. For a very different position that views friendship as "woven into the ontology of IR [international relations]," see Smith (2014:48). The notion of international friendship offered in these chapters is neither as pessimistic as what King and Keller argue, nor as necessarily pervasive as Smith suggests.

6. See also Oelsner and Koschut (2014b:7–8) for a response to Keller that turns on the breadth of usage associated with friendship.

7. For example, American president George Washington viewed entangling alliances with Europe as a function of passionate attachments. In his farewell address, he noted that "a passionate attachment of one nation for another produces a variety of evils" (1796). Or, to cite another example, Arnold Wolfers wrote that "close and effective interstate amity as among allies should tend to promote emotional friendship" (1962:33). Wolfers's view of this sort of relationship appears to depend on the connection that a people may have to the image of another nation. Perhaps just as we develop emotional ties to the image of our own nation (Benedict Anderson, for example, talks about the "affective bonds of nationalism" [1991:64]), we could develop emotional ties to our allies.

8. A similar distinction will be highlighted in chapter 9's discussion of Andrea Oelsner's idea of international friendship.

9. I suspect that my differences with Eznack and Koschut go deeper into moral theory and the role of reason (at least at the level of states). In their discussion of international friendship, they appeal to Francis Hutcheson's idea of moral sense (2014:76). In discerning that moral sense, Hutcheson argues that our passions and affections are not under our direct control and that we naturally approve of affections that are benevolent and recoil from affections that are selfish. In these responses, reason is purely instrumental and cannot explain our actions (Schmitter 2014). In contrast, much of the discussion of international friendship that I offer rests on the possibility of reason being able to motivate state action. If Hutcheson's approach suffuses Eznack and Koschut's position, then my position, from their perspective, is misguided at this deeper level. Whatever may be true at the individual level, I am presuming that reason can and should play some role in state interactions. Moreover, the reasons that motivate state action should have a public character and be accessible to all.

10. Quoted in Bumiller (2010).

11. As I understand it, the "practice-turn" of international theory seeks to set out and explore the commonsensical or unthought aspects of international relations (e.g., Adler and Pouliot 2011a, 2011b; Neumann 2002; Pouliot 2007, 2008, 2010). The possibility that the language of friendship reinforces a particular way to understand the relationships between states would be compatible with a practice approach that looked to actual state behavior. The difference, however, is that the claims that I have made are largely speculative. In addition, the goal of these chapters is not to offer a practice account of state behavior, but a theoretical account of international friendship.

12. Although Graham Smith concludes that Schmitt "must be considered no friend of friendship" (2011a:223), he does argue that Schmitt is a theorist of friendship, albeit offering a theory that is "askew" (221; 2011b:18). Schwarzenbach calls the notion of a cooperative venture formed purely in response to a threat, a "negative friendship" (2009:254; 2011:31).

13. There is some slippage in the way in which Schmitt employs these terms in these two contexts (the domestic versus the international), and that will appear later in the discussion.

14. It may be helpful to note that unlike a form of realism that focuses on the systemic balance of power, Schmitt is concerned with the perception of threats to a state's way of life. It is a balance of perception of threat to one's identity—an identity that itself may be broadly conceived. Consequently, the political is not structured by a balance of power that could be assessed from a neutral, academic position, but by the decision of a state to publicly establish certain opponents as enemies because they are deemed to threaten its way of life.

15. In contrast, Smith argues that "friendship is simply the binary opposite of enemy" (2011a:222).

16. If true, this may dilute the notion of friend at the domestic level. If compatriots step up and die for a way of life, then that makes them friends, but only after the fact. They are not dying for one another because they are friends, they are friends because they are dying (or willing to die) for each other. What may motivate compatriots is not friendship, but a "politically distinct consciousness." The unity of a nation now becomes based on things such as a "common language, common historical destiny, traditions and remembrances, and the common political goals and hopes" (Schmitt 2008:261–62). International allies are friends in Schmitt's technical sense of the term and are not united by these elements.

17. In their analysis of friendship treaties, Devere, Mark, and Verbisky argue that throughout history, most treaties of friendship have been based on utility and the cynical manipulation of the notion of friendship. These arrangements, "claim to give mutual benefit to each party, but while there is some reciprocal exchange agreed to, the treaties are not altruistic. Often they are used by the larger powers to make an agreement about the use of the other nation's resources, in return for some protection" (2011:64; see also Roschin 2011:88). The argument of this chapter is that, unlike interpersonal friendships, interstate friendship can be based on self-interest. In the international realm, self-interest is not a deficient reason. In contrast, Devere, Mark, and Verbisky suggest that these friendships are false friendships insofar as the underlying motivations are not merely utility but also manipulating and dominating one's partner. Their hope is that interstate relations can be directed by more than utility. They derive their notion of interstate friendship and goodwill from the work of Jawaharlal Nehru. The chapters that follow agree with Devere, Mark, and Verbisky to the extent that there are reasons beyond narrow self-interest that can form the basis for interstate cooperation.

18. This sketch is indebted to Glen Snyder's analysis in *Alliance Politics* (1997), but it is not meant as a summary of his position, nor does it encompass the intricacies of economic, game theoretic, or sociological approaches of alliance formation and their relationship to practical reason.

19. It is important to note that the idea of states as rationally self-interested actors who deploy instrumental reason to secure and promote their goals is a familiar but contested one in international relations. For example, in seeking to understand interstate cooperation, constructivists point to the importance of "shared identities, values, and meanings" (Adler and Barnett 1998:31; Tusicisny 2007:427–28); democratic peace theorists point to such things as domestic political structures and culture (Doyle 1997, 2005; Oneal and Russett, 1997; Starr 1992:208; Weart 1998); and early advocates of security communities noted the significance of

"processes and transaction flows," "mutual needs," and the willingness of states to offer "mutual concessions" (Deutsch et al. 1957:91). These alternative approaches call into question the adequacy of the realist descriptive and/or explanatory account of why states align or ally with one another. For the most part, however, these explanations tend to remain within a causal framework and are less concerned with the normative question of what reasons should be compelling to state actors.

9. INTERNATIONAL FRIENDSHIPS OF CHARACTER

1. See Osgood and Tucker (1967:282–83).
2. It could be argued that there is an important distinction between governments and states that is being lost in the discussion. Governments come and go, but states as creatures of international recognition and law remain. Alternatively, the blurring of governments and states ignores the importance of national identity to the protection of institutions and claims to the homeland. Internationally, the state does provide what Michael Walzer (1977) called a "shell" which allows political communities the opportunity to work out their own political destinies within certain parameters. The argument here does blur the government/state distinction because the shell of the state ultimately rests on the idea of the state as an indispensable condition of value and on the claim that states can, in fact, play that role. The role that nationalist arguments play in the discussion is considered briefly later in the chapter.
3. One may add that they are willful in the sense that they have their conceptions of what makes a good life and seek to pursue it as best they can which generates a robust pluralism and, potentially, a robust notion of individuality (Flathman 1992).
4. Acknowledging that as international law has evolved—for example in the case of the responsibility to protect—territorial integrity has become less sacrosanct.
5. This view does not deny that other states may be concerned about the interests of the United States out of fear of her power or because of whatever advantages may be gained by aligning with such a powerful partner. Nor does it deny that in many instances the actions and policies that are alleged to be in the interest of the United States are actually in the interest of a few private individuals or groups.
6. Assuming that the necessary resources and other conditions for establishing a just state are present.
7. Other reasons for cooperation such as balancing and bandwagoning may not be distinguishable from motives of utility and self-interest narrowly construed.
8. In the radical conception of ideology, motivations are ideological if they fail to recognize the way the world really operates, close down alternative plausible

views of reality, legitimize a given power structure, or cut off the possibility for debate and inquiry.

9. A somewhat different constructivist approach to international friendship is provided by Felix Berenskoetter who sees friendship as a "special relationship of choice that does not simply form on the basis of geographic proximity, close trade links or an otherwise high level of 'interaction,' but through a mutual commitment to use overlapping biographical narratives for pursuing a shared idea of international order" (2014:57). This is a view of international friendship that shapes and reinforces the identities of the friends (67), which can be anxiety-controlling, provide ontological security and serve as a source of power (58).

10. Perhaps the proximity analogy for individuals is raised when friends become lovers. In that situation, the metaphorical melding seem to push us to say that they are "more than" friends.

11. The terms *alignment* and *alliance* are sometimes used interchangeably, but more generally alignments tend to be seen as looser forms of association in which the expectations of the states have not be formally negotiated and set down on paper. In contrast, alliances are frequently stipulated to be "formal associations of states for the use (or nonuse) of military force, in specific circumstances, against states outside their own membership" (Snyder 1997:4; Lai and Reiter 2000:205; see also Fedder 1968:68–69). Their formal character usually entails a promise or a contract setting out the conditions under which force will or will not be called upon (Cha 2000:265n9; Snyder 1997:6–7). Both alignments and alliances are frequently understood to refer to associations in which there exist expectations for military assistance. They are, to put it in George Liska's succinct terms, "against, and only derivatively for, someone or something" (Liska 1962:12; Wolfers 1962:27). International friendships would be alignments unless they were formalized into alliances. In contrast to Liska, such alliances are "for" and only derivatively against someone or something.

10. THE POLITICS OF INTERNATIONAL FRIENDSHIP

1. It is important to note that within the realist and neorealist traditions, a fairly well-developed body of literature explores alliance formation and management. Less attention, however, has been devoted to alignments (Weinstein 1969:43; Duncan and Siverson 1982; Snyder 1990:105, 1997:6–8, 21–22). Central works concerned with alliance formation are Morgenthau (1959), Liska (1962), Holsti, Hopmann, and Sullivan (1973), Walt (1987), Keohane (1989), Christensen and Snyder (1990), Duffield (1992), McCalla (1996), Christensen (1997), and Snyder (1997). The central questions within the issue of alliance formation are why, when, and with whom one allies and how they divide the alliance payoffs and burdens (Snyder 1997:129). Important works that consider alliance management

include Fox and Fox (1962), Olson and Zeckhauser (1966), Osgood (1968), Bennett, Lepgold, and Unger (1994), Goldstein (1995), and Snyder (1997). The central issues of alliance management concern the preservation of the alliance and managing the risks of abandonment and entrapment. As will become evident, a number of these issues will crop up in the discussion of international friendships. The question that I am interested in pursuing is how the idea of international friendship could fit into a state-centric logic of international relations—a logic that also informs the conventional accounts of alliances and alignments.

2. Such a situation is not quite bandwagoning as understood by Stephen Walt (1987) or by Randall L. Schweller. States are neither aligning because minimally just states are dangerous nor are they aligning because they expect profit and easy gain (Schweller 1997:928). It is, however, closer to the general constructivist claim that "ideational context" can play in bandwagoning, if the norm is that of acting on justifiable reasons (Lebovic 2004:168).

3. In his discussion of his empirical evidence, Snyder fine-tunes these conclusions by arguing that "Easing the fear of abandonment does not necessarily mean accepting an increased risk of entrapment; it merely requires adapting one's policy more closely to the ally's desires" (1997:317). The question is whether the state is willing to accept the costs of tailoring its policies to those desires (318). When a distinction is made between alliances and alignments, where the latter lack the formal establishment of responsibilities and obligations, alignments may not have the same political pressures as alliances. On the one hand, it could be argued that because alignments lack the formalized creation of obligations, the fear of abandonment will be far greater than the fear of entrapment. The process of allying with another state is a way to get closer to them. On the other hand, it could be argued that states which are locked into the formal structure of an alliance have more wiggle room in begging off situations that look like entrapment. On this reading, alignments are all about performance—that is all one can go by. In contrast, alliance partners can look to the reassurances set out in a piece of paper if they have questions about a partner's commitments. In the case of an alliance, Snyder argues, "one can withhold support on issues outside the limits without calling into question one's loyalty on issues inside them." In the case of an entente or an alignment, there are no clear limits. Consequently, "any show of reluctance to support an ally on any issue casts doubt on one's reliability over all issues and incurs a risk that the ally will defect." Confidence, in the case of an entente, will turn more on performance than on a verbal promise. The opposite is true in the case of an alliance (347).

4. See Snyder (1997:19).

5. I am taking this term (although not its value nor subscribing to its predicted effects) from a story Snyder tells about Raymond Poincaré's firing of French ambassador Philippe de Crozier after his attempted rapprochement with the Austrio-Hungarian Empire before the First World War. Poincaré believed

that such a move would generate a conflict if the Triple Entente drove a wedge between Germany and Austria-Hungary. Snyder writes,

> Crozier's subordinate at Vienna, Count de St. Aulaire, expressed Poincaré's own sentiments when he wrote: "We could not [make such an agreement with Austria] without falling prey to the deadly system of the penetration of the alliances, of which it has been said, so rightly, that it is 'a cause of international decomposition just as pacifism is a cause of national decomposition.' The penetration of alliances, in fact, corrupts and dissolves them. By upsetting the balance and by obscuring the clarity of the situation, in reality it leads to ambiguity and instability. In doing so, it eventually weakens the guarantees for peace while claiming to increase them by the chimera of universal harmony."
>
> (1997:332)

Perhaps critics could argue that if minimally just states did ally with unjust states for purposes of security there would be similar risks of corruption or, at least, the risk of appearing to endorse the unjust regimes' internal arrangements. Undoubtedly, these risks can generate what I call a "politics of penetration" as the unjust states seek entrance into the international friendships of minimally just states. Nevertheless, if security is the reason for the alliance, then once that reason dissipates so should the alliance.

6. The enormous democratic peace literature lends some empirical plausibility to this idea. The notion of international friendship, however, raises the normative issue of whether justice should be the operative term as opposed to democracy.

7. A politics of penetration can occur when one or both parties are motivated to elide the distinction between friendships of utility and friendships of character. From the perspective of the minimally just state it may be easier to ally with an unsavory partner who is portrayed as progressive or making a good faith effort toward protecting basic rights. From the perspective of the autocrat, it may come to believe that eliding that distinction provides greater international legitimacy ("How bad can we be, if these democratic states are willing to do business with us?") or if it believes that the elision could yield increased levels of respect, consultation, support, and long-term commitment that it desires. From a Derridean point of view, politics arises because these are not stable assessments of the relationship and one or both parties may see it as necessary to remind the other that what is at stake is really utility ("Just remember, we're fighting the good fight against your enemies—whoever they happen to be.").

BIBLIOGRAPHY

Adler, Emanuel, and Michael Barnett. 1998. "A Framework for the Study of Security Communities." In *Security Communities*, edited by Emanuel Adler and Michael Barnett, 29–66. Cambridge: Cambridge University Press.

Adler, Emanuel, and Vincent Pouliot. 2011a. "International Practices." *International Theory* 3:1–36.

——, eds. 2011b. *International Practices*. New York: Cambridge University Press.

Allan, Graham A. 1989. *Friendship: Developing a Sociological Perspective*. London: Harvester Wheatsheaf.

Allen, Danielle S. 2004. *Talking to Strangers: Anxieties of Citizenship Since Brown v. Board of Education*. Chicago: University of Chicago Press.

Anderson, Benedict. 1991. *Imagined Communities: Reflections on the Origin and Spread of Nationalism*. London: Verso.

Annas, Julia. 1977. "Plato and Aristotle on Friendship and Altruism." *Mind* 86: 532–54.

——. 1993. *The Morality of Happiness*. Oxford: Oxford University Press.

Aquinas, Thomas. 1991. "Questions on Love and Charity (from *Summa Theologiae*)." In *Other Selves: Philosophers on Friendship*, edited by Michael Pakaluk, 146–84. Indianapolis: Hackett.

Arendt, Hannah. 1958. *The Human Condition*. Chicago: University of Chicago Press.

——. 1963. *On Revolution*. London: Penguin Books.

——. 1968. *Men in Dark Times*. Orlando: Harcourt, Brace and Company.

Aristotle. 1985. *Nicomachean Ethics*. Translated by Terence Irwin. Indianapolis: Hackett.

——. 2013. *Eudemian Ethics*. Translated by Brad Inwood and Raphael Woolf. Cambridge: Cambridge University Press.

Arnold, Laura W., Rebecca E. Deen, and Samuel C. Patterson. 2000. "Friendship and Votes: The Impact of Interpersonal Ties on Legislative Decision Making." *State and Local Government Review* 32:142–47.

Badhwar, Neera Kapur. 1993. "Introduction." In *Friendship: A Philosophical Reader*, edited by Neera Kapur Badhwar, 1–36. Ithaca: Cornell University Press.

Bailey, D. R. Shackleton. 1999. "Introduction." In *Letters to Atticus*, vol. 1, edited and translated by D. R. Shackleton Bailey. Cambridge, MA: Harvard University Press.

Baker, Ross K. 1999. *Friend and Foe in the U.S. Senate*. Acton, MA: Copley Publishing.

Barnett, Michael, and Raymond Duvall. 2005. "Power in International Politics." *International Organization* 59:39–75.

Barnett, Michael N., and Jack S. Levy. 1991. "Domestic Sources of Alliances and Alignments: The Case of Egypt, 1962–73." *International Organization* 45:369–95.

Baron, Marcia. 1984. "The Alleged Moral Repugnance of Acting from Duty." *Journal of Philosophy* 81:197–220.

——. 1991. "Impartiality and Friendship." *Ethics* 101:836–57.

Beitz, Charles R. 2000. "Rawls's Law of Peoples." *Ethics* 110:669–96.

Bell, Sandra, and Simon Coleman. 1999. "The Anthropology of Friendship: Enduring Themes and Future Possibilities." In *The Anthropology of Friendship*, edited by Sandra Bell and Simon Coleman, 1–19. Oxford: Berg.

Bennett, A., J. Lepgold, and D. Unger. 1994. "Burden-Sharing in the Persian Gulf War." *International Organization* 48:39–75.

Bennett, D. Scott. 1997. "Testing Alternative Models of Alliance Duration, 1816–1984." *American Journal of Political Science* 41:846–78.

Berenskoetter, Felix. 2007. "Friends, There Are No Friends? An Intimate Reframing of the International." *Millennium: Journal of International Studies* 35:647–76.

——. 2014. "Friendship, Security, Power." In *Friendship and International Relations*, edited by Simon Koschut and Andrea Oelsner, 51–71. London: Palgrave Macmillan.

Bickford, Susan. 1996. *The Dissonance of Democracy: Listening, Conflict, and Citizenship*. Ithaca: Cornell University Press.

Bloom, Allen. 1993. *Love and Friendship*. New York: Simon and Schuster.

Blum, Lawrence A. 1980. *Friendship, Altruism, and Morality*. London: Routledge & Kegan Paul.

——. 1990. "Vocation, Friendship, and Community: Limitations of the Personal-Impersonal Framework." In *Identity, Character, and Morality: Essays in Moral Psychology*, edited by Owen Flanagan and Amelie Oksenberg Rorty, 173–97. Cambridge, MA: MIT Press.

Bolotin, David. 1979. *Plato's Dialogue on Friendship: An Interpretation of the Lysis, with a New Translation*. Ithaca: Cornell University Press.

Boym, Svetlana. 2009/10. "Scenography of Friendship." *Cabinet Magazine*, no. 36. http://cabinetmagazine.org/issues/36/boym.php.

Brink, David O. 1992. "A Puzzle About the Rational Authority of Morality." *Philosophical Perspectives* 6:1–26.

Brunkhorst, Hauke. 2005. *Solidarity: From Civic Friendship to Global Legal Community*. Cambridge, MA: MIT Press.

Bueno de Mesquita, Bruce, and David Lalman. 1992. *War and Reason: Domestic and International Imperatives*. New Haven: Yale University Press.

Bull, Hedley. 1966. "The Grotian Conception of International Society." In *Diplomatic Investigations: Essays in the Theory of International Politics*, edited by Herbert Butterfield and Martin Wight, 51–73. Cambridge, MA: Harvard University Press.

Bumiller, Elisabeth. 2010. "Gates on Leaks, Wiki and Otherwise." *New York Times*, November 30. http://thecaucus.blogs.nytimes.com/2010/11/30/gates-on-leaks-wiki-and-otherwise/?scp=2&sq=Gates&st=cse.

Burridge, Kenelm O. L. 1957. "Friendship in Tangu." *Oceania* 27:177–89.

Caldeira, Gregory A., and Samuel Patterson. 1987. "Friendship in the Legislature." *Journal of Politics* 49:953–75.

Canellos, Simon. 2009. *The Last Lion: The Fall and Rise of Ted Kennedy*. New York: Simon and Schuster.

Caney, Simon. 2005. "Global Interdependence and Distributive Justice." *Review of International Studies* 31:389–99.

Canovan, Margaret. 1988. "Friendship, Truth, and Politics: Hannah Arendt and Toleration." In *Justifying Toleration: Conceptual and Historical Perspectives*, edited by Susan Mendus, 117–98. Cambridge: Cambridge University Press.

Carrier, James G. 1999. "People Who Can Be Friends: Selves and Social Relationships." In *The Anthropology of Friendship*, edited by Sandra Bell and Simon Coleman, 21–38. Oxford: Berg.

Cha, Victor D. 2000. "Abandonment, Entrapment, and Neoclassical Realism in Asia: The United States, Japan, and Korea." *International Studies Quarterly* 44:261–91.

Chambers, David L. 2001. "For the Best of Friends and for Lovers of All Sorts, a Status Other than Marriage." *Notre Dame Law Review* 76:1347–64.

Childs, Sarah. 2013. "Negotiating Gendered Institutions: Women's Parliamentary Friendships." *Politics & Gender* 9:127–51.

Chong, Kim-Chong. 1984. "Egoism, Desires, and Friendship." *American Philosophical Quarterly* 21:349–57.

Christensen, T. 1997. "Perceptions and Alliances in Europe, 1865–1940." *International Organization* 51:65–97.

Christensen, T., and J. Snyder. 1990. "Chain Gangs and Passed Bucks: Predicting Alliance Patterns in Multipolarity." *International Organization* 44:137–68.

Cicero. 1991. "On Friendship." In *Other Selves: Philosophers on Friendship*, edited by Michael Pakaluck, 77–116. Indianapolis: Hackett.

———. 1999a. *Letters to Atticus*, vol. 1. Edited and translated by D. R. Shackleton Bailey. Cambridge, MA: Harvard University Press.

———. 1999b. *Letters to Atticus*, vol. 2. Edited and translated by D. R. Shackleton Bailey. Cambridge, MA: Harvard University Press.

———. 1999c. *Letters to Atticus*, vol. 3. Edited and translated by D. R. Shackleton Bailey. Cambridge, MA: Harvard University Press.

———. 1999d. *Letters to Atticus*, vol. 4. Edited and translated by D. R. Shackleton Bailey. Cambridge, MA: Harvard University Press.

———. 2009. *The Republic and the Laws*. Translated by Niall Rudd. Oxford: Oxford University Press.

Cocking, Dean, and Jeanette Kennett. 1998. "Friendship and the Self." *Ethics* 108:502–27.

Cohen, Gerald Allan. 2008. *Rescuing Justice and Equality*. Cambridge, MA: Harvard University Press.

———. 2009. *Why Not Socialism?* Princeton: Princeton University Press.

Cohen, Joshua. 2004. "Minimalism About Human Rights: The Most We Can Hope For?" *Journal of Political Philosophy* 12:190–213.

———. 2006. "Is There a Human Right to Democracy?" In *The Egalitarian Conscience: Essays in Honor of G. A. Cohen*, edited by Christine Sypnowich, 226–48. Oxford: Oxford University Press.

Cohen, Yehudi A. 1961. "Patterns of Friendship." In *Social Structure and Personality: A Casebook*, edited by Yehudi A. Cohen, 351–83. New York: Holt-Rinehart-Winston.

Constantin, Cornelia. 2011. "'Great Friends': Creating Legacies, Networks and Policies that Perpetuate the Memory of the Fathers of Europe." *International Politics* 48:112–28.

Cooper, John M. 1993. "Political Animals and Civic Friendship." In *Friendship: A Philosophical Reader*, edited by Neera Kapur Badhwar, 303–26. Ithaca: Cornell University Press.

Copeland, Jordan Joel. 2007. "Rehearsals for Engagement: The Moral Practice of Friendship and the Cultivation of Social Concern." PhD diss., University of Iowa.

Corera, Gordon. 2013. *The Art of Betrayal: The Secret History of MI6*. New York: Pegasus Books.

Cozby, Paul C. 1973. "Self-Disclosure: A Literature Review." *Psychological Bulletin* 79:73–91.

Davidson, Lee. 2009. "Hatch, Kennedy Made Political Theater as 'Odd Couple.'" *Deseret News*, August 27. http://www.deseretnews.com/article/705326039/Hatch-Kennedy-made-political-theater-as-odd-couple.html?pg=all.

Dawson, Raymond, and Richard Rosecrance. 1966. "Theory and Reality in the Anglo-American Alliance." *World Politics* 19:21–51.

de La Boetiè, Ètienne. ca. 1548. "Slaves by Choice." Unknown English translator. Accessed August 17, 2012. http://www.constitution.org/la_boetie/sbc.htm.

Deneen, Patrick, and Susan J. McWilliams. 2011. "A Better Sort of Love." In *The Democratic Soul: A Wilson Carey McWilliams Reader*, edited by Wilson Carey McWilliams, Patrick J. Deneen, and Susan J. McWilliams, 1–18. Lexington: University of Kentucky.

Derrida, Jacques. 1988. "The Politics of Friendship." *Journal of Philosophy* 85:632–44.

——. 1997. *Politics of Friendship*. London: Verso.

Deutsch, Karl, Sidney A. Burrell, Robert A. Kann, and Maurice Lee Jr. 1957. *Political Community and the North Atlantic Area: International Organization in the Light of Historical Evidence*. Princeton: Princeton University Press.

Devere, Heather. 2014. "Friendship in International Treaties." In *Friendship and International Relations*, edited by Simon Koschut and Andrea Oelsner, 182–98. London: Palgrave Macmillan.

Devere, Heather, Simon Mark, and Jane Verbitsky. 2011. "A History of the Language of Friendship in International Treaties." *International Politics* 48:46–70.

Digeser, P. E. 2001. *Political Forgiveness*. Ithaca: Cornell University Press.

——. 2009a. "Friendship Between States." *British Journal of Political Science* 39:323–44.

——. 2009b. "Public Reason and International Friendship." *Journal of International Political Theory* 5:22–40.

——. 2013. "Friendship as a Family of Practices." *Amity: Journal of Friendship Studies* 1:34–52.

Doyle, Michael. 1997. *Ways of War and Peace: Realism, Liberalism, and Socialism*. New York: Norton.

——. 2005. "Three Pillars of the Liberal Peace." *American Political Science Review* 99:463–66.

Du Bois, Cora. 1974. "The Gratuitous Act: An Introduction to the Comparative Study of Friendship Patterns." In *The Compact: Selected Dimensions of Friendship*, edited by Elliot Leyton, 15–32. Newfoundland: University of Newfoundland.

Duffield, J. 1992. "International Regimes and Alliance Behavior: Explaining NATO Conventional Force Levels." *International Organization* 46:819–55.

Duncan, G., and R. M. Siverson. 1982. "Flexibility of Alliance Partner Choice in a Multipolar System." *International Studies Quarterly* 26:511–38.

Eisenstadt, S. N. 1956. "Ritualized Personal Relations." *Man* 56:90–95.

Emerson, Ralph Waldo. 1991. "Friendship." In *Other Selves: Philosophers on Friendship*, edited by Michael Pakaluk, 218–32. Indianapolis: Hackett.

Epstein, Joseph. 2006. *Friendship: An Expose*. New York: Mariner Books.

Eznack, Lucile. 2011. "Crises as Signals of Strength: The Significance of Affect in Close Allies' Relationships." *Security Studies* 20:238–65.

Eznack, Lucile, and Simon Koschut. 2014. "The Sources of Affect in Interstate Friendship." In *Friendship and International Relations*, edited by Simon Koschut and Andrea Oelsner, 72–88. London: Palgrave Macmillan.

Fedder, Edwin H. 1968. "The Concept of Alliance." *International Studies Quarterly* 12:65–86.

Fischer, Claude S. 2009. "The 2004 GSS Finding of Shrunken Social Networks: An Artifact?" *American Sociological Review* 74:657–69.

Flathman, Richard E. 1992. *Willful Liberalism: Voluntarism and Individuality in Political Theory and Practice.* Ithaca: Cornell University Press.

———. 1998. *Reflections of a Would-be Anarchist: Ideals and Institutions of Liberalism.* Minneapolis: University of Minnesota Press.

———. 2003. *Freedom and Its Conditions: Discipline, Autonomy, and Resistance.* New York: Routledge.

———. 2005. *Pluralism and Liberal Democracy.* Baltimore: Johns Hopkins University Press.

———. 2006. "Perfectionism Without Perfection: Cavell, Montaigne, and the Conditions of Morals and Politics." In *The Claim to Community: Essays on Stanley Cavell and Political Philosophy*, edited by Andrew Norris, 98–127, 349–53. Stanford: Stanford University Press.

Forster, E. M. 1938. *Two Cheers for Democracy.* New York: Harcourt, Brace, & World.

Fox, W. T. R., and A. B. Fox. 1962. *NATO and the Range of American Choice.* New York: Columbia University Press.

Frank, Jill. 2005. *A Democracy of Distinction: Aristotle and the Work of Politics.* Chicago: University of Chicago Press.

French, Peter. 1984. *Individual and Collective Responsibility.* New York: Columbia University Press.

Friedman, Marilyn. 1993. *What Are Friends For? Feminist Perspectives on Personal Relationships and Moral Theory.* Ithaca: Cornell University Press.

Fuller, Timothy. 2008. "Plato and Montaigne: Ancient and Modern Ideas of Friendship." In *Friendship and Politics: Essays in Political Thought*, edited by John von Heyking and Richard Avramenko, 197–213. Notre Dame: University of Notre Dame Press.

Garofano, John. 2002. "Institutions and the ASEAN Regional Forum: A Security Community for Asia?" *Asian Survey* 42:502–21.

Gilbert, Margaret. 1989. *On Social Facts.* London: Routledge.

———. 1996. *Living Together: Rationality, Sociality, and Obligation.* Lanham, MD: Rowman and Littlefield.

———. 2000. *Sociality and Responsibility: New Essays in Plural Subject Theory.* Lanham, MD: Rowman and Littlefield.

Godbeer, Richard. 2009. *The Overflowing of Friendship: Love Between Men and the Creation of the American Republic.* Baltimore: Johns Hopkins University Press.

Goldstein, A. 1995. "Discounting the Free-Ride: Alliances and Security in the Postwar World." *International Organization* 49:39–71.

Goodrich, Peter. 2004. "The Immense Rumor." *Yale Journal of Law and the Humanities* 16:199–233.

———. 2005. "Friends in High Places." *International Journal of Law in Context* 1:41–59.

Govier, Trudy. 2002. *Forgiveness and Revenge.* London: Routledge.

Gowa, Joanne. 1995. "Democratic States and International Disputes." *International Organization* 49:511–22.

Grieco, Joseph. 1988. "Anarchy and the Limits of Cooperation: A Realist Critique of the Newest Liberal Institutionalism." *International Organization* 42:485–507.

Griffin, Miriam. 1986. "Philosophy, Cato, and Roman Suicide: I." *Greece & Rome* 33:64–77.

Grunebaum, James O. 2003. *Friendship: Liberty, Equality and Utility.* Albany: State University of New York Press.

Guichard, M., P. Heady, and W. G. Tadesse. 2003. "Friendship, Kinship and the Bases of Social Organization." In *Max Planck Institute for Social Anthropology Report 2002–2003,* edited by Günther Schlee and Bettina Mann, 7–17. Halle, Germany: Max Planck Institute for Social Anthropology.

Hardimon, Michael. 1994. "Role Obligations." *Journal of Philosophy* 41:333–63.

Hatch, Orrin. 2009. "The Ted Kennedy I Knew." *Politico,* August 26. http://www.politico.com/story/2009/08/the-ted-kennedy-i-knew-026482?o=1".

Heider, F. 1958. *The Psychology of Interpersonal Relations.* New York: John Wiley.

Helm, Bennet. 2005. "Friendship." In *The Stanford Encyclopedia of Philosophy,* edited by Edward N. Zalta. http://plato.stanford.edu/archives/sum2005/entries/friendship/.

Holsti, O. P. T. Hopmann, and J. D. Sullivan. 1973. *Unity and Disintegration in International Alliances: Comparative Studies.* New York: Wiley.

Honig, Bonnie. 2001. *Democracy and the Foreigner.* Princeton: Princeton University Press.

Hopf, Ted. 1998. "The Promise of Constructivism in International Relations Theory." *International Security* 23:171–200.

Hutter, Horst. 1978. *Politics as Friendship: The Origins of Classical Notions of Politics in the Theory and Practice of Friendship.* Waterloo, Canada: Wilfrid Laurier University Press.

Hyatte, Reginald. 1997. *The Arts of Friends: The Idealization of Friendship in Medieval and Early Renaissance Literature.* Leiden, Netherlands: Brill Academic Publishers.

Jackson, Robert H. 1997. "The Political Theory of International Society." In *International Relations Theory Today,* edited by Ken Booth and Steven Smith, 110–28. Cambridge: Polity Press.

Jeske, Diane. 1997. "Friendship, Virtue, and Impartiality." *Philosophy and Phenomenological Research* 57:51–72.

——. 1998. "A Defense of Acting from Duty." *Journal of Value Inquiry* 32:61–74.

——. 2008. *Rationality and Moral Theory: How Intimacy Generates Reasons.* New York: Routledge.

Kahn, R. A. 1976. "Alliances Versus Ententes." *World Politics* 28:611–21.

Kant, Immanuel. 1991. "Lecture on Friendship." In *Other Selves: Philosophers on Friendship,* edited by Michael Pakaluck, 208–17. Indianapolis: Hackett.

Karst, Kenneth L. 1980. "The Freedom of Intimate Association." *Yale Law Journal* 89:624–92.

Keller, Simon. 2004. "Friendship and Belief." *Philosophical Papers* 33:329–51.

———. 2009. "Against Friendship Between Countries." *Journal of International Political Theory* 5:59–74.

———. 2013. *Partiality*. Princeton: Princeton University Press.

Keohane, Robert. 1989. *International Institutions and State Power: Essays in International Relations Theory*. Boulder: Westview Press.

Kierkegaard, Søren. 1991. "You Shall Love Your Neighbor." In *Other Selves: Philosophers on Friendship*, edited by Michael Pakaluck, 233–47. Indianapolis: Hackett.

King, Preston. 2007. "Friendship in Politics." *Critical Review of International Social and Political Philosophy* 10:125–45.

Kirkland, Justin H. 2011. "The Relational Determinants of Legislative Outcomes: Strong and Weak Ties Between Legislators." *Journal of Politics* 73:887–98.

Konstan, David. 1997. *Friendship in the Classical World*. Cambridge: Cambridge University Press.

Koschut, Simon, and Andrea Oelsner, eds. 2014. *Friendship and International Relations*. London: Palgrave Macmillan.

Kristof, Nicholas D. 2008. "Obama, Misha and the Bear." *New York Times*, November 20.

Lai, Brian, and Dan Reiter. 2000. "Democracy, Political Similarity, and International Alliances, 1816–1992." *Journal of Conflict Resolution* 44:203–27.

Lane, Melissa. 2014. *The Birth of Politics: Eight Greek and Roman Ideas and Why They Matter*. Princeton: Princeton University Press.

Langer, Ullrich. 1994. *Perfect Friendship: Studies in Literature and Moral Philosophy from Bocaccio to Corneille*. Geneva: Droz.

Lebovic, James H. 2004. "Unity in Actions: Explaining Alignment Behavior in the Middle East." *Journal of Peace Research* 41:167–89.

Leib, Ethan. 2007. "Friendship & the Law." *UCLA Law Review* 54:631–707.

———. 2009. "Friends as Fiduciaries." *Washington University Law Review* 86:665–732.

———. 2010. "Contracts and Friendships." *Emory Law Journal* 59:649–726.

———. 2011. *Friend v. Friend: The Transformation of Friendship—and What the Law Has to Do With It*. Oxford: Oxford University Press.

Lewis, C. S. 1960. *The Four Loves*. New York: Harcourt, Brace.

Lincoln, Abraham. 1861. "First Inaugural Address." Accessed July 2012. http://avalon.law.yale.edu/19th_century/lincoln1.asp.

Linklater, Andrew, and Hidemi Suganami. 2006. *The English School of International Relations: A Contemporary Reassessment*. Cambridge: Cambridge University Press.

Liska, George. 1962. *Nations in Alliance: The Limits of Interdependence*. Baltimore: Johns Hopkins University Press.

Long, A. A., and D. N. Sedley, eds. 1987. *The Hellenistic Philosophers*, vol. 1. Translated by A. A. Long and D. N. Sedley. Cambridge: Cambridge University Press.

Lu, Catherine. 2009. "Political Friendship Among Peoples." *Journal of International Political Theory* 5:41–58.

Ludwig, Paul W. 2010. "Without Foundations: Plato's *Lysis* and Postmodern Friendship." *American Political Science Review* 104:134–50.

Lynch, Sandra. 2005. *Philosophy and Friendship*. Edinburgh: Edinburgh University Press.

MacIntyre, Alasdair. 1999. *Dependent Rational Animals: Why Human Beings Need the Virtues*. Chicago: Open Court.

MacIntyre, Ben. 2014. *A Spy Among Friends: Kim Philby and the Great Betrayal*. New York: Crown.

Malle, B. F. 1999. "How People Explain Behavior: A New Theoretical Framework." *Personality and Social Psychology Review* 3:21–43.

Mason, Andrew. 1997. "Special Obligations." *Ethics* 107:427–47.

May, Larry. 1987. *The Morality of Groups: Collective Responsibility, Group-Based Harm, and Corporate Rights*. Notre Dame: University of Notre Dame Press.

——. 2012. *After War Ends: A Philosophical Perspective*. Cambridge: Cambridge University Press.

McCalla, R. 1996. "NATO's Presence After the Cold War." *International Organization* 50:445–76.

McCarthy, David. 1997. "Rights, Explanation and Risks." *Ethics* 107: 205–25.

McEvoy, James. 1999. "The Theory of Friendship in the Latin Middle Ages: Hermeneutics, Contextualization and the Transmission and Reception of Ancient Texts and Ideas, From c. AD 350 to c. 1500." In *Friendship in Medieval Europe*, edited by Julian Haseldine, 3–44. Thrupp, UK: Sutton Publishing.

McGeer, Victoria, and Philip Pettit. 2009. "Sticky Judgement and the Role of Rhetoric." In *Political Judgement: Essays for John Dunn*, edited by Richard Bourke and Raymond Geuss, 47–72. Cambridge: Cambridge University Press.

McPherson, Miller, Lynn Smith-Loving, and Matthew E. Brashears. 2006. "Social Isolation in America: Changes in Core Discussion Networks over Two Decades." *American Sociological Review* 71:353–75.

Mearsheimer, John J., and Stephen Walt. 2007. *The Israel Lobby and U.S. Foreign Policy*. New York: Farrar, Straus, and Giroux.

Meyer, Michael J. 1992. "Rights Between Friends." *Journal of Philosophy* 89:467–83.

Millar, Fergus. 1988. "Cornelius Nepos, 'Atticus' and the Roman Revolution." *Greece and Rome* 35:40–55.

Miller, Richard. 1981. "Marx and Aristotle." *Canadian Journal of Philosophy* 7:323–52.

Mitchell, Joshua. 2008. "It Is Not Good for Man to Be Alone: Tocqueville on Friendship." In *Friendship and Politics: Essays in Political Thought*, edited by John von Heyking and Richard Avramenko, 268–86. Notre Dame: University of Notre Dame Press.

Moles, J. L. 1992. Review of *Cornelius Nepos, a Selection, Including the Lives of Cato and Atticus* by Nicholas Horsfall. *Classical Review*, New Series, 42:314–16.

Montaigne, Michel de. 1991. "On Friendship." In *Other Selves: Philosophers on Friendship*, edited by Michael Pakaluck, 185–99. Indianapolis: Hackett.

Moore, Barrington. 1954. *Terror and Progress—USSR: Some Sources of Change and Stability in the Soviet Dictatorship*. Cambridge, MA: Harvard University Press.

Morgenthau, Hans. 1959. "Alliances in Theory and Practice." In *Alliance Policy in the Cold War*, edited by Arnold Wolfers, 189–212. Baltimore: Johns Hopkins University Press.

Morrow, James D. 1994. "Arms Versus Allies: Trade-offs in the Search for Security." *International Organization* 47:207–33.

Nehamas, Alexander. 2010. "The Good of Friendship." *Proceedings of the Aristotelian Society* 110:267–94.

Nepos, Cornelius. (1929) 2005. *Atticus* in *Cornelius Nepos*. Translated by John C. Rolfe. Cambridge, MA: Harvard University Press.

Neumann, Iver B. 2002. "Returning Practice to the Linguistic Turn: The Case of Diplomacy." *Millennium: Journal of International Studies* 31:627–51.

Nichols, Mary P. 2009. *Socrates on Friendship and Community: Reflections on Plato's Symposium, Phaedrus, and Lysis*. Cambridge: Cambridge University Press.

Nixon, Jon. 2015. *Hannah Arendt and the Politics of Friendship*. London: Bloomsbury Academic.

Norris, Andrew. 1998. "Carl Schmitt on Friends, Enemies and the Political." *Telos* 112:68–89.

Nussbaum, Martha. 1986. *The Fragility of Goodness: Luck and Ethics in Greek Tragedy and Philosophy*. Cambridge: Cambridge University Press.

Oakeshott, Michael. 1975. *On Human Conduct*. Oxford: Oxford University Press.

——. 1991. *Rationalism in Politics and Other Essays*. Indianapolis: Liberty Press.

——. 1999. *On History and Other Essays*. Indianapolis: Liberty Fund.

Oelsner, Andrea. 2007. "Friendship, Mutual Trust, and the Evolution of Regional Peace in the International System." *Critical Review of International Social and Political Philosophy* 10:257–79.

——. 2014. "The Construction of International Friendship in South America." In *Friendship and International Relations*, edited by Simon Koschut and Andrea Oelsner, 144–62. London: Palgrave Macmillan.

Oelsner, Andrea, and Simon Koschut. 2014a. "Conclusion." In *Friendship and International Relations*, edited by Simon Koschut and Andrea Oelsner, 201–8. London: Palgrave Macmillan.

——. 2014b. "A Framework for the Study of International Friendship." In *Friendship and International Relations*, edited by Simon Koschut and Andrea Oelsner, 3–31. London: Palgrave Macmillan.

Oelsner, Andrea, and Simon Koschut, eds. 2014c. *Friendship and International Relations*. London: Palgrave Macmillan.

Oelsner, Andrea, and Antoine Vion. 2011. "Friends in the Region: A Comparative Study on Friendship Building in Regional Integration." *International Politics* 48:129–51.

Oldenquist, Andrew. 1982. "Loyalties." *Journal of Philosophy* 79:173–93.

Olson, M., and R. Zeckhauser. 1966. "An Economic Theory of Alliances." *Review of Economics and Statistics* 48:266–79.

Oneal, John, and Bruce Russett. 1997. "The Classical Liberals Were Right: Democracy, Interdependence, and Conflict, 1950–1985." *International Studies Quarterly* 41:267–94.

Osgood, Robert E. 1968. *Alliances and American Foreign Policy*. Baltimore: Johns Hopkins University Press.

Osgood, Robert E., and Robert W. Tucker. 1967. *Force, Order and Justice*. Baltimore: Johns Hopkins University Press.

Pahl, Ray. 2000. *On Friendship*. Oxford: Polity Press.

Paine, Robert. 1974. "Anthropological Approaches to Friendship." In *The Compact: Selected Dimensions of Friendship*, edited by Elliot Leyton, 1–44. Newfoundland: University of Newfoundland.

——. 1999. "Friendship: The Hazards of an Ideal Relationship," in *The Anthropology of Friendship*, edited by Sandra Bell and Simon Coleman, 39–58. Oxford: Berg.

Palmerston, Henry John Temple. 1848. "Remarks in the House of Commons Defending his Foreign Policy." In *Hansard's Parliamentary Debates*, 3rd series, vol. 97, col. 122.

Pangle, Lorraine Smith. 2003. *Aristotle and the Philosophy of Friendship*. Cambridge: Cambridge University Press.

Patsias, Caroline, and Dany Deschenes. 2011. "Unsociable Sociability: The Paradox of Canadian-American Friendship." *International Politics* 48:92–111.

Patterson, Samuel C. 1959. "Patterns of Interpersonal Relations in a State Legislative Group: The Wisconsin Assembly." *Public Opinion Quarterly* 23:101–9.

Penner, Terry, and Christopher Rowe. 2005. *Plato's Lysis*. Cambridge: Cambridge University Press.

Plato. 1966. "Epistle 1." In *Plato in Twelve Volumes*, vol. 7, translated by R. G. Bury. Cambridge, MA: Harvard University Press.

——. 1968. *The Republic of Plato*. Translated by Allan Bloom. New York: Basic Books.

——. 1980. *The Laws of Plato*. Translated by Thomas Pangle. Chicago: University of Chicago Press.

——. 1991. "Lysis." In *Other Selves: Philosophers on Friendship*, edited by Michael Pakaluck, 1–27. Indianapolis: Hackett.

Pogge, Thomas W. 2004. "An Egalitarian Law of Peoples." *Philosophy and Public Affairs* 23:195–224.

Pouliot, Vincent. 2007. "'Sobjectivism': Toward a Constructivist Methodology." *International Studies Quarterly* 51:359–84.

——. 2008. "The Logic of Practicality: A Theory of Practice of Security Communities." *International Organization* 62:257–88.

——. 2010. *International Security in Practice: The Politics of NATO-Russia Diplomacy*. New York: Cambridge University Press.

Powell, Robert. 1994. "Anarchy in International Relations Theory: The Neorealist-Neoliberal Debate." *International Organization* 48:334–38.

Raines, Howell. 1991. "Grady's Gift." *New York Times Magazine*. Accessed August 20, 2012. http://wp.stockton.edu/gah1293/files/2012/01/Howell-Raines-Gradys-Gift-New-York-Times-Magazine-12-1-91.pdf.

Ramage, Edwin S. 1967. "Review of *Cicero's Letters to Atticus* by D. R. Shackleton Bailey." *Classical Journal* 62:318–20.

Rawls, John. 1971. *A Theory of Justice*. Cambridge, MA: Belknap Press of Harvard University Press.

——. 1999. *The Law of Peoples*. Cambridge, MA: Harvard University Press.

——. 2005. *Political Liberalism*. New York: Columbia University Press.

Raz, Joseph. 1989. "Liberating Duties." *Law and Philosophy: International Journal for Jurisprudence and Legal Philosophy* 8:3–21.

Reeder, Glenn D., John B. Pryor, Michael J. A. Wohl, and Michael L. Griswell. 2005. "On Attributing Negative Motives to Others Who Disagree With Our Opinions." *Personality and Social Psychology Bulletin* 31:1498–510.

Reidy, David A. 2004. "Rawls on International Justice: A Defense." *Political Theory: An International Journal of Political Philosophy* 32:291–319.

Reina, Ruben E. 1959. "Two Patterns of Friendship in a Guatemalan Community." *American Anthropologist*, New Series, 61:44–50.

Rhodes, James M. 2008. "Platonic *Philia* and Public Order." In *Friendship and Politics: Essays in Political Thought*, edited by John von Heyking and Richard Avramenko, 21–52. Notre Dame: University of Notre Dame Press.

Rolfe, John C. 1929. "Introduction." In *Cornelius Nepos*, translated by J. C. Rolfe. Cambridge, MA: Harvard University Press.

Rosenbury, Laura A. 2007. "Friends with Benefits?" *Michigan Law Review* 106:89–242.

Roshchin, Evgeny. 2006. "The Concept of Friendship: From Princes to States." *European Journal of International Relations* 12:599–624.

——. 2011. "Friendship of the Enemies: Twentieth Century Treaties of the United Kingdom and the USSR." *International Politics* 48:71–91.

——. 2014. "Friendship and International Order: An Ambiguous Liaison." In *Friendship and International Relations*, edited by Simon Koschut and Andrea Oelsner, 89–106. London: Palgrave Macmillan.

Rousseau, David L. 2002. "Motivations for Choice: The Salience of Relative Gains in International Politics." *Journal of Conflict Resolution* 46:394–426.

Salkever, Stephen. 2008. "Taking Friendship Seriously: Aristotle on the Place(s) of *Philia* in Public Life." In *Friendship and Politics: Essays in Political Thought*, edited by John von Heyking and Richard Avramenko, 53–83. Notre Dame: University of Notre Dame Press.

Santos-Granero, Fernando. 2007. "Of Fear and Friendship: Amazonian Sociality Beyond Kinship and Affinity." *Journal of the Royal Anthropological Institute* 13:1–18.

Schall, James V. 1996. "Friendship and Political Philosophy." *Review of Metaphysics* 50:121–41.

Scheffler, Samuel. 2001. *Boundaries and Allegiances: Problems of Justice and Responsibility in Liberal Thought.* Oxford: Oxford University Press.

——. 2010. "Morality and Reasonable Partiality." In *Partiality and Impartiality: Morality, Special Relationships, and the Wider World*, edited by Brian Feltham and John Cottingham, 98–130. Oxford: Oxford University Press.

Schmitt, Carl. 1996. *The Concept of the Political.* Chicago: University of Chicago.

——. 2008. *Constitutional Theory.* Translated by Jeffrey Seitzer. Durham: Duke University Press.

Schmitter, Amy M. 2014. "17th and 18th Century Theories of Emotions." In *The Stanford Encyclopedia of Philosophy*, Spring 2014 edition, edited by Edward N. Zalta. http://plato.stanford.edu/archives/spr2014/entries/emotions-17th18th/.

Schmitz, David F. 2006. *The United States and Right-Wing Dictatorships, 1965–1989.* New York: Cambridge University Press.

Schubertwalker, Lilly, and Paul H. Wright. 1976. "Self-Disclosure in Friendship." *Perceptual and Motor Skills* 42:735–42.

Schwartz, Daniel. 2007. *Aquinas on Friendship.* Oxford: Clarendon Press.

Schwarzenbach, Sibyl A. 1996. "On Civic Friendship." *Ethics* 107:97–128.

——. 2009. *On Civic Friendship: Including Women in the State.* New York: Columbia University Press.

——. 2011. "Fraternity and a Global Difference Principle: A Feminist Critique of Rawls and Pogge." *International Politics* 48:28–45.

Schweitzer, Ivy. 2006. *Perfecting Friendship: Politics and Affiliation in Early American Literature.* Chapel Hill: University of North Carolina Press.

Schweller, Randall J. 1997. "New Realist Research on Alliances: Refining, Not Refuting Waltz's Balancing Proposition." *American Political Science Review* 91: 927–30.

——. 1998. *Deadly Imbalances: Tripolarity and Hitler's Strategy of World Conquest.* New York: Columbia University Press.

Scorza, Jason A. 2004. "Liberal Citizenship and Civic Friendship." *Political Theory: An International Journal of Political Philosophy* 32:85–108.

Shanley, Mary Lyndon. 1993. "Marital Slavery and Friendship: John Stuart Mill's *The Subjection of Women*." In *Friendship: A Philosophical Reader*, edited by Neera Kapur Badhwar, 267–84. Ithaca: Cornell University Press.

Sharp, Ronald A., and Eudora Welty, eds. 1991. *The Norton Book of Friendship.* New York: Norton.

Shklar, Judith. 1984. *Ordinary Vices.* Cambridge, MA: Belknap Press of Harvard University Press.

——. 1998. "A Friendship." In *Redeeming American Political Thought*, edited by Stanley Hoffmann and Dennis Frank Thompson, 14–27. Chicago: University of Chicago Press.

Simmel, Georg. 1950. *The Sociology of Georg Simmel*. Edited and translated by Kurt H. Wolff. New York: Macmillan Publishing.

Simon, Rich, and Claudia Luther. 2009. "Edward Kennedy Dies at 77; 'Liberal Lion of the Senate.'" *Los Angeles Times*, August 26. http://www.latimes.com/local /obituaries/la-me-ted-kennedy26–2009aug26-story.html#page=1.

Singer, J. D., and M. Small. 1968. "Alliance Aggregation and the Onset of War: 1815–1945." In *Quantitative International Politics: Insights and Evidence*, edited by J. D. Singer, 247–86. New York: Free Press.

Slomp, G. 2007. "Carl Schmitt on Global Terrorism and the Demise of the 'True Friend.'" *Critical Review of International Social and Political Philosophy* 10:99–214.

Smith, Graham M. 2011a. *Friendship & the Political: Kierkegaard, Nietzsche, Schmitt*. Exeter: Imprint Academic.

——. 2011b. "Friendship and the World of States." *International Politics* 48:10–27.

——. 2014. "Friendship, State, Nation." In *Friendship and International Relations*, edited by Simon Koschut and Andrea Oelsner, 35–50. London: Palgrave Macmillan.

Snyder, G. 1984. "The Security Dilemma in Alliance Politics." *World Politics* 36:461–95.

——. 1990. "Alliance Theory: A Neorealist First Cut." *Journal of International Affairs* 44:103–24.

——. 1997. *Alliance Politics*. Ithaca: Cornell University Press.

Starr, Harvey. 1992. "Democracy and War: Choice, Learning and Security Communities." *Journal of Peace Research* 29:207–13.

Stocker, Michael. 1976. "The Schizophrenia of Modern Ethical Theories." *Journal of Philosophy* 73:453–66.

——. 1981. "Values and Purposes: The Limits of Teleology and the Ends of Friendship." *Journal of Philosophy* 78:747–65.

——. 1991. "Duty and Friendship: Toward a Synthesis of Gilligan's Moral Concepts." In *Women and Moral Theory*, edited by Eva Feder Kittay and Diana T. Meyers, 56–68. Lanham: Rowman and Littlefield.

——. 1993. "Values and Purposes: The Limits of Teleology and the Ends of Friendship." In *Friendship: A Philosophical Reader*, edited by Neera Kapur Badhwar, 245–63. Ithaca: Cornell University Press.

Stockett, Kathryn. 2011. *The Help*. New York: Amy Einhorn Books/Putnam.

Stroud, Sarah. 2006. "Epistemic Partiality in Friendship." *Ethics* 116:498–524.

Sullivan, Andrew. 1998. *Love Undetectable: Notes on Friendship, Sex and Survival*. New York: Vintage.

Sweeny, Kevin, and Paul Fritz. 2004. "Jumping on the Bandwagon: An Interest-Based Explanation for Great Power Alliances." *International Organization* 66:428–49.

Tamir, Yael. 1993. *Liberal Nationalism*. Princeton: Princeton University Press.

——. 1995. "The Enigma of Nationalism." *World Politics* 42:418–40.

Tan, Kok-Chor. 2000. *Toleration, Diversity and Global Justice*. University Park: Pennsylvania State University Press.

Telfer, Elizabeth. 1991. "Friendship." In *Other Selves: Philosophers on Friendship*, edited by Michael Pakaluk, 248–67. Indianapolis: Hackett.

Thomas, Laurence. 1987. "Friendship." *Syntheses* 72:217–36.

Thucydides. 1910. *History of the Peloponnesian War*. London: J. M. Dent; New York: E. P. Dutton. http://data.perseus.org/citations/urn:cts:greekLit:tlg0003.tlg001.perseus-eng3:5.89.1.

Tocqueville, Alexis de. 2011. *Democracy in America*. Translated by Harvey C. Mansfield and Debra Winthrop. Chicago: University of Chicago Press.

Tusicisny, Andrej. 2007. "Security Communities and Their Values: Taking Masses Seriously." *International Political Science Review* 28:425–49.

Vernon, Mark. 2006. "Plato, Thomas and the Daring Ethics of Friendship." *Theology and Sexuality* 12:203–16.

———. 2010. *The Meaning of Friendship*. Houndmills: Palgrave Macmillan.

Vion, Antoine. 2007. "The Institutionalization of International Friendship." *Critical Review of International Social and Political Philosophy* 10: 281–97.

Vlastos, Gregory. 1981. *Platonic Studies*. Princeton: Princeton University Press.

von Heyking, John. 2010. "Friendship in Democracy and in Tocqueville's *Democracy*." Paper presented at the Annual Meeting of the American Political Science Association. September 1–5, 2010. Washington, D.C.

Wahlke, John C., Heinz Eulau, William Buchanan, and Leroy C. Ferguson. 1962. *The Legislative System: Explorations in Legislative Behavior*. New York: John Wiley.

Walt, Stephen. 1987. *The Origins of Alliances*. Ithaca: Cornell University Press.

Waltz, Kenneth N. 1979. *Theory of International Politics*. Reading, MA: Addison-Wesley.

Walzer, Michael. 1977. *Just and Unjust Wars: A Moral Argument with Historical Illustrations*. New York: Basic Books.

Wang, Hua, and Barry Wellman. 2010. "Social Connectivity in America: Changes in Adult Friendship Network Size from 2002 to 2007." *American Behavioral Scientist* 53:1149–69.

Washington, George. 1796. "Farewell Address," September 19, 1796. Online by Gerhard Peters and John T. Woolley, *The American Presidency Project*. http://www.presidency.ucsb.edu/ws/?pid=65539.

Weart, Spencer R. 1998. *Never at War: Why Democracies Will Not Fight One Another*. New Haven: Yale University Press.

Weinstein, F. 1969. "The Concept of Commitment in International Relations." *Journal of Conflict Resolution* 13:39–56.

Welch, Kathryn E. 1996. "T. Pomponius Atticus: A Banker in Politics?" *Historia: Zeitschrift für Alte Geschichte* 45:450–71.

Wellman, Christopher Heath. 2001. "Friends, Compatriots, and Special Obligations." *Political Theory: An International Journal of Political Philosophy* 29:217–36.

Wendt, Alexander. 1994. "Collective Identity Formation and the International State." *American Political Science Review* 88:384–96.

——. 1995. "Constructing International Politics." *International Security* 20:71–81.

Wheeler, Nicholas J. 2000. *Saving Strangers: Humanitarian Intervention in International Society.* Oxford: Oxford University Press.

Wheeler, Nicholas J., and Timothy Dunne. 1996. "Hedley Bull's Pluralism of the Intellect and Solidarism of the Will." *International Affairs* 72:91–107.

Whiting, Jennifer E. 1991. "Impersonal Friends." *The Monist* 74:3–29.

Wittgenstein, Ludwig. 1973. *Philosophical Investigations.* Upper Saddle River, NJ: Prentice Hall.

Wolf, Eric R. 1977. "Kinship, Friendship, and Patron-Client Relations in Complex Societies." In *Friends, Followers, and Factions: A Reader in Political Clientelism,* edited by Steffen W. Schmidt, Laura Guasti, Carl H. Landé, and James. C. Scott, 167–77. Berkeley: University of California Press.

Wolf, Susan. 1992. "Morality and Partiality." *Philosophical Perspectives* 6:243–59.

Wolfers, Arnold. 1962. *Discord and Collaboration: Essays on International Politics.* Baltimore: Johns Hopkins University Press.

Xenophon. 1925. "Hiero." In *Xenophon in Seven Volumes,* vol. 7, translated by E. C. Marchant. Cambridge, MA: Harvard University Press. http://www.perseus.tufts.edu/hopper/text?doc=Perseus%3Atext%3A1999.01.0210%3Atext%3DHiero%3A chapter%3D3.

Yack, Bernard. 1985. "Community and Conflict in Aristotle's Political Philosophy." *Review of Politics* 47:92–112.

——. 1993. *The Problems of a Political Animal: Community, Justice, and Conflict in Aristotelian Political Thought.* Berkeley: University of California Press.

——. 2006. "Rhetoric and Public Understanding." *Political Theory: An International Journal of Political Philosophy* 34:417–38.

Young-Bruehl, Elizabeth. 1982. *Hannah Arendt: For Love of the World.* London: Yale University Press.

INDEX

ethics, of international friendships, 261–63

Eudemian Ethics (Aristotle), 106, 136

exchange relationships, 58, 112, 130, 138–39, 297n8, 316n14, 321n17

exclusion/inclusion, politics of, xix, 260, 268–69, 274, 275

extrinsic value of friendship, 42–45

Eznack, Lucile, 220–22, 319n1, 320n9

fairness, xii–xiii, 128; in institutions, 173–75; in rules of cooperation, 232, 239; self-interest and, 313n25

false friends: distinguished from true friends, 57, 181–82, 183, 190; flatterers, 182–83; motivations of, 57–58, 321n17; state producing, 186–92

family of practices: friendship as, xiii, xv, 16, 23, 39, 52, 144–45, 200, 281, 286n8; overview of, xv; politics and, 144–45, 295n4

family resemblance concept: friendship as, xiii–xiv, 5–6, 9–11, 24, 174, 200–201, 281, 286n8, 288n11; implications of, 10; language and, 9

fiduciaries, friends as, 206–7, 208, 209, 212

Flathman, Richard: on individuality, xvii, 74, 77, 81, 84–92, 99, 301n9, 302n10, 302n14, 322n3; on Montaigne, 87–89

flatterers, 182–83

forgiveness, 71–72, 198, 306n9

formal equality, value of, 175

Forster, E. M., 93, 119–20, 217, 220

fortune, 16, 143, 162–67, 169, 170–72, 312n21

fragility, of friendship, 193–97

Frank, Jill, 138–40, 283n1, 309n25, 309n27

fraternity, 146, 148, 310n8, 310n10

Friedman, Marilyn: on affection, 290n2; on friendship, 14, 29, 35–36, 82, 90, 181, 283n1, 288n14, 289n1, 290n2, 294n1, 302n15, 317n17

friendliness, as part of a thin theory of civic friendship, 111–14, 306n10

friendly actions: friendship not solely a function of, 25, 55–57, 170, 255; as part of friendship, 33–34, 170–71; of states, 255

friends: actions of, 13–15; with benefits, 202–3; circle of, 30, 57, 96, 236, 247, 255–58, 269, 273, 274; as enemies, 304n21; false, 57, 181–82, 183, 186–92, 321n17; as fiduciaries, 206–7, 208, 209, 212; friendship and, 3–4, 295n4; impersonal, 243; in international politics, 217–34; motives of friends, 15, 25–31; number of, 306n6; perspectives valued by, 263; philosophic, 304n22; privileges of, 197, 204–6; states as, 219–20; stool pigeons and, 186–92

friendship: affected by self-interest, 123; in ancient Greece, 7–9, 56, 62, 125, 127, 147–48, 150, 284n6, 294n2; barriers to, 180–81, 192–93; beginnings and ends of, 210–11; bridging/bonding, 74; characteristics of, 11, 200, 286n8; Cicero and, 4, 22–23, 58, 93, 106, 128, 145, 153, 159, 168, 284n5, 289n1; comeback of, xi–xii; conditions of, 11, 23–28, 31, 39–40, 54, 84; conventional morality and, 93–95; corruption and, xii, 157, 158, 174, 176–78; decline of, 194–95; deep, 37–39; defined, 199–203, 257; Derrida on, xix, 8, 36, 62–63, 219, 270–71, 277, 278, 280, 293n21, 297n10, 312n22; discourse linked to, 146–52, 169, 306n11; diversity of, xiii, 5–9, 23, 55, 196, 198–203, 284n5, 288n18; duty and, 54–55, 63–73, 318n21; dyadic, 113–14; elasticity of, 71–72; emotional, 57; equality required by, 109, 127, 129, 181, 185, 201, 291n7, 304n1, 305n4, 308n20, 315nn7–10, 317n19; explanation of, 39–41; family resemblance of, xiii–xiv, xvi, 4–5, 6, 9–11, 23–24, 39, 52, 144–45, 174–75, 200–201, 281, 286n8, 288n11; flexibility of, 6–8; forgiveness and, 71–72, 198; fragility of, 193–97; Friedman on, 14, 29, 35–36, 82, 90, 181, 283n1, 288n14, 289n1, 290n2, 294n1, 302n15, 317n17; friendly actions are not sufficient for, not solely a function of, 25, 55–57, 170, 255; friends and, 3–4, 295n4; gay, 292n16; goods of, 42–44, 46, 194; guest, 7, 56, 62, 150, 294n2; impartiality and, xii–xiii, 42, 173–80, 288n14, 294n25, 299n16, 305n3; indirectly encouraged, 192–93; individuality and, 18, 95, 301n8, 302n12, 304n22; individuality and bridging/bonding, xvii, xx, 74, 82–93, 300n2, 300n4, 302n16, 302n18; individuality, Emerson, and, 306n11; individuality, Flathman, and, xvii, 74, 77, 81, 84–92, 99, 301n9, 302n10, 302n14, 322n3; individuality as a motive of, 77; individuality, Nietzsche, and, 301n6; individuality and practices of, xiv; individuality as an unwelcome part of, 96–101, 302n11; instrumental, 57, 294n3; intimacy in, 96–99, 109, 110, 127, 133, 147–48, 152, 185, 200, 293n17, 295n4, 305n3, 310n7, 316n14; Jeske on, 9, 10, 12, 50, 65–66, 100, 284n4, 286n8, 288n12, 290n6, 294n1, 305n5; justification of, 39–41, 52, 193; Kant on, 27, 30, 33, 75, 181, 184, 291n10,

303n19; King on, 27, 112–14, 126, 183, 284n4, 287n10, 297n11, 303n20, 315n7, 319n5; kinship distinguished from, 202; law of, xv, 23, 93, 174, 196–203, 211, 213–14, 318n20, 318nn23–24; love and, 17, 30–31, 47–48, 112, 147, 182, 217, 297n9, 315n8, 317n16, 323n10; Lynch, Sandra, on, 9, 10, 65, 68–69, 94, 97, 145, 284n5, 286n8, 287n10, 291n8, 293nn21–22, 294n2, 296n7, 301n8; mirror conception of, 292n13, 293n22, 302n16; as model for political relationships, xi–xii; modernity and, xiv, 46, 96–99, 316n14; Montaigne on, 16–17, 33, 74–75, 87–89, 91, 98, 289n1, 302n12, 302n14; mutability of, 199–203; online, 291n11; Pahl on, 5, 17–18, 97, 285n4, 292n14, 293n17, 293n23, 315n7, 316n14; passions of, 26, 31, 320n9; philia, 8, 106, 127, 134, 137, 147, 149–50, 225, 284n6, 285n3, 288n18, 290nn3–4, 294n2, 296n7, 304n1, 306n10, 308n21, 310n7; of pleasure, 8–9, 28–29, 46, 58–59, 60, 75, 277, 288n18, 290n6, 296nn5–6, 308n24; politics of, 62, 255, 274, 276–78, 280, 297n10; power influencing, 129, 162, 181–86, 192, 203, 260–61, 315n9, 321n17, 322n5; public, 152, 170; pure, 307n12, 308n18, 315n7; relationships view of, 41–52; self as product of, 37–38; self-interest and, 313n25, 318n21; self-interest and attributing motives to 110, 137–38, 183, 255; self-interest and international 218–19; self-interest as a complex motive in, 58–63; self-interest as material advantage or utility and, 58–60, 139, 208–9, 245, 255, 281, 291n10, 297n8, 308n24; self-interest, cooperation, and, 140–41;